From Elite to Mass Politics

From Elite
to Mass
Politics

Italian Socialism
in the Giolittian Era,
1900–1914

James Edward Miller

THE KENT STATE UNIVERSITY PRESS
Kent, Ohio, and London, England

HX
288
.M56
1990

© 1990 by The Kent State University Press, Kent, Ohio 44242
All rights reserved
Library of Congress Catalog Card Number 89–20043
ISBN 0–87338–395–8
Manufactured in the United States of America

Library of Congress Cataloging-in-Publication Data

Miller, James Edward.
    From elite to mass politics : Italian socialism in the Giolittian Era,
    1900–1914 / James Edward Miller.
        p.   cm.
    Includes bibliographical references.
    ISBN 0-87338-395-8 (alk. paper)
    1. Socialism—Italy—History—20th century.   2. Italy—Politics and
government—1870–1915.   I. Title
HX288.M56   1990
320.5′31′0945—dc20   89-20043
                                                                  CIP

British Library Cataloging-in-Publication data are available

Contents

Preface and
Acknowledgments

How and why do organizational issues affect the ability of political parties to operate in their environments? This study argues that between 1900 and 1914 questions of organization played a significant and largely unappreciated role in defeating the efforts of the Italian Socialist party (PSI) to achieve the radical transformation of Italy's society. Specifically, it contends that the leaders of both the Party's left- and right-wing factions consciously chose and maintained an organizational structure that made the PSI the representative of a small portion of Italian industrial and agrarian workers. It argues that by limiting the PSI's size and failing to support the extension of voting rights to the mass of Italians, particularly Southern farm labor, the PSI reduced its political options. Finally, it attempts to demonstrate that the PSI's choice of political organization had a deleterious effect on the Italian socialist movement throughout the period 1900–1914 but especially in the triennium 1911–14 when the Party attempted to halt Italy's involvement in colonial expansion and war.

Party organization was only one factor, albeit a significant one, in the PSI's inability to master its political environment. Conflicts over ideology, mistaken political strategy, shifting economic conditions, and personal rivalries posed significant obstacles to the Party's success. Moreover, the creation of a mass-based political party was no guarantee that the PSI could achieve its objectives. The mass-based European socialist parties of the era were unsuccessful in achieving the radical transformation of bourgeois society or in mastering the crisis of July–August 1914, when Marxist internationalism collapsed before the power of nationalism. The German Social Democrats (SPD), European Marxism's most influential mass movement and model of political organization, never seriously threatened conservative control of Germany. On the other hand, the Bolshevik faction of the Russian Social Democrats, a tightly knit elite of professional revolutionaries that disdained mass participation in decision making, ultimately became the most successful Marxist movement of the era. In 1917 the Bolsheviks seized the leadership of a popular revolution and erected history's first proletarian dictatorship.

The political situation in Italy between 1900 and 1914 was profoundly different from that of prewar, prerevolutionary Russia. A reactionary, incompetent autocracy governed Russia, forcing the Socialists to adopt clandestine methods of operation. Differences with the situation of the SPD, while less dramatic, were still significant. In Germany, despite a universal suffrage law and fairly wide political liberties, the Social Democrats operated as a tightly controlled opposition, a pariah party with little influence on the national government. In Italy, reform-minded middle-class governments dominated politics between 1900 and 1911. Their leader, the nation's perennial prime minister, Giovanni Giolitti, was eager to bring both the Catholic and Socialist movements into a governing coalition, albeit on his terms. The Catholics proved on a number of occasions, particularly during the 1913 elections, that a party with mass support had an unusual opportunity to capitalize on these numbers to gain bargaining leverage with Giolitti. Even when the PSI became an uncompromising opponent of the Italian government, a mass base could have helped the Party mount a more effective resistance to the foreign and domestic policies it opposed.

In the long history of the Italian Socialist party, few periods are more instructive than the Giolittian era (1900–1914). Founded in 1892 by a handful of visionaries, many of middle-class origin, the Party played an important role in organizing part of Italy's small but growing working classes and a segment of its agrarian laborers into a political force. At the end of the nineteenth century, the young Socialist party, in coalition with other progressive forces, defeated conservative efforts to limit freedom of political association and action. The Zanardelli-Giolitti government, created by the victorious reformers, ushered in a new chapter in Italy's history, one pregnant with the possibility of major social change. For the PSI, however, reform and frustration went hand in hand. The successive governments of Giovanni Giolitti enacted major social, economic, and political reforms while a national labor organization coalesced and soon enrolled nearly 350,000 workers. Simultaneously, the Socialist party's claim to be the exclusive political voice of the Italian working class was eroded on all sides:

by Giolitti, by organized labor, and by a growing Catholic political and labor movement. The PSI's inability to guide either the agenda or the pace of reform unleashed a fierce internal struggle which eventually resulted in the defeat of the Reformist current and in experiments with other types of political organization and strategies. In the immediate post–World War I years, the PSI adopted a mass party structure, recruiting over 200,000 members. This new organization brought the Socialists tantalizingly close to control of the state in spite of a poorly chosen strategy that exacerbated class conflicts and built support for fascism.

This study focuses on the years 1908–14, when Reformism proved incapable of achieving its objectives and the left or "revolutionary" wing of the Party organized, gained control of the PSI, modified its organizational structure, and changed its strategy. The first section (chapters 1 through 3) examines the evolution of party organization from the PSI's origins to 1900; dissects the organizational structure of the Reformist-dominated Party to illuminate the relationship of ideology, class, political organization, and strategy choices; and then discusses the PSI's developing internal split.

The second section (chapters 4 through 6) examines the basic structural weaknesses of the Reformist Party and then discusses both the proximate causes of schism within Reformist ranks and the alternatives which the dissidents offered for the solution of the PSI's internal crisis.

As Reformism unraveled, the Party's usually factious leftists coalesced. The third section of this book (chapters 7 through 9) explains how the left captured a majority among the rank and file and then carried out a major reorganization of the PSI. Italy's plunge into a major colonial war gave the left its opportunity. The onset of World War I less than three years later revealed that the left lacked strategic alternatives to the politics of parliamentary reform. The left was building a vehicle through which the PSI could harness the potentially vast power of Italy's growing working classes. The Reformists, however, continued to offer the only coherent formula for successfully employing the power of these numbers.

The effects of the internal crisis of 1908–14 long haunted the Socialist party. During these years, the majority of Italian Socialists rejected the parliamentary gradualism of Reformist leader Filippo Turati in favor of ineffective opposition to Italy's nascent parliamentary democratic system. This choice had great impact on both Italian socialism and Italian democracy. By adopting the strategy of "revolutionary intransigence" and rejecting Turati's reformist socialism, the left inadvertently helped to set the stage for the triumph of fascism. The issue of whether the Socialist party was to operate as a revolutionary organization or as a social democratic political party continued to burden the PSI throughout its long struggle against fascism, becoming especially acute during the armed resistance and postwar reconstruction (1943–50).

In the post–World War II era, the continued inability of Italian Socialists to determine whether they should follow a policy of parliamentary reform or of revolutionary opportunism caused the Party to waver between an uneasy alliance with the Italian Communist party (1945–56) and membership in a series of Christian Democrat–dominated coalition governments in the 1960s and 1970s. In both cases the PSI found itself the junior partner. The declining strength of Italian socialism after 1946 is directly traceable to the PSI's inability to determine what its role should be within Italy's new democratic system. In the mid-1970s, the Party returned to Turati's vision and opted for democratic reformism. By then, its bases of support had been eroded by the Christian Democrats, Communists, and a host of intraparty schisms. After a decade of patient reconstruction and reformist politics, the PSI finally made significant gains at the polls but remains Italy's third party.

This book stands on the shoulders of a great deal of first-class scholarship. The importance of the birth, growth, and internal struggles of the PSI were recognized by a number of acute contemporary observers. Robert Michels's studies of the Party remain classics of history and political theory.[1]

The triumph of fascism impeded the study of the PSI. After Italy's 1945 liberation, intense concern over the causes of the collapse of the parliamentary system, the Socialist party, and working-class movement stimulated renewed work on the origins of Marxism in Italy. Interest in these problems was particularly keen on the political left, where the two working-class parties that descended from the Giolittian-era PSI were struggling for the leadership of the lower socioeconomic classes and simultaneously confronting a Catholic mass party which collected a significant part of its support from urban and agrarian labor. Recognizing that the parties of the left must secure their interests within the framework of a parliamentary democracy, Marxist historians and party leaders examined both the origins of the socialist movement and of parliamentary democracy in Italy.[2] Communist party chief Palmiro Togliatti contributed an interesting evaluation of the role of Giovanni Giolitti.[3]

The publication of the correspondence, documents, and periodicals of the early socialists began in the 1950s. The Istituto Giangiacomo Feltrinelli of

Milan has had a significant role in this effort.[4] The Einaudi family also encouraged the work, rendering an invaluable service to scholarship through the publication of the Turati-Kuliscioff correspondence.[5]

The first two decades of the postwar era were marked by a number of major studies of the origins of the Italian Socialist movement and of the "struggle of the currents" during the Giolittian era. By the early 1970s, a trend toward regional and local studies deepened our knowledge of grass roots politics in the Giolittian era and provided needed information on the sections and federations of the PSI.[6] The easy availability of primary sources has stimulated valuable monographic work and the production of important syntheses of the previous two decades. The socialist historian Maurizio Degl'Innocenti has studied the links between the development of the working class and the evolution of a socialist party. He has also provided a convincing and detailed account of the Italian Socialist party's reaction to the Libyan War of 1911–12.[7] Brunello Vigezzi has pored through the Turati correspondence to produce works which challenge the traditional views of the Reformist leader's collaboration with Giolitti.[8] Spencer DiScala's work on Filippo Turati and Reformism stresses the continuing centrality of the Reformist vision of democratic socialism.[9]

In general, these studies have not connected the issues of strategy, class, and ideology with that of political organization. Reformism, for example, was more than a series of policy choices. It defined a specific view of Socialist party organization. The Reformists insisted on building and maintaining a party dominated by middle-class deputies who enjoyed a remarkable independence from the control of the rank and file. Reformist party organization severely limited the PSI's ability to broaden its base of popular support. The lack of a broad base, in turn, played a significant role in undermining the Reformists' ability to enact their political program. For all of the personal attractiveness of Turati, Kuliscioff, and other Reformists as well as the intellectual appeal of their politics, their failure to build a mass base of support for their objectives seriously weakened their faction.

This book initially took form as a Ph.D. dissertation at the University of Illinois in the early 1970s, prompted by my interest in the process of political polarization that affected all the major states of Europe in the years prior to World War I. In Italy, this polarization interrupted a process of democratization that appeared to be well along the way toward completion. The Italian Socialist party had been on the cutting edge of both the process of democratization and the revolt against Giolitti's reformism that ushered in the xenophobic politics of wartime and postwar Italy and ultimately set the stage for the triumph of fascism. Reviewing the manuscript after a decade of work in other areas, at times I had the feeling of reliving my first serious romance: a mixture of pleasure and bemusement. However, I believe that both the research and the thesis stand up well. An extended period of research in Italy permitted me to update the bibliography, explore new sources, and revise the manuscript. I again would like to express thanks to all those who aided in the original dissertation research, particularly David E. Sumler, and add to this list the staff members of the Archivio Centrale dello Stato in Rome and the Istituto Socialista di Studi Storici of Florence. Special thanks are due to Spencer DiScala and Richard Drake, who read and offered helpful criticism of the revised manuscript, and to Professor Charles Delzell, whose rigorous reading of this text saved me from numerous grammatical and a few factual errors.

The book is dedicated to my parents, who with patience and good humor provided a stable home environment and the lavish financial support that enabled me to complete a university education and begin the study of history.

Introduction

Political movements are born in medias res and must come to grips immediately with both the specific issues which necessitated their birth and with a broader range of problems that involve the nation. At the end of the nineteenth century, Italian society was in a ferment as new forces fathered by industrialization changed the social, economic, and political character of the nation, while conservative elites attempted to repress change with force.

THE HERITAGE OF THE RISORGIMENTO

Italy's mid-nineteenth-century political unification, the Risorgimento, while frequently hailed as a masterpiece of liberal nationalism, left the new state with many unresolved problems. United Italy was the creation of an energetic and talented minority that imposed a relatively advanced political structure on an economically backward society. The minority employed a very restricted suffrage and force as needed to preserve the new state from the threat that internal enemies might organize the peasant masses to overthrow constitutional government.[1]

While excluding the masses from political participation, united Italy's new rulers simultaneously embarked on domestic and international policies designed to make their state a great power. At home, this policy included favoring capital accumulation over consumption. Regressive taxes on foodstuffs and other basic items of consumption placed the costs of economic development unevenly and most heavily on the peasant masses. The Italian government's objective was aiding its entrepreneurial sector to rapidly accumulate capital for investment. A speedy expansion of the nation's industrial sector combined with agricultural modernization was the best, and indeed the only, guarantee of achieving social stability and great power status for Italy.

As a modern industry and agriculture developed slowly in the 1870s and 1880s, the Italian state began to claim great power status. Otto von Bismarck, Germany's cynical but perceptive chancellor, cuttingly remarked that the Italians possessed a large appetite but poor teeth. Throughout the nineteenth century, Italy was an economically and militarily weak power burdened by the grand ambitions unleashed by the Risorgimento. A society that attempted to achieve great power status with such limited means needed massive popular backing for its undertaking. The Italian state was unable to organize this popular consensus. Massimo D'Azeglio, the poet and Piedmontese prime minister, had been correct: Italy had yet to create Italians. The ideology of the Risorgimento had little appeal to the peasantry or to powerful institutions like the Roman Catholic church. Without access to cheap sources of raw materials, a modern agricultural base, a highly developed industry, or a commonly accepted ideology, Italy's efforts to play the role of a great power were extremely dangerous to its internal social and political stability.[2] During the 1890s, the degree of this instability was fully revealed.

ELEMENTS OF THE ITALIAN CRISIS

Between 1896 and 1914, Italian industrial development accelerated rapidly. Cavour and his successors laid the foundations of an industrial society, building an infrastructure of roads, railroads, and canals while establishing a primary role for the state in economic policy. However, Italy's development was handicapped throughout most of the nineteenth century by a lack of capital and of basic raw materials, especially coal and iron. By the mid-1890s, these defects had been sufficiently corrected to allow Italy's industrial development to accelerate. The main agents of change were the formation with foreign capital of industrial development banks, such as the Banca Commerciale Italiana, the increasing use of hydroelectric power as a substitute for coal, and a government policy of intervention to support developing industries.[3] Italy's industrial revolution got off to a shaky start in the wake of the European "Great Depression" (1873–96) and a major domestic financial crises which nearly destroyed the nascent industrial banking system. By 1899, however, Italy was experiencing an economic boom. Taking 1900 as 100, industrial output stood at 75 in 1896 and rose to 184 by

1913. The period of most rapid growth was 1896–1906, when annual industrial output increased by 6.7 percent. This increase in production was accompanied by a rise in real wages and in the general standard of living. At the same time, the highest rate of emigration in Italy's history relieved pressure on the labor market. Advances continued against illiteracy. The number of *analfabeti* between the ages of six and twelve dropped from 64.1 percent in 1881 to 46.6 percent in 1901 to 35.3 percent in 1911.[4]

Nevertheless, the political crisis deepened between 1890 and 1900. The crisis was constitutional in nature: a struggle over the right of the Italian government to restrict individual freedom. By generating greater wealth while concentrating growing numbers of Italians in the expanding cities of the North, industrialization created pressure for political change in a nation which had inherited a set of problems of massive proportions. By the early 1890s, the political and economic demands of a growing working class were added to the three great inherited problems of united Italy: the Southern Question, the position of the Catholic church within the Liberal state, and the legitimacy of a political system based on the practices known as *trasformismo*. Before Italy's dominant classes could peacefully enjoy the fruits of the nation's economic surge, they would have to either make an accommodation involving a fairer distribution of wealth and political power with the masses or sacrifice their hard-won individual liberties to an authoritarian ruler in the hopes of preserving their economic predominance.

The Southern Question was multifaceted: exhaustion of the soil, illiteracy, "amoral familism," dietary imbalance, overpopulation, lack of capital, unequal land distribution, and a rigid class structure all contributed to impoverishing Southern Italy. To ameliorate these problems the government had to attack an economic and social structure not far removed from feudalism in order to create a modern agrarian sector. Meanwhile, industrialization was exacerbating the problems of the South. The heart of Italy's industrial revolution lay in the most northern sector of the nation: the triangle of Turin, Milan, and Genoa. Certain other central and northern provinces, among them Venice, Bologna, and Florence, were making progress in industrial development. Within the area bounded by Turin to the west, Venice to the east, and Florence to the south, the agricultural sector had modernized and was able to provide a level of production and consumption adequate to support the new industries. An industrial state inside the Italian state came into being. The South, too backward to support its own industry, became an economic colony for Northern industrialists. Italian tariff policies cut the South off from the cheaper production of foreign industry. The

Southern peasant paid for the protection provided to Northern industry. The peasant masses of the *Mezzogiorno* (South) were caught in a rent and price squeeze created by their landlords' rising level of consumption and the increased costs of the necessities they could not produce for themselves.[5]

After national unification, the peasantry reacted to growing exploitation from the North with outbreaks of "social banditry." Supported by elements of the old nobility and the Church, the peasants fought an unsuccessful guerrilla war against the new government. The midnineteenth-century South, however, was not a seething cauldron of revolution with the army sitting on its lid. The conditions of the postunification peasantry were too depressed to provide the base for a social revolution, as Bakunin and other anarchists discovered. By 1900, however, Southern peasants were reaching a stage of elementary political consciousness. The strikes by organized peasantry known as the Sicilian *Fasci* (1893–94) indicated that the introduction of very rudimentary socialist ideas could transform millenarian expectation into something more durable: "the permanent and organized adherence to a revolutionary social movement."[6] Faced with the threat of an organized peasantry, the Southern ruling classes recognized that traditional means of control such as the *mafia* and the local clergy were inadequate and looked to the government to neutralize or eliminate the threat posed by socialist ideology.[7]

The ruling classes of the South had long since reached a favorable accommodation with Northern leaders. After the national unification, Northerners had treated the South as a conquered land. In reaction, the Southern ruling elite built an initial electoral alliance with ex-Garibaldians and Mazzinians who were equally discontented with the policies of Cavour's successors, the *Destra* ("Right"). Together, they formed core elements of the *Sinistra* ("Left"), the party of "democratic" opposition to Cavourian liberalism. In 1876, the *Sinistra* came to power and Southern leaders were in a position to firm up their control at home. In order to preserve their semifeudal economic and social position, they organized themselves into a permanent governmental bloc. A bargain was struck between Northern industrialists and Southern landowners. The Southerners accepted a policy of high tariffs and Northern economic hegemony in exchange for a free hand in dealing with the peasantry.[8]

The Southern Question was thus intimately linked with another of Italy's major problems: the inadequacy of its political system. Liberal Italy was governed by methods known as *trasformismo*. At different times and under different names, analogous practices have existed in the parliamentary systems of other Western nations. The necessary elements of *trasformismo* were an executive with wide powers of political patronage, a limited political class, and a restricted suffrage. The practices of *trasformismo* had been foreshadowed by Cavour's "marriage" of the left and right center of Piedmont's parliament in 1852. This alliance had united most of the middle class around Cavour and his policies, isolating the "clericals" of the old right and the followers of Mazzini and Garibaldi.

In 1876 the *Destra* split along regional lines over the issue of the nationalization of the railways. King Victor Emmanuel II asked Agostino Depretis, the leader of the left, to form a new ministry. Depretis called new elections that gave the *Sinistra* a sweeping victory. The press spoke of a "parliamentary revolution," but it failed to materialize. In spite of a large majority in parliament, neither Depretis nor Benedetto Cairoli, the other leader of the left, was able to form a stable government and the two men played musical chairs in the prime minister's office for four years. Finally, in 1881, Depretis hit upon a solution. He recognized that a single, highly restricted governing class could not support two distinct political parties. Since the satisfaction of specific, usually local, interests rather than broad issues of ideology and policy were at the root of much of the distinction between the two Liberal "parties," a rational distribution of favors would bring enough of the left and right together to form a stable majority. Depretis assumed the portfolio of minister of the interior, thereby taking control of the distribution of political patronage.

The other element in the *trasformismo* equation was the deputy. The "Liberal party" to which a vast majority of the deputies gave their allegiance was nonexistent. No central organization, no party paper, no common platform united Italian "liberals":

> The liberals were the local notables: landlords, businessmen, industrialists, lawyers, professional men: all those with a taste for politics. Usually they belonged to a loose "constitutional club" or organization which came to political life only at election times to promote certain men. This system produced men whose function was to act as agents for local interests . . . probably a provincial lawyer well versed in local problems, well connected with the notables, without roots in Rome, without political ambitions, who rarely let great issues get in the way of local problems.[9]

The deputy usually joined an organized political grouping only after he entered parliament. Governments were formed around these groups. The minister of the interior dealt with the groups and with the individual deputies, purchasing their support with a "judicious distribution of state patronage and expenditure or by the negative favor of a blind eye to local abuses or [by] the transfer of an awkward official."[10] In the absence of organized political parties, *trasformismo* kept the state functioning. Even in the advanced mass political societies of the present-day West, more than a slight application of the tactics of *trasformismo* is necessary to keep democratic government operating. *Trasformismo*, however, became the standard method of political operations in Italy at a time when the entire concept of parliamentary government was under attack throughout Europe. Moreover, *trasformismo* encouraged and magnified the worst abuses and failures of the parliamentary system: favoritism, electoral corruption, and localism. Public respect for representative institutions declined in the face of these defects and parliament's inability to provide solutions to national problems.[11]

No problem facing united Italy was more intractable than Church-state relations. The position of the Catholic church and the Papacy within Italy had vexed secular politicians since the fall of the Roman Empire. A united Italy without Rome was unthinkable to Italian nationalists, and Cavour's successors completed the unification and put an end to the temporal powers of the popes by seizing the city in 1870. The capture of Rome appeared to settle the territorial issue but left open the question of the legal and diplomatic position of an international church with its central administration inside the borders of a national state. Both the Church and the Italian leadership recognized that the initial solution offered by united Italy was a stopgap. This solution was a compound of the Law of Guarantees (1871), which offered monetary compensation for Rome together with pledges of equitable treatment for the Church, and an official policy of anticlericalism. Pope Pius IX's total condemnation of the Italian state was equally a stopgap measure.[12]

Pius died in 1878. His successor, Leo XIII, and the Italian government slowly groped their way toward a modus vivendi. Leo refused to abandon the Church's claim to temporal power. The Papacy's claim to universality would be compromised if the pope in effect accepted Italian citizenship by placing himself under the protection of Italy's government. Leo insisted that the relationship between Church and state had to be governed by a negotiated settlement.[13]

Liberal governments stood firm on the principles of the territorial unity of the Italian state and of the power of the state over the activities of the Italian Catholic church. In their view, the repeated attempts of Pius IX and

Leo XIII to turn the "Roman Question" into an international issue invited foreign powers to dismember Italy.[14]

The Vatican ordered Italian Catholics to refrain from participation in national politics. This decision limited the Catholic church's ability to bring its power to bear in parliament in proportion to its hold over the loyalties of a large share of the Italian population, thus assisting Liberal efforts to secularize the state. However, Catholic nonparticipation in public life also meant that this same large group was alienated from its Liberal rulers and from the state they were creating. Keenly aware that they were a tiny minority, the Liberals feared a Catholic mass movement. In addition, the ostentatious nonparticipation in the political and social life of the capital by Rome's "black [papal] nobility" underlined the depth of the Church's influence among the upper classes.[15]

Efforts by Italy's leaders and Pope Leo to find a compromise were unsuccessful until the dramatic events of 1890–1900 threatened to destroy the existing social structure, breaking down many of the barriers between the two sides. Fear of the "red menace" united Liberals and Catholics. The move toward reconciliation was further stimulated in 1903 when Pope Pius X succeeded Pope Leo. The new pope, a political reactionary, permitted Catholics to enter public life in order to bolster the Liberal state against socialism. The main issues of the Church-state relationship remained unresolved.[16]

The organization of a small portion of the Italian working class into trade unions and into the new Socialist party provided the catalyst for the partial and tactical reconciliation of Church and state. As late as 1914 neither movement made great inroads among the masses. Prior to 1919, the Socialist party membership never exceeded 50,000. In 1911, the year of its greatest expansion, the Confederazione Generale del Lavoro (CGL), Italy's national labor organization, had 383,770 members, approximately 5 percent of the working classes.[17]

Nevertheless, a number of factors combined to give the worker's movement a political impact greater than its size appeared to warrant. First, this movement was concentrated in the centers of Italy's economic and political life: Rome, Piedmont, Lombardy, and Emilia-Romagna. Second, the diminutive size of the Liberal ruling group made any movement which counted an active membership in the tens of thousands a potent force. Third, the PSI enjoyed considerable support among propertied skilled workers and artisans, the aristocracy of labor, which gave it a disproportionate weight within Italy's restricted electoral body. Finally, the growing political consciousness of industrial and agricultural workers increased pressure for the enactment of social and economic policies that would initiate a fundamental redistribution of wealth, threatening the social preeminence and political influence of Italy's entrepreneurial class.[18]

I

The Reformist Party

The PSI

and the

Giolittian System

During the last decade of the nineteenth century the maturation of the Italian Socialist movement paralleled the deepening crisis of the Liberal state in Italy. Beginning as a workers' self-help society oriented more toward symbolic political protest than practical achievement, Italian socialism rapidly developed into an electoral machine with well-defined political objectives. The coordination of the twin processes of organizational and ideological transformation was the work of a few men led by Filippo Turati and organized around the journal *Critica Sociale*. In contrast with the other factions which had a hand in the formation of the Italian Socialist party, Turati's group displayed superior organizational as well as intellectual ability and distinctly middle-class origins. The root of its influence was the *Critica Sociale* group's hold over the Party press and the parliamentary group. Following the formation of the Party in 1892, Turati and his allies controlled the Party's national newspapers together with its most important theoretical journal while providing both the bulk of the PSI's parliamentary representation and its most influential deputies.

THE BIRTH OF THE PSI, 1881–93

Anarchism dominated the Socialist movement in Italy until the 1880s. Thereafter, its hold rapidly weakened. The failure of anarchist-inspired uprisings in Bologna (1873) and Benevento (1877), the death of Michael Bakunin (1876), and the defection to Marxism of his chief Italian lieutenant, Carlo Cafiero (1882) were serious blows to the Italian anarchist movement. Anarchism lost its hold over large segments of the laboring classes as well as many intellectuals, who were disenchanted with the gospel of in-surrection and began to involve themselves in programs for the political education of the working class and in the creation of working-class organizations. The leader of this movement from insurrection to political education was Andrea Costa (1851–1910). In 1881 Costa played a major role in the formation of a Socialist Revolutionary party in the Romagna. In 1882 he became the first socialist to sit in the Italian parliament.

The same year a group of workers and artisans formed the Sons of Labor in Milan. The Sons' program stated that the "emancipation of the working class will only be accomplished through the efforts of the working class itself," and limited its membership to "workers in the most restricted sense of the word."[1] In 1883, this group began publishing a weekly newspaper, *Il Fascio Operaio,* directed by Costantino Lazzari. On September 1, 1884, the Milan Sons of Labor and similar organizations in four nearby cities founded the Regional Federation of North Italy of the Italian Workers Party (POI). They soon dropped the words *Regional Federation of North Italy* from the title, but the new party never exercised much influence outside Lombardy.

The Milan Socialist League grew up alongside this exclusively workers ("operaist") movement. The League was an organization for middle-class socialists whose leaders included Osvaldo Gnocchi-Viani, Enrico Bignami, and Filippo Turati. Initially, both the League and the Workers party supported the separation of the two organizations. The Workers party leadership viewed the League as an "intellectual reserve" which would "furnish the workers movement with the literary and scientific thought nec-essary for its development" and at the same time diffuse socialist views among the general Italian public. The middle-class intellectuals who made up the League accepted this dual role of brain trust and propaganda appa-ratus for the Workers party. Turati was delighted to write an anthem for the party. He commented that "the workers have economic, moral and histor-ical reasons to act for themselves" and that the formation of a multiclass socialist party on the German model was premature in Italy.[2]

Prime Minister Francesco Crispi dissolved both the Workers party and Costa's Socialist party in 1890. Crispi's subsequent actions convinced many socialists that the movement could only survive the frequent sequestration of its newspapers and the long jail terms handed out to many of its militants by building a new organization. A second factor driving the socialist fac-tions into closer association was their desire to publicly divorce the move-ment from the anarchists.[3]

Costa and Turati assumed leadership in the effort to unify all Italian socialists. A change in the political climate favored their efforts. Crispi fell in
February 1891. The conservative di Rudini succeeded him and dropped the
harshest antisocialist measures. The first ministry of Giovanni Giolitti,
which succeeded the di Rudini government in May 1892, took a tolerant
approach toward the groups of the far left. Profiting from the suspension of
police repression, the socialists reorganized. Initial efforts by Costa to unify
the various socialist groups failed. Many of the former members of the
Workers party continued to mistrust middle-class intellectuals, while some
middle-class socialist intellectuals feared the results which a fusion of the
classes would have on workers' self-initiative. Nonetheless attempts to
achieve fusion continued until Turati successfully brought it about. At the
1891 Congress of Milanese Workers, Turati secured the adoption of a resolution calling for the creation of an Italian Workers party with a membership open to all associations of working men. The Milanese workers also
voted to hold an organizational congress the following year and appointed a
commission to prepare for this meeting.[4]

ignificant step in the process of orga-
ly. On January 1, 1891, the first edi-
ica Sociale, appeared in Milan. For
cioff, *Critica Sociale* was the starting
vorkers' movement and ultimately the
arx. The group which formed around
young, university-educated, northern,
venty who formed its inner circle of
degrees: eight in law, three in medi-
s social sciences. In 1900 the average
n were under thirty, another six were
rom Piedmont, three from Lombardy,
one, the historian Gaetano Salvemini,
hip of the group was furnished by the
ties, parliamentary deputies by 1900,
ialist movement since the 1880s. The
ini, Leonida Bissolati, and, of course,

–15, 1892) began the formidable task
. An anarchist minority with support
nined to obstruct this effort. After a
the Marxist socialists out of the meet-

ing. That evening, one hundred and fifty of the Marxist delegates met at a local restaurant and agreed to hold a rump congress, excluding both the anarchists and their allies. Speaking to this meeting the following day, Turati proposed that a new, interclass Partito dei Lavoratori Italiani (PLI) assume full responsibility for the conquest of political power by the proletariat, leaving control over economic affairs to organized labor. The Turati proposals were approved by the delegates who also passed a party platform, soon to become famous as the "Maximal Program," with only four dissenting votes.[7]

The Maximal Program called for the socialization of the means of production "by the action of a proletariat organized in a party of class, independent of all other parties." The task of this party would be conquering power in elections with the ultimate objective of transforming "the organs of oppression and exploitation . . . into instruments of the political and economic expropriation of the ruling classes."[8]

Critics, including Antonio Labriola, Italy's foremost academic student of Marx, continually berated the new party for its lack of intellectual coherence and the shallowness of its leaders' understanding of Marx. They were substantially correct. In order to bring divergent and often mutually hostile intellectual groups, the *operaisti,* labor organizations, and mutual assistance societies into a single Marxist movement, Turati stressed lowest common denominators. The factions that made up the new organization never achieved more than a common agreement that their party was Marxist. Moreover, the middle-class intellectuals who dominated the movement until the eve of World War I were highly influenced by positivism. They frequently substituted the optimistic view of evolution ("a linear theory of progress") that characterized positivist thought for Marx's vision of a long, difficult, and violent class struggle as the motor that drove human society toward a socialist revolution. Nevertheless, the Reformist current that Turati guided fit easily into the mainstream of European socialism. Similar movements existed in the French and German parties, the major centers of Marxist socialism. Throughout the pre–World War I era, Reformism was the only consistently coherent faction within the PSI, a factor that enabled it to survive many inherent organizational weaknesses and dominate the Party during much of the Giolittian era.[9]

After adopting the Maximal Program, the congress created a structure for the new party. Its key decisions were to permit its local units to participate in elections and to grant them wide administrative autonomy. The *Statuto* ("constitution") of the PLI opened its membership to "all federations, leagues, . . . and independent societies which adhere to [its] program'' and to ''all workers associations . . . which aim at [their members'] economic and social improvement.'' Each of these societies would have one vote at the national congresses. The delegates created a central committee responsible to the congress for its conduct to oversee the daily activities of the PLI. Each of the societies belonging to the PLI was to pay dues in proportion to the size of its membership. Failure to pay meant the loss of the right to vote at the national congress. The delegates designated the Milanese weekly, *Lotta di Classe,* which Turati discreetly edited, as the Party newspaper.[10]

Overall, the new party bore the imprint of Filippo Turati. He had cajoled diverse factions into a small centralized party that openly proclaimed itself Marxist. At Turati's insistence, the Party program excluded the use of violence. Turati was behind the creation of a central committee. Most importantly, he prevailed on the issues of giving the PLI a program with a distinctively Marxist flavor and on a multiclass membership. A party that openly proclaimed its Marxism would attract limited numbers of recruits, but Turati preferred to rely on a small body of committed militants. He mistrusted the masses, particularly the Southern peasantry, believing they were easily exploited by reactionary forces. Turati saw the Socialist movement as the necessary intermediary between the masses and Italy's ruling elites.[11]

For the first time in its history, Italy had a centralized political movement. Its national and regional congresses and the annual accountability of the central committee safeguarded the Party's internal democracy. The central committee, however, enjoyed broad powers of intervention to enforce the decisions of the Party Congress. A ''national'' weekly newspaper would diffuse a single Party line.

On the other hand, despite the declarations of the Maximal Program, the PLI was basically a society for mutual assistance with vague political aims, rather than a parliamentary political party. Its organization was based on workers' societies, generally of the mutual aid variety, and much of the money collected by the Party was earmarked for assisting the victims of governmental persecution.[12] Finally, the *Statuto* made no provision for the existence of a socialist parliamentary group (GPS), although ''socialist'' deputies already sat in parliament.

With its program and constitution determined, the Congress divided responsibilities. The influence of the POI reasserted itself through the selection of a Central Committee made up of seven workers from Milan, among them, the chiefs of the defunct Workers party. Milan's dominance of the new party was rooted in its advanced state of industrialization and resultant heavy concentration of workers, labor organizations, and socialist intellectuals. The delegates sanctioned this leadership role with their decision that both the Central Committee and Party newspaper would reside in that city. In order to lessen the impression of Milanese control of the Party, the delegates selected Prampolini, who already published the successful *La Giustizia,* as the titular editor of Turati's *Lotta di Classe.*[13]

The operaist faction controlled the PLI's Central Committee, but its members exercised little control over the Party. The mutual assistance orientation of the PLI was one reason.[14] The Party's membership was another: organizations not individuals joined the PLI. "At Reggio Emilia [1893], the Italian Workers Party comprised 294 societies and 107,830 members, 65,932 from Sicily alone. . . . A good half of [them], one can say without fear of exaggeration, were in the Party either without their knowledge, or against their will."[15] Very few of these 100,000 members had any knowledge of Marx. Party leaders lacked a program outlining immediate political objectives. Antonio Labriola, the influential socialist intellectual, complained that the Party was completely unprepared for an election campaign. Meanwhile, the Sicilians, whose socialism tended toward millenarianism, impatiently demanded that the PLI act immediately to achieve the Maximal Program. Finally, Turati emerged as Party leader and spokesman because of his control of the press and his carefully nurtured ties with organized labor. *Critica Sociale* had easily established its preeminence as the Party's theoretical journal. Claudio Treves, the new editor in chief of *Lotta di Classe,* was Turati's most trusted lieutenant. The preeminence of the Turati faction fueled a latent rivalry with the operaist group.[16]

CREATING A CADRE PARTY, 1893–1900

The Congress of Reggio Emilia (1893) tied up many of the loose ends left over by the Genoa meeting, in particular, defining the PLI's immediate political objectives. Taking up the important question of political tactics, the Congress adopted a resolution stating its opposition to any form of alliance with middle-class parties. It then provided rules for the conduct and organization of the five socialist parliamentary deputies, approving a Giuseppe Croce resolution that instructed the deputies to form a parliamentary group and maintain a united front against the middle-class parties.[17] The resolution also required that the deputies maintain close contact with the PLI leadership through an elected secretary and accept the Party's direction. It subjected their conduct to review by the Party congress. Finally, the resolution instructed the deputies "in no case can the parliamentary faction give a vote of confidence to a government."[18]

The attempt to create a disciplined parliamentary group was a major innovation in Italian political practice. Moreover, recognizing the need for a coherent program on which the Party's parliamentary group could run for election and conduct its legislative business, the delegates adopted the first of a series of "minimal" programs that defined the objectives of the socialist parliamentarians. The Congress also voted to change its name to the Socialist Party of Italian Workers (PSLI). Finally, the congress again elected members of the operaist faction to the Central Committee. Turati's group retained control of the Party press.[19]

Reggio Emilia gave the PSLI a political arm by establishing a parliamentary group and providing it with a program. Structurally, however, the Party remained a national society of mutual assistance groups rather than an electoral organization. Crispi forced the socialists to restructure their party. In December 1893 the Giolitti government fell in the wake of a banking scandal. At almost the same time, the disorders caused by the groups known as the Sicilian *Fasci* came to a head. Giolitti had attempted to deal with these disorders by ameliorating their causes. Crispi invoked martial law. By the end of January 1894, he had suppressed the *Fasci* and either imprisoned its leaders or driven them into hiding. The PSLI was decimated in the police actions and deeply implicated in what Crispi believed was a foreign plot against Italian unity.[20]

Taking advantage of a parliamentary recess, Crispi dissolved the PSLI by royal decree and arrested the members of the Central Committee (October 22, 1894). Before reporting to their designated place of confinement, the Central Committee members convoked an emergency congress to discuss the reorganization of the Party. Police action prevented a scheduled meeting at Bologna, but the delegates convened secretly in Parma on January 13, 1895. Reorganization was the first order of business for the clandestine congress. Piedmontese representatives proposed abandoning the existing organization based on workers societies in favor of the creation of a party based on local electoral circles. The Milanese socialists insisted that membership in the Party must be on an individual basis. The congress adopted a resolution reorganizing the Party around "local socialist groups composed of individual members paying minimum dues of 1.20 lire per year." The Italian Socialist party (PSI) was born.[21]

Meanwhile, Turati had challenged the continued value of a policy of absolute separation from reform-minded middle-class parties and organizations. In the February 1894 edition of *Critica Sociale,* Turati published a carefully edited letter from Engels entitled "The Future Italian Revolution and the Socialist Party." Engels's letter noted the failure of the Italian bourgeoisie "to complete its victory" over the old ruling class in the Risorgimento. Since the Socialist party was "too young and, because of the economic situation, too weak to hope for an immediate victory of socialism," Engels gave his blessing to the strategy of creating alliances with middle-class reformers.[22]

Turati's brief support for a strategy of total opposition to middle-class parties ("intransigence") had been purely tactical. Since the middle of the 1880s, he had favored cooperation with more progressive elements of the middle classes. In an 1892 article in *Critica Sociale,* Turati gave a Marxist justification to these views:

> Certainly, if one part of the bourgeois class accepts one of our ideas, fights privilege with us, works to disarm another faction of the middle class, it obviously takes its advantage from the fleeting instant and, in reinforcing us, ends, as a class, in damaging itself . . . [T]he ranks of the powerful . . . always hasten their own fall with their own hands, attempting to raise themselves to greater power . . . When we have a stronger *bourgeoisie* in Italy, we will have a much stronger proletariat.[23]

In September 1894, following the publication of the Engels letter, Turati supported the establishment of a middle-class-led Milanese "League of Liberty" to oppose Crispi's reactionary policies. Although Bissolati criticized this action as going too far in the direction of cooperation with the middle class, Turati defended his move by urging Italian Socialists to follow a policy of "continuous adaptation" to changing circumstances. Turati's independent stand soon passed acceptable limits for one member of the Party Central Committee. Lazzari appeared at the editorial offices of *Critica Sociale* with a rebuttal article in hand. After a "violent argument," Turati refused to print the article. "From that moment on there was a continuous polemic on tactics," in which Lazzari and the other supporters of "intransigence" were at a serious disadvantage because they lacked editorial control over any important Party journal.[24]

While the quarrel over tactics grew, the reorganization of the Party's structure went ahead. The Fourth Congress of the Italian socialist movement met in Florence in the fall of 1896. Lazzari presented a Central Committee resolution that instructed the sections to organize and recruit with the aim of winning elections and limited membership in the PSI to individuals who were dues-paying members of the sections.[25]The motion was attacked by the Party's left. The young Neapolitan intellectual, Walter Mocchi, warned that "in a country without universal suffrage and without a correspondence between the working class and the electoral body, one can not speak of organization on an electoral base."[26]

Bissolati offered an amendment to the Lazzari resolution stressing the division of responsibility between the political (PSI) and economic arms of the working-class movement. Enrico Ferri then offered a compromise resolution which permitted local socialists to determine their mode of organization. In the voting the unamended Lazzari resolution triumphed.

One of the last acts of the Congress of Florence was to approve the establishment of a new national daily newspaper. On December 25, 1896, that newspaper, *Avanti!*, published its first edition. *Avanti!*'s director was Leonida Bissolati. A socialist national Congress had again strengthened the *Critica Sociale* group's control over the Party press. The delegates' decision that only the Party's national congress could supervise and review the activities of *Avanti!*'s director reinforced Bissolati's position.[27]

The Maximal Program's call for the conquest of power by political means foreshadowed the victory of the concept of an electoral political organization over a party based on workers' mutual assistance. The staking out of positions by three influential middle-class intellectuals was the most interesting development at the Congress of Florence. Mocchi's statement, which emphasized that the labor movement was the key to a successful revolution, capsulized the developing viewpoint of the future Revolutionary Syndicalists, a group of southern socialists, led by Arturo Labriola. Electoral success was to be subordinated to the creation of class solidarity. The PSI would be a spear carrier for the working class. Ultimately, the young Syndicalists decided that the Party constituted a roadblock to their plans for an Italian revolution. They recognized that the emphasis on compromise that was at the center of parliamentary politics undercut the social tensionsthat create revolutionary situations. The young Syndicalists' objective was a revolution. Their strategy was class confrontation. Radicalized unions,not a political party, were the best vehicle for achieving this goal.

Ferri's suggestion that the Party organization be based in some areas on local electoral organizations and in others on workers' self-help societies was typical of his political style. Throughout his PSI career, Ferri's strength rested on his ability to express the fears of the rank and file that too much fighting over tactical issues would destroy the Party's unity. Ferri's political actions always revolved around his personal ambitions. He had little interest in the finer points of strategy or organization.

Bissolati outlined the views of Turati's faction on political organization by emphasizing the division of labor between the political and economic organizations of the working class. Turati and his allies wanted to strictly limit the PSI's involvement with the day-to-day business of the labor movement and permit the Party to concentrate its full attention on parliamentary politics. Turati's faction always measured the success of the socialist movement in terms of vote totals and parliamentary seats. Their objective was the reform of the existing state. The strategy was class cooperation in parliament. The "Reformists" relied on the cadre party both to organize the working classes around this program and to achieve credibility with Italy's governing classes.

The victory of Lazzari's resolution was the last significant success for the operaist current of the PSI. Among the factors which led to their decline were financial scandals that touched Lazzari and other central committee members, the cumbersome nature of the Party in its earlier forms, and Turati's control of the press. However, the most important factor in the decline of the operaist faction was the Party's new electoral organization. In an electoral party, the deputy became an independent power center. Moreover, deputies were unsalaried in Liberal Italy. This fact practically mandated that the deputies come from the professional middle class or wealthy aristocracy. The Italian Socialist party relied upon middle-class intellectuals to form its parliamentary group. After the elections of 1897, the Party held fifteen (later sixteen) parliamentary seats. All were occupied by middle-class politicians. More importantly, seven of the sixteen were closely associated with Filippo Turati. Creating an electoral organization for the PSI meant specialization: the middle-class deputy and professional journalist. The *Critica Sociale* group provided these specialists. Lazzari and his group, with their limited skills, income, and power base, lost influence. The dramatic events of 1898–1900 pushed them into political oblivion and confirmed the Party on a parliamentary course.[28]

The parenthesis of relative calm following the fall of Crispi's government in 1896 had permitted the Socialists to rebuild their party. This parenthesis came to an abrupt end in the fall of 1897, when a poor harvest doubled the already heavily taxed cost of bread. During the winter of 1897–98 rising prices provoked food riots in the South. The rioting spread into northern

Italy during the spring of 1898. The attempts of the di Rudini government to meet the crisis were ineffective. On May 6, 1898, an insurrection, the *fatti di maggio*, broke out among the alienated poor of Milan. On May 7, the di Rudini ministry proclaimed martial law and sent the army into Milan to restore order. The soldiers put down the insurrection with force, killing at least eighty civilians and arresting hundreds, including every major Socialist party leader in the city. In the trials which followed, Turati, who had attempted to halt the disturbances, was sentenced to twelve years in prison. The government suppressed *Critica Sociale*.

Public reaction to the government's actions was negative, and di Rudini resigned in June 1898. King Umberto I asked General Luigi Pelloux to form a new ministry. Pelloux's nomination was a royal gesture of conciliation toward the left. The general had close ties to the Court but was also known for his liberal views and had developed good working relationships with many elements of the moderate left. The Court hoped that Pelloux would utilize these contacts to dampen the crisis. Instead, the new prime minister succeeded in taking the struggle off the streets and bringing it into the halls of parliament. In the process, the problem of restoring order became a constitutional question of the government's right to restrict freedom of speech and of the press in the name of internal security. Parliament became the cockpit for this struggle, and a coalition of Liberals, Republicans, and Socialists emerged to defend not only their political right to exist but also the whole system of parliamentary government. Urged on by his whip, the conservative Baron Sidney Sonnino, Pelloux moved to increasingly extreme positions. The Socialists countered with a series of increasingly extreme parliamentary tactics: filibustering, overturning voting urns, and finally, mass resignation. During a year and a half of political warfare, the left defeated Pelloux's efforts to increase the powers of the Crown at the expense of parliament. The frustrated prime minister called new elections. The left increased its support, and although he still held a diminished majority in parliament, Pelloux resigned on June 24, 1900.

The experience of 1898–1900 confirmed both Turati's faith in a parliamentary strategy and his leadership of the Party. During Turati's imprisonment, Bissolati assumed the leadership of the *Critica Sociale* current and made *Avanti!* the rallying point for the forces of the left. The pages of the Socialist daily became a meeting place for the views of all those fighting for civil liberties.

As part of his civil liberties campaign, Bissolati employed *Avanti!* to agitate for the release of Turati and other Socialist prisoners. Simultaneously,

Bissolati and Enrico Ferri led the Socialist parliamentary deputies in the battle to block the government's efforts to restrict individual rights.[29]

Turati and Bissolati drew the same conclusions from the experience of 1898–1900: socialism could only succeed if basic constitutional rights were strengthened and guaranteed. Maintaining these rights necessitated the defense of parliament. To ensure their ultimate triumph, the Socialists would have to abandon notions of violent revolution for what both Bissolati and Turati were convinced was the slower but ultimately more secure method of mustering the parliamentary majorities needed to gradually transform Italy into a socialist society. Successful parliamentary politics required not only alliances with the other parties of the far left but also cooperation with democratically inclined Liberals like Giuseppe Zanardelli and Giovanni Giolitti.

Shortly after he was imprisoned, Turati wrote his mother that a Giolitti government offered the best hope for his early release from confinement. At about the same time, Giolitti began to take an increasingly active role in the parliamentary opposition to Pelloux. Although he did not support the obstructionist tactics of the Socialists, Giolitti repeatedly underlined his opposition to the government's measures. Simultaneously, he used his influence to improve the treatment of the government's political prisoners.[30]

Shortly after his 1899 release from prison, Turati resumed publishing *Critica Sociale,* and a Claudio Treves article summed up the view which the Turatian Socialists had formed of Giolitti:

> There is on the other side a man who understands us. . . . Giolitti understands the causes of the discontent of Italy and realizes that the PSI expresses this discontent. He also understands that [Italy] must choose between imperial ventures and economic well being at home. He is aware of the tyranny of the bureaucracy over the lives of the people, and of the lack of justice. Giolitti also understands that the rising forces in the state cannot be suffocated by violence (and he appreciates their size and power) but rather he realizes that they must be allowed to grow. Together with the Socialists, he demands liberty, although his final aims are not those of the Socialists. He does not envision the future socialist society. [It is] enough that this man has understood that infringing liberty is . . . foolish and dangerous.[31]

In the 1900 parliamentary elections, the PSI doubled its vote and its parliamentary representation rose from sixteen to thirty-two. Membership in the Party also doubled. Since the conservatives still held a diminished majority in parliament, the creation of a reform ministry would require at least the tacit support of the Socialist party. Thus, the Socialists had to decide whether the advantages of supporting a left-center government were great enough to warrant the abandonment of the successful tactics of the previous seven years and, if so, what price they would demand for their support.

On January 1, 1900, Turati and Kuliscioff outlined their vision of a socialist parliamentary strategy, soon known as Reformism. They called for the creation of a democratic government whose program was the restoration of the rule of law. The other parts of the Reformist program were the election of magistrates subject to recall, reduction of military expenditures, abandonment of colonial ambitions, tax reforms, reorganization of the police forces, and legislation protecting laboring women and children. Turati and Kuliscioff envisioned a coalition government based on the "popular" parties of the left and the progressive elements of the Liberal party which would enact this program of reform. The Socialist party should demand only one thing as its price for supporting such a coalition government: "that it [the government] adapt itself to create conditions favorable to the civil development of our country."[32] They opposed direct PSI participation in the central government, arguing that this would be the last step in the revolutionary process which a democratic government would put into motion:

> For us, the revolution comes from events. We await it and live in expectation. Every school that opens, every mind which is unclouded, every backbone which is straightened, every cancerous abuse which is eradicated, every elevation of the tenor of life of the oppressed, every law protecting labor . . . all . . . coordinated to a very clear and conscious end of social transformation. . . . There will come a day when these snowflakes will form an avalanche. To augment this latent force, to labor everyday for it, is to make revolution a daily work. . . . This is the revolutionary path which we follow every day.

After the fall of Pelloux's ministry, Italian politics passed through an entr'acte. The Saracco government (June 1900–February 1901) was a caretaker regime whose mission was to do nothing to upset the political truce until the various parliamentary factions sorted out their objectives. This political truce held despite the July 29, 1900, assassination of King Umberto by an anarchist. The new king, Victor Emmanuel III wanted to avoid a repetition of the political upheavals of the previous three years.

On September 8, 1900, the Sixth Congress of the Italian Socialist party met at the Teatro Eldorado in Rome. The congress was a historic watershed for the Party. After a lively debate, it approved a resolution presented by

Ivanoe Bonomi of the Turati faction which authorized Socialist sections to take control of local governments wherever conditions permitted. The congress also authorized the sections to run candidates on combined lists with other parties, to support local governments, and to participate on special commissions.[33]

The congress next approved a Treves resolution which granted full autonomy to its local organizations to form electoral alliances with the middle-class parties of the *estrema* (extreme left) in order to elect parliamentary deputies. The PSI's Central Committee, however, retained the right to veto any agreement which seemed to conflict with the Party's objectives.[34]

The congress also reorganized the Central Committee (*Direzione*), changing the composition of its membership to increase the weight of the parliamentary group and Party press in the leadership of the PSI. Finally, it heard a report by Treves on a new minimal program, and after considering the objections of Arturo Labriola, the congress approved the new program by acclamation.[35]

Commenting on the significance of the 1900 minimal program, one Italian historian summarized the judgment of many Italian scholars:

> As a platform of propaganda and agitation, the Minimal Program was of little value because of the generalness of its affirmations. In its ideological meaning it acquired a much greater importance. . . . It announced that the roads to revolution and the socialist society were long and unforeseeable and that the realization of the socialist society was to be put off *sine die*.[36]

In fact, nothing in the 1900 minimal program warrants this judgment. The Socialist party had been adopting and refining minimal programs since 1893. The 1900 program simply improved the political platform on which the Party's deputies could run. Further, all the PSI's factions agreed that the creation of a socialist society lay in the distant future. The 1900 minimal program acquired its special significance because it represented a list of concessions which the Reformists hoped to win from a reforming government.[37]

The adoption of a reformist strategy and the reorganization of the *Direzione* represented the triumph of Turati's conception of the Party. This victory was gained with a minimum of opposition. The arguments of opponents of a policy of class cooperation focused on the dangers to the "immature" PSI from dealing with the bourgeoisie rather than on the political or ideological implications of this approach. They were extolling the virtues of virginity to a daughter who had taken a lover years earlier.

The PSI already had entered into a close cooperation with the parties of the *estrema* and factions of the Liberal left. The Rome congress recognized this fact and regularized the relationship.[38]

A Ferri resolution reorganized the *Direzione*. It ensured the dominance of Reformism within the PSI by giving five seats on the eleven-man Central Committee to the members of the parliamentary group and another to the director of *Avanti!*. The two strongholds of Reformism were freed from any effective control except that exercised by the national congresses.[39]

The Rome congress marked both the triumph of Reformism and the end of the heroic age of Italian Socialism. From a feared, persecuted, and often clandestine movement, the PSI had become an accepted part of the Italian political system. Its support was essential for the formation of a reform government. The Party now faced the formidable task of making its political programs a reality through parliamentary action.[40]

GIOLITTI AND THE PSI

In February 1901 King Victor Emmanuel III asked the elderly Giuseppe Zanardelli to form a government which would pacify the nation through a policy of prudent reform, abandoning the repressive tactics of the previous decade. Giovanni Giolitti, who became the minister of the interior in the new government, was fifty-nine years old.

Giolitti began his career in the bureaucracy and, after establishing a reputation as an exceptional career civil servant, entered politics. He first won election to parliament in 1882 and held his seat until his death in 1928. Banking scandals almost finished his career in 1894, and Zanardelli turned to Giolitti for help in forming and maintaining a government as much for the lack of an alternative as for Giolitti's great parliamentary skills. The King had vetoed a Giolitti government, but no left-center ministry could be formed without the support of Giolitti and his bloc of deputies. Giolitti got the powerful interior ministry as the price for his support.[41]

Giolitti is one of the most controversial figures in modern Italy's history. In his memoirs, the Piedmontese statesman referred to the events of 1900–1901 as a conscious decision by the Italian nation to "return" to Liberal traditions. Giolitti seems to have meant a cautious reformism leading to a gradual and perhaps incomplete democratization of the Italian state. Such liberalism, personified in the work of Cavour, Cairoli, Zanardelli, and Giolitti, would be based on economic prosperity and the rejection of imperial involvements.[42]

For Giolitti the "tradition of liberalism" also meant established Italian political methods, especially *trasformismo*. Giolitti accepted *trasformismo*, improved its techniques, and adapted it to accommodate two major new political movements: socialism and political Catholicism. However, he faced a major dilemma: the greater the success of reform, the greater the peril to the Liberal state and the privileged groups it represented. The creation of political institutions designed to accommodate the masses could mean the end of *trasformismo*, of Giolitti, and of the Liberal state. The inclusion of the Socialist and Catholic mass movements within the Italian state necessitated carrying the Liberal ruling classes toward democracy while simultaneously restraining the ambitions and demands of two powerful new movements. This audacious attempt to head off social upheaval through judicious and timely reform was conceived and carried forward by an individual thoroughly rooted in tradition. More extraordinary still, Giolitti appeared to be on the verge of carrying off his program when he abandoned his anti-imperialist foreign policy and plunged Italy into a divisive colonial war in Libya (1911).[43]

Giolitti's electoral techniques best reveal the contradictions which plagued his program. In the South, where the masses remained substantially disenfranchised, Giolitti permitted corruption, violence, and direct interference by the government's prefects to ensure a progovernment majority in elections. In the North, he employed much subtler methods of influencing elections. However, as one of his harshest critics admitted, even illegal activities in the South were marked by a certain restraint under the new minister of the interior: "Giolitti was, in sum, dictator only on election day, only where it was necessary, and within the limits of necessity." This policy of moderate corruption for the best of ends had an effect opposite from that which Giolitti's admirers, Socialists among them, expected: "It is a labor of Sisyphus: the result is that democracy is paralyzed and disorganized rather than conquered."[44]

The Italian Socialist party remained at the center of Giolitti's plans until 1912. Giolitti was one of the first Italian politicians to recognize the significant role which the socialist movement would play in Italian politics. He was convinced that the socialist movement could be mastered within a parliamentary system and that the threat to established institutions posed by the left could be resolved by a policy of intelligent economic, social, and political reform. The threat of socialism built Catholic support for the Piedmontese leader. Catholic leaders made little differentiation between the Reformists and the more radical elements inside the PSI, since all socialists were united in their opposition to the Church. However, a truly revolutionary Socialist party would deprive Giolitti of his political options and drive him into the arms of the right. Giolitti needed the continued predominance of Turati's Reformists as well as the presence within the PSI of a noisy but ineffective left-wing minority to achieve his objectives. Belief in a "red peril" made Catholic leaders and other conservatives more amenable to reform. With Turati and other moderates dominating the Socialist party and the socialists continuing their anticlerical propaganda offensive, Giolitti successfully played on the tensions between Catholics and Socialists and between the Reformists and their "revolutionary" opponents.[45]

Giolitti got a second chance to see what judicious reform could do when he became the minister of the interior in 1901. The new government seemed destined to a brief life. Conservatives still held a majority in the Chamber. The governing coalition was formed around the blocs of Zanardelli and Giolitti (about 125 deputies) together with the Socialists and the other deputies of the *estrema* (75 members). These forces gave the government a solid group of 200 seats in a chamber of 508 deputies. Giolitti had to round up the additional votes needed for a working majority in the Chamber.[46]

Luckily for Giolitti, all of the parties of the *estrema* were under compelling pressure to cooperate with the new government in order to avoid a return to the politics of repression practiced by the right. The only alternative to Zanardelli appeared to be an authoritarian ministry led by Sonnino. Nevertheless, keeping a government in power required Giolitti to manage skillfully both issues and personalities. The Socialist deputies had to be able to show their restive constituents significant economic and political gains from cooperation with the bourgeoisie in order to retain the backing of the rank and file for the experiment in class cooperation.[47]

The Socialist parliamentary group voted to support the Zanardelli-Giolitti government on June 15, 1901, in defiance of a May decision by the *Direzione*. Turati insisted that the *Direzione*'s formula of supporting the cabinet on a "case by case" basis was unworkable. The GPS had to commit itself to preserving the Zanardelli-Giolitti government "as long as it maintained its policy line." He won the majority of the group to this view. Significantly, Enrico Ferri opposed Turati's motion of support. He insisted that the GPS could support the government on a vote of confidence and then vote against it on the specific issue of Italy's military alliances to remain consistent with its antimilitarism policy. Turati was incredulous. He could see no sense in a policy that would result in the collapse of a reform-oriented government and its probable replacement with a reactionary cabinet under Sonnino.[48]

The Socialist deputies were able to point to significant legislative gains from cooperation with the Zanardelli-Giolitti ministry. Parliament passed new regulations on the conditions of working women and children. It established two national bodies to care for the unemployed and the handicapped. Government-sponsored public works cut down unemployment, while other programs promoted the establishment and growth of workers' cooperatives.[49]

Meanwhile, the new minister of the interior was repaying the government's other political debts. The Zanardelli ministry took a new line on strikes, declaring its neutrality in labor disputes. The government's attitude was a major step toward the fulfillment of part of the PSI's political program. The Italian working classes, long accustomed to government support for the owners, found the new policy "almost revolutionary."[50] They acted immediately to test the sincerity of the ministry.

In the first major tests of the new policy, the Italian government emerged as a mediator between capital and labor.[51] Instructing his prefects on the approach to take in one important agricultural strike, Giolitti outlined his philosophy:

> Obviously we are faced with an irresistible economic movement which tends toward the improvement of the *contadini* [peasantry]. . . . It would be useless and perhaps impossible to oppose such a movement. Therefore the object of the government must be to regulate it so that the demands of the workers are within reasonable limits, and that the proprietors examine them with benevolence and with the intention of accepting them when they are just.[52]

Nevertheless, Giolitti was ready to use force to protect the property rights of the owners, and in spite of his repeated warnings to the prefects to act with caution, clashes broke out between strikers and government troops.[53]

The Socialists, however, remained within the coalition supporting the government. The strike at Molinella provides a case study of both Giolitti's techniques and the attitudes of the Socialist party's leadership. Molinella lay within the province of Bologna, and its parliamentary representative was Leonida Bissolati, the number-two man in the Reformist leadership. The city had been a center of labor unrest for years. In 1901, strikers attempted to coerce other workers into joining their walkout. The prefect of Bologna called in heavily armed police to protect nonstriking workers. After receiving his prefect's report on the situation, Giolitti sent a copy to

Bissolati together with a request that the Socialist deputy take a hand in the negotiations aimed at settling the strike. Bissolati agreed immediately and the strike was settled in May 1901, although only after further outbreaks of violence left one striker dead. Throughout the complex negotiations which led to a settlement, Giolitti generally accepted the specific recommendations of Bissolati but backed the decisions of his prefect concerning the use of police. The May 25 killing of a striker forced Bissolati to choose between accepting a compromise solution or breaking off the negotiations and his contacts with Giolitti. He chose continued cooperation with Giolitti in great part because he feared that a serious split with the government would lead to its overthrow and a return to the repressive practices of the 1890s.[54]

The strike at Molinella quite clearly revealed the Reformists' dilemma. They believed that the PSI needed Giolitti and Zanardelli more than the Liberal reformers needed them. The Reformists had no alternative to the Zanardelli-Giolitti government. Giolitti was determined that he would guide the pace of reform and that the improvement of working conditions would take place within limits defined by the government. The PSI remained divided on the policy of class cooperation. Reformist control depended on its success in winning concessions from the Giolitti-Zanardelli ministry. Giolitti played upon this weakness to keep the PSI within the governing coalition on his terms.[55]

Meanwhile, Giolitti used his wide powers as minister of the interior to put the individual Socialist deputies in his debt. He was the channel through which the government distributed favors to individual deputies. In certain instances, Giolitti threw the support of the government behind Reformist deputies in internal Party struggles. In some cases he even intervened to see that a favored Reformist candidate was elected. Giolitti was particularly concerned when internal Party struggles forced Turati to resign his seat and run in a special election in the spring of 1902.[56]

By 1904 Giolitti succeeded in "transforming" a large number of individual Socialist deputies through a combination of economic reforms and political favors. In the process, by meeting many of the outstanding demands of the urban and rural working classes, he weakened the appeal of the Socialists at the same time that his policy of support for the Reformists widened their internal divisions. Giolitti gave the Liberal state a new lease on life.[57] The organizational structure that the Reformists imposed on the PSI played a significant role in facilitating Giolitti's success.

Reformism

and

Party

Organization

In 1899, one of the most perceptive students of the Italian Socialist party, Antonio Labriola, wrote, "Here Party means Parliamentary Group and *Avanti!*. There is nothing else. . . . "[1] Studies of the PSI's early history have frequently ignored this shrewd observation about the nature of the Party. Yet, the question of political organization was inextricably bound with the issue of which of the conflicting socialist programs the PSI would adopt. Any analysis of the collapse of Reformist control within the PSI must deal with the connection of political strategy and organization.

EUROPEAN SOCIALISM

A recent study of the period of the Second International (1889–1914) defined that era as the "golden age of Marxism." The political movement that took its inspiration from the writings of Karl Marx was a rising force throughout the European continent. Marxism had not yet been codified into a stultifying dogma. Both socialist theorists and politicians were blending Marx's views with other ideas and traditions to create Marxist parties that shared many common features but also displayed unique national characteristics.[2]

The development of "revisionist" Marxism was a natural reaction to the breadth of the intellectual heritage that confronted Marx's disciples. The philosopher and political pamphleteer of the 1840s was a far different Marx from the social scientist of the 1870s and early 1880s. Moreover many of Marx's key suppositions were incorrect. Perhaps most troubling for post-Marx socialists was the evident failure of capitalist development to produce the impoverishment of the proletariat. The working classes were gaining a limited share of the wealth that their labor created. As the workers joined in the prosperity created by industrialization, the likelihood of a proletarian revolution appeared to decline. Socialist politicians and thinkers began exploring alternatives to the concept of a revolutionary dictatorship of the proletariat. In particular, they began to adjust their thinking about parliamentary government, exploring the possibility of utilizing parliament and universal suffrage to smooth the path toward eventual working-class control of the state.[3]

Frederich Engels, Marx's aging but influential associate, sensed a danger that "revisionist" ideas would cause the Marxist movement to fragment and lose its international character. From the mid-1880s to his death in 1895, Engels strove to create a body of doctrine, a Marxist orthodoxy, that would be the common patrimony of all socialist parties. In this effort, Engels enjoyed the cooperation of a number of German Social Democrats, most prominently Karl Kautsky, and, most ironically, Eduard Bernstein.[4]

On the critical issue of the process of revolutionary change, Engels simplified Marx's views of dialectical materialism under the influence of Darwinian theories of evolution and Hegel's "inner, hidden laws" of history. Throughout his life, Marx struggled with the problem of determinism. In attempting to turn the study of the historical processes into a science, he increasingly relied upon the concept of an impersonal "historical necessity" to drive society toward a proletarian revolution. Marx, however, avoided the embrace of determinism. History was not a mechanicalprocess. He insisted that the socialist labor movement would be the primary agent of change. Historical necessity propelled change, but revolution was a conscious act, understood and guided by the theorist (Marx) and theworking class organized around socialist theory.[5] "Engels—and following him Kautsky and the orthodox school in general . . . transform[ed Marx's] vision of a unique historical breakthrough into the doctrine of a casually determined process analogous to the scheme of Darwinian evolution."[6]

Engels embraced the determinism Marx rejected. In so doing, he reduced the importance of rational action and put emphasis on the inevitability of the process of change. This simplified view of Marx's theory had two unintended and paradoxical results. Its reassuring view that the proletarian revolution was inevitable tended to encourage passivity among many left-wing socialists while simultaneously spurring the movement's moderates to experiment with class collaboration inside parliamentary bodies.

31

Engels's association with German socialists was logical given both his national background and the development of the Sozialdemokratische Partei Deutschlands (SPD). During the 1890s, the German party consolidated its position as the largest and best organized of Marxist movements. The French socialist movement, the only other continental group capable of challenging the German model because of its revolutionary tradition and size, was splintered into contending factions. Moreover, France lagged behind Germany in industrial development. The SPD emerged as the most influential Marxist Socialist party. Its organization and its doctrine had enormous impact on the other European Marxist parties.[7]

From the beginning the German Socialists recognized the value of recruiting the largest possible number of workers into the SPD. By 1900, the SPD had over one million dues-paying members, becoming the first mass political party.

In his classic study of political parties, Maurice Duverger differentiated between the middle-class "cadre" party and the Socialist mass party. The cadre party was

> the grouping of notabilities [*sic*] for the preparation of elections, conducting campaigns and maintaining contact with candidates. Influential persons in the first place, whose name, prestige, or connections can provide a backing for the candidate and secure him votes; experts, in the second place, who know how to handle the electors and how to organize a campaign; last of all financiers, who can bring the sinews of war. Quality is the most important factor: extent of prestige, skill in technique, size of fortune.[8]

Duverger explained that a mass party is defined by both size and structure. While the middle-class parties of nineteenth-century Europe evolved from factions or caucuses within a parliament, mass parties were created outside of parliament. Mass parties tended to have a greater degree of centralization. They were usually organized from a single center around an existing ideology. "Their committees and local groups are set up through the drive from a pre-existing center, which can therefore restrict their liberty of action."[9] They insisted on a large degree of control over the action of individual members as well as local bodies, a marked contrast with the middle-class parties that dominated European politics. Moreover, their financing differed greatly from existing political practice. Traditionally, parliamentary parties relied upon a few wealthy individuals for economic support. "[T]he mass party spreads the burden over the largest possible number of members, each of whom contributes a modest sum."[10]

Finally, a mass party stresses the identification of the individual with the movement:

[T]he recruiting of members is a fundamental activity, both from the political and financial standpoints. In the first place, the party aims at the political education of the working class, at picking out from it an elite capable of taking over the government and the administration of the country: the members are therefore the very substance of the party, the stuff of its activity. Without members, the party would be like a teacher without pupils. Secondly, from the financial point of view, the party is essentially based upon the subscriptions paid by its members: the first duty of the branch is to ensure that they are regularly collected.[11]

The SPD's position as Europe's leading Marxist party owed a good deal to the particular circumstances in which it developed. Bismarck played a major role in defining the mass character of the SPD through his legislative enactments. Universal suffrage (1871) encouraged SPD efforts to build a large membership and voter base. Antisocialist laws (1878) locked the German party into the role of perpetual opposition with tainted legitimacy in the eyes of the government. Bismarck's constitution restricted the role of the popularly elected Reichstag, effectively negating the power of the ever-larger SPD parliamentary delegation. As a result, the SPD enjoyed the unwanted luxury of defining its precedent-setting organization and strategy without facing the difficult choices that other socialist parties encountered when they had the opportunity to participate significantly in national government.[12]

By the 1890s the twin issues of cooperation with bourgeois parties to win reform and participation in middle-class-led reform governments were of critical importance in a number of parties. In Germany, Engels's former collaborator, Eduard Bernstein, disputed orthodox Marxism on the theoretical level. Bernstein challenged the whole notion that workers' control of the state was historically predetermined. He "considered socialism desirable but not inevitable. It would come only if people desired it and worked for it."[13] Bernstein argued that gradual reform through cooperation with the progressive middle class was the best, and possibly the only, way to achieve the transformation to socialism. European socialists could not simply await for the hidden hand of dialectical materialism to work.[14]

At the same time that Bernstein attacked the theoretical base of orthodoxy, French parliamentary socialist leaders launched a pragmatic experiment in class cooperation. Jean Jaurès, the dynamic leader of one faction, insisted that the socialists collaborate with the middle-class defenders of

Captain Dreyfus. Alexandre Millerand, an independent socialist, went further, joining a reformist government in 1899.

The defenders of orthodoxy responded strongly to these challenges. In Germany, Kautsky, unleashed a major counterattack on Bernstein's views and won two official condemnations of "revisionism" at the 1899 and 1903 SPD congresses. Jules Guesde, the leader of left-wing French socialists, sought the Second International's condemnation of his rival Jaurès.

THE ITALIAN VARIANT

Italian Socialists were intensely involved in the theoretical debate sparked by the French and German parties. Both the Reformists and their "revolutionary" opponents adopted ideas from the northern European parties. The PSI's left-wing factions paraded their association with foreign movements and ideas. The Party's traditional left, men like Lazzari and Giovanni Lerda, were particularly anxious to associate their faction with the "orthodox" SPD. Enrico Ferri attempted to reinforce his claims to Party leadership through association with the French socialist Guesde and by high-profile participation in the 1900 and 1904 congresses of the Socialist International.[15]

Turati's Reformism had much in common on a tactical level with Jaurès's parliamentary socialism. On the theoretical level, Italian Reformists were frequently in accord with Bernstein. Nevertheless, Turati and other Reformists avoided too close identification with either French or German "revisionism."[16]

The Reformists recognized the tactical importance of remaining within the confines of Marxist orthodoxy. They sought to portray Reformism as a via media between the extremes of foreign revisionism and the "revolutionism" of the Italian left. In the article "The Socialist Party and the Current Political Situation" (1901), Turati laid down a set of "fundamental principles" that derived directly from Engels's version of the dialectical process. The PSI's role, Turati explained, was to aid in the "natural evolution" that leads to the substitution of communal for private property. Class struggle, Marx's engine of social change, remained part of Turati's formula. However, the transformation of society would be "slow and gradual." Thus, Socialist party strategy should focus on what Turati defined as "the division within the possessing classes" exemplified in Italy by the split between the Liberals and their Radical and Republican opponents. The place to exploit these divisions, Turati argued, was parliament, where the internal struggles of the bourgeoisie were played out. The PSI could exploit these divisions by allying with one faction against the other. Moreover, Turati stressed, the pragmatic utilization of parliament to carry on the class struggle fit the objective situation of the Party. Due to the immature state of development of the Italian workers movement, the Party could not think of revolution but rather had to concentrate on solidifying and expanding the gains that the proletarian movement had made during the 1890s.[17]

Turati had followed Engels in substituting a Darwinian model of evolution for Marx's concept of the active mediation of a socialist movement at the center of the dialectical process. He went a step further by making parliament the motor of change.[18]

The PSI's traditional left was incapable of offering a successful rejoinder to Turati on the ideological plane. The various left-wing factions were very weak in the area of Marxist theory. Few Marxist texts were available in Italy during the 1880s and 1890s. More importantly, the left relied on the authority of Engels, Kautsky, and other members of the orthodox school for the interpretation of Marx's thought. They embraced Engels's simplified version of the dialectic and followed Turati's lead in stressing the importance of parliament, agreeing that the proletariat was too immature for social revolution. If anything, the influence of Darwinian ideas was greater on the PSI's left than on the right. Ferri, a major spokesman for Italian positivism, was a fervent Darwinian who ceaselessly stressed the mechanical certitude of a socialist revolution. Lazzari, Lerda, and the other leaders of the traditional left were also believers in a "scientific socialism" that stressed historical inevitability. Moreover, Turati's contacts with Engels enabled the Reformist leader to assume the mantle of chief Italian disciple and interpreter of the master. As a result theoretical debate within the PSI centered on what type of parliamentary tactics would accelerate the pace of change. The left and right agreed that the PSI's ability to extend its influence among Italian workers was closely linked to its ability to expand and defend their economic, social, and political interests. Parliament was the logical area for this struggle. Therefore, the real dispute between the factions was what tactics would accelerate the process of change.[19]

The rival factions also shared basic agreement on the question of Party organization. The role of the PSI was twofold. First, it had to organize to contest elections. Second, it was to build class consciousness. Given the political immaturity of the Italian proletariat, violence was a danger to the survival of the Socialist party. Thus, both left and right worked to restrain violent outbreaks among the working class and to channel discontent into political and economic organizations.[20]

The traditional left, of course, continued to await a violent revolution somewhere in the future. The role of the Party would then change from one of building class consciousness to leading the final stage of the conquest of power. In the meantime, the major dangers to the Party were premature proletarian violence and a strategy of class cooperation that would inhibit the formation of the workers' class consciousness. The PSI's activity in parliament, the left insisted, had to reinforce class struggle not ameliorate it.[21]

The theoretical weaknesses and practical politics of the PSI's two major wings drove Italy's major "orthodox" socialist thinker into despair. Antonio Labriola, a Neopolitan philosophy professor, maintained a lively correspondence with the major figures in "orthodox" socialism, including both Engels and Kautsky. He had initially hoped to transfer the organizational model of the SPD into Italy and build a German-style movement. Labriola was a consistent and caustic critic of the PSI's contending factions and its organization. In spite of his impressive contacts and acknowledged mastery of Marx's thought, Labriola had little influence on the Italian socialist movement. He clashed frequently with Turati during the Party's formative years and, disdaining the left, remained outside the official organization. Moreover, Labriola's critique of the PSI was fragmentary and generally consigned to his personal correspondence with foreign socialist leaders. Labriola published little in his lifetime, even in the area of Marxist theory.[22]

A REFORMIST PARTY

Labriola's limited influence, the traditional left's divisions and lack of theoretical options, and the success of its defensive strategy helped to secure Reformist ascendancy at the beginning of the twentieth century. The Reformists built a political organization that mirrored their ideological and tactical presuppositions.

The Reformist PSI's model was the German Social Democratic party. Like its German counterpart, the Italian Socialist party came into being at an early stage in the development of the working-class movement. In fact, the organization of a Socialist party predated the creation of a national labor movement. During the Giolittian era, the small, middle-class-led Socialist party found its real source of strength in its decision to concentrate on the achievement of liberal democratic goals. This decision allowed the

PSI to collect a significant part of its support from middle-class voters.[23] Table 1 illustrates the relation of the Party's organizational and electoral strength.

Information on the General Confederation of Labor has been included in table 1 to show that the PSI's influence extended beyond the elite of politically conscious workers. The creation of a national labor organization does not seem to have materially affected the electoral pull of the PSI. In the election of 1909, the Party picked up only 21,000 more votes than in 1904 despite the active support of the newly created labor confederation. There does seem to have been a correlation between the PSI's membership size and the increase of its total vote. Strong advances in the Socialist party's vote occurred in 1900, 1904, and 1913. In each case a dramatic rise in PSI membership paralleled or immediately followed electoral success.[24]

The PSI's small membership and the correlation of Party size with electoral success underline the Italian Socialist party's status as a cadre party with a small, active membership that concentrated on winning elections and drew much of its support from non-Party members who sympathized with parts of its program. The organizational history of the PSI between 1892 and 1914 revolved around a dichotomy. In the quarter century which passed between the PSI's creation and World War I, most major structural reforms introduced by the Party built the foundations of a mass organization similar to the German model. However, the PSI remained an elite party. It lacked the linkages with the developing workers movement which the German Social Democratic party had built. The SPD organized consensus for its politics among the German working classes through the trade unions, a young socialist movement, education programs, women's organizations, and a

TABLE 1
Electoral and Organizational Strength of the PSI, 1892–1914

Year	PSI		CGL		GPS	
	Sections	Members	Members	Votes	%	Seats
1892	—	—	—	27,000	—	5
1895	—	—	—	76,359	6.2	15
1897	682	27,281	—	108,086	9.0	16
1900	546	19,194	—	164,946	12.9	33
1904	1236	45,800	—	326,016	21.3	29
1909	989	28,835	307,925	347,615	19.0	41
1913	1490	37,151	327,302	883,409	17.7	52

SOURCES: PSI, *Relazione politica della Direzione; Statistica delle elezione generale politiche; La CGL nel sessennio.*

highly developed and responsive party bureaucracy. The Social Democrats created a state within the German state.

The Reformists built a party that reflected their mistrust of the masses and their belief that they knew what was best for Italy's working classes. Their party was an intermediary that expressed the needs of the organized and politically active minority of workers and agricultural laborers of North Italy to the nation's governing elite.

The Reformist leadership consciously kept all extra-Party organizations out of the control of the PSI's *Direzione*. Turati, who played a leading role in the establishment of cooperatives, educational organizations, and other workers' self-help and improvement societies, frequently cooperated with Republican and Radical leaders to build these groups. He utilized them as part of his personal political power base and guarded them from interference by the *Direzione*. In spite of resolutions passed by the 1900 Rome Party Congress, relations between the PSI and the union movement generally existed only at the highest level in the form of a joint leadership. After separating the functions of Party and labor movement, the Reformists insisted on maintaining that division. The Party's activities were directed toward the next election. The extra-Party organizations existed to create a working-class culture, while the unions would organize labor and press its salary demands. The labor movement, moreover, became increasingly jealous of its independence from all the parties of the left, the Socialists included.[25]

Strategy and ideology played important roles in the Reformists decision to opt for a cadre party organization that placed maximum reliance on the actions of the parliamentary group and *Avanti!*. Four interrelated factors influenced their choice: the multiclass makeup of the Party's membership, the Italian electoral system, a concern about the political maturity of the masses, and a conscious elitism.

From its origins, the PSI was a multiclass party in which the proletariat composed a large minority. In 1903, workers constituted approximately 42.3 percent of the Party's 42,451 members. Agricultural laborers made up another 21 percent of the membership, while artisans provided about 15 percent and the middle classes 10.5 percent of the rank and file. The PSI was always the home of multiple class constituencies, and as a result, its political program was designed to maintain the support of diverse social and economic groupings.[26]

Tactical necessity reinforced ideological pragmatism. The PSI was operating inside a system based on limited suffrage that required it to seek the votes of the middle class in order to elect Socialist deputies.[27] In order to hold on to its multiclass base and to consolidate support among the middle classes, the PSI downplayed Marxist ideology and offered a political program with a wide appeal. The Party's minimal program was a shopping list of social and political reforms that both the progressive middle-class voters and industrial and agrarian workers could support. The minimal program, with its accent on building democracy rather than a socialist society, helped create a solid middle-class voting bloc for the PSI.[28]

The Reformists' deep-seated fear of the results of prematurely bringing the uneducated masses into political activity as much as their need for middle-class support led them to embrace a cadre party organization. Reformist fear of the political immaturity of the masses was rooted in the practical experiences of the *Fasci Siciliani* and *fatti di maggio*. Bringing a mass of poorly educated and undisciplined peasants into the PSI would play into the hands of radical elements within the Party. The masses would be easy prey for anarchists or extreme leftists, who would lead them into a frontal confrontation with the Italian state. The Reformists knew from recent, painful experience that the PSI would lose a confrontation. Further, a violent clash with the Italian state would trigger the flight of the entire middle class into the hands of the right and bring a return to reactionary rule.[29]

As a result, the Reformists relied on elite leadership, a small party, and the gradual education and integration of the masses into Italy's existing political system to produce social reform. The Reformists made no excuses for the elite nature of their party. In 1909, the Reformist Fausto Pagliari explained the rationale for the Reformist emphasis on elite Party leadership. Pagliari argued that the concentration of power in a few hands was an iron law of politics. In the Socialist party, however, the growing power of the working classes forced leadership elites to make policy in their best interests. "The workers movement produces forces that counterbalance oligarchic tendencies and . . . tend toward the most perfect and secure forms of democracy."[30] The Reformists' consistent problem, Treves admitted, was convincing the working-class rank and file that the Party's leadership elite was able to keep their interests primary rather than abandoning class struggle for immediate political objectives that primarily benefited middle-class interests.[31]

The Reformists' reliance on a cadre party organization was rooted in the practical experience of trying to organize mass support for political action. Faced with large-scale illiteracy, regional diversity, and widespread working-class indifference to the activities of its local political organizations, the Reformists relied on a committed elite to remake Italian society.[32]

These same factors strengthened the Reformists' reliance on parliamentary politics and encouraged their efforts to collect middle-class voting support by taking political positions that favored the growth of capitalism and democracy.[33]

The PSI's support for legislation that would promote Italy's industrialization grew out of Reformist conviction that the development of a capitalist economy was an inevitable and generally favorable development. The Party supported free trade, since cheap foreign imports would reduce the cost of living for the working classes. Conversely, it was suspicious of protected private monopolies and opposed government control of industries because it believed that state capitalism weakened long-term capitalist development.[34]

The Party's opposition to militarism and the crown's expensive civil list involved both deep antimilitarist conviction and a judgment that these expenses hindered economic development. However, the PSI took a relatively soft stand on the issue of the monarchy because the institution commanded widespread respect, particularly with middle-class voters, who associated the crown with Risorgimental nationalism.[35]

The Reformists' stand against violence, which had its roots in the sincere pacifism of men like Turati, paid political benefits with middle-class voters by disassociating the PSI from anarchists and other proponents of terrorist action.[36]

Finally, the PSI's stress on controlling municipal institutions aided its efforts to build electoral alliances with the middle classes. The Reformists consistently supported wide autonomy for local Socialist sections in order to permit them to arrive at compromises with the progressive elements of the middle classes that would simultaneously improve the situation of the working class and reinforce support within the middle-class electorate.[37]

The result of these policy and organizational choices was a Party which was often cut off from the workers it was supposed to represent and an easy prey for Giolitti's *trasformismo*. Reformism's critics, including Kuliscioff and, at times, even Turati, saw reformist socialism drifting toward a sterile parliamentary politics in which the PSI was chained to Giolitti for lack of any alternative. In the effort to serve its multiclass constituency, the Party found it increasingly difficult either to motivate reforms or to escape being submerged in ever-widening governing coalitions. The Socialists increasingly played the role of a left-wing opposition within the existing political system. The Party of protest against the bourgeois system was becoming part of that system.[38]

LOCAL ORGANIZATION IN THE ITALIAN SOCIALIST PARTY

From 1900 to 1919, the PSI was the organizational embodiment of Reformist ideology. The 1900 Rome Party Congress had severely limited central control over the activities of *Avanti!* or the parliamentary group. Power within the Italian Socialist party was effectively decentralized.

In a decentralized Party, power rested with those organizations which could claim constituencies larger than the Party—*Avanti!* and the GPS—and with the basic organizational unit, the section.

The PSI had a highly symmetrical organization. The shape of the whole organization was the mirror image of its smallest component. The smallest Party unit was the section, composed of a minimum of ten members, eighteen years of age or older, who resided in the same geographic area: the *comune.* Only one section could be established in a *comune.* Since the size of the *comuni* varied greatly, the size of the sections also varied. The Milan section had 1150 members in 1904, while the section of Isernia, the only Socialist organization in the entire province of Molise, had the minimum 10 members. Larger sections were authorized to form smaller groups. In the case of Milan, for example, the local organization was subdivided into six bodies that corresponded to the city's six electoral colleges. Another possible form of subdivision was into clubs: intellectuals, university students, women, factory workers. Generally these clubs ran educational programs. Whatever their activities, such groups had only limited official standing in the eyes of the Party. They could not make decisions that were binding upon their members. The Party constitution reserved this function for the unitary assembly of the section. Moreover, the sections alone had the power to authorize the formation of these groups.[39]

Membership in a Socialist party section was a matter of personal choice and brought with it automatic membership in the national Party. Membership was not automatic for any category of applicant, including workers. A candidate made his application to the governing body of the section, which then, in theory, investigated his character and political views. "Joining the Socialist Party implies accepting its general principles as well as observing the discipline and methods of struggle and political action which have been decided by the [Party] congresses."[40] Prospective members quite often had sponsors within the section and had to be able to demonstrate a knowledge of the Party's basic objectives. If accepted by the section, the new member then purchased his *tessera* or membership ticket. The *tessera* was valid for one calendar year (January to December) and in theory, the member had to renew it if he wished to continue to participate in the activities of the section and the Party. In fact, being in arrears in membership dues was commonplace for Italian Socialists. In general, the sections allowed members in arrears as much time as they needed to pay their dues: they could not afford the loss of members which strict enforcement of the rules would entail. Members were often several years in arrears. Nonpayment of dues was a major and continuing problem for the PSI throughout its first two decades of existence. Income realized from dues was divided between the sections and the central organs of the PSI. The lack of dues payments meant that both the national and local structures of the PSI were chronically short of money. One incentive for calling a national congress every two years appears to have been filling Party coffers. Sections could not participate in a congress unless they paid their yearly quota. In the days which immediately preceded the national congresses, *Avanti!* was full of reports of last-minute payments.[41]

The sections possessed wide powers of discipline over individual members. They could expel or suspend members for either political or moral transgressions. In the first major case of a section's powers of expulsion, a national congress backed the decision of the Naples section to expel the deputy Enrico De Marinis for deviations from the Party line. The rights of accused members were safeguarded. They were guaranteed the right to be informed of the exact nature of the charges against them and of the conclusions of the investigations of these charges. They were guaranteed the right to a personal defense. They could only be expelled from the section by a majority vote and had the right to appeal an expulsion or other disciplinary action to higher Party bodies.[42]

Ferment characterized the life cycle of the sections. They were born and died within the space of a few years. New sections were continuously formed and old ones reestablished only to dissolve within a short space of time. Data from three provincial federations illustrates this life cycle of the sections. Milan was among the most industrialized areas of Italy; Ravenna, an agrarian province in northeastern Italy, had strong working-class organizations; Foggia was a southern agrarian area with weak working-class organizations but with a history of continuous Socialist organizational activity.

Over the ten-year period surveyed, all three areas experienced a high turnover rate. Local Party leaders faced great difficulties in their efforts to keep their organizations functioning. A high percentage of the individuals within the Socialist movement were constantly in need of indoctrination and the number of trained organizers was always small. Neither the Reformists nor the middle-class factions which opposed them were able to build up a solid majority when 25 to 40 percent of the local organizations melted away in any given year.[43] (See table 2.)

The life of the section was organized around two bodies: the assembly and the central committee. The assembly consisted of all the paying members of the section. Usually it met at least one time a month to discuss local affairs, decide policy, choose its representatives to regional or national

TABLE 2
Stability and Turnover in the Sections of the PSI, 1904–14

Province	Year	No. of Sections	New Sections	Reestablished Sections	Turnover
Milan	1904	15	—	—	0
	1906	8	3	—	37.50
	1908	15	4	3	46.66
	1910	17	6	2	47.05
	1911	26	7	4	42.30
	1912	29	5	3	27.58
	1914	33	8	4	36.36
					39.57 (average)
Ravenna	1904	50	—	—	0
	1906	50	15	—	30.00
	1908	54	15	7	40.74
	1910	67	10	6	23.88
	1911	65	10	1	16.92
	1912	59	4	5	15.25
	1914	59	9	8	28.81
					25.93 (average)
Foggia	1904	8	—	—	0
	1906	4	0	—	0
	1908	11	5	2	63.63
	1910	6	0	0	0
	1911	6	1	1	33.33
	1912	9	0	3	33.33
	1914	19	9	2	57.89
					31.36 (average)

SOURCE: PSI, *Resoconti dei VIII–XIV congressi*, 1904–14.

meetings, elect new members, select its own leadership, or hear the reports of the elected representatives of the Party. Special sessions usually took place on the eve of major events such as national or local elections or Socialist party congresses. The administration of the section was handled by its central committee. The size of these committees varied greatly, but they normally exercised the same functions: overseeing the activities of individual members and of the local Party press (if it existed), collecting money, presiding over the meetings of the sections, and propaganda. Within the central committee an elected secretariat handled day-to-day paperwork. The central committee normally met weekly. Two other organs common to most sections were the treasurer and the *probiviri,* a committee that investigated the political and moral conduct of applicants and members.[44]

The most interesting feature of the Socialist section's organization was its nearly total lack of a standing bureaucracy. Generally only two officials, the secretary and the editor of the local newspaper, were full-time Party employees. This meant that the ability of the sections to organize election campaigns was limited. Like their Liberal rivals, the Socialists preferred to rely on the gifted but part-time amateur to organize election campaigns. However, the year-round existence of the section gave it a marked advantage over Liberal election clubs by permitting it to continually organize for the next campaign. In addition to its role in political campaigns, the section was a collecting point for new recruits, contributed to the political education of workers through its library, and provided a base for union organization. Most importantly, the section, with its constitutional organization, its monthly meetings, and its sharing of responsibility, was a school of democratic education for the working class.[45]

REGIONAL AND NATIONAL ORGANIZATION

The next stage in the PSI's organizational hierarchy was the collegial or provincial federation. The decision on whether to establish a collegial (that is electoral) or provincial (geographic) federation reflected the extent of Socialist influence in a given area. In general, the creation of collegial federations was a sign of Socialist strength in agrarian areas. A provincial federation was then erected on top of a number of collegial federations, rather than directly upon the sections, as occurred in more urbanized areas. These provincial federations corresponded to the administrative divisions of Italy and enabled the Socialist party to build an electoral machine which paralleled that controlled by the ministry of the interior. The size of these provincial bodies varied. In 1904 the Campobasso provincial federation comprised one section with a total membership of ten. The Reggio Emilia federation had 4031 members in 94 sections. Clearly, in the case of Campobasso, the provincial federation was a third wheel in the Party's organization. In other areas like Reggio Emilia, it knit together a large number of sections with small membership.[46]

Constituent elements of the federation were the regional congress, an assembly of delegates chosen by the sections, and, normally, an executive committee. Its secretary served as the federation's representative to the PSI *Direzione*. The secretariat and executive committee oversaw the activities of the sections and acted as a court of appeals in the disputes of individual members and sections and between sections. When requested to do so by the *Direzione*, the federation collected economic and statistical data.[47]

The region, the largest subdivision of Italy, had historic rather than legal standing. No regional organization was sanctioned by the Party constitution, but delegates from areas such as Lombardy frequently caucused prior to the Party congress with the objective of adopting a common policy.[48]

The Party's national organization was built on top of the provincial federations. The *Direzione*, the Party executive, represented the PSI at the national level. The size of the *Direzione* as well as the composition of its membership was determined at the PSI national congress. The duty of the *Direzione* was to enforce the policy laid down by the national congress. Within this broad charge, the *Direzione* had special assignments: overseeing (but not disciplining) the parliamentary group, acting as an appeals court for those contesting the decisions of the provincial federations, distributing propaganda materials and plans, keeping the PSI in constant communication with the Socialist International, and overseeing the work of *Avanti!*'s director.[49]

The seat of the *Direzione* was Rome. The director of *Avanti!* and at least one member of the GPS always belonged to the *Direzione*. Beyond this, the structure of the *Direzione* was repeatedly modified by the contending forces who controlled it and by the needs of the workers' movement. For example, an economic secretariat existed within the *Direzione* between 1900 and 1903. The PSI disbanded this office after the union movement created the Secretariat of the Resistance. The delegation of the GPS on the *Direzione* was reduced from five members to one when Ferri's coalition captured control of the Party in 1904 and membership in the *Direzione* was redistributed on a geographic basis in 1906. An executive committee was established within the *Direzione,* and this Rome-based group had full power to act in the name of the enlarged *Direzione.*[50]

The heart of the *Direzione* was its secretariat. The political and administrative secretaries of the PSI were permanent paid employees of the Party. They handled the day-to-day operations of the Party with the aid of a small clerical staff. The *Direzione* existed to handle exceptional and urgent matters which could not be put off until the next congress. Potentially, the political secretary was a figure of considerable power who could utilize his office to give a definite direction to Party policy. The primary function of both secretaries was organization: establishing new sections and keeping accounts of dues payments and disciplinary problems. A secondary activity was compiling statistical data. The publication and distribution of propaganda was a third function. In 1901, the PSI set up the *Casa Editrice Mongini* under the supervision of the *Direzione,* together with a lending library to ensure that Socialist literature reached the rank and file.[51]

The national congress was the Party's supreme legislative and judicial body. Normally meeting every two years, the national congress made policy for the PSI, set standards for membership, appointed the Party's administrators, and passed judgment on their work.[52]

Initially, each section of the Party was allowed to send a single voting delegate to the national congress. Until 1904, this delegate cast one vote. At the Congress of Bologna that year the delegates approved a system of proportional representation in which the delegate or delegates representing a section cast a number of votes equal to the number of paying members of the section. The effects of this reform were to weaken the voice of the South within the PSI and to strengthen the influence of urban sections. Only rural sections organized into voting blocs, such as Reggio Emilia, could enjoy real weight in the congress. The votes of the representatives of Rome, Turin, and Milan could give a powerful thrust to any project on which they agreed. The system failed to make allowance for representing the viewpoint of minority factions within the sections.[53]

A decision on how a section or provincial federation would vote on a given issue was normally taken shortly before a national congress met. The "revolutionary" faction of the *Rome Socialist Union* usually held a bare majority in these precongress votes. The Roman representative or representatives cast all the votes allotted to the section (normally more than 500) for a left-wing resolution. In effect, this action ignored the views of almost half the Roman Socialists. The Milan section tried to correct this inequity by adopting proportional representation and dividing its vote.[54]

The *Direzione* drew up the agenda of the national congress. Its ability to control debate was limited by a statutory requirement that the agenda of the congress be presented to the sections three months in advance of the meeting. This provision ensured that the sections would have the right to propose amendments. Moreover, amendments could be offered either prior to the congress or during its sessions. The order of discussions at the congresses rarely varied: first, election of officers, followed by the reading of the reports of the permanent organs of the PSI, followed by a discussion. The congress then turned to matters of policy. Generally, the discussion focused on one subject. Finally, and in great haste, the congress considered policy issues of less weight, appointed a new *Direzione,* and adjourned.[55]

Due to the congresses' potential power over the Party, it is important to determine the degree to which its decisions reflected the attitude and values of the rank and file. One means is by an analysis of the social composition of the congresses, although raw data are limited. In 1908, Robert Michels estimated that workers made up less than one-third of the delegates. A more recent study of the first half of the Giolittian era, citing the lack of available information, has termed Michels's figures "very approximate" and then claimed "a great increase in the weight of proletarian representation" between 1900 and 1904.[56] Lists of attendance are available for the 1904 and 1906 congresses, and a Party census was compiled in 1903.

On December 31, 1903 (four months before the Congress of Bologna), workers constituted 42.27 percent of the PSI's membership. If we accept Michels's estimate that workers' participation at the 1904 congress was less than 33 percent, this class was somewhat underrepresented at the PSI's chief policy-making body. Middle-class professionals, on the other hand, constituted 2.2 percent of the PSI's total membership in 1903, yet 151 of the 925 delegates to the 1904 congress clearly identified themselves as professional men (16.4 percent). Of those nominated to present the positions of the contending Party factions at national congresses between 1906 and 1914, 62.5 percent were middle-class professionals. All the available statistical evidence indicates the disproportional weight which the middle class enjoyed within the Party.[57]

The PSI national Congress was something of a parody of the Italian parliament. During its sessions, the "revolutionaries" always sat ostentatiously on the left side of the hall in ascending order of militancy, while the Reformists, whose numbers included the vast majority of the deputies, had to content themselves with seats on the right. Sessions were usually tumultuous with heckling, interruptions from the floor, and, on one occasion, an attempt by discontented delegates to seize the podium by force. Sessions invariably started late and often dragged on into the early morning hours. An inordinate amount of time was consumed with such meaningless formalities as the reading of telegrams of good wishes from foreign parties and welcoming speeches. Even when the congresses got down to serious business, florid oratory was the order of the day. Very few speakers paid the slightest attention to the gag rules which weary delegates repeatedly enacted. Under these circumstances, it is little wonder that so many delegates showed up late and left for home as soon as possible. The Italian parliament, with its long sessions, could accept all these types of delay as annoying but rarely serious hindrances to its work. National congresses of the Socialist party normally lasted four or five days. The PSI national congress under the circumstances was little short of pandemonium, and its concentration upon a single major issue was a necessity. Even so, this concentration had grave drawbacks. The issue dealt with in depth was invariably one of political tactics. Tactical questions approached within the framework of a relatively stable political situation by the leaders of a Marxist party could produce only a few plausible alternatives. By 1906, if not earlier, all the reasonable tactical options open to the PSI had been explored ad nauseam. The result of continuing to debate these issues was a sterility in the congresses and eventually in the life of the Party down to its lowest level. The Party congresses ran in place: exerting tremendous energy while going nowhere.[58]

In the absence of a firm direction from the congress, daily Party policy was usually made by *Avanti!* and by the parliamentary group. The organizational framework of section, federation, *Direzione*, and congress led to a focus on the internal dynamics of the PSI: preparing for elections, educating the rank and file in Marxism, developing a sense of democratic procedure inside the Party. Contact with non-Socialist Italy, propaganda, recruitment, the defense of Party interests, and practical dealing with the men and institutions that ran Italy was the mission of these two peripheral and largely unsupervised organs. From its foundation in 1896 to 1903, Leonida Bissolati directed *Avanti!* with the aid of a staff that was predominantly Reformist. Bissolati pursued his objectives with little effective opposition from the Party's left wing until 1902. Prior to 1900, he was responsible only to a national congress that did not meet between 1897 and 1900 and that was under firm Reformist control in 1900 and 1902. Even after the 1900 congress placed the editor of *Avanti!* under the supervision of the *Direzione*, Bissolati was effectively independent since the *Direzioni* elected in 1900 and 1902 were also Reformist. *Avanti!*'s fatal weakness lay in its effort to reach a reading public in the lowest and poorest economic strata. Newspapers were a luxury for the poor. Moreover, the vast majority of Socialist party sections were continually in dire economic straits and unable to contribute to the support of the Party daily. Only the *Direzione* was in a position to coordinate the economic support the paper required.

Financial problems potentially placed the editor of *Avanti!* under a measure of Party control. No such ties weighed down the members of the GPS. By 1900, the parliamentary group had taken over the leadership of the PSI. In part this leadership rested on the heroic and effective obstruction campaign of 1898–1900. Other factors also contributed to the GPS's hegemony. One was the desire of most Socialists to have visible evidence of the growth of their movement. Such statistical reassurance came less from the often erratic growth of the PSI than from dramatic increases in the size of the Socialist vote. Further, the men who represented Italian Socialism in parliament were frequently luminaries in their nation's public life. Ferri, for example, was a world-famous criminologist; Ettore Ciccoti, a well-known historian; Prampolini, an important labor leader; and Costa enjoyed a certain fame or notoriety as a result of his youthful role in the anarchist and socialist movements. Their individual reputations and achievements further strengthened the independence of the individual deputy. Neither the national congress nor the *Direzione* had any effective means to discipline either the GPS or its individual members except through expulsion, which meant the probable loss of a parliamentary seat to the Party. Moreover, the allegiance of the deputy was of necessity given first to his electors. Since Socialist party members usually provided less than a quarter of the total vote that the Party won, conflicts of interest were bound to develop. Finally, prior to 1904, the deputies enjoyed a majority on the *Direzione*. The net effect of these factors was to hand control of the daily administration of the PSI over to its peripheral wings. The GPS ended by making the critical policy decisions for the Party.[59]

The Socialist parliamentary group was a youthful, well-educated group of men whose agreement on common principles in an atomized political system should have given them a cohesion and weight far greater than their still small numbers allowed. Not only were Socialist gains in the 1900 elections impressive in numerical terms, they were lasting. In a number of colleges, Socialist candidates piled up large enough margins to create "safe seats" for themselves and the PSI. This relative security reinforced the independence of the individual deputy from Party controls. The support which the majority of deputies gave to Reformism is hardly surprising since it insisted upon the supremacy of the deputy over the Party structure and gave him the leading role in the struggle for the emancipation of the working class.[60]

Thus, the PSI was characterized by confused lines of authority that rendered its central organs relatively helpless in their efforts to give direction to the activities of the Party. Initiative rested with the base and with the peripheral organizations of the Party rather than with the *Direzione*. In the mass parties which were to dominate European politics after World War I, communist, socialist, christian democratic, and fascist, all the organizations of each movement acted at the command of a central body. In turn, this body has frequently been dominated by one individual. Within the PSI of the Giolittian era, the *Direzione* operated effectively only when it put itself in line with the views of the peripheral organizations of the Party. From 1901 to 1903, the Party machine functioned well because the Reformists controlled the *Direzione, Avanti!,* and the GPS. Between 1903 and 1908, the Party was in a state of confusion because Ferri-led coalitions held control of the *Direzione* and *Avanti!* but were unable to tame the GPS. In 1908, the Reformists regained control of both the *Direzione* and *Avanti!* and the Party again presented a united front. When Reformism split over the Libyan War in 1911, a new "revolutionary" coalition took over the leadership of the PSI. Profiting from Ferri's experience, the left attempted to end the confusion that plagued the PSI by centralizing its control over all political activities and organizations under the *Direzione*. The experiment was only a partial success. The GPS remained an independent power center until the introduction of a system of proportional representation after World War I. Only then did the *Direzione* finally solidify its control over the Socialist party.[61]

The revolutionary *Direzione* also reduced the sections to effective control. The independence of the section prior to 1912 rested upon its freedom from effective control from the regional or provincial federations. Decisions taken by these bodies were subject to appeal to the national congress where the federation was not directly represented. Decisions of a federation were binding only within a federation and only if approved by a national congress. This permitted the sections to overturn any action which struck at their freedom. Selection of congress delegates took place within the section. Modern mass parties frequently select the delegates to national bodies within their central committees, thus strengthening their control over the local bodies. In addition, the sections, which played a key role in recruiting and electing Socialist deputies, retained special ties with the members of the GPS. This gave them a voice in national affairs and enabled the deputies and sections to cooperate to frustrate actions of the central organizations which might adversely affect their common interests. Finally, individuals paid their dues through the local bodies rather then directly into a national treasury, which gave the sections a larger measure of financial independence from the *Direzione* and, in fact, left the central committee dependent on the local organizations.[62]

From 1900 to 1914, the PSI was structurally a Reformist party. The interdependence of deputy and section and their mutual independence from control by a Party central authority meant that the PSI was designed to achieve its political objectives in parliament. The "revolutionary" opposition early grasped the crux of their problem. In 1904, Walter Mocchi clearly expressed their concern, warning that the danger posed by Reformism lay precisely in the leading role of the GPS in Party affairs. The parliamentary group was taking the PSI down "the road that leads to collaboration with the monarchy."[63] The lack of an alternative to the existing political organization of the PSI hampered efforts by the left to reverse this situation as did the small size of the PSI. A small party was of necessity heavily dependent on those members who could rally mass support for its programs: the deputies. Prior to the passage of a second universal suffrage law in 1919, the leftists, who campaigned vigorously against the middle classes, were rarely able to win enough support to be elected to parliament. Moreover, as noted, the traditional left lacked an alternative vision to the Reformist Party. With the notable exception of the Syndicalists, most "revolutionaries" shared the same conceptual framework as their Reformist opponents. They anticipated a distant triumph for socialism. Like the Reformists, the traditional left paid great attention to the activities of the GPS because it accepted the idea that parliament was the stage upon which the contemporary act in the struggle of bourgeois and proletariat was being played out. Finally, these revolutionaries were as eager as the Reformists to promote social changes that would benefit the working classes through parliamentary action. Thus, prior to 1912 a triumph of the left did not automatically mean the end of the Reformist Party. Instead, tactical changes within the existing political framework were the most frequent outcome of a left-wing victory.[64]

The basic structural change upon which the left-wing groups insisted was strengthening the hand of the *Direzione* in its relationship with both the GPS and *Avanti!*. Their attempts to centralize and discipline the PSI did not aim at bringing the masses into the Party but simply made such a development possible. The ideology of the left, except for the Syndicalists, emphasized confrontation with bourgeois Italy inside parliament. The evolution of the PSI's organizational structure into a mass party was largely accidental, the result of a series of pragmatic choices made to correct and improve on a cadre party organization that neither the left or the right was able effectively to control.[65]

While the revolutionaries were uncertain about what type of party structure to adopt, Reformists were adamant in claiming that the cadre organization they had created "signifies the maturation of the Party."[66] Reformist spokesman Garzia Cassola summed up their viewpoint in 1901:

> Our *Direzione* always lacks political sense. It is a good organization for the solution of small personal contests; and it can be a good organism for the distribution of administrative duties. But it cannot direct. And perhaps this is for the best. It would be dangerous to concentrate in a few [men], even if they are among the best, a power which is almost dictatorial. The life of the Party will be more spontaneous and more fertile when the productive organs of its complex social functions are left free: the press, the Parliamentary Group, and the economic and political organizations [of the Socialist movement] acquire, with independence, a sense of responsibility and develop . . . [into] the directive force of the Party.[67]

Within the type of structure favored by the Reformists, political power depended on a system of personal relationships and power positions analogous to those of *trasformismo*. In fact, some of Turati's comments indicate that he viewed the cadre structure of the PSI as "mature" precisely because it permitted a style of political operations which was similar to that which flourished under *trasformismo*.[68] The parallels between the two systems were important. The deputy was the key figure in both. With his wide-ranging contacts, the deputy provided the services which individual electors or sections required. The only man with similar influence was the director of a periodical or newspaper, and it is significant that a majority of the PSI's deputies were also editors: Prampolini, Treves, Turati, Canepa, Podrecca, Bissolati, Morgari, and Ettore Ciccotti to name some of the most prominent. Arturo Labriola cited the close ties which Turati developed with the unions and cooperatives, the Popular University of Milan, and the city's *Società umanitaria* as one of the key factors in his long preeminence in the PSI. And Turati was not the only deputy who built up a large personal clientele within the Party. Ferri, too, created a wide body of support by doing favors and building personal ties with local organizations.[69]

In building a cadre party, the Reformists relied upon *Avanti!* and the GPS to create a democratic and progressive Italian society through a strategy of class cooperation. This strategy divided the Party and strengthened Giolitti's political control at the same time that it promoted reform. Opposition to Reformist strategy emerged even as the GPS began collaborating with the Zanardelli-Giolitti government in 1901. By 1903 a coalition of left-wing Socialists was mounting a strong challenge to Reformist control of the PSI.

Challenges
to Reformism,
1901–1907

LEADERS AND TENDENCIES OF THE LEFT

The groups which coalesced in opposition to Turati's faction had little in common except their abiding dislike of Reformism. One current, the weakest, comprising the survivors of operaist movements, was led by Lazzari, who continued to wage a highly personal battle against Turati.[1] Turati had formed a negative opinion of Lazzari as early as the 1880s and in 1901 attempted to purge him from the Milan Socialist Federation (MSF). The attempt failed and only increased the bitterness which existed on both sides.

Aided by the faction captained by Arturo Labriola, Lazzari not only escaped expulsion but forced Turati to break with one of his power bases, the MSF. Turati immediately created a rival body, the *Unione Socialista Milanese*, from which the Reformist leader eventually recaptured control of the local Party. In the struggle, however, Turati turned his antagonist into a martyr in a struggle which pitted a ''worker'' against a middle-class intellectual. Still, Lazzari lacked a power base within the Milan socialist movement and had to attach himself to the Labriola group of young, mostly southern, intellectuals. This alliance must have been a bitter pill for Lazzari to swallow. He retained a lifelong distrust of middle-class intellectuals. Nevertheless, a deal was struck. Lazzari needed these particular allies for his struggle against Turati because they had everything he lacked: a coherent ideology, an organization, and a newspaper.[2]

The Italian historian Luigi Cortesi has observed that the young men who entered the socialist movement in the 1890s were the first generation with the opportunity to study Marx from the sources. Instead, Cortesi notes, both the young men who rallied around Turati as well as his youthful opponents read and adopted the ideas of intellectuals on the fringes of the Marxist movement. The young of both right and left converged on the same program: syndicalism.[3]

The members of this third generation of Italian socialists were part of the Europe-wide intellectual movement which rediscovered the irrational in human behavior. In Italy, this investigation of human consciousness took place under the influence of Benedetto Croce. During the second half of the 1890s, Croce devoted himself to the study of Marxism. At about the same time, Georges Sorel, a retired engineer, was working on similar ideas in France. Croce's interest in Marx waned after 1900, but he continued to patronize Sorel and to promote the diffusion of the Frenchman's work in Italy.[4]

French syndicalism was an offshoot of anarchism. It took root in the 1890s among French trade unions when the chronically divided French socialist movement failed to establish a predominant influence over organized labor. French socialists, particularly the left-wing followers of Jules Guesde, fought without success to limit syndicalist influence inside the unions and to contain the spread among socialists of syndicalist theory, particularly its tactical emphasis on the general strike as the weapon to overthrow bourgeois society.[5]

Georges Sorel was an attentive student of the syndicalist movement, although he had little direct contact with or influence over French syndicalists. Ironically, his writings provided the major vehicle for the spread of a syndicalist theory. Sorel's glorification of myth and violence, his attacks on bureaucracy and on the elites who create and perpetuate it, and his development of the theory of the general strike endeared him to the rising generation of young, anti-Reformist intellectuals whose leaders included Labriola, Enrico Leone, E. C. Longobardi, and Walter Mocchi. In their revolt against Turati's leadership, they found Sorel's antirationalism a powerful weapon against the Enlightenment faith in reason embodied in Reformism. The issue of parliamentary reform tactics became embroiled in a struggle of generations, of intellectual systems, and of organizational plans, between a leadership elite and its would-be successor.

Revolutionary Syndicalism in both its premises and its objectives was the antithesis of Reformism. The movement was antiparliamentary, suspicious of political parties, and contemptuous of the notion that meaningful reform of the bourgeois state was possible. Syndicalists argued that the ruling classes would never willingly surrender power. The working classes had to seize control of the state by means of a violent revolution. Reformism with its emphasis on class cooperation, gradualism, and parliamentary action was simply the most recently developed tool for preserving the bourgeoisie's control over the working class. Under Reformist leadership the PSI had become a willing participant in the bourgeois political system.

The Syndicalists' alternative to corrupt Reformist politics was to build a mass-based revolutionary union movement. The unions were the authentic political expression of the proletariat that created them. They could perform the essential functions of educating, mobilizing, and radicalizing the working classes, accustoming them to taking an active role in the control of the means of production. In addition, the unions would serve as the basic institutions on which to construct a postrevolutionary society.

According to Syndicalist theory, organized labor would utilize the political strike to radicalize and mobilize the working classes to overthrow the old order. Syndicalists viewed the strike as a revolutionary act motivated by economic necessity. The continuing clash between workers and owners over the allocation and division of Italy's limited resources would build working-class political consciousness and radicalism while drawing an ever-widening number of industrial and agricultural workers into political action. Milan, the heart of the developing Italian industrial society, was the center of their struggle against both the bourgeois state and Reformism.[6]

Syndicalism was the antithesis of Reformism in three areas: its stress on involving the working classes directly in political action, its emphasis on violence, and its rejection of parliamentary politics. In one area, however, Syndicalist views were similar to those of their opponents. The Syndicalists, like the Reformists, were convinced that the working classes were politically immature and offered themselves, a group of middle-class intellectuals, as the general staff of the revolution. They were prepared to organize and lead the aroused masses to the overthrow of the Italian state. Unlike the French, Italian Syndicalists were determined to carry on their fight against Reformism within the Socialist party. Their aims were to drive out the Reformists, take control of the Party and utilize it in exacerbating class warfare. In their struggle with the Reformists for control of the PSI, the Italian Syndicalist movement developed distinctive political characteristics.[7]

The dominant figure in this emerging Italian Syndicalism was Arturo Labriola. Labriola was born on January 21, 1873, in Naples to a middle-class family and held a degree from the University of Naples. In 1894, soon after joining the socialist movement, he was arrested for his involvement in the Sicilian *Fasci* and sentenced to eighteen months in prison. During these initial years of Socialist party membership, Labriola was a protégé of Turati. In 1898, however, he left Italy to avoid arrest for his role in the *fatti di maggio*. After a brief sojourn in Switzerland, Labriola made his way to Paris. The French capital was enmeshed in the Dreyfus affair, and Labriola was later to stress the importance of his exile in Paris in forming his syndicalist views. He left France, Labriola stated, "a Marxist and a republican" but also came into contact with "individualist currents of thought," specifically with Sorel and the anarchists. Sorel initially had a low opinion of the young Italian socialist but changed his mind after he got to know Labriola. Labriola, on the other hand, later remarked that contact with Sorel led him to lower his opinion of the French intellectual as a man while admitting his great debt to the writer and thinker. Certainly, the relationship was fruitful for Labriola, who returned to Italy in 1900 to lead a strong theoretical and practical challenge to Reformism.[8]

During his exile in France, Labriola kept in contact with fellow Neapolitan E. C. Longobardi and other like-minded Socialists.[9] Returning to Naples, he found that his fellow dissidents had built up an anti-Reformist power base in the city around the newspaper, *La Propaganda*. From Naples, they prepared to carry their war to Turati's Milan.

The Syndicalists held Turati and his faction responsible for turning the Socialist party into a constitutional party of social reform. Labriola was incensed by the Reformists' indifference to the "institutional question" of a republican or monarchist Italy. He believed that the monarchy "because of its traditions and its origins was necessarily tied to authoritarian and illiberal solutions" and therefore represented a "fatal obstacle" to progressive and democratic tendencies. The weakness and reactionary nature of the monarchy had been amply demonstrated by its actions during the 1890s. Instead of cooperating with other progressive forces to bring down the crown, Reformist indifference to the institutional question was reinforcing the monarchy. A third point in the Syndicalist critique was the charge that the Reformists' commitment to parliamentary action was separating the PSI from its natural base of support, the working class. While the Reformist-led PSI concentrated on parliamentary action that conserved existing social and political institutions, the Syndicalists charged, the Reformist-led unions were abandoning their true role of creating class consciousness to support small-scale reform. Moreover, the Syndicalists stressed that even the passage of reform legislation would not necessarily bring benefits to the working class. Italy's large, permanent state bureaucracy was profoundly antidemocratic. Without radical restructuring, the bureaucracy would delay or leave unenforced the reform laws that parliament passed.[10]

In 1901 the Syndicalists moved boldly into Milan to challenge Reformism in its citadel. Syndicalist boldness paid high dividends. Shortly after the arrival of this new "revolutionary" force, the labor unions began to suffer serious reverses in their struggle with the owners. The overwhelming and easy successes of 1901 strikes were not repeated the following year. The owners' resistance to further concessions stiffened, and by March 1902, the number of successful strikes had declined precipitously. When the Socialist deputies were unable to gain government intervention in support of the strikers' demands, Reformism came under growing attack from the rank and file within both the Party and the labor movement.[11]

Nevertheless, the forces of Lazzari and Labriola could never have conquered a majority within the PSI. Neither faction had enough support among the rank and file. The third factor in a successful left-wing challenge to Reformism was a leader who could appeal to the Party as a proponent of unity: Enrico Ferri. Ferri was a very contradictory individual. A major figure in Italian sociology, a proponent of positivist thought, Ferri was a clever orator and skilled parliamentarian. By birth, by education, by inclination, he belonged among the Reformists. However, when Ferri entered the Party he established an independent position to the left of Turati. During the crisis of 1898, Ferri played a significant role in directing the opposition to the government. He briefly assumed the post of editor of *Avanti!* during Bissolati's imprisonment. Later he had a leading role in parliamentary obstruction of the Pelloux government. At the 1900 Party congress, Ferri insisted on continuing with the policy of separation from the parties of the middle class. He argued that the Party was not yet "mature" enough to grant autonomy to its sections and that this policy would arrest the development of the Italian Socialist movement. Then he introduced the resolution that reorganized the *Direzione* and handed the Reformists the effective control of the PSI.[12]

Ferri's desire to become the PSI's undisputed leader explains his rapid swings. In 1900, Antonio Labriola, who despised Ferri, made an uncannily accurate prediction of his future course:

> Our monarchist ministers have been for the most part former republicans—and so it will be with the future ex-Socialists. . . . Ferri, who has played the intransigent at [the Socialist International Congress at] Paris, is the most determined of all to play Millerand [the former French Socialist became a minister in a bourgeois government].[13]

Arturo Labriola had few illusions about Ferri:

My opinion of him is that he has never changed and has remained a conservative. You can be a Socialist and a conservative, as for example [Ettore] Ciccotti is. Both [men] have a mad woman's fear of the revolution and of the republic.[14]

Nevertheless, Arturo Labriola was eager to join forces with Ferri in 1901. Ferri had the ability to feel the pulse of the Party and to leap in the direction the rank and file was moving. Because his real aim was to be the undisputed leader of the PSI, Ferri had little interest in the finer points of ideology. Ferri was a sort of anti-Bernstein, who reversed the motto of the German revisionist socialist to read, "The end is everything, the means nothing."[15] "Revolutionary," "Integralist," "Reformist" were tags which meant little to Ferri, who was all three in the space of ten years. Similarly, Ferri showed little interest in questions of political organization. He viewed these issues, like all others, through the optic of his ambition. Ferri embraced any organization that promoted his claims to Party leadership. In 1906, at the ninth national congress of the Party, Ferri deftly read the Syndicalists out of the PSI and, in the process, neatly spelled out his conception of his special role: Ferri believed he was a balancing factor correcting the deviations of the Reformists or the Syndicalists.

Ferri's reasoning had wide appeal and was not without its solid points. While Labriola and Turati insisted that the PSI follow a single strategy, Ferri replied that it must be flexible in its tactics. When Turati's parliamentary politics and Labriola's revolutionary designs led both men to propose major modifications in the Party's organizational structure that would deny a major role to the PSI, Ferri insisted the Party had a continuing central role. Ferri's great popularity rested on his ability to express forcefully the feeling of the rank and file that the struggle of the two factions had gone too far and that both sides must accept a concept of Party, as opposed to factional, loyalty. Had Ferri been less consumed with personal ambition, he might have been able to reconcile the two factions and achieve his ambition of leading a united Party. Instead, he followed an opportunistic course until the endless contradictions of his stances left him isolated from the rank and file.[16]

On a tactical plane, Ferri's programs were an attempt to talk Italy into a revolution. He believed that the "essence of revolution is the formation of socialist consciousness within the proletariat by means of propaganda. . . . I tire myself by repeating . . . *ad nauseam*: collective property and class struggle, collective property and class struggle."[17] Ferri's emphasis on propaganda accorded with the views of Labriola's faction. Beyond violent speech, however, lay violent action, and here Ferri took leave from his Syndicalist allies.[18]

REFORMISM UNDER FIRE, 1901–4

From Labriola's arrival in the fall of 1901 until the seventh national Congress of the PSI in September 1902, Milan was the cockpit of the struggle against Reformism. Turati's failure to purge Lazzari from the Party led to a split within the MSF. A series of strikes in February and March 1902 resulted in resounding defeats for the workers. The manner in which Giolitti broke a strike by railway workers was a particularly graphic demonstration of his ascendancy over the Socialist parliamentary deputies. Turati was reduced to the position of a petitioner before the powerful minister of the interior. He pleaded with Giolitti that failure to find an acceptable compromise on this strike would be a serious blow to the Reformists and throw the workers into the arms of the PSI's left wing.[19]

Turati was under constant attack by Arturo Labriola, who had become a regular contributor to the Milanese Republican party paper, *L'Italia del Popolo*. In an effort to counter Labriola's increasingly effective offensive, the Reformists took full control of another Milanese daily, *Il Tempo,* on April 14, 1902. A few weeks later, however, Reformism's long hold on the national Socialist party press was finally broken when Ferri published the first edition of a new bimonthly magazine, *Il Socialismo.*

Adding to Turati's troubles was the rising number of strikers killed by armed police and troops during labor disturbances. In the first eighteen months of the Zanardelli-Giolitti cabinet, two clashes between strikers and troops resulted in 4 deaths and 27 injuries. A third clash, which left 5 dead and 10 wounded, took place on September 8, 1902, during the Socialist national Congress at Imola. The pace of the violence accelerated, and by the time Giolitti left the Ministry of the Interior in March 1903, government troops and police had killed 14 strikers and wounded 87.

When the Congress of Imola met, the Reformists were on the defensive. In an effort to conciliate the more moderate part of the opposition, Bonomi introduced a hazily worded resolution obfuscating and smoothing over differences between the factions. After affirming that the fundamental principles of the Party were class struggle and collective property, the resolution declared: "The Congress affirms that the action of the Party is reformist because revolutionary, and revolutionary because reformist, that is to say of the Party that it is simply Socialist."[20] In dealing with the critical issues of autonomy of the sections and of the parliamentary group, however, the Bissolati resolution took an unmistakably Reformist line while making numerous bows in the direction of central control, orthodoxy, and other ideas dear to the left. The Bissolati resolution carried by a two-to-one margin over the motion offered for the left by Ferri.[21]

During the last day of the Congress, the delegates discussed the organization of the PSI. Turati introduced a motion to abolish the *Direzione* and grant full autonomy to the Party sections, to *Avanti!*, and to the parliamentary group. The resolution also would have set up a commission to revise the *statuto*. When a vote on his resolution resulted in a tie, Turati withdrew it.[22] He apparently judged that an attempt to force a radical revision of the Party's organization might lead to a serious split.

Turati freely admitted that his proposal was radical. It was, however, in keeping with the evolution of Reformist thought and showed the influence of the two-year experiment of cooperation with the Zanardelli-Giolitti ministry. Turati's proposal would have turned the PSI into a cadre party similar to the middle-class parties which dominated most European parliaments of the era. Without a *Direzione,* all decisions affecting the Party and the working class inevitably would be made in parliament. The sections would become permanent standing electoral committees for the individual deputies. Turati was proposing that the PSI bring its structure into line with that of the ''Liberal party'' in order to integrate the Socialist movement more successfully into the existing political system. The Socialist deputy would become a representative of local interests who gave homage, and probably little else, to a series of broad principles labeled ''socialism.''

Although the Turati resolution failed to gain a majority, Reformism had triumphed at the Imola Congress. Bonomi observed that the ideological split within the Party was not severe enough to endanger its unity and admonished the left to take a closer look at the experiences of the Socialist movement since the publication of the *Communist Manifesto.* Ferri, however, was equally pleased with the results his faction achieved at Imola. The left opposition had been strongly represented in spite of continued Reformist dominance of the national and local Party press.[23]

Moreover, the Reformists had little time to savor their triumph. Their dominance over the Milan Socialist press was decisively broken when the left began publishing a new weekly, *Avanguardia Socialista* in December 1902. As the Reformists admitted, *Avanguardia* was a formidable opponent for *Il Tempo*. Treves's paper, traditionally a spokesman for the entire left, attempted to reach a wider reading public than Milanese socialists and thus focused much of its coverage on national political affairs. *Avanguardia Socialista* was an avowedly Socialist paper which concentrated its coverage on the activities of the Milanese socialist section and working class. Labriola served as the editor in chief of the new newspaper. He centered his attacks on the failures and weaknesses of Italian Socialism, singling out one inviting target for blame: the archrevisionist Filippo Turati. Turati, he charged, was a man "more Bernsteinian than Bernstein."[24]

By early 1903, the left-wing coalition of Reformism's enemies controlled newspapers in Naples and Milan as well as Ferri's national review, *Il Socialismo*. Then, on April 1, 1903, a well-orchestrated campaign forced Bissolati to resign as the director of *Avanti!*. Ferri took over control of the Party's official newspaper, bringing a new editorial staff with him. The Syndicalist Enrico Leone became editor in chief of *Avanti!*. Six months after the Reformist victory at Imola, the positions of the contending factions were dramatically reversed. Ferri, through his control of *Avanti!* and *Il Socialismo*, established his position as the spokesman of a new majority within the PSI.

Under Ferri's leadership, *Avanti!* launched a campaign against corruption in the armaments industry. While a political success, the court costs which followed soon placed the PSI's national newspaper in a perilous financial situation. Ferri also faced other problems within his press empire. Attempting to edit both *Avanti!* and *Socialismo* proved too much even for a man of Ferri's energy. Within six months, he was forced to hand over editorial control of *Socialismo* to Giovanni Lerda, an orthodox leftist of considerable independence and stature. Moreover, Ferri had problems controlling Leone, who frequently took a divergent political stance from that of *Avanti!*'s director. Nevertheless, Ferri could be highly satisfied with the successes which he had achieved. The left was a growing force within the PSI. Ferri and his allies spoke for the Party and were in a position to take action against both the government and its Reformist supporters.[25]

The Zanardelli government was limping toward its end. The prime minister's health was failing. In the spring of 1903, he decided to introduce a divorce bill in parliament; an action which was political dynamite in Catholic Italy. Giolitti, with one eye on the emerging Catholic political movement, tried to dissuade Zanardelli. When he failed, Giolitti resigned. Ferri led the group into the opposition to the government with Turati's approval. The government struggled on for another six months before it fell on October 29, 1903. Giolitti then formed his second ministry, on November 3, 1903.

Turati, aware that the Zanardelli government was doomed, busily improved the Party's ties with Giolitti in anticipation of a reform government led by the Piedmontese statesman. Both Turati and Kuliscioff were convinced that Giolitti was the one Italian leader capable of guiding a reform package that favored the interests of the working class. They also believed that he would have to rely on Socialist support to maintain a government in power. Giolitti decided to cement this support. He invited Turati "to enter my ministry. I thought that since my intention and program of government were to continue without reservation . . . in that politics of liberty to which the Socialist Party had always given its support that it was logical for this party to participate in the ministry."[26]

Turati was acutely embarrassed by Giolitti's offer. He admitted that he could not even go to Rome for consultations with Giolitti for fear of the effects that such a meeting would have within the PSI. The Party, he confided, was "out of my hands." Joining the new government would play into the hands of his enemies and create an irreparable split in the PSI.[27]

Giolitti, of course, was aware of Turati's dilemma. By offering the Reformists a place within the government, he was trying to force them to face the full implications of their political strategy. Reformism, as the left ceaselessly pointed out and the right relentlessly denied, taken to its logical consequences led to Socialist participation in a government.[28] In 1903, however, neither Turati nor Bissolati accepted this conclusion. Fearing with reason that the working classes would not accept a decision to participate in a government, the Reformists held back. Giolitti, meanwhile, had healed the basic rifts among Liberals. Many conservative deputies were quite willing to support a government which had shown its ability to control the working classes. Giolitti no longer needed Socialist support to survive. After Turati rejected his offer of a cabinet position, Giolitti turned to the Catholics for support. Meanwhile the Reformists, who were unable either to participate in a government or force the ministry to accept their reform program, waited passively for Giolitti to take the lead in reforming.

THE TRIUMPH OF FERRI'S COALITION

While the Reformists repeatedly demonstrated their inability to force the pace of reform, the left-wing coalition aligned with Ferri continued its conquest of the Party. In February 1904, Turati's opponents, led by Labriola, took control of the Lombard Socialist federation. A regional congress at Brescia narrowly adopted a radical resolution introduced by Labriola, signaling the left's control in this critical part of the Italian working-class movement.

The Reformists were disconcerted by their defeat and by the language in the Labriola resolution. One Reformist deputy acidly commented, "Our Party ought to change its name from Socialist Party to the Anarchist Party."[29] More importantly, the Ferri faction triumphed on the eve of the national Party Congress at Bologna.

Maurice Duverger has pointed to the more than symbolic importance which the selection of a site for a political gathering can have.[30] The 1900 PSI Congress was held at Rome, in the wake of the parliamentary group's triumphs. Imola was the fiefdom of Reformism's "grand old man," Andrea Costa. Bologna, however, was a city with a strong revolutionary tradition within a region with a long history of left-wing politics.[31] The city was the ideal site for staging the triumph of the Party's left wing.

Robert Michels, the representative of the German Social Democratic party, set the tone of the 1904 Congress by warning the delegates of the imminent threat to the existence of the Party posed by parliamentarism. He urged discipline and unity as the solutions for the PSI's problems. The delegates then adopted a Lazzari-Labriola resolution praising the *Direzione* and reiterating the need for Party unity.[32]

During the next two days, as the two factions outlined their differences, a split emerged within the left-wing coalition. The Syndicalists were obviously moving away from the mainstream of the Party. A center faction, dedicated to the preservation of Party unity, emerged under Ferri's leadership. Reformism and Syndicalism became the two extremes which threatened this unity.[33] A Reformist resolution proposed by Bissolati easily defeated one offered by Labriola 316 votes to 198 but lacked an absolute majority. Ferri and labor leader Labriola introduced two "centrist" resolutions. The Ferri motion defeated a Rinaldo Rigola proposal 424 to 377.[34]

The 1904 Party Congress is the first for which the statistical data are sufficient to permit an analysis of the strengths of the contending factions in terms of geographic distribution and economic situation.

Certain patterns emerge clearly. The Reformists were strongest in the northern part of Italy and among sections with a membership of one hundred or less. The center of Reformist strength was the agrarian Emilia-Romagna area. In the rest of northern Italy the strength of the Reformists was evenly matched by that of the Syndicalists. An important exception to this generalization was Turin, a center of heavy industry, where Labriola found enough support to cancel out the Reformist advantage among the smaller, primarily agrarian sections of the province. In Central Italy, the pattern of Reformist strength in smaller, primarily agrarian, sections, was repeated in Tuscany and the Marche. However, from Umbria down to the southern tip of the mainland, the pattern reversed itself. The Syndicalists found strong support in these areas where only a few small Socialist party sections existed. Finally, the islands of Sicily and Sardinia also had contrasting voting patterns. The Reformists found strong support in Sicily, where a relatively long tradition of Socialist organization existed. Conversely, Syndicalism found some support in Sardinia, where the PSI had only recently begun its organizational activities. (However, all the sections of this island then supported the Ferri resolution.)

Reformism, then, was strongly rooted in the agrarian areas of the North where its leaders had played a major hand in the foundation of the National Organization of Agricultural Workers (Federterra) in 1901. The distribution of PSI seats in parliament followed this pattern. Eleven of the Party's seats lay in the Emilia-Romagna region. Seven of the PSI's remaining fourteen seats lay in agrarian areas contiguous to the Emilia-Romagna region. Reformism was weak in the South because the agrarian workers in that area were mostly unorganized and lacked the vote.[35]

In addition to a base of support among the agrarian areas of the South, Syndicalism enjoyed its greatest support in the largest cities in Italy. The Milan, Turin, and Rome sections all voted for the Labriola resolution, as did the Socialist organizations of Naples, Bologna, and Venice. The Reformists managed to offset Syndicalist support in Milan but enjoyed support only among the smaller urban centers of Reggio Emilia and Imola, the fiefs of Reformist leaders Costa and Prampolini.[36]

The Syndicalists returned to their shaky alliance with Ferri for the second vote, while the Reformists backed the Rigola resolution. In the voting, the Reformists showed their strength in the Emilia-Romagna. They also held their own numerically in Central Italy but were defeated by a vote for the Ferri resolution which doubled and, at times, tripled the support given to Labriola. Tuscany shifted its support from Reformism on the first ballot to Ferri on the second. The Ferri resolution also picked up substantial support in southern Italy and in the islands. In Sicily, Ferri's calls for Party unity were apparently as effective as a decade of Reformist organizational work. Overall, the Ferri resolution found support in every area of Italy and among all types of Socialist sections. Success was tempered by the failure of Ferri's resolution to win support in the two most industrialized cities: Milan and Turin. Both sections abstained on the second ballot. Ferri's resolution did receive the support of the sections of Rome, Venice, Naples, Bologna, and Florence. None of these cities, however, were major industrial centers. The Reformists, united behind labor leader Rinaldo Rigola, with first-ballot support in Milan and second-ballot backing in Genoa, had a better claim to be in tune with the views of the industrial proletariat than Ferri. The most important sources of support for the Rigola motion were the smaller industrializing Italian cities of the North.[37]

The victory of Ferri's resolution gave his coalition control of the Party's directive organs. Given the opportunity to reorganize the PSI, Ferri and his supporters declined to act. They sidestepped the issue of the autonomous section of Milan, instructing the *Direzione* to hold a referendum on the problem at an unspecified later date. The victors did reorganize the *Direzione*, reducing its membership from eleven to seven by limiting the parliamentary group to one representative. Recognizing that their own activities within the previous *Direzione* were partially to blame for its paralysis, the left excluded the Reformist minority from the Party central committee. Ferri was easily reelected director of *Avanti!*, which brought with it membership on the *Direzione*. The Congress then adjourned.[38]

The Congress of Bologna provided proof both of the fragility of the Ferri-led coalition of the left and of the enduring strength of the Reformists. Ferri's coalition was a marriage of irreconcilables. The Syndicalists made no secret of their disdain for the "revolutionary-reformism" of the center. Mocchi brushed off the centrist position as inconsequential, stressing that "the struggle is between two antithetical views of the future of Socialism."[39] Ferri referred to the Syndicalists as "secessionists" who would abandon the Party if it refused to accept their views. The Ferri maneuver, which pitted the Syndicalist's resolution against Bissolati's motion, was a clever tactical move. The Syndicalists were badly beaten, as Ferri foresaw, and were then faced with a stark choice: either to support Ferri and ride to victory with him or to forego political power for ideological purity. Once again they were forced to recognize their dependence on Ferri. However, getting the Syndicalists to acknowledge his leadership was one matter, keeping them under control once the coalition held power was another. Organizationally, they were more cohesive and stronger than the groups of the center, which, as they claimed, were incapable of defining any political aim except the need for Party unity. Ferri did little more than ensure that a left-center *Direzione* was installed in power, since this was the absolute minimum requirement for ensuring his continued leadership. He did nothing to correct the power imbalance which existed between the Party's central bodies and the parliamentary group. The members of the GPS, officially a part of the opposition, remained autonomous and continued to pursue their constituents' interests through cooperation with and support for the Giolitti ministry. Policy continued to be made in parliament rather than in the *Direzione*. Ferri was unwilling to upset the existing Party organization because he was one of its chief beneficiaries. He was both a deputy and the director of *Avanti!*. If he subordinated the PSI to the tight control of a powerful *Direzione*, Ferri would have had to accept the same discipline himself. The prize which he had long sought was the leadership, not membership on a directing committee of seven.[40]

Ferri, therefore, introduced only minor changes in the Party's political structure. An unmodified organization permitted the Reformists to operate freely, but major modifications would threaten Ferri's primacy and play into the hands of the more disciplined Syndicalists. By maintaining a balance of tensions, Ferri successfully played the Reformists off against the Syndicalists, solidifying his position as Party leader.

When Ferri's position finally eroded, the Reformists were able to regain control. Command of the *Direzione* was never central to their plans, but autonomy for the deputies and sections was. Since the Congress of Bologna did nothing that would limit the independence of either the GPS or the sections, their defeat was not too serious. Turati, however, had made a major error at Bologna by ignoring Ferri to seek a confrontation with the Syndicalists. At an April 8 caucus of the Reformists, Turati fought against a proposal that they back a centrist resolution instead of opposing the Labriola motion with one of their own. Turati insisted that the introduction of the Bissolati resolution would drive a wedge between the center and the Syndicalists.[41] In his April 10 speech to the Congress, he took a hard line: "Within this Congress, there exist not two spirits within the same Party, but two parties, and it is time for the delegates to decide which is the true Socialist Party."[42] After Turati called for a purge, Ferri rose to insist on the unity of the PSI, "a fact which the minorities must respect."[43] Turati recognized that his inflexibility had played into Ferri's hands and damaged the Reformists' position. At the next Congress, he would be ready to lift the mantle of champion of Party unity from Ferri's shoulders.

THE HIGH TIDE OF SYNDICALISM, APRIL–SEPTEMBER, 1904

After his personal triumph over both Reformists and Syndicalists at the Bologna Congress, Ferri quickly lost the political initiative to his left-wing allies. Seeking to create class consciousness within the Italian proletariat, the Syndicalists relied upon the political strike and violent clashes with the forces of the law. They chose the Chambers of Labor as a vehicle for organizing a crescendo of strikes and violence leading to a general strike and the overthrow of the state.

Like Syndicalism, the Chamber of Labor had its origins in France. The first Italian Chamber was organized in Milan in 1891. The chambers attempted to "soften labor conflicts, stabilizing the possibility of [class] contact."[44] The Chamber, like the Socialist section, was a school in which the workers could learn to manage their economic affairs and a training ground in democratic practice. As the number of Chambers increased they took on more specialized functions, such as organizing strikes and propaganda. Simultaneously, the Chambers began to develop a national organization. Because the Chambers organized workers on a geographical basis rather than according to industrial specialization, their ability to negotiate with owners was limited. After 1900, the Chambers were rapidly supplanted by national trade union organizations. However, it was precisely the undifferentiated character of the Chambers of Labor which appealed to the Syndicalists. Since the Chambers were ineffective bargaining agents, their membership was easily oriented toward political action. Further, because their members were employed in so many types of industry and agriculture, the Chambers of Labor were excellent places in which to recruit and train revolutionary cadres who could simultaneously disrupt a number of different segments of the national economy. Reformists had originally sponsored the creation of the Chambers, which remained solidly Reformist in sympathy until the labor movement ran into serious trouble in 1902–3. By 1904 the Syndicalists had made major inroads among their rank and file, especially in Milan.[45]

When the short honeymoon between the Zanardelli-Giolitti ministry and labor ended in 1902, employers took heart. Their resistance to workers' demands stiffened, and the number of unsuccessful strikes rose from 29 percent in 1901 to 54 percent in 1902. The number of strikes also diminished, but the level of violence increased. By 1903 the strikers' goals were changing from economic to political. The general strike was more widely utilized. The first general strike took place in Rome in March 1903. After the strike was put down with force, its organizers damned the Reformists for their faint-hearted support. The tempo of these political strikes picked up throughout 1903 and continued to grow in 1904. So did the number of deaths resulting from police action. After the Congress of Bologna left the

Reformists momentarily paralyzed, the Syndicalists tried to exploit their opponents' weakness and thoroughly radicalize the working classes through a combination of an effective propaganda campaign and the expansion of general strike tactics. The Syndicalists, moreover, found a highly useful source of support in the recently organized Young Socialist Movement.[46]

In September 1904, the Syndicalists finally achieved a national general strike. After clashes between strikers and troops on September 4 and 14, 1904, left five workers dead and thirty wounded, the Milan Chamber of Labor called a general strike (September 15). By September 17, the strike was spreading throughout Italy. It finally collapsed at the beginning of October, defeated by masterful inactivity on the part of Giolitti. The prime minister recognized that this strike lacked economic causes and that political objectives could not unite the workers for long. He concluded that it would not threaten Italy's constitutional arrangements.[47]

The Reformists were disconcerted by the general strike, which they opposed as "utopian" and counterproductive. Ferri took a similar position and suffered a serious loss of prestige. He supported a September 14 *Direzione* resolution which condemned the use of the general strike. The union movement, too, lost heavily in financial and organizational terms as well as in political prestige. The unions had been unable to control the spontaneous general strike. The Syndicalists, who could claim a success, were rudely shocked when Italy's middle-class voters coalesced and handed the PSI a major setback in the November–December 1904 general election.[48] Giolitti, too, was a loser. Although, he later claimed, with some justification, that his policies helped the Italian middle class to "recover from their fright of the social[ist] peril,"[49] the memory of the 1904 strike left an indelible mark on the psyche of Italy's bourgeoisie. Twenty-five years later, Luigi Albertini remembered, "The morning after the first day of the general strike, Milan seemed to be abandoned to itself. Public force disappeared . . . It seemed that the government had been the first to obey the order for a general strike for it had deserted its functions."[50] Tommaso Tittoni, a member of Giolitti's government, also recalled the "sad impression" made by a Milan "abandoned to the subversives."[51] In the elections which followed, the Italian electorate swung right and Giolitti followed them.[52]

The general strike of 1904 was both the high point of Syndicalist influence within the PSI and the beginning of the final rupture between Syndicalism and Socialism. Labriola was disillusioned with the PSI. In December 1903, he wrote fellow Syndicalist Longobardi, "Every day that passes I become more aware of an incompatibility between us and the official socialists."[53] He also faced grave difficulties trying to keep *Avanguardia Socialista* afloat, disliked life in Milan, and complained that he was increasingly isolated from the intellectual and political life of the Party. In the aftermath of the strike, Ferri was tacking to the right, publicly endorsing the gradual development of socialism. The Syndicalists realized that their alliance with Ferri was finished. *Avanguardia Socialista* editorialized that Ferri had been "frank and resolute" in opposing the Syndicalists "before, during, and after the general strike." Walter Mocchi accused Ferri of abandoning the class struggle. To further emphasize their isolation from the rest of the Party, the Roman Syndicalists began publishing their own theoretical journal, *Il Divenire Sociale* on January 1, 1905.[54]

FERRI'S PROGRESS TO THE RIGHT, OCTOBER 1904–OCTOBER 1906

While the Syndicalists moved toward an open break with the PSI and the Reformists regrouped, Enrico Ferri held center stage within the Socialist party. In the two and a half years between the congresses of Bologna and Rome, he completed his metamorphosis from "revolutionary" to "integralist."

Throughout the period, Ferri engaged in a fierce struggle with his Syndicalist former allies for the control of *Avanti!*. The combination of Ferri as director and Leone as editor in chief of the paper was unworkable. With both *Avanguardia Socialista* and *Il Divenire Sociale* struggling for their existence, the Syndicalists were determined to retain their foothold on the editorial board of the Party daily. Ferri's *Socialismo* was also near financial collapse, and he had to assert his control over *Avanti!* or lose the Party leadership. By February 1905, Leone's days as editor in chief were numbered. Labriola feared that Ferri would speedily ally with the Reformists and that the paper would fall under Reformist control. "Without a deputy in the chamber and with the Party daily in the hands of the Reformists, we will return to the situation [which existed] before [the Congress of] Imola."[55]

Ferri had no intention of sharing power with his adversaries. In June 1905, he used changes in the paper's format as a screen to reshuffle *Avanti!*'s staff, dismissing Leone and the Syndicalists. Ferri completed the rupture with his former allies in February 1906 when he convinced the GPS to support a Sonnino ministry over Turati's objections. The government that Ferri claimed would help to "moralize Italian politics" lasted for three months. Then a general strike in Turin forced the GPS to withdraw its support from Sonnino. Giolitti returned to power. Ferri faced the 1906 Party Congress in the wake of a serious political failure and with few positive achievements to show for his thirty months as the Party leader.[56]

THE CONGRESS OF ROME: TURATI'S *TRASFORMISMO*

At the 1906 Party Congress at Rome, Turati gave evidence that he was an able pupil of Giolitti and quite capable of applying the master's methods to dominate the internal struggles of the PSI. With Giolittian methodicalness, Turati embraced "Integralism" and gutted it so completely that by its 1908 Congress, the Party had a new right-center majority under his leadership. The Integralists were reduced to a splinter group.[57]

Ferri defended his actions in an October 9 address to the Congress, rejecting the theory of a revolutionary upheaval in favor of the slow evolutionary development of socialism. He claimed that the Sonnino ministry had offered a beneficial program of reforms for the proletariat. Ferri even defended the autonomy of the GPS.[58] The only solid success which Ferri could claim for his thirty months of leadership, forcing Giolitti's 1905 resignation, was negated by the Piedmontese leader's return to power.

Turati spoke after Ferri. He was conciliatory, even condescending toward the Integralists but once again warned that two parties existed within the body of the PSI. Syndicalism, he stated, was simply anarchism, driven from the Party in 1892 only to return in a new guise. An internal struggle against this new form of anarchism was a "luxury" which the Party "could not permit." Turning to the Integralists, Turati accused them of "zig-zag politics" which had weakened the PSI. He added, however, that no real differences existed between the Reformists and the Integralists. The Integralists were politically immature and eventually the majority of them would become Reformists.[59]

The 1906 Congress also witnessed the birth of a new faction: the "Revolutionary Intransigents." Giovanni Lerda, a founder of the Genovese socialist movement and an old opponent of Reformism, was one of their major spokesmen. The new faction comprised left-wing Socialists who were unwilling to move to the right with Ferri and unable to accept the Syndicalists' positions. Lerda denied that the proletariat was ready to support a middle-class ministry through its parliamentary representatives, much less participate in a government. The masses, he claimed, were not ready to judge political issues; they needed to be led. (A point on which the Reformists fully agreed.) Syndicalist doctrines, Lerda continued, opened the way for the bourgeoisie to penetrate the Party and the workers' movement. Finally, he accused the Socialist deputies of continually opposing the spontaneous actions of the working class in the name of the proletariat and demanded that they end this action.[60]

Revolutionary Intransigence was a simple but powerful appeal for the overthrow of all the middle-class theoreticians—Turati, Ferri, Labriola—and a return to the policies and outlook of 1892: war with the bourgeoisie. The simplicity of its analysis and its appeal to an heroic age just past, gave Revolutionary Intransigence a latent potency. As Socialist parliamentarism continued to fail and the Party began to decay, Lerda's faction would be able to rally the disenchanted.

Shortly after Lerda's speech, Prampolini told the Congress that the Reformists would support the Integralist motion. Instantly, Ferri was on his feet protesting. But, with Reformist backing, the Ferri resolution received 26,943 votes against 5,278 for the Syndicalist motion and 1,100 ballots for a Lerda resolution. The Syndicalists had been routed. The entire South, including their original base of Naples, supported Ferri's resolution. Only four larger sections voted for the Syndicalist resolution: Ancona, Parma, Bologna, and a part of Milan.[61]   •

Both the Integralist-Reformist majority and the Syndicalists increased their support among northern agrarian sections. Certain pockets of leftist support were identifiable. One was the area around Genoa, where a fierce struggle between Reformists and Syndicalists had been underway for six years.[62] Another area was among the sections of the eastern Emilia-Romagna: Ravenna, Bologna, Mantova, Ferrara, and Rovigo. In Lombardy, support for Syndicalism was particularly strong in Como. Agricultural Parma, located adjacent to the Reformist heartland, Reggio Emilia, went Syndicalist. During the next two years, Parma would be the center of Syndicalist activity. The voting pattern at Rome showed a significant switch in Syndicalism's base of support. The industrial workers of the North had been abandoning it since the unsuccessful 1904 general strike. The failure of a 1905 railway workers strike accelerated the decline. After 1906, the Syndicalists built their organization among the agricultural workers of the North. The Revolutionary Intransigents, moving from a very limited base in the agrarian Emilia-Romagna, would eventually capture the industrial cities of North Italy.[63]

Once the left had been defeated, the Integralists opened a discussion of the conduct of the parliamentary group and *Avanti!*. Ferri won an easy reconfirmation as director of *Avanti!*. Next, speaking fot the "Integralist majority," he proposed that the new *Direzione* consist entirely of Integralists in order to "overbalance the . . . parliamentary group," and also suggested a geographic distribution of its members. The Integralists asked some union leaders to sit on the new *Direzione* in recognition of the growing importance of organized labor. Within an expanded *Direzione* of thirty-four, Ferri proposed the creation of a central directing committee of nine which would reside at Rome to handle the Party's daily business. The Congress approved the motion.[64]

While Ferri claimed victory, Turati had gained what he wanted at the Congress of Rome. His pre-Congress goals included the triumph of Integralism over the left, for "if the mish-mash of Integralism prevails . . . we will triumph through them."[65] Turati's other key objective was driving the Syndicalists out of the Party. Labriola recognized that "Italian Syndicalism can never hope to be the majority in the Italian Socialist Party," and called for a break with the Party. Within eight months of the Rome Congress, the Syndicalists formally left the PSI. However, for all practical purposes, their participation in the Party ended at the Rome Congress.[66]

REFORMISM RECAPTURES THE LABOR MOVEMENT, 1904–7

Shortly before the Congress of Rome, the Reformists had effectively sealed their renewed control of the labor movement, defeating the Syndicalist challenge. The general strike movement of 1904 was a warning to the Reformists that they were losing their grip on the labor movement. Bissolati credited his removal as *Avanti!*'s director and the subsequent defeats suffered by Reformism through the Bologna Congress to the loss of organized labor's support. The Syndicalist attempt to turn the Italian labor movement into a school for creating revolutionaries threatened to knock out one of Reformism's chief props. Fortunately for the Reformists, a majority of labor leaders also saw the Syndicalists as a threat and were predisposed toward gradualism. Combining forces, they stole a march on the Syndicalists by creating national labor organizations which successfully brought local labor unions under their control.[67]

During the first third of the Giolittian era (1901–5), national trade and craft unions took root in Italy. The earliest of these vertical unions, the book printers union, was organized in 1872. In 1894, the railwaymen's union came into being after a fifteen-year organizational struggle. With the greater freedom to organize under the Zanardelli-Giolitti ministry, these union federations mushroomed. So rapid was their development that in November 1902 representatives of the federations and Chambers of Labor established a "Central Secretariat for Resistance" to function as a coordinating body for union organization and the effective distribution of propaganda. A Reformist, Angiolo Cabrini, was the first elected secretary of this organization.[68]

Reformists took the lead in organizing the federations of craft organizations that soon replaced the Chambers of Labor. With the single but important exception of the railwaymen's union, all these federations supported the Reformists in their struggle with Syndicalism. The Reformists, moreover, continued to contest the Syndicalists' control over the Chambers of Labor, and in January 1905, at the national congress of the Chambers, the Reformists retained control of the national organization. As the Syndicalists shifted their base of operations to rural Italy, the Reformists won back control of many of the local Chambers, including that of Milan. The Syndicalists received a further hard blow when the government broke the 1905 railway workers strike and nationalized the railroads.

In February 1906, the leaders of the Italian Federation of Metalworkers (FIOM) issued a call for the creation of a national confederation of Italian unions which would take over the coordination functions of the Secretariat of the Resistance and actively press the working class's economic demands. Once again, the Reformists were able to steal a march on their Syndicalist opponents. When the congress of labor federations met in Milan, the Reformists, who knew what kind of national confederation they wanted, were able to defeat the proposals of their disorganized opponents: Syndicalists, anarchists, and apolitical conservatives.[69]

The new organization, the General Confederation of Labor (CGL) faced many serious difficulties, including its relationship with the PSI. The CGL's leaders wanted to avoid a deepening involvement in the Socialist party's internal struggles, fearing its effect on the labor movement. However, when forced to take sides, they generally supported the Reformists.

While the leaders of the CGL agreed with the Reformists' insistence on a parliamentary approach to politics and on gradualism, the preeminent factor motivating their support was the Reformists' hands-off attitude toward the internal politics of the labor movement. The chiefs of the CGL developed a strong sense of independence from the PSI. Like their Reformist colleagues in the Party leadership, they believed in a strict separation in the activities of PSI and CGL. The Syndicalists, Revolutionary Intransigents, and even the Integralists all posed the threat of Party control over the labor movement.[70]

The CGL underlined its insistence on independence from the control of the PSI early in its existence. On July 29–30, 1907, a meeting of the CGL's Directive Council adopted a resolution stating:

1. Direction of agitation and strikes must be the responsibility of the CGL.
2. Party newspapers must have editors and reporters favorable to the labor movement. They must support the labor movement.
3. The GPS must create a secretariat responsible for keeping it in contact with the CGL.
4. The *Direzione* of the PSI must develop its economic program in conformity with that of the CGL and . . . individual members [of the Party] must conform to the statutes of Party and Confederation in their conduct.[71]

The leaders of the CGL were especially anxious that the members of the GPS act as their representatives in parliament. On October 14, 1906, two weeks after the creation of the CGL, its Directive Council sent three delegates to a meeting with the GPS. The CGL delegation carried a list of programs on which the Confederation wanted action. The demands of organized labor on the loyalties of the Socialist parliamentary deputies conflicted with the concept of an organized and disciplined political party. One immediate if unforeseen outcome of these conflicts was to force a number of PSI leaders to cut back their ties with the Party in order to meet their union responsibilities. Socialist deputies were increasingly forced to decide if they represented the Party or organized labor. Ultimately, a number of Reformists concluded that the Socialist party had outlived its usefulness and decided to replace it with a new organization, directly subordinated to the demands of organized labor.[72]

THE ERA OF MIDDLE-CLASS HEGEMONY

In assessing Ferri's impact on the PSI, relatively little has been said about the organization of the Party because his coalition modified so little of the political structure or mind set which it inherited from the Reformists. As the ruling coalition and its leader moved from the left to the center and then toward the right, the rationale for such changes diminished. Nevertheless, Integralism represented a departure from Reformism in one organizational area, albeit a small one. Ferri's insistence on creating a more representative *Direzione* probably saved that body from extinction. When the Reformists returned to power, Turati made no effort to abolish it. By increasing the membership on the *Direzione*, giving it a regional representation, and including prominent labor leaders among its members, Ferri increased its legitimacy. Further, by insisting that its members be selected only from the majority, Ferri ended the paralysis which characterized the *Direzione* under Reformist leadership. With a united *Direzione*, Ferri tried in a half-hearted manner to impose the will of the Party's central directing organism on the parliamentary group and the PSI's local organizations. Ferri gave renewed impetus to efforts to impose greater discipline within the PSI. At the same time, however, he was increasing his independence and that of *Avanti!*.

Middle-class intellectuals like Ferri and Turati rarely were amenable to the idea of Party discipline. Their inherited system of values pointed in the other direction: toward individualism. They shared these outlooks with the middle-class intellectuals who led Syndicalism. While all of these would-be leaders were ready to take command of the Party, they balked at accepting discipline imposed by a majority led by their opponents. The Syndicalists, who broke with the PSI after their 1906 defeat, were always in the forefront of those calling on the Reformists to accept Party discipline. The Syndicalists, however, repeatedly rejected all efforts to control or limit their activities. With Ferri, individualism reached its zenith. Ferri identified himself and the PSI so closely in his own mind that one could fairly say that he viewed Italian Socialism as simply an emanation of Enrico Ferri. When the Socialist party began to show signs of disaffection with its self-appointed messiah, Ferri abandoned the PSI. Having won personal preeminence, he was unwilling to accept any diminution of his status or to submit to Reformist leadership.[73]

The Reformists behaved in a different manner. They played the role of loyal opposition between 1904 and 1906. Turati, however, was rarely tolerant of opposition and attempted to expel such opponents as Lazzari and Labriola. Within the Reformist camp, personality clashes played a major role in politics, a characteristic normally associated with the less disciplined middle-class party.[74] Ultimately, middle-class individualism would play a major role in eroding the Reformists' control over the PSI.

By the end of 1907, Turati and Reformism stood victorious over rival middle-class-led political factions. These victories in internal party battles did not ensure the success of Reformism. Reformism continued to stake its future and that of the PSI on the ability of two largely independent bodies,

Avanti! and the GPS, to foster significant economic, social, and political change through cooperation with the middle classes. However, both the group and the newspaper were gripped with serious internal crises. The continuing weakness of these two bodies and their consequent inability to function effectively as agents of change opened major schisms within the dominant factions. The inability of these two organizations to perform their assigned tasks within Reformist grand strategy led directly to the splintering of the dominant faction and to the emergence of a new and more radical internal opposition.

II

The Crises

of

Reformism

The Continuous

Crisis:

Avanti!,

1896–1911

In a modern civilization, the newspaper is everything. . . . A political organization lives through the press.

—*La Avanguardia*, Dec. 18, 1910

THE PROBLEMS OF A SOCIALIST NEWSPAPER

With radio and motion pictures in their infancy, the young Italian Socialist party had only one means of mass communications with Party members and potential recruits: the newspaper. Keenly aware of its need to establish communication with the masses, the newly founded Socialist party designated the Milanese weekly, *Lotta di Classe,* as its official newspaper while encouraging the development of a local socialist press.[1] These actions were an important first step toward propagating the Party's ideals and organizing the masses. However, as Gaetano Salvemini noted, the PSI would be in position to compete with its middle-class opponents only when it too possessed a mass circulation daily. "For us, this is an even stronger need than for others because we rely on continuous propaganda."[2]

In 1896 the Party was able to set up its own daily. The *Direzione* nominated a committee of seven to study the technical problems involved in creating a new newspaper in August 1896. Acting on the advice of this committee, the *Direzione* set one thousand prepaid subscriptions as the minimum financial support needed to launch the new enterprise. In September *Lotta di Classe* began a subscription drive for the new daily. Enrico Ferri traveled throughout Italy seeking pledges of support. By mid-November 1896, the subscription drive produced the needed support and the *Direzione* met with the members of the committee and the newly nominated director of the paper to set a publication date. They picked December 25, 1896.[3]

Avanti! was the first attempt to publish a newspaper in Italy which would be national both in outlook and in circulation. At the same time, *Avanti!* was the paper of an emerging working class, covering events of interest to workers and running articles designed to meet their educational needs within a format similar to that of its powerful local competitors: *La Stampa, La Nazione, Il Resto del Carlino, Corriere della Sera.* In line with these aims, the Socialists decided to publish the new paper in Rome, the political and administrative center of the nation. Salvemini prophetically warned that this symbolic gesture endangered the survival of the paper. Rome was two hundred miles south of any major concentration of Socialist support as well as five hundred miles north of Sicily, the only area in the *Mezzogiorno* where the PSI was well established. By the time the paper reached the masses of the North and Sicily, its reporting would be hours and even days behind its local competitors. Moreover, the limited Italian reading public diminished the farther south the paper traveled. Most Rome newspapers struggled for survival. *Avanti!* was entering an overcrowded market. Establishing a home for the Party newspaper, Salvemini argued, must follow organizing work, not precede it. For this reason, he and other Socialists urged publishing *Avanti!* in Milan where a market existed. Salvemini's argument was sound. However, the conditions of 1896 Italy forced the Party to publish in the capital. The PSI was struggling to protect and expand elementary political rights—among them its right to existence—and Rome was the arena in which this battle was being fought.[4]

The decision to publish in Rome placed *Avanti!* in a state of continuous financial crisis. The core of *Avanti!*'s problem was its need to maintain a large volume of subscription sales. Paradoxically, a healthy newsstand run only increased the paper's troubles. *Lotta di Classe* experienced the same problem. In 1892, it was selling an average 15,000 copies per issue but, due to the added expenses of newsstand distribution, was losing two centesimi per copy per day. "In other words, the more we sell, the more we lose."[5] Subscription sales cut out the costs of middle men and enabled the paper to balance the inevitable losses derived from newsstand sales. *Avanti!*, moreover, could not raise prices to cover its losses. It had to keep its price low to encourage subscriptions, to be competitive, and to reach a working class audience. In addition, the paper faced other serious drains on its limited cash reserves. Court costs arising from civil suits and sequestration were unpredictable but omnipresent. *Avanti!*'s efforts to carry the Socialist message to the working class met with active opposition from the Italian government. The degree of official harassment employed by the government varied from cabinet to cabinet and at times was supplemented by independent actions of local authorities. The distribution of *Avanti!* was frequently impeded. All of these factors forced the paper to an endless series of subscription drives. Almost any occasion provided a pretext to solicit subscriptions: May Day, Party Congresses, the beginning of a serialized novel, election campaigns, even the introduction of telegraphic news services from Northern Europe. Despite a capitalistic odor, *Avanti!* was soon utilizing contests and offering special prizes to lure new subscribers.[6]

ORGANIZATION

Avanti! was organized on the pattern of most Italian dailies of that era. Press and editorial offices were located in Rome. An editorial board composed of the director, an editor in chief, and four editors decided on the layout of the daily edition. Party members served as correspondents. An individual nominated by the section provided news of the local sections. Leading members of foreign Socialist parties served as special correspondents for *Avanti!*. The salaries of these "comrade correspondents" varied. Those in Berlin, London, Brussels, and Vienna received 50 lire per month. The newspaper paid its Paris correspondent "three times as much because of the importance of his service." Other collaborators were paid 10 to 25 lire per article or a set monthly fee. Salaries of the editors ranged from 200 to 250 lire per month. The management of *Avanti!* was in the hands of an administrator, a treasurer, and four clerks who received salaries ranging from 115 to 200 lire per month. Both the administrator and the director were nominated by the Party Congress and were responsible to it.[7]

The scattered sources available permit a brief but accurate reconstruction of the activities of *Avanti!*'s staff. Before 1904 and again after its move to Milan in 1911, *Avanti!* was published as a morning edition. Under Enrico Ferri, *Avanti!* became an evening paper in Rome in an attempt to corner a larger local market. (It continued to appear as a morning edition in the rest of Italy.) As an evening edition, the paper went to press about ten hours earlier. However, the pattern of activities surrounding its publication remained essentially the same.

The editorial staff of *Avanti!* normally arrived for work about six hours before the paper was to go to press. By the time they arrived most of the information which would be included in the next day's paper had already arrived: letters, copies of telegraphic messages from correspondents, information taken from the government press agency, Stefani, copies of the opposition press, and the reports from the Party's special correspondents. Each editor had a well-defined area of responsibility. Under Bissolati, for example, political matters were divided among Bissolati, Ivanoe Bonomi, and two editors. Guido Podrecca dealt with "clerical affairs," while Luigi Bottazi was in charge of a daily "variety" column. Once assembled, the editors normally met with the director and editor in chief to decide on the layout for the next edition. They evaluated the news of the previous day and decided what sort of articles to include in the upcoming edition. The director then delegated members of the editorial staff to write the appropriate stories and editorials. After they agreed to the final layout and wrote their assigned pieces, the editors were free to go home. Normally, the paper went to press about three hours before it would appear on the streets.[8]

Under Italy's press censorship laws, government censors examined the content of a newspaper while the first edition was being printed. If an offending article, sentence, or even word was discovered, the entire edition was declared sequestered. However, the newspaper could publish a second edition with the sequestered material removed. The standard practice at *Avanti!* was to leave the censored area blank as a form of protest. In addition, changing the format to fill the void was a costly, time-consuming process, especially after the paper's editors had already left for the evening. The censorship law was one reason that the director usually remained in his office until the paper was being distributed. One peculiarity of the censorship law did favor the newspaper. Only copies intended for newsstand sale were subject to sequestration. Subscription copies, which were normally sent by mail, were not disturbed. This meant that subscribers would receive the newspaper at the usual time and that *Avanti!* saved part of the costs which a second press run entailed.[9]

In layout, as in organization, *Avanti!* did not differ markedly from its competitors. The paper published a four-page edition until 1905. From 1905 to 1911, the Sunday edition was six pages. In May 1906, *Avanti!* began putting out a six-page Saturday edition as well. The first page of the four-page format was devoted to national and international news and to major news from the Socialist movement. Whether in five- or six-column format, the first column of the paper was usually devoted to a lead editorial (often by the director), and the last column to intellectual and cultural affairs. The center columns provided coverage of the major stories of the day. Use of the boldface headlines varied with director. Ferri employed them more frequently (1903–8) than Bissolati during his two terms (1896–1903,

1908–10). Benito Mussolini (1912–14) was the first director to fully exploit the dramatic impact of the headline.

Pages two and three of *Avanti!* were devoted to local (Roman) news, theater, parliamentary activity, and obituaries. As the journal of the working class, *Avanti!* also offered information on the activities of the Party's local formations and on the labor movement. Page four was devoted primarily to advertising, with the top quarter of the page normally reserved for the serialization of a popular novel. When the paper was published in six-page format, advertising took up one and a quarter or one and a half pages. Most of the remaining space was devoted to coverage of the local Party organizations and labor movement. Rinaldo Rigola, the chief of the General Confederation of Labor, served as a special editor during much of the Ferri era. [10]

Avanti! accepted advertising, a compromise to keep the newspaper afloat. These advertisements frequently were in conflict with the paper's mission of educating the working class. Much of the advertising was for legitimate products. But a number of quack remedies and charlatans, including hair-growing tonics, cures for impotence, and fortune tellers also advertised in *Avanti!*. While many other dubious advertisements were for harmless patent medicines, their appearance in *Avanti!* appeared to give them the Socialist party seal of approval. [11]

THE REFORMIST PAPER, 1896–1903

Avanti!'s history between 1896 and 1911 had a certain rhythm. Successive directors took control during financial crises, which they partially ameliorated. They left *Avanti!* as another and usually more serious crisis broke over the newspaper. Each director marked a new stage in the continuous financial crisis of *Avanti!* until Claudio Treves finally stabilized the paper in a new location. By then, however, time had run out on Reformist socialism.

Despite its shaky financing, *Avanti!* appeared to be off to a good start in 1897. Its initial press run was 40,000 copies. Although this quickly leveled off to a daily run of 13 to 14,000 copies, the paper received 66,204 lire in donations during its first year and had 3500 paid subscribers. Bissolati quickly set the tone of the new newspaper. Antimilitarism tied to anticolonialism in the wake of the Adowa disaster became one of the staples of the paper, together with investigations of economic corruption. The political cartoon made its appearance with the work of the talented Gabriele Galantra ("Rata Langa"). In keeping with the Reformism of its director, *Avanti!*

published the complete texts of important parliamentary speeches as two-page supplements to its regular editions.[12]

By May 1898 *Avanti!* had already outgrown its original equipment and headquarters. The newspaper purchased new presses that were to be transferred to new quarters in the aptly named Via della Propaganda, together with the editorial, administrative, and distribution offices of *Avanti!*.[13]

Before the move could be made, the *fatti di maggio* broke out in Milan. Bissolati and most of the paper's staff were arrested. On May 13, 1898, at the request of the *Direzione,* Ferri took over the direction of the paper, with Bonomi as his editor in chief. *Avanti!* was hard hit by the period of reaction which followed. Delivery to Milan was cut off for four months, with a resultant serious loss of revenues. Meanwhile, post office and other government officials, with the apparent approval of the Pelloux government, frequently delayed and confiscated *Avanti!*. Government censors were more attentive than usual to *Avanti!*'s content. The many arrests which followed the revolt in Milan severely reduced the number of correspondents available to the paper. The Party delayed the movement to the newspaper's new quarters, and the editors established a temporary new command post over a local printing press. The changes of location increased the paper's problems since many correspondents sent their stories to incorrect addresses. The staff of the paper was frequently decimated by arrests. Moreover, *Avanti!* lost two costly lawsuits and was still paying court costs in 1900.[14]

Ferri and Bonomi held the paper together. They got *Avanti!* established in its new quarters on May 19, 1898. Correspondents in Italy and abroad were urged to send important news by telegraph in spite of the higher costs to *Avanti!* that this means entailed. Bissolati was released and resumed command in September. He immediately reorganized the correspondent service and established new norms for reporting. By the end of the year, *Avanti!* expressed confidence that it had mastered its internal problems. In a message to its readers, the newspaper promised fuller coverage of the activities of the right, more variety, more cultural coverage, and increased foreign affairs reporting.[15]

By the beginning of 1899 *Avanti!* was devoting its coverage to organizing a campaign for amnesty for those still imprisoned or exiled as a result of the *fatti di maggio.* The paper created a special subscription campaign designed to aid the families of the detained. The fund collected 21,500 lire within three months.[16] In the summer of 1899, these efforts and those of thousands of other Italians of differing political views drove the government to release the vast majority of its prisoners. Most of the exiles were amnestied in 1900.

Despite these successes, *Avanti!* remained in its formative journalistic stages. Surveying the paper's progress with his customary condescension, Antonio Labriola wrote Wilhelm Liebknecht:

> *Avanti!* does as well as it can. Bissolati has practiced grand politics for only two years. Before that he lived in little Cremona. The other writers of *Avanti!* are young men who are not really informed about the situation abroad. Besides that they are burdened with their work. *Avanti!*—and I mean not only the small folio, but also the editorial office—must do so many things;—that is, defend the Party—substitute for the *Direzione* of the Party because the Central Committee (in Milan) has not existed for a year—represent and cover the parliamentary faction that very rarely assembles at Rome—hold together the very divergent tendencies of the comrades of the Party, as much as this is possible, etc! All this with such modest intellectual means and with such poor preparation.[17]

Technically, *Avanti!*'s most serious defect was its inability to utilize the front page to full effect. Bissolati shunned the headline as too demagogic. The first page was crowded with short articles, many of them fillers. Major news stories were insufficiently developed. Moreover, Bissolati gave news of local Party organizations a very low priority, much to their distress. Many Socialists also objected to the heavy coverage given to intellectual and cultural matters.[18]

Moreover, in a period of growing intellectual ferment within the socialist movement in Italy, the Reformists were unprepared to deal with the confusion created by various "revisionist" movements, usually of anarchist inspiration, that challenged more orthodox Marxism. "In these circumstances, *Avanti!* does itself little good. The liberal and conservative press have been conducting a true crusade against Socialism in the names of Bernstein and Sorel. . . . *Avanti!* has replied with a few jokes and impertinences and then has done nothing."[19] At times the anarchists used more direct tactics in their effort to stir confusion among PSI members, such as publishing a fake May Day edition of *Avanti!*.[20]

By 1900, Bissolati was aware of many of the defects of the paper and was attempting to correct them. The front page had fewer articles, with more content. In an effort to reach a larger reading public, *Avanti!* devoted more coverage to popular, nonpolitical issues. In 1900, for example, the paper sent a special correspondent to Paris to cover the great Exposition. A regular column, *Avanti e indietro* ("Forward and Backward"), dealt with political and social issues in a lighter vein. In August 1899, following a major publicity buildup, *Avanti!* became the first newspaper to serialize Tolstoy's newest novel, *Resurrection*. The quality of serializations appearing thereafter improved markedly. *Resurrection* was followed by Turgenev's *Summer Nights*, Tolstoy's *Memoirs,* and Balzac's *Le Père Goriot,* and *Slaves*. In July 1901 the paper introduced *Avanti! della Domenica*, a Sunday supplement devoted to political issues and featuring the cartoons of Galantra at a special subscription price of 1.50 lire for six months.[21]

Despite these efforts to boost sales, *Avanti!*'s financial situation remained precarious. In November 1900, the paper admitted that its subscription drive was going poorly. The use of telegraphic reporting to improve news coverage drove up publication costs. The paper pleaded with its subscribers to find new subscribers, offering special rates. In December, Bissolati and the paper lost a costly slander case. This was the tenth major court battle in the five years of the paper's existence and legal debts were mounting rapidly. In March and April 1902, *Avanti!* suspended its serial and devoted the space to extra advertising.[22]

In an effort to stimulate subscriptions, the administration of *Avanti!* offered special rates with increasing frequency after 1899. In 1900 the paper began offering special package subscriptions to *Avanti!, Critica Sociale,* and the anticlerical review *L'Asino. Avanti!*'s fifth anniversary provided the opportunity for a fund-raising dinner.[23]

Bissolati's pessimistic report to the 1902 Party Congress on *Avanti!*'s financial state induced the Party to set up a special investigation committee with the task of surveying the operations of the paper. The commission submitted its report in February 1903. It endorsed Bissolati's leadership. The "bookkeeping is done regularly, [financial control] is continuous, and the audit has been quick and easy." Expenses were "contained within the strict limits of necessity," with a gradual diminution of ordinary fixed expenses and a careful allotment of the savings to the technical improvement of the paper. The report concluded that responsibility for the paper's problems lay with the Party's rank and file. Donations to *Avanti!* had declined seriously, subscription drives received scarce support, and the rank and file were unwilling to match the efforts made by the paper's administrators to save *Avanti!*.[24]

In response to the report, the *Direzione* and the administration of *Avanti!* requested all sections of the Party to comment on the paper's situation and pledge additional financial support. In mid-March 1903, the *Direzione* called a special meeting to discuss the paper's problems. On the eve of the meeting, Bissolati resigned, citing the demands of a small number of sections that he be removed before they would contribute to the paper. The resignation came in reaction to a carefully orchestrated campaign against Bissolati by Ferri's faction. The Reformist leadership calculated they could force a vote of confidence for both Bissolati and the Reformist *Direzione*. Their plan failed. On the second day of the special meeting, Turati introduced a resolution rejecting Bissolati's resignation and giving him a vote of confidence. Ferri and his allies succeeded in amending two of the three paragraphs of the Turati resolution, turning it into a vote of no-confidence. When the weakened revised resolution passed over the opposition of Turati and other Reformist members of the *Direzione*, Bissolati had no alternative but to resubmit his resignation. On April 3, 1903, the *Direzione* offered the position of director of *Avanti!* to Enrico Ferri. Turati privately calculated that losing control over a financially strapped *Avanti!* might not be all bad. He expected that the paper would die under Ferri's control, discrediting his rival. Meanwhile, the Reformists controlled *Critica Sociale* and the Milan-based *Il Tempo*.[25]

THE FERRI YEARS

Under Ferri's leadership, *Avanti!* entered into a new phase. Overnight it became the platform for a coalition of "revolutionaries" who made Giovanni Giolitti, "the arch corrupter," and his supporters, "the blood-suckers" of Italy's military-industrial complex, their chief targets.[26]

Ferri brought a new team of collaborators with him, led by Enrico Leone, his Syndicalist editor in chief. Only two of Bissolati's collaborators remained. Ferri made frequent use of full-column headlines and moved Galantra's cartoons to the front page. He introduced a new political column, *Fischi e applausi* ("Jeers and Cheers"). A crude but vigorous anticlericalism became another trademark of Ferri's *Avanti!*. Space devoted to Party and labor news on the second and third pages increased. However, the most dramatic change in the new *Avanti!* was its emergence as the mouthpiece of Enrico Ferri. Bissolati had regarded *Avanti!* as an expression of the whole Party and downplayed his own role. Ferri's signed articles appeared frequently on page one, and his activities merited constant front-page attention. The violence of Ferri's attacks on Giolitti's governments also brought a return to the censorship that the Piedmontese prime minister had all but eliminated during the years of his collaboration with the Reformists. Although not as frequent or as heavy-handed as under previous ministries, these sequestrations underlined the fragility of the "regime of liberty."[27]

Ferri's most lasting contribution to *Avanti!* was the worsening of its financial crisis. The same drive and imagination which enabled Ferri to resurrect the paper's slumping fortunes in 1903 led him to plunge *Avanti!* into even greater difficulties.

Ferri made acceptance of *Avanti!*'s directorship conditional on the approval of the sections of the Party in the form of cash pledges to the paper. By the time he assumed active control of *Avanti!* on May 11, 1903, the sections had pledged over 30,000 lire. Appropriating one of Bissolati's marketing techniques, Ferri offered the first of many special subscriptions on June 2. He published *Avanti!* as an evening edition in Rome in the hope of increasing subscription sales. In 1904, he reported to the national Congress that *Avanti!*'s debts were nearly paid off. In September of the same year, Ferri moved his expanding operation into new quarters near the Pantheon.[28]

In October 1904, at Ferri's request, the *Direzione* set up another commission to report on the paper's condition. The commission's report praised Ferri's work and warned that *Avanti!*'s typographical equipment was dangerously outdated. It recommended raising additional funds to purchase new machinery. In March 1905 Ferri came forward with a grandiose plan for improving the newspaper. He promised that *Avanti!* would begin publishing a large format with more correspondence, improved parliamentary coverage, and new features on May 1, 1905. The additional cost to the Party would be 20,000 lire per year for the following four years. On May 2, the first edition of the six-page, six-column *Avanti!* came off the presses. The six-page edition was published every Sunday, while six-columns became a standard feature of *Avanti!*. Ferri's goal was a daily six-page edition.[29]

In April 1906, *Avanti!* purchased two large rotary machines and their electric motors at a cost of 52,000 lire. Publication of a six-page Sunday newspaper added another 15,000 lire per year to the Party's expenses. As a result, rank and file contributions of over 30,000 lire in 1905 were offset and *Avanti!* needed an additional 20,000 lire to keep pace with its rising expenses. In an effort to encourage more contributions, Ferri promised that *Avanti!* would publish two six-page editions per week if the response to his appeal was "good" and a daily six-page edition if the response to his appeal for additional funds was "very good." To stimulate further support, *Avanti!* offered special "working-class subscriptions" of one lira per month. In July 1906, the paper began accepting classified advertising to raise more money.[30]

The response to Ferri's appeal was "good." In May 1906, *Avanti!* commenced publication of a six-page Saturday edition. Ferri apparently was encouraged to continue planning for the publication of a six-page daily. In August he negotiated a deal for six new composition machines to complement his recently acquired rotary machines. In order to pay for this latest addition to its plant, *Avanti!* needed another 60,000 lire in contributions. Ferri, however, had gone to the well once too often. He had lost the political and financial support of large parts of the left. His quarrels with the Syndicalists mounted and his alliance with more orthodox leftists frayed. Ferri purged most of the Syndicalists from *Avanti!*'s staff in May 1905. The *Direzione* backed Ferri's action, but his support within the Party was evaporating slowly. Contributions fell as Ferri continued to pile additional expenses on *Avanti!*.[31] (See table 3.)

Ferri maintained that a rising subscription rate enabled the paper to remain debt-free. This is difficult to believe in the face of the extraordinary expenses which he heaped on *Avanti!*.[32]

In March 1907, Ferri, always innovative, tried another expedient to remedy the financial shortages of the newspaper and achieve his objective of a six-page daily. After negotiating a special deal with the two major Italian insurance companies, *Avanti!* offered a special non-job-related insurance policy to new subscribers at an additional cost of three lire for a full year's coverage. The paper would receive a percentage of the premiums as agent for the companies, and Ferri hoped to combine this money with the funds raised through new subscriptions to reach the goal of a six-page daily newspaper.[33]

The insurance scheme failed to get off the ground. A few weeks later, Ferri's already declining personal prestige received a serious blow from his former allies, the Syndicalists. After purging the Syndicalists in May 1905, Ferri replaced them with Integralists and Reformists. The Syndicalists, with

TABLE 3
Contributions to *Avanti!*, 1903–6

1903 (8 months)	10,544 lire
1904	16,772 lire
1905	32,567 lire
1906 (8 months)	5,094 lire

Source: *Avanti!*, Aug. 26, 1906.

the support of a reactionary noble and government official named Scarano, founded their own journal, *L'Azione,* in Rome. Morgari revealed the Syndicalists' ties to Scarano in a March 30, 1907, article in *Avanti!*. On April 2 Ferri hinted that Leone, now an editor of *L'Azione,* had somehow siphoned off funds from *Avanti!* to *Azione.* The Syndicalists charged that *Avanti!* was being financed by the Bank of Italy. The *Direzione* conducted a four-day inquiry but was unable to find conclusive proof that *Azione* was being financed by funds intended for *Avanti!*. Its final report concluded that the finances of the Syndicalists' journal were "highly suspect." The main loser was Ferri, not the Syndicalists, who had left the PSI. Although no evidence of impropriety existed in either his dealings with the Bank of Italy or with the insurance companies, the fact that *Avanti!*'s director was dealing with capitalists did nothing for either Ferri's standing or that of his newspaper. Further, Ferri's management of *Avanti!*'s finances obviously required improvement if Leone could carry away thousands of badly needed lire over a period of two or three years.[34]

Ferri and his following on the *Direzione* pressed ahead with the campaign for a six-page daily edition. At the conclusion of the investigation into the finances of *Azione,* the *Direzione* voted full confidence in Ferri and agreed to make another effort to reach a six-page daily edition. On May 1, 1907, the PSI mailed thousands of copies of the special edition of *Avanti!* free to a list of nonsubscribing Socialists. On May 5, *Avanti!* offered special new prices, together with three prizes for each new subscriber. In August the *Direzione* sent Morgari to the sections to explain the Ferri plan. Two days later, as *Avanti!* began to use the first of its new linotype machines, Ferri promised that when all these machines were installed in October, he would publish special editions for the North and South of Italy as well as a Rome edition. Coupled with the promise was a plea for money. In October, apparently as an economy move, the administration of the paper took *Avanti!*'s publicity campaign away from the private firm which had been directing it. Ferri made a personal fund-raising trip throughout Italy and collected 80,000 lire in pledges. Even with this aid, the editors of *Avanti!* had to face the inevitable. One hundred thousand lire in debt for new machinery and with publication costs rising, they were unable to publish three four-page editions of *Avanti!*, much less a six-page daily edition. They decided instead to publish two four-page editions, one for Rome and the other for the rest of Italy.[35]

The failure of this latest attempt seems to have convinced Ferri of the futility of his efforts. After four years of fund-raising without parallel, the

The Continuous Crisis

newspaper was deeper in debt than when he took over from Bissolati. (See table 4.) At the same time, his personal base of support within the PSI was eroding rapidly. Physically worn down by the hectic efforts of four years, Ferri resigned as director of *Avanti!* on January 22, 1908.

Oddino Morgari, Integralism's founding father, took on the unenviable task of holding the paper's staff together until the Party Congress of Florence could bail out *Avanti!*. Meanwhile, the *Direzione* assessed Ferri's performance. By the time the Socialists met in Florence, the *Direzione* had discovered that the debt was actually more than 100,000 lire.

In order to support Morgari's efforts, the *Direzione* authorized a special tax of one lira per head on all members of the PSI, to be paid by March 31, 1908. The money was not forthcoming. By mid-August 1908 only 21,000 lire had been collected despite threats of suspension or expulsion.[36]

THE RESCUE OPERATION

When the Congress of Florence convened on September 19, 1908, *Avanti!* was once again in a deep crisis. The financial report and the proposals of *Avanti!*'s administration recommended removing the administrative control over the paper from the supervision of the *Direzione* and placing it under the jurisdiction of a council of administration, setting limits on the paper's expenditures, and enacting another forced contribution of one lira per member and ten lire per section. Two major creditors renounced debts of 10,000 lire each owed by *Avanti!*. A confused debate followed in which only one point of consensus emerged: no matter what the cost, *Avanti!* must continue to publish. Finally, with the debate leading nowhere, labor leader Argentina Altobelli proposed that the PSI establish a commission to survey the problem and report back to the Congress.[37]

G. E. Modigliani delivered the commission's report the following morning. The commission found that the paper needed 40 to 50,000 lire just to carry on until the end of the year and reported that it had already rounded

TABLE 4
Balance Sheet of *Avanti!*, 1903–7

December 31, 1903	+20,104.66 lire
December 31, 1904	−12,598.83 lire
December 31, 1905	−26,246.72 lire
December 31, 1906	−27,704.86 lire
December 31, 1907	−35,000.00 lire

SOURCE: PSI, *Avanti!: Resoconto del giornale,* 1908; *Avanti!,* Feb. 6, 1908.

93

up pledges covering that sum. Modigliani also reported that numerous Party members were voluntarily renouncing the debts that the paper owed them. A tax of one lira would be placed on all Socialists financially able to pay. Profiting from experience, the commission estimated 20,000 could pay. To cover the costs of publication for 1909, the commission recommended that all Socialists able to afford a fifteen-lire subscription cost sign up or face expulsion. Another proposal was that the Congress levy a special contribution on professional men and raise the cost of the *tessera* to 1.50 lire. On the technical and administrative side, the commission endorsed the plan of the paper's administration to create a new council of administration to oversee *Avanti!*. Finally, to improve the quality of the news appearing in *Avanti!*, the commission recommended that the newspaper appoint local correspondents. Modigliani's report, formulated into a resolution, was approved by unanimity less one vote. The Congress then returned to its usual business, the political struggle between Reformism and its opponents. Turati's forces won a major victory. As a result, Bissolati regained direction of *Avanti!*.[38]

Returning to *Avanti!* after five years, Bissolati pledged that the paper would take a leading role in the struggle for a democratic Italy.[39] To begin, he gave the journal a face-lifting. Its coverage was reoriented toward parliament. Cartoons and such columns as *Fischi e applausi* and *Avanti e indietro* disappeared. Coverage of Socialist sections and the labor movement slowly declined from the levels of the Ferri years. Foreign affairs and news of Rome got more space. On the whole, the tone of the paper was higher, but it was a good deal duller.

The Reformist *Direzione* attempted to give *Avanti!* the support it needed to survive. The *Direzione* adopted a series of tough guidelines to ensure that financial support was forthcoming. The paper launched a new subscription drive. Neither threats of expulsion nor subscription drives produced completely satisfactory results. To increase subscription sales, Bissolati began publishing a Tuscan edition. Like the Rome edition, the Tuscan version of *Avanti!* went to press in the early evening so that it would be on the streets of the region's cities the following morning.[40]

The year 1910, like 1909, opened with a major subscription drive and poor results. Nor did the required contributions come in great numbers. When the section of Molinella came to the aid of *Avanti!* with a contribution of 1000 lire, the paper noted with some resentment that for a few, at least, the decisions of the Congress of Florence were not a dead letter. On July 24, 1910, in an effort to stimulate contributions, the *Direzione* listed all sections which had not paid their 1909 quota and set July 30 as the cutoff date for payment. After this, the sections would not be able to participate at the upcoming national Congress at Milan. In September, for the first time in a decade, the question of the relocation of the paper was discussed at a meeting of the *Direzione*. Bissolati's second term as director of *Avanti!* coincided with a sharp decline in Party membership. During 1909 the PSI lost approximately 15,000 members. These losses cost *Avanti!* subscriptions and contributions. By undertaking drastic economies, Bissolati succeeded in reducing the paper's total debt. Even with the aid of the *Direzione*, however, *Avanti!* was unable to find new subscribers among the rank and file, and its average daily press run dropped from 22,000 to 10,000. Bissolati's editorial policy was out of tune with the views of a majority of his readers, whether Reformist or left wing. They bought fewer papers.[41]

At the 1910 Congress of Milan, Bissolati was at odds with the Reformist majority on many issues and resigned. Turati's alter ego, Claudio Treves, replaced him. Treves, who had vast experience as the editor of *Lotta di Classe* and *Tempo*, brought a return of popular journalism. He introduced new subscription and advertising rates. The cartoon reappeared with a talented new cartoonist, Giuseppe Scalarini. Treves gave more focus to labor news and stronger support to the drive for a universal suffrage law. Despite these improvements, *Avanti!*'s financial situation remained perilous.

Relief arrived only in 1911. As long as Turati and Kuliscioff controlled *Tempo*, they could view *Avanti!*'s financial problems with a certain detachment. The failure of Ferri's management could only reinforce their position. While *Tempo* remained financially viable, Turati opposed moving *Avanti!* from Rome to Milan. By late 1909, however, a general deterioration of the financial base of the entire Socialist press, plus the need to reduce the influence of the right-wing Reformists, including Bissolati, gave impetus to the idea of moving *Avanti!* to Milan and merging it with the city's other Socialist papers. The Reformist leadership remained concerned that moving *Avanti!* to Milan would resurrect fears of Lombard domination of the PSI. Nevertheless, by early 1910, a majority of the *Direzione* favored a move. Further, both *Tempo* and *Critica Sociale* were in severe financial straits. Kuliscioff warned Turati that the newspaper could not survive until the end of the year and that saving the review would require a major personal retrenchment.[42]

The Party leadership, however, temporized throughout 1910. Turati was attached to the idea of publishing *Avanti!* in the capital. Easing Bissolati out of the direction of the paper was a slow process. The Reformist leadership finally acted in 1911. Between January and March, the PSI's leadership held a series of secret meetings on the future of *Avanti!*. The paper's financial condition was so bad that on more than one occasion the highly emotional Treves suggested liquidating it. Turati, despite a lingering reluctance to move *Avanti!* from Rome, took the more rational view that the transfer must take place and that the local Milanese Socialist press had to be sacrificed. At times even Turati wondered if a "catastrophe" could be avoided and considered the likely effects of replacing the Party daily with a bulletin. *Avanti!*, Treves reported, received little financial support from the PSI's sections, from the cooperatives, or from the labor movement. Its debt had reached 90,000 lire and was continuing to rise. He suggested broadening its subscription base by returning to the *Tempo* strategy of publishing a paper which appealed to the more progressive elements of the middle class.[43]

Finally, in May 1911, the *Direzione* took drastic action to save the paper. It formed the *Società editrice socialista*. This company, that would eventually be capitalized at 1,220,000 lire, was to sell stock in the paper at 100 lire per share. In order to keep *Avanti!* under Party control, a majority of the shares (eventually 6050) were purchased by the *Direzione*. Sales of the remaining shares were limited to Party members, PSI sections and federations, together with labor organizations and their members. Turati was elected the first president of the Society. At a joint meeting with the *Direzione*, the Society decided to move *Avanti!*.[44]

Under the leadership of Turati and Treves, the new corporation shored up the financial position of *Avanti!*. By June 13, 1911, the Society reported that it had pledges of 500,000 lire and planned to raise its capitalization from 1 million to 1,200,000 lire. It set July 9 as the final day for paying off 30 percent of the money pledged. With this money in hand, the Society could sign articles of incorporation and become a legal entity. Small delays occurred, but the Society was incorporated on July 23, 1911. On July 28, the Society outlined its initial objectives. The *Direzione* provided it with a list of all sections which had not paid their contribution, and the two bodies agreed to work together to extract the money. *Avanti!* would be published as a six-page daily in Milan with eight-page weekend editions on the condition that it could obtain 20,000 new subscriptions. The corporation set October 1 as a tentative date for the move to Milan.[45]

The reforms introduced by Turati and Treves put *Avanti!* on a competitive footing and laid the basis for a vast expansion of its circulation. In short order, *Avanti!* began to make a profit. (Regrettably for the Reformists, they were unable to test the full potential of the paper. Following the victory of the PSI's left wing, the young extremist Benito Mussolini inherited the editorship of a reorganized *Avanti!* and graphically illustrated the potential of a mass circulation newspaper in recruiting and organizing the working classes.)

On September 7, the movement of *Avanti!*'s machinery began. By mid-September the subscription drive was going well enough for the Society to authorize a six-page edition. New features of the paper included sports coverage, commercial bulletins, and stock exchange reports, together with photographs. The Society also decided to leave a number of *Avanti!*'s editors in Rome to provide complete political coverage.[46]

Despite the paper's desperate state, opposition to *Avanti!*'s move was strong. The left objected that a decision to move had been made by the Reformist *Direzione* rather than by the upcoming national Congress. They feared that the incorporation of a publishing company was a maneuver to cement Reformist control over *Avanti!*.[47]

The first edition of the Milanese *Avanti!* came off the presses on October 9, 1911. In the month that had elapsed since the movement of the machinery began, the political climate of Giolittian Italy had changed drastically. The Italian government attacked Libya, and *Avanti!* spoke for all the currents which opposed the war. Located in the heartland of the workers' movement and leading a determined campaign against Giolitti, *Avanti!*'s sales rose dramatically. By February 1912, its daily press run was averaging 40,000 copies. Expenses fell and subscriptions doubled.[48]

Treves put a lasting imprint on the Milan *Avanti!*. Advertising was limited to three-quarters of page six. Photography and the cartoons of Scalarini gave the paper a greater impact, as did the three or more columns of page five devoted to late-breaking news. A judicial column appeared. In another innovation, headlines were introduced in the inside pages. When Treves stepped down in July 1912, he could justly claim to have rebuilt *Avanti!* into a mass circulation newspaper.[49]

The move of *Avanti!* to Milan was a success for the PSI but quickly became a major disaster for the Reformist current. By closing down its own local press and relying on *Avanti*, the Reformists inadvertently opened the way for their opponents to solidify a dominant position when the 1912 Party Congress gave them a majority and control of the *Direzione*. As Turati foresaw, a Milanese *Avanti!* was much less susceptible to the influence of Reformist deputies. The left wing's control of both the *Direzione* and through this, the Society, gave it a firm hold over editorial policy. As *Avanti!*'s director, Mussolini mounted an intense assault on Reformist Socialism.[50]

Between 1900 and 1910, *Avanti!*'s successive directors proved incapable of overcoming the paper's financial crisis. This failure was a serious blow to Reformist hopes. The financial difficulties caused by the paper's placement in Rome and the personal limitations of the directors who preceded Treves meant that *Avanti!* never achieved its goal of becoming an influential mass circulation daily. At the same time *Avanti!* was struggling to achieve a press run of 20,000 copies daily, *Corriere della Sera* was selling 200,000 newspapers. The inability of a Rome-based *Avanti!* to attract a large circulation base frustrated the efforts of Reformists to reach either a majority of the working classes or sympathetic elements of the middle class, building and solidifying their support for gradualistic socialism.

Ironically, the Reformists eventually did rescue the paper and put it on a modern basis that would permit them to reach the masses. At this point, however, they lost control of both *Avanti!* and the Party. The left reaped the benefit of their efforts. Under Mussolini's direction, *Avanti!* built mass support in a manner that horrified the Reformist leadership and also reinforced their doubts about the political maturity and reliability of the Italian working classes.

The Eye
of the Storm:
The Socialist
Parliamentary Group,
1900–1910

Parliamentary government is, like all other, an historic form, responding to the needs of a large and concentrated state in which classes with antagonistic interests operate. It is the mechanism for expressing the collective will, which is presently monopolized by the predominant classes. It is, therefore, the indispensable mechanism that the subject classes grasp in order to give weight to their own interests. . . . The day that they become arbitrators of this mechanism, they must utilize it to abolish the causes of class antagonisms, thus completing their own emancipation.

—Leonida Bissolati (1895)

The Reformists' belief that parliament was the key to the triumph of the working classes meant that this institution inevitably became the focus of their political efforts. If Reformism was to hold on to its dominant position in the PSI, the men who formed the Party's parliamentary group (GPS) had to provide tangible success in the form of significant reform legislation. The debate over whether Reformism was a success or failure occupied center stage at the Party Congresses between 1902 and 1912. The efforts of the GPS were monitored, criticized, and defended. Yet the group lived a life of its own, seemingly as indifferent to the demands of its leftist critics as it was to the plans and pleas of its Reformist defenders. Ironically, the Reformists' insistence that the group possess the widest possible autonomy ultimately undermined their leadership because the GPS never achieved the type of successes which would have justified its continued independence from the control and direction of the Party. Parliament was the nemesis of Reformism.

THE SOCIALIST PARLIAMENTARY GROUP

The GPS was organized simply. Normally, the Socialist deputies elected one of their number to serve as secretary of the group for the duration of the legislature. The secretary handled liaison between the group and the *Direzione*, proposed a division of work assignments among the deputies, and prepared and delivered a report on the group's activities to the national Congress. In addition, he monitored the legislative calendar and kept the often-absent Socialist deputies informed when their presence was required in Rome for important debates and votes. For this reason, the secretary resided in Rome throughout the parliamentary session.[1]

The assembly or caucus of the deputies completed the formal organization of the GPS. The deputies who attended these caucuses were members of the GPS and normally, but not always, members of the Party. Likewise, at various stages of their careers, a number of dues-paying Socialist deputies were not members of the group, usually when they belonged to a minority faction within the PSI. After an organizing meeting at the beginning of each legislature, meetings of the GPS usually took place on the morning or evening prior to an important vote or debate. The caucuses normally debated tactical issues: selecting a spokesman for a given debate, distributing work loads, and deciding how to vote on a particular issue. In theory, a unit rule was in effect which required the Socialist deputies to vote in a bloc. However, this rule was frequently ignored, particularly on issues which might have special significance in a particular district.[2]

Between 1900 and 1914, ninety-four men sat in parliament as part of the GPS. They were a highly homogeneous group. An analysis of the social composition of the 1900 group shows that they were little different from parliamentary deputies anywhere in Western Europe. The majority came from the professional middle class and had university degrees. Twenty-one of the thirty-two Socialist deputies who sat at the opening session of the Twenty-First Legislature (1900) had a degree (*laurea*), another had a diploma from a *scuola superiore*, and one had completed part of his university education. The 1900 group included twelve lawyers, two doctors, six university professors, an engineer, four Party functionaries (journalists and propagandists), five other members of the middle classes, and two newly elected workers. These two men, Pietro Chiesa and Rinaldo Rigola, were the first members of the working class to enter Italy's parliament. By contrast, the German Socialist parliamentary group included fifty-three workers and only thirteen university-educated middle-class professionals. Middle-class PSI deputies greeted Chiesa and Rigola with both pride and obvious relief: at last, the workers' party was represented in parliament by bona fide members of the working class. Turati proudly announced their arrival to the Chamber: "Gentlemen, Labor is entering." Aside from its middle-class composition, the most striking feature of the 1900 group was its youth. Eleven of its members were under 40; sixteen more were under 50, most in their early forties. Only four deputies were over 50, and the oldest of them was only 55. The average age of the group was 39.5 years.[3] (See table 5.)

The pattern of a youthful, middle-class professional parliamentary group continued throughout the Giolittian era. Over the next fourteen years, the average age of the GPS rose to approximately forty-four and the number of working-class deputies increased slightly in the last legislature of the pre-

TABLE 5
Composition of the GPS, 1900–1914

	1900	*1904*	*1906*	*1909*	*1913*
Seats	33	29	26	42	52
Laureati	21	20	18	30	40
Without university degree	11	9	8	12	12
Occupation					
Lawyer	12	12	10	20	27
Physician	2	4	3	5	8
Professor	6	4	5	5	4
PSI functionary	4	5	3	5	4
Engineer	1	0	0	0	1
Other, middle class	4	2	2	4	3
Working class	2	2	0	2	5
Age					
30–39 years	11	12	6	6	14
40–49 years	16	11	12	19	19
50–59 years	4	4	3	2	6
60 plus years	0	0	1	3	0
Average age	39.48	42.81	40.68	42.66	43.87

SOURCES: *I 508;* Cerchiari, *L'opera;* Ghisalberti; *Dizionario biografico; Enciclopedia biografica;* "I 508 moribundi," *Avanti!,* Aug.–Dec. 1904; PSI, *Relazione del gruppo parlamentare socialista,* 1902, 1908, 1912, 1914.

war era. The majority of Socialist deputies were elected from the northern one-third of the nation—particularly the Po Valley, the industrialized cities of Turin and Milan, and the rapidly industrializing province of Biella in northern Piedmont. The PSI remained very weak in northeastern Italy, a traditional Catholic stronghold. Two decades of intense organizational work in Sicily finally yielded a small harvest of Socialist deputies in the 1913 elections, but they were members of the Reformist Socialist party, expelled from the PSI in 1912. By 1913, the parliamentary group was strongly entrenched in Tuscany, but it had lost two seats that it captured in Rome after the 1909 elections to the Reformist Socialist party. In the rest of Italy, the progress of the Socialist movement, as measured both in total vote and parliamentary seats, was slow and uneven.[4] (See table 6.)

The Socialist deputy wore many hats. Normally, he was a legislator, propagandist, professional man, local and national Party official, all at the same time. While it would be impossible to say which of these duties ranked first in the minds of individual deputies, for the PSI rank and file the deputy was above all a propagandist. As *Lotta di Classe* stated in 1894, "Our candidates . . . must not be legislators, but agitators." Because membership in the GPS normally reaffirmed rather than created the public eminence and Party leadership of the deputy, he was always in great demand as a speaker at rallies. Turati drew thousands to an April 1900 meeting in Milan. Nine years later, at the height of the 1909 election campaign, he had to publish a brief statement in *Critica Sociale* that he could not accept or even reply to the flood of requests for his presence coming from all over Italy. During the 1902 local government elections, *Avanti!* published a statement by the deputies that none of them could accept further speaking engagements. Even in nonelection periods, the demands on the deputies' time were so great that, in 1902 and again in 1904, the *Direzione* attempted to equalize and limit the propaganda loads carried by GPS members. The *Direzione* also hired professional propagandists to take some of the burden off the overworked deputies. When Mario Todeschini, one of the most active propagandists in the GPS, lost his seat in the 1904 elections, the *Direzione* agreed that it would propose him as a candidate to the sections in whatever parliamentary district the first vacancy occurred.[5]

In a nation with an underdeveloped transportation and communication system, the life of a propagandist was rugged. The sole financial relief available to the deputy was a pass that enabled him to travel free on the railways. Oddino Morgari traveled deep into the Romagna from his native Turin to hold a meeting in the small city of Follonica. When he finally

TABLE 6
Geographic Distribution of GPS Seats, 1900–1914

	1900	1904	1906	1909	1913 PSI	1913 PSRI*
North						
Piedmont	6	6	4	10	12	1
Liguria	1	0	0	2	2	2
Lombardy	6	7	6	7	7	4
Veneto	2	3	2	2	4	1
Emilia Romagna	11	11	8	13	15	1
Total	26	26	20	34	40	9
Center						
Tuscany	2	1	1	6	7	2
Marche	0	1	1	0	0	0
Umbria	0	0	0	0	0	0
Lazio	0	0	0	1	0	1
Abruzzi	0	0	0	0	0	0
Total	2	2	2	7	7	3
South						
Campania	2	0	0	1	2	2
Puglia	0	0	0	0	1	0
Basilicata	0	0	0	0	0	0
Calabria	0	0	0	0	0	0
Total	2	0	0	1	3	2
Islands						
Sicily	2	2	3	3	0	4
Sardinia	0	0	0	0	1	0
Total	2	2	3	3	1	4

*PSRI = Italian Socialist Reformist Party.
SOURCE: *Avanti!*, 1909, 1914.

arrived Morgari discovered that the local Socialists had been unable to rent a hall. He ended up giving a series of talks in private homes. Angiolo Cabrini was less fortunate. In 1901 he set out for Hungary for a speaking engagement. On his arrival, Hungarian authorities arrested and expelled Cabrini. A few years later, Morgari was physically attacked in Ariano and had to take cover in the house of a local Socialist leader. The visit of Dino Rondani to Udine province provides a picture of a successful and uneventful propaganda trip. Arriving on October 20, 1900, Rondani visited the small towns of San Daniele and Ponzano in the morning and afternoon, then moved on to Udine city and Felletto for two evening meetings. On October 21, he returned to Udine for a second meeting before going to Serva where he gave a talk that evening. In large urban areas, the Socialist party pioneered meetings on a grand scale. On January 1, 1901, a meeting in Milan's sixth electoral college featured two deputies together with a number of other Party notables. The schedule for January 3 in the same college called for the participation of five deputies at a mass meeting.[6]

Late in 1901, the deputy and historian Ettore Ciccotti observed that on top of the demands on the GPS member's time posed by these meetings and conferences, he had to give an equally large amount of his time to normal parliamentary business. In addition, the deputies had to earn an outside income since their position was unsalaried. While most deputies belonged to the middle class, few were independently wealthy. In order to support himself and his family, the average deputy needed professional employment. Since the PSI lacked a large bureaucracy, few deputies could devote full-time to the Party and the workers' movement. The needs of their families and frequent calls for their services by local PSI organizations led to widespread parliamentary absenteeism among the deputies of the GPS.[7]

Within the structure of the PSI, the deputy occupied an anomalous position. As a member of a section, he was subject to Party discipline, but as a deputy, he had received a grant of complete autonomy of action from the PSI. No organ or individual within the Party structure had oversight responsibilities for the deputies or the power to discipline them. The deputy was ultimately responsible only to his electors, a majority of whom were normally neither Socialists nor members of the working classes. Only the sections of his electoral district could exercise influence on him since they nominated the candidates and normally provided campaign workers for the election battles. The deputy usually kept in close contact with the sections of his district.[8]

The most important services which the deputy provided his local supporters were the favors that he obtained from the government. Normally he devoted a good deal of time to supporting organizational candidates in local elections. He could also be influential in bringing a national Party Congress, with the profits and prestige it entailed, into his district. Andrea Costa, for example, arranged to hold the 1894 and 1902 Congresses in his city of Imola. By providing these services, the deputy quickly weakened whatever local control initially existed over his activities. The relation of deputy to section was mutually advantageous, and the sections were loathe to part with the services of their deputy. In November 1909, Enrico Ferri gave a newspaper interview in which he announced that he was available for a ministerial post. The GPS met on December 13, 1909, and again on

December 22 to discuss the Ferri action and both times agreed to take no action despite his clear violation of Party rules. The official explanation was that Ferri's actions showed that he was no longer a member of the PSI. The deputies also recognized that any move against Ferri would force the sections of the Gonzaga electoral district to break with the Party. Ferri underlined his independence from Party control by calling a meeting at which he delivered a slashing attack on his opponents within the PSI. The Gonzaga sections then passed a resolution expressing full confidence in their deputy. The anomalous situation in which an independent was the parliamentary representative of the Socialist party of Mantua lasted until 1912 when Ferri joined the new Socialist Reformist party and led his sections out of the PSI.[9]

Ferri also provides an example of how the deputy could use his local ties to improve his leadership position at the national level. In 1904, he ran in thirty-four electoral colleges, was elected in two, and won a significant portion of the total vote in eight others. By running as a candidate in so many places, Ferri illustrated his national popularity, reinforcing his claims to Party leadership, while building up bases of local support in a large number of sections. He would cash in these political debts at succeeding national Congresses.[10]

Every PSI national Congress from 1902 to 1912 hotly debated the issue of the deputies' autonomy. The Congresses granted formal autonomy, the right of the group to decide its own policy, in 1900 and then withdrew it in 1912. However, the autonomy of the deputies went far beyond the question of who decided how the GPS would vote on an issue before parliament. So long as the deputy kept his special relationship with the section, he was de facto autonomous. The subordination of the deputy to the dictates of the Party would occur after World War I, when the bureaucratization of the PSI, the creation of a mass party, and the introduction of proportional representation gave the PSI the opportunity to replace the middle-class deputy with organization men who were dependent on the Party machine for their parliamentary seats.[11]

THE SEARCH FOR A "GREAT REFORM," 1900–1910

The tragedy of Reformism lay in the expectations it placed on the GPS. Somehow these thirty to forty parliamentary Archimedeses had to find a way to exert enough leverage on the government and the other 460 plus deputies to reform the Italian state along the lines set out in the PSI's pro-

105

grams. In 1897 Bissolati's *Avanti!* editorialized, "The Socialist Party is the only one, as its adversaries confess, that struggles for principles . . . and whose disciplined democratic organization makes . . . its members the conscious executors of the will of the Party.[12] The idea that principles might at times be a hindrance in dealing with the less principled, or that democracy and discipline might at times be at variance with successful political action apparently had not yet occurred to the editorial writers of *Avanti!*. Within a few years, critics would castigate the GPS for too much compromising.

Worse, the Reformists created an overly optimistic view of the capabilities of the group among the Party rank and file. As early as 1894, *Lotta di Classe* had to remind Party members that the range of options open to five overworked and unsalaried deputies was very limited.[13] Little more than a year later, however, with fifteen Socialist deputies sitting in parliament, *Lotta* sang a different tune: "In the previous parliament . . . the principal duties of our Group were affirmation and propaganda. Today with increased numbers and a larger electoral base . . . [the deputies] must . . . assume the duties of legislators.[14]

Encouraged by Reformist propaganda, this habit of overestimating the capabilities of the GPS became deeply ingrained in the psyche of the Socialist party. While the GPS and its individual deputies achieved a number of significant legislative successes during the Giolittian era, their accomplishments never met the demands of the Party's rank and file or its leaders. Reformists claimed that the obstructionist campaign of 1898–99 was conclusive proof of the parliamentary group's ability to move parliament. Enrico Ferri, however, pointed out that the defensive tactics practiced by the group in this crisis were fairly easy to coordinate and could be carried out by a tiny minority. The real proof of the GPS's influence would come when it attempted to write its legislative program into law. Even a cursory reading of *Avanti!* during the crisis confirms Ferri's analysis. *Avanti!*'s Reformist editors frequently noted that the alliance with the middle-class parties of the left was a marriage of convenience based on the convergence of immediate aims. Moreover, it was a convergence within the political territory of the Italian middle class, an alliance based on constitutional rather than on social issues. The 1900 campaign slogan of the PSI was "The Choice before Italian voters is a representative democratic regime or a return to despotism."[15]

The electoral success of 1900 seemed to open the way to still greater legislative success. Turati urged the deputies of the *estrema* to agree on a coordinated program of reform while they enjoyed the psychological and moral advantage over a disorganized opposition. After the 1900 Socialist Congress approved a program of legislative cooperation and Zanardelli formed his ministry with the support of the GPS, the road to meaningful reform appeared to be open.[16]

Under the illusion that they could control the agenda of the new ministry, the Socialist deputies heatedly debated how far the GPS could allow itself to be tied to a bourgeois ministry. At a May 28, 1901, joint meeting, the parliamentary group and the *Direzione* adopted a "case-by-case" policy. The Socialists would decline to join the new government's formal majority but would pledge their support for Zanardelli on an issue-by-issue basis. Turati dissented. In a June 1, 1901, article in *Critica Sociale*, he urged the left to clarify its own goals and then closely cooperate with Zanardelli to win them. At Turati's urging, the GPS adopted a policy of support for the ministry in mid-June. The group had committed the Party to collaboration with the Zanardelli-Giolitti government.[17]

For two years a symbiotic relationship, born of fear of the alternatives, existed between the cabinet and its Socialist supporters. The government gradually gained the advantage. The Socialists lacked an alternative to Zanardelli and Giolitti, and the Reformists believed that cooperation with the government would permit them to slowly modify the political and economic system. Moreover, the PSI never achieved a satisfactory relationship with the other parties of the *estrema*. A number of deputies mistrusted the middle-class democrats. The Socialists generally resented the alliances that the Radicals and Republicans formed with organized labor. The Socialists and middle-class democrats frequently had divergent positions on major issues such as the military budget. Their rivalries and mutual mistrust grew as Giolitti turned the Radicals into a stable part of his governing coalition. Isolation from the other parties of the *estrema* deepened Socialist dependence on Giolitti.[18]

The government had its options. Faced with demonstrations of the unreliability of the Socialist party as a coalition partner, the ministry relied upon *trasformismo* to solidify its position and secured a reliable majority by adding the votes of conservative deputies. By 1903, the PSI's influence had diminished greatly.

Within the Chamber of Deputies, the Socialists worked with some success to strengthen constitutional guarantees. Savino Varazzani asked for an investigation of the legal procedures under which he and others were tried in 1899. The government complied. Gregorio Agnini concerned himself with the rights of illiterate soldiers. Bissolati urged that the ministry show

greater restraint when confronted by public demonstrations. Agostino Berenini presented a bill for divorce to the lower house in December 1901, commenting that the measure was of greater utility to the Italian middle classes
than to workers. His objective, Berenini stated, was creating a more progressive society and reinforcing the "moral and judicial integrity of our
liberty and independence."[19]

Regrettably, the group exercised no weight in the two areas where it
sought to promote significant reform in the economic and political structure
of Liberal Italy: the reduction of military expenses and customs barriers.
Socialist proposals to reduce military expenses and lower the duties on ce-
real grains were repeatedly rejected. Even a relatively mild resolution calling on the government to "proportion military expenses to the economic
power of the nation and to initiate the gradual transformation of the present
military order into another more consonant with . . . the needs of national
defense" was voted down 296 to 64. The size of Italy's military budget was
determined by secret clauses in the Triple Alliance. The king insisted on
maintaining the nation's military force at levels above the minimums set by
its alliance commitments. Giolitti never challenged this policy. He was
equally reluctant to mount an assault on a tariff arrangement that sustained
his government and the entire system of *trasformismo*.[20]

By the spring of 1902, rival factions were capitalizing on dissatisfaction
with the accomplishments of the GPS to undercut Reformism. Arturo Labriola claimed that the small concessions granted by Zanardelli had completely paralyzed the "revolutionary action" of the working class. Inside
the group, Ferri successfully reworked a Bissolati resolution removing all
references to close cooperation by the GPS with the other parliamentary
groups of the *estrema*. Ferri claimed that the GPS was preoccupied with
fears of another reactionary ministry. He confidently insisted that after two
years of unrestricted organizing, the working class could easily defeat a
reactionary government. Arturo Labriola pointed out that Reformism's
plans rested on the now discredited belief that Giolitti and Zanardelli were
captives of the GPS. The group's efforts to exploit this relationship had
resulted in a class cooperation which negated the Party's influence while
making the GPS the sole center of Socialist political activity.[21]

Faced with a strong challenge to both his personal position and to Reformism, Turati examined the work of the GPS and concluded that the failure of parliamentary action was due to a lack of motivation on the part of
the Socialist deputies. To offset the inherent weakness created by the small
size of the GPS, Turati sought a remedy through effective and intense co-

operation with the other parties of the *estrema*. He recognized the importance of securing an indemnity for the deputies and the need for firm discipline within the group.[22]

Nevertheless, Turati did not find the situation of the GPS totally discouraging. The work of Reformism was necessarily a slow process since it involved convincing a sizeable portion of the middle classes of the correctness and value of the Socialist position. Moreover, a parliamentary system normally worked slowly even under the best of circumstances.[23]

The GPS never achieved any real unity of purpose. The pressures of local interests and self-advancement were too great. By 1903, Turati was complaining bitterly about the group's lack of discipline. He bluntly told Kuliscioff that neither the GPS nor the parliament was capable of carrying forward the reform process. However, Turati himself contributed to this indiscipline when he refused to bow to the will of the majority within the Milan Socialist Federation or accept any control over his actions as a deputy.[24]

The critical weakness of Reformist parliamentary tactics was its lack of options. The struggles between Turati and Ferri led both men, but Turati in particular, to put their personal prestige behind a single tactical approach to Italy's complex political problems. Any deviation from a policy of cooperation with a reform-minded ministry became a serious blow to Turati's standing within the Party. As a result, Turati's public analysis of the failures of the GPS always centered on its lack of motivation and never indicated that his tactical approach might be mistaken.

In the spring of 1903, Ferri assumed a dominant position within the PSI as a result of the inability of the GPS to enact major reforms and the crumbling financial position of *Avanti!*. He launched a campaign to break the Group's alliance with the *estrema* and bring down the Zanardelli-Giolitti ministry. Concentrating on the Southern Question, Ferri hammered home the message that the Southern bourgeoisie was totally corrupt and that the PSI could expect no help from middle-class democrats as it attempted to meet the problems of the *Mezzogiorno*. When Zanardelli reorganized his ministry in June 1903, Ferri led the GPS into the opposition. Meanwhile, he attempted to create greater unity among the deputies. A February 1903 joint meeting of the *Direzione* and the parliamentary group approved a Ferri plan to establish a committee of three to direct a parliamentary and propaganda campaign against "unproductive expenses" such as the armed forces and the civil list of the kingdom. Ferri's objectives were uniting democratic elements within Italy around the PSI while simultaneously deepening the split between the Party and the *estrema*. Turati opposed this plan and created a competing committee to establish a program of action for the Chamber of Deputies. Ferri's committee was composed of three left-wing members of the PSI, Turati's committee consisted of three Reformists.[25]

During the next eighteen months the Turati-Ferri struggle within the group mirrored their contest for leadership of the Party. After a series of initial victories by Ferri, Turati regained the upper hand within the GPS in the wake of the 1904 general strike. The turning point in the two men's struggle came at an October 16, 1904, meeting of the GPS. Turati and Ferri clashed over relations with the other *estrema* parties. Ferri tabled a resolution that condemned the Republicans and Radicals for their lack of concern over police violence against workers. Turati countered with a resolution which called for new laws restricting police activities and for other social reforms. The resolution condemned the apathy of the other *estrema* parties but reaffirmed the need for cooperation between the PSI and the Radicals and Republicans. Checked on this issue, Ferri demanded that the group conform to the known views of the *Direzione* and limit its dealings with the other parties of the *estrema*. The deputies balked, dealing Ferri a further setback. Turati won a second victory when the GPS voted that his relations with the *Direzione* were outside the competence of the group. In effect the deputies were rejecting the right of the *Direzione* to interfere in the activities of the GPS while simultaneously strengthening Turati's hand in his battle with the dominant left wing within the Milan Socialist party.[26]

In this exchange, Turati found the weapon with which to defeat Ferri: the autonomy of the parliamentary group. On November 30, 1904, the GPS met to reorganize after its election setback. Ferri immediately tabled a proposal which held out the prospect of financial support from organized labor if the GPS was better disciplined. Turati countered with a resolution that rejected cash support from organized labor, charging it was a first step toward the subjection of the GPS to the unions.[27]

Further setbacks in parliament and within the Party over the next two years, together with the financial crisis of *Avanti!*, seriously weakened Ferri's position. He decided to support the formation of a government under Giolitti's conservative foe, Sidney Sonnino. The collapse of the first Sonnino ministry in May 1906 after little more than three months in power was a severe blow to Ferri's hold over the Party and the group.[28]

After the Sonnino debacle, Turati and other Reformist chiefs reevaluated the GPS and its prospects. Italian politics came full circle as Giolitti returned to head the government. The time seemed right for another round of cooperation with the middle-class parties in pursuit of reform. However, the fundamental question remained: how could the GPS bring more weight to bear on the government and drive it toward meaningful reform? Adolfo Zerboglio, the Reformist deputy from Alessandria, offered a penetrating analysis of the group in *Critica Sociale*. He noted that while individual Socialist deputies often carried considerable weight within parliament, the GPS was unable to exploit this advantage. One cause of the GPS's weakness was its growing absenteeism. However, Zerboglio rejected the idea that paying a salary to the deputies would lead to greater attendance. As an alternative, he proposed to seek a solution to absenteeism in two other areas. The group was hampered by its lack of both organization and a reasonable division of labor. He suggested that each deputy be assigned a specific legislative function and become expert in it. At the same time, Zerboglio noted, the Party must reassess and reduce its expectations. It must limit the demands it made on deputies, especially for propaganda, and permit them to concentrate on legislative matters.[29]

The Zerboglio essay was the prelude to a major debate within the PSI on reforming the group. Turati outlined his views in the January 1, 1907, *Critica Sociale*. He offered a diagnosis of the symptoms of the malaise of the GPS and invited others to join in the search for effective solutions. The problem, Turati wrote, was not that the "Socialist Parliamentary Group does not function. Worse, it functions badly." The group lacked linkage with the Party. Although the deputies had mastered the parliamentary game, they had never been able to achieve a major reform. These factors were even more disheartening in view of the great success which the GPS enjoyed in defending the constitutional system in its moment of peril in 1898–1900. Moreover, while the Party continued to show its vitality, the group was losing its few working-class members and the most heavily working-class electoral colleges. Finally, except at election times, Turati believed that the Socialist rank and file were totally uninterested in the activities of their deputies.[30]

Zerboglio replied in the January 16, 1907, edition of *Critica Sociale*. He reversed his previous position by calling for paying salaries to the deputies. Turati, in a comment, agreed with this suggestion but added that the causes of absenteeism were deeper than monetary.[31]

The young Socialist historian, Gaetano Salvemini, found that the chief weakness of the group was its lack of specialization. As long as deputies were fighting for basic constitutional rights, they held their own. This group of middle-class dilettantes were out of their depth trying to deal with the complexities of social legislation. The deputies, like the PSI, represented only the small aristocracy of labor. They were out of contact with the needs of the vast majority of Italians. Thus, Salvemini argued, the solution of the group's problems would have to await a solution to the problems of the Party. Until the labor unions had organized the masses and were able to convey their needs to the Party, the group would be unable to carry out its function effectively.[32]

While the Reformists debated, pressures built for a solution to the group's problems. In March 1907 both the Integralist *Direzione* and the leaders of the new General Confederation of Labor expressed concern with the performance of the GPS. The Confederation called a conference to discuss the group's performance and find "the best ways to reinvigorate it." The *Direzione* publicly accused the deputies of gross neglect of their duties. Turati replied, rejecting the heavy-handed intervention of the Integralists in the affairs of the GPS. He charged that the Integralists had led the Party into a quagmire of inaction. Only cooperation between workers and Reformists, outside official Party channels, could revitalize the movement and the group. This new clash with the Integralists suggested an alternative method of revitalization of the GPS to Turati: closer cooperation with the local units of the Party to get around the barriers which he believed Integralism had erected against successful parliamentary reform.[33]

The failure of the parliamentary group to seriously influence the course of the Giolitti ministry over the following eighteen months was a great blow to Turati. Giolitti's return to power had reignited debate among Reformists on the benefits of cooperation with the Piedmontese leader. At times, both Turati and Kuliscioff found the prospect inviting because of Giolitti's unmatched parliamentary skills and his commitment to reform politics. After forming a new ministry in May 1906, Giolitti enacted a series of economic and financial reforms, sponsored an investigation of the conditions of the population of the South, and maintained social peace. As a government of reform and social pacification, Giolitti's third ministry was a major success. In 1908, Turati wrote Kuliscioff that Giolitti was "the only serious statesman in the Chamber," adding, "I confess to you that I am Giolittian to the bone." Kuliscioff responded that "I too feel the old love."[34] Neither of the two Reformists was blind to the conservative nature of Giolitti's majority. Turati, however, believed that he could force the pace of reform in the direction the PSI desired if he could build a solid bloc of just twenty deputies. At the same time, he contemptuously dismissed both the *estrema* and the GPS as filled with "charlatans and empty heads."[35]

Avanti! agreed with Turati's private analysis. In June 1908, the Party's national voice scored the absenteeism and general neglect of duty on the part of the group. Coupled with this admonition was the threat of a purge of the GPS prior to the next general elections. Commenting on *Avanti!*'s editorial, the conservative *La Nazione* of Florence predicted that this threat would not in the least trouble the Socialist deputies. The majority, the paper noted, had joined in Giolitti's system of deals and favors. These deputies now had close ties with the local officials of the government, and they had received a lasting impression of Giolitti's power in 1904. The Socialist deputies knew who the real master was.[36]

By 1908, the absorption of the group into Giolitti's system of deals and favors was a fait accompli. Typical was the case of Giuseppe DeFelice Giuffrida. The hero of the Sicilian *fasci* was always more of an emotionally than intellectually committed Marxist. As a result of the favors and deals the prime minister offered, De Felice Giuffrida was so bound to Giolitti that he repeatedly broke with Party discipline. Ultimately he led most of the Sicilian socialists out of the PSI rather than oppose the Libyan war.[37]

Absenteeism was on the rise throughout the Giolittian years. (See tables 7 and 8.) Both Reformists and Integralists deplored this development and proposed remedies to meet it. However, Benito Mussolini, an obscure left-wing Socialist, put his finger on the crux of the problem when he noted that for the success of legislation, "It is enough that Giolitti is there." The success of Giolitti's *trasformismo* was so complete that the group was powerless. Under these circumstances, the deputies were probably rendering the PSI a greater service by staying in their home districts and tending to local Party matters.[38]

Both the Party and the parliamentary group appeared to lack alternatives to continued subjugation to Giolitti. Cooperation (1901–3) begot *trasformismo*. Giolitti easily circumvented the Party's official "opposition" of 1904–9 and won further successes with the votes of Socialist deputies. The deputies ruled out a return to an obstruction campaign. Changes in parliament's rules after 1900 made obstruction an impractical alternative policy.[39]

Reformists and Integralists agreed that a solution to the group's problems must include both paying salaries to the deputies and energizing the GPS through the struggle for a "Great Reform." However, Turati, Bissolati, and many of their followers insisted that the GPS enjoy total autonomy and supported continued alliance with the other parties of the *estrema*.

TABLE 7
Parliamentary Absenteeism, 1900–1909

	% Absent	
	All Deputies	*PSI Deputies*
21st Legislature (1900–1904)		
Key roll calls*	26.3	38.5
All roll calls	27.2	54.0
22nd Legislature (1904–1909)		
Key roll calls*	26.9	43.9
All roll calls	31.1	57.3

*Key roll calls are those involving legislation which the Party had designated as of special importance.
SOURCE: *AP*, Camera, XXI and XXII legislatura, 1900–1909.

Two key questions remained unanswered: could the GPS find a means to move the government toward the enactment of major reforms, and what reforms should it support? Turati, who by 1908 was again the Party's major spokesman, was at the center of both debates. He insisted that the group could make its weight felt only as part of a compact *estrema*. The problem, Turati readily admitted, was that the group and the *estrema* were equally undisciplined.[40]

The choice of reforms was equally troubling. A project for a vast expansion of Italy's suffrage gained support among Party leaders, largely as a result of the tireless promotion of Gaetano Salvemini. Universal suffrage had enabled the German Social Democrats to build a powerful parliamentary group and had been a primary factor in the creation of a mass party. Turati, however, had serious doubts that the expansion of suffrage to the mostly illiterate peasantry of the South would produce similarly positive results. He suspected that the Southern ruling class would be capable of controlling the vote of the Southern peasantry, offsetting increased Socialist support in the North. The Party's right wing also doubted the utility of suffrage reform.[41]

Turati and other Reformist skeptics were hard pressed to define alternatives to the idea of a universal suffrage reform. The complexity of the issues before parliament already created serious divisions among the Socialist deputies. Many issues, such as colonialism and reducing military expenses, were unlikely to interest the Party rank and file. Anticlerical activities, although popular with large segments of the Party, threatened to polarize the nation to the benefit of extremists on the far left and right.[42]

TABLE 8
Absenteeism at Special GPS Meetings, 1901–11

Date	Present	Total Members	% Absent
Dec. 21, 1901	15	33	54.5
March 13, 1902	21	33	36.4
Nov. 28, 1902	14	33	57.6
Feb. 5, 1903	16	33	51.5
Nov. 30, 1903	19	33	42.4
May 25, 1904	10	33	69.7
Sept. 22, 1904	23	33	30.3
Dec. 1, 1904	20	29	31.0
March 5, 1905	11	29	62.1
March 23, 1905	17	29	41.4
May 8, 1906	16	29	44.8
Dec. 22, 1909	20	42	52.4
April 29, 1910	26	42	38.1
April 7, 1911	27	42	35.7
Total	255	474	46.2 (average)

SOURCE: *Avanti!*, 1901–11.

Reluctantly, Turati began to give grudging support to the idea of employing the universal suffrage issue to revitalize the group. He continued to resist the plans of Salvemini, Kuliscioff, and others to utilize the campaign for universal suffrage to politicize the masses of the South.[43] Turati insisted that parliament was the stage upon which to carry out reform. "In Italy we are not negative forces facing governmental action. . . . We can influence it, we are an indirect part of the government."[44] If the *estrema,* or at least part of it, would unite under his lead, Turati continued to believe that they could put Giolitti "on the spot" and quite possibly force a change in his policies.[45]

The reality, Turati confessed in June 1908, was that the left was too divided to seriously challenge Giolitti. Still, he and other Reformists clung to their belief that a reorganized *estrema* could effect major reform and counted on the 1909 parliament elections both to enlarge the left and revitalize its component parts.[46]

These hopes quickly evaporated. In June 1909, a frustrated Turati admitted, "The government has excluded us from everything." Giolitti systematically cut the Socialist deputies out of membership in important parliamentary committees even as he supported the election of Andrea Costa to the largely ceremonial position of vice president of the Chamber. The deputies responded by making their individual deals with the prime minister. At the same time, the divisions among the parties of the *estrema* were so deep that effective cooperation of its constituent elements was impossible.[47]

Turati hoped to "revitalize" the group by adopting an "intransigent" opposition to the government. As a first step, he planned a special meeting of Socialist deputies to coordinate the effort. G. E. Modigliani, the Reformist deputy from Livorno, responded that these projects were doomed to failure until the Party had organized the masses behind it by means of a campaign for universal suffrage.[48]

The group was divided over the universal suffrage issue as well as over the question of supporting the successive ministries of Giolitti, Sonnino, and Luigi Luzzatti. Backers of a mass campaign for universal suffrage were in a minority. Turati wavered, torn between his doubts about the effects of a suffrage expansion and his recognition of its usefulness in revitalizing the group.[49]

In April 1910, shortly after assuming the prime ministership, Luzzatti announced his government's commitment to suffrage reform. For Bissolati, Bonomi, and the other deputies of the right, Luzzatti's action provided the necessary pretext for the GPS to support the government. A majority within the group initially resisted this course. Turati and Treves were "perplexed." Turati admitted that supporting a government that offered suffrage reform made sense but shared the distaste of the GPS majority for the wily, conservative Luzzatti.[50]

Ultimately, the group agreed by a narrow margin to support the government on the traditional case-by-case basis. Turati dutifully endorsed both the decision and the concept of a major suffrage reform. However, he continued to doubt the efficacy of suffrage reform unless it was linked to legislation creating proportional representation and paying salaries to the deputies. He also wanted to keep parliamentary action and mass agitation separate.[51]

In December 1910, Luzzatti unveiled his suffrage reform proposal. The bill was too restrictive for the Socialist party's majority. When Giolitti presented a plan for a much broader extension of the suffrage, the group withdrew its support from the government. At the same time, the GPS made clear its willingness to support a ministry that offered a far-reaching suffrage bill. Giolitti was the only Liberal political leader capable of offering such a reform. Turati waited apprehensively for the Piedmontese leader to once again gather the GPS into his control.[52]

The debate over universal suffrage revealed the central weakness of Turati's Reformism. The Reformists were unwilling to mobilize the masses. They were convinced that except for the working and farming elites of the North the masses were too immature to participate directly in the nation's political processes. Without mass support, the GPS was incapable of challenging Giolitti's control of parliament. Even with mass support Giolitti calculated that he could control parliament as long as the suffrage reform was not linked to proportional representation. The GPS cooperated with Giolitti by failing to link suffrage reform to proportional representation. The Socialist deputies went along with Giolitti in the face of overwhelming evidence that the single-college electoral system consistently worked against the PSI. In elections in 1900, 1904, 1909, and 1913, the Socialists received two to three times fewer seats under the single-college system than they would have won under a system of proportional representation irrespective of the size of the voting body. The PSI declined to press for proportional representation because of its fear of the Catholics' ability to mobilize the uneducated peasant masses. A Catholic mass party drawing support from both the peasantry and large segments of the middle class could obstruct Socialist reform programs and probably would be an overwhelmingly attractive coalition partner for Giolitti. A coalition of Giolitti and the Catholics would reinforce conservative forces and end the possibility of effective parliamentary reform.[53]

At the end of 1910, the paralysis of Reformism was evident. *Avanti!* was in the midst of a full-scale economic crisis. The GPS had proven incapable of promoting the "great reform" that would rebuild rank-and-file support for Reformism or justify its continued autonomy from Party control. Opposition to continuing the group's autonomy was growing on both the left and right of the PSI. The search for solutions to the paralysis which gripped both Party and faction created schisms within Reformist ranks and opened the way for the successful conquest of power by the left. The next chapter will examine the breakup of the Reformist faction.

The Indian
Summer of Reformism,
1908–1910

Between 1908 and 1910 both the Reformist faction and the Italian Socialist party began to unravel. The inability of *Avanti!* and the GPS to promote reform or widen the Party's base of support were the root causes of the decline of the PSI and Reformism. Other factors contributed to the crisis of Reformism, primary among them a growing challenge to the Party's political leadership from the CGL and a deepening economic crisis which gradually radicalized an increasing part of the labor movement and the Party rank and file. The Party's inability to master these challenges deepened the fissures within the Reformist camp. Reformist unity began to fray at the 1908 Party Congress. By 1910 Reformism was divided into warring camps.

RECESSION AND THE LABOR MOVEMENT

Both Reformism and the Giolittian system were rooted in the economic prosperity which flowed from Italy's industrial takeoff. In 1907, however, the rapid expansion of Italy's economy came to a halt and a recession began. A series of bank failures triggered cutbacks in production and employment. The economic slowdown was gradual but persisted until the eve of World War I. As unemployment rose, so did the number of strikes and the level of labor militancy. Employers were increasingly successful in breaking strikes and in cutting their labor costs. The PSI proved incapable of confronting the economic crisis with parliamentary action. The leaders of the CGL intensified the search for a vehicle which would build their political influence and offset the power of the factory owners and propertied classes, who were building their own national confederations. The internal debate over the future of the PSI became entwined with the efforts of organized labor to create an independent political power base.

While Reformist infighting sapped the vitality of the PSI, the General Confederation of Labor was isolating the Party from the labor movement. Labor leaders were more comfortable with Reformists at the head of the PSI but remained insistent on preserving their independence from Party control even after Turati's faction replaced the Integralists in command of the Socialist party. While its leaders frequently affirmed their desire to let the Party handle political issues, the Confederation was involved in parliamentary activity from its inception. Since the CGL claimed to represent the interests of workers of all political affiliations, its officials began cooperating with the deputies of all the parties of the *estrema*. The Confederation bypassed the *Direzione* to deal directly with Socialist deputies and refused to let the PSI act as its bargaining agent in negotiations with other parties.[1]

The CGL reaffirmed this independent stand with monotonous regularity. On June 4, 1907, for example, the Executive Committee of the Confederation instructed Rigola to "recall the PSI to a line more in conformity with that of the Confederation." In March 1908, the *Direzione* censored the CGL for attempting to create a common platform of action for all the parties of the left. The CGL's Executive Committee "rejected" the PSI protest. At their 1908 national congress CGL delegates passed a resolution which strictly limited those areas in which Party interference would be tolerated. CGL leaders, however, continued to support Reformist dominance of the PSI because the Reformists backed the CGL's efforts to build a solidly disciplined labor movement. One of the ironies of the Giolittian era was that the Reformists vigorously supported the Confederation's attempt to discipline the working classes while simultaneously fighting to keep the PSI decentralized. The Reformists remained concerned about the political immaturity of the workers. They wanted to organize the working classes as much to prevent them from joining an insurrection as to shape them into a force that could extract concessions from the propertied classes.[2]

THE CONGRESS OF FLORENCE

The PSI's growing isolation paralleled an internal stagnation. The Party's membership declined dramatically after the Reformists recaptured full control of the PSI at the 1908 national Congress. They confirmed their hold at the Party's 1910 meeting in Milan. The opposition was fragmented. Integralism withered away. The Syndicalists had left the PSI. The small band of "revolutionaries" who remained within the Party were divided. At the height of Reformist success, however, the Party first crumbled and then stagnated. In the first year that the Reformists regained control, Party membership dropped by 15,000. Although membership then leveled off, the Reformists were unable to recapture a significant number of militants who abandoned the PSI. Defections to the Syndicalists account for some of the losses, but more Socialists apparently left the Party out of a sense of frustration with Reformist leadership.[3] (See table 9.)

The Tenth National Congress of the PSI met in Florence on September 19, 1908. After two days of discussions devoted primarily to *Avanti!*'s problems, and two evenings of inconclusive caucuses among the factions, the delegates finally began debating the issues of the Party's future political course and its relations with the labor movement on the morning of September 21. Rigola assured the delegates that labor still needed the PSI's cooperation but pointedly warned the Party to stay out of union business. He claimed that the CGL alone had the power to call and direct strikes. Longobardi, the former Syndicalist leader, lashed out at the Reformist leaders in both the Confederation and the Party. The Reformists, he warned, were mistaken in thinking that Giolitti's Italy was a democratic state over which they could successfully exercise influence. The CGL's chiefs were equally wrong in believing that they represented the laboring masses. "Our Confederation . . . represents an aristocracy . . . it is not a mass movement." Finally, Longobardi accused the CGL's leadership of trying to practice "political polygamy" in their relations with the parties of the *estrema*.[4]

Gaetano Salvemini tried to draw the Congress's attention to the problem of defining a program of reforms for the GPS to enact. He attacked the Northern delegates for their failure to give serious attention to the problems of the South and stressed that the passage of a universal suffrage act was

TABLE 9
Party Membership, 1906–11

Year	Sections	Members
1906	1,279	43,654
1907	1,340	43,953
1908	1,222	43,788
1909	989	28,835
1910	1,125	31,960
1911	1,092	30,220

SOURCE: *Avanti!*, April 22, 1914.

the key to unlocking the South to the PSI. Salvemini warned that major reforms would not come from cooperation with Giolitti but had to be won over the opposition of the interests which Giolitti represented.[5]

At the end of the third day of meetings, the weary delegates voted to limit the number of orators. Turati assumed Ferri's role of Party unifier. He denied that any significant difference existed between Reformists and Integralists and minimized the differences which separated these two factions from the Party's left wing. Replying to Salvemini, Turati claimed that the PSI was in such good condition that it could risk a policy of careful cooperation with Giolitti. The "unity" resolution which Turati introduced at the end of his discourse triumphed easily in a floor vote.[6] The result of the vote was:

"Unity"	18,251
Integralist	5,957
"Revolutionary"	5,384
Abstentions	144

The voting pattern at this Congress showed that the Reformists dominated in North and North Central Italy and were also strong in the South and the islands. The Integralists found supporters in North Central Italy but very little backing in the *Mezzogiorno*. Integralism also retained some support in Morgari's home base, Piedmont, and in Forli and Ravenna in the Romagna. The Revolutionaries increased their support almost fivefold to the level which the Syndicalists had enjoyed in 1906. Their bases of support were in the South and among the agrarian sections of Lombardy and Piedmont. The left received backing from some sections in Latium and Umbria. Except for 150 votes which they received from Milan, the Revolutionary faction had scant support in Italy's industrial centers.[7]

Before adjourning, the Congress modified the structure of the *Direzione*. It reduced membership to fifteen: twelve representatives elected by the congress, the director of *Avanti!*, the political secretary, and a representative of GPS. The Congress rejected a Turati resolution which would have permitted more than one section to exist in the same area. Finally, it elected Bissolati director of *Avanti!*.[8]

The Reformist victory was nearly total. Integralism was dissolving. The left remained weak. One Revolutionary leader commented that the only bright spot for the defeated left was that the Reformists would now have to shoulder Party leadership openly and alone. The pressure was on a badly divided majority to produce results.

The Reformists had a difficult time producing the concrete results needed to justify their claims to lead the Party. Giolitti pushed through the greater part of his economic package without Reformist aid. The 1909 elections proved the limits of Reformist power. The PSI ran as a Party of the opposition, but this claim was rather transparent since so many Socialist deputies were firmly enmeshed in Giolitti's system of favors and deals. The Party's showing was unimpressive. Its total vote increased only slightly over 1904 levels. The Party's only significant achievement was electing Bissolati as the first Socialist deputy from Rome.[9]

Moreover, the GPS remained ineffective. In 1907, Salvemini had commented acidly, "The Socialist Party is not ill: it is dead; it is now only a specter and the Parliamentary Group is but the specter of a specter."[10] Turati admitted, "The Group suffers from a double absenteeism that paralyzes its efforts while reinforcing the antiparliamentary prejudices of doctrinaire and sentimental anarchists." He defined these two absenteeisms as the personal absenteeism of deputies from parliament's sessions and their lack of a coherent and agreed upon political program.[11]

The Reformist Ettore Ciccotti quit the GPS, writing Salvemini that the group lacked men with "guts" who were willing to do the research and work necessary to be effective legislators.[12] Within the group, the activities of Giacomo Ferri became a public scandal. Ferri gained control of a number of local public service monopolies in San Giovanni Perscieto with the aid of the city's Socialist mayor. His actions violated Party policy, which opposed both monopolies and private control of public services.[13]

REFORMISM DISSOLVES: THE NEW SYNDICALISM

As evidence of the PSI's political ineffectiveness mounted, the left and right wings of Reformism attempted to develop workable alternatives to the policies which Turati championed. Turati himself began to question the traditional approaches. He planned to initiate structural reform within both the PSI and the Reformist faction at future Party Congresses. This process began at Milan in 1910 but was cut short by the outbreak of the Libyan war.[14] Meanwhile, two other groups of Reformists attempted to redirect the PSI. Both groups showed an increased awareness of the development of mass movements on the fringes of the Socialist party, but neither dealt with the issue of a structural reorganization to exploit the growing political maturation of the masses.

The program of the right, championed by Bissolati and Bonomi, owed much to the views of the German revisionist socialist, Eduard Bernstein, and to the practical example of the British Labor party but also had common roots with the syndicalism of Arturo Labriola. In 1905, Antonio Graziadei, a young Reformist, published "Syndicalism, Reformism and Revolutionism" in *Critica Sociale*. Graziadei's thesis was that Reformists should take a second look at Syndicalist theory. Stressing Marx's great sympathy for the British trade union movement, Graziadei rejected the notion that syndicalism was inherently antiparliamentary: a group of extremists had captured Syndicalist theory. Graziadei correctly predicted that they would be unable to hold the support of the working class. The workers would soon reject the long-term objectives of the Syndicalists in favor of the satisfaction of their immediate needs. Reformism, Graziadei affirmed, was the ideal vehicle for bringing the working classes to political consciousness. In fact, "Reformism well understood is the master road through which the Socialists can reach syndicalism."[15]

As the Syndicalists left the PSI in 1907, Ivanoe Bonomi returned to the question of the Party's relationship with organized labor. In the first section of his *Le vie nuove del socialismo*, Bonomi stressed the evolution of Marx's thought in the twenty-three years which elapsed between the publication of the *Communist Manifesto* and the Paris Commune. He readily admitted that in 1847 Marx had excluded the possibility of a gradual development of a socialist society, although not the possibility that the proletariat might cooperate with other classes to overthrow the dominating class. During these years, Bonomi pointed out, the centerpiece of Marx's thought was the certainty that an economic crisis would ignite the proletarian revolution. Marx believed in the "increasing impoverishment" of the working class. However, Bonomi noted, this impoverishment did not occur. Instead the wages of the average worker rose. By 1871, Marx had second thoughts about the possibilities of interclass cooperation, and by the time of his death in 1883, he was convinced that the advance of the working class must be "position by position." A new tactical approach, blessed by Engels, permitted the European socialist parties to complete the reduction of the bourgeois state at a pace they judged best while they simultaneously trained the workers to assume full control of the state. A dictatorship of the proletariat was no longer necessary.[16]

The strategy of Reformism arose from the belief that after its victory over eighteenth-century monarchist absolutism, the bourgeoisie had split into a number of competing factions. The working class could ally first with one faction and then another to gain its ends. In Italy, where the victory of the middle classes was recent, the working classes had been able to employ this tactic for the first time in 1901: "The government ceased to belong to one class and must [thereafter] subordinate itself in part to the will of the proletariat and the small and middle bourgeoisie." Moreover, the reforms produced by class cooperation "are of identical nature to those reforms which revolutionary theorists put off to a future dictatorship of the proletariat."[17]

In the second part of his book, Bonomi stressed the importance of workers' organizations. He defended the support that Reformism gave to the expansion of the economic power of the state, arguing that it prepared the way for working-class penetration of capitalism.[18]

The final section of Bonomi's book provided an historical analysis of the development of the workers' movement. After decades of leading the struggle for the emancipation of labor, Europe's socialist parties were entering a new period:

> Twenty years of propaganda and action have by now enabled the workers' leagues, cooperatives, craft unions to make their own decisions, without the need of being constantly instructed, guided, represented by a party composed of Marx's followers. This party is certainly not yet decomposing, but it is being reabsorbed by the workers' movement which it has sustained but which can no longer submit to it. . . . The party lives as an organ serving the will of the unions and not as before as the directive body of the unions.[19]

For Bonomi, the crisis of Reformism was the result of the process of renovation of the Italian socialist movement.[20]

Bonomi's analysis appealed to organized labor's leaders who found their position raised from partners with the Socialist party to its masters. It also offered a fairly simple diagnosis of the PSI's ills. If the Party no longer functioned effectively, replace it or reduce its scope of action.[21] Finally, this analysis seemed to be mirrored in the history of the GPS. As the parliamentary group had liberated itself from the Party's control between 1893 and 1902, individual deputies shook off the group's control during the next decade. The deputies would complete that process by transferring their allegiance from the Party to the Confederation.

While Bonomi acted as the ideological spokesman for the right-wing Reformists, Bissolati was the faction's indisputable leader. *Avanti!*'s editor was a dominating moral figure within Italian Socialism. Angelica Balaban-off, an uncompromising Revolutionary, remarked:

> Although I disagreed with him politically, I came to have a great personal admiration for him. He was the personification of the antidemagogue. Just as courageously as he had defied public opinion in his native province when he joined the labor movement, he later faced the disapproval of the masses and his comrades. . . . In neither case was he concerned about, nor would he make the slightest concession to, public opinion.[22]

The son of a Garibaldian ex-priest, Bissolati was strongly committed to the Risorgimento ideals of Italian nationalism. His support for Giolitti reflected his desire to build an Italian social democratic movement that reflected the risorgimental tradition. During the Giolittian era, Bissolati slowly moved rightward, attempting to reconcile Marxism with Italian nationalism. In the process he adopted many positions that conflicted with the official program of the PSI.

Bissolati's evolution away from Socialist orthodoxy was most striking in issues relating to defense and foreign policy. After 1905 Bissolati, the Party's "expert" on these issues, began to support reasonable outlays for defense. Bissolati believed that the nation's traditional enemy and current ally, the Austrian empire, posed a direct military threat to Italy's national unity and independence. Bissolati and Turati first clashed over defense issues in 1908, and their discord grew as Bissolati's support for military outlays became more pronounced. Turati was a convinced antimilitarist who opposed any budgetary outlays for armaments.[23]

Bonomi and Bissolati were gradualists. They planned to move slowly in creating a labor party in Italy. Instead of mounting a direct challenge to the Party, Bissolati and his allies increasingly utilized their positions in the Party press and parliamentary group to act as the representatives of an emerging labor party. In the process they challenged numerous Party dogmas. In addition to their support for "reasonable" budgetary outlays for national defense, Bonomi and Bissolati ceased to oppose the continued existence of the monarchy. The right Reformists openly began to discuss the advantages of a Socialist participation in a ministry. Rigola, then aligned with the right, argued that "every sane and vital parliamentary party must participate in government and even assume the governing of the nation. There is no contrast, and never was, between the spirit of class struggle and the Socialist ascent to power."[24]

REFORMISM DISSOLVES: UNIVERSAL SUFFRAGE
AND THE SOUTH

Bissolati and his followers were only one of Reformism's internal factions. Their vision of replacing the PSI with a labor party aroused the opposition of a group on the left which was seeking to revitalize the Italian Socialist party. Anna Kuliscioff provided discreet support for these critics of Reformist practice. She recognized that legislative achievements alone could not resuscitate the Party or Reformism. The Party had to create new links to the masses, particularly the Southern peasantry. Kuliscioff, however, remained in the background, seeking to build understanding between the left and Turati. The two most visible leaders of left Reformism were Gaetano Salvemini and G. E. Modigliani. Salvemini provided the intellectual critique of Reformist practice and, acting as the movements tactical leader, sketched out a strategy for winning control of the PSI at the 1910 national Congress.[25]

For Salvemini, resurrecting both Reformism and the PSI required that both reverse their stated positions on three issues: the Southern Question, universal suffrage, and Giolitti.

"There are only two . . . true tendencies of Italian Socialism: the prevalent economic tendency of the North, the prevalent political tendency of the South," Salvemini wrote in the aftermath of the 1902 Congress of Imola.[26] Because of its backwardness, the South's representatives to the Party's national organizations would always be out of step with their Northern colleagues. While Northerners already enjoyed a large amount of political freedom and were preoccupied with social reform, the South's poor had to conquer their elementary political rights before they would be able to force social and economic concessions from the landowners of the *Mezzogiorno*. Since the Reformists consistently ignored the needs of the South and since they could expect no quarter in their struggle with their landlords, Southern Socialists usually joined the ranks of the extreme left.[27] In taking extreme positions, however, they placed themselves at odds with the real needs of the South: "If there is any place where the socialist revolution is a distant and fantastic abstraction, it is certainly Southern Italy. What can we hope to socialize in the South? Misery?"[28]

Salvemini added that in ignoring the needs of the working people of the South, the Reformists were ignoring the interests of the vast majority of the working population of Italy.

The solution to the Southern problem lay in the passage of a universal suffrage act: "In the North the conservative deputy is obliged to act with a certain prudence; many times he even puts on the mask of a democrat; gives the appearance of being a friend; fears election results. But the Southern deputy fears only the government in elections; he puts the peasant, who cannot vote, under his feet, crushes him, and moves onward."[29] A universal suffrage act would force Southern deputies, like their Northern colleagues, to respect the demands of the masses. However, the Northern Reformists were blocking progress toward suffrage reform. A majority of Northern workers could successfully pass the requirements of the existing suffrage law, and the Socialist deputies, who came exclusively from the North, therefore saw no pressing need for voting reform. They were content to continue to cooperate with the government and ensure the passage of the social reform legislation that their clients desired. By adopting this attitude, the Reformists were missing important opportunities to improve the PSI's position. With universal suffrage, the Party would make major gains in its parliamentary representation. Participation in a political process would awaken the people of the South to the need to confront their problems. Finally, Northern Liberals would have to abandon their Southern allies and the base of *trasformismo* would collapse. A new Southern deputy, representing the people rather than the government, would enter parliament.[30]

If the Socialist party was to revitalize itself, Salvemini warned, it had to take the lead in the fight for universal suffrage. To accomplish this, the PSI, and specifically the GPS, had to firmly and definitely break with Giovanni Giolitti. Salvemini regarded Giolitti as the arch-corrupter: "From 1860 until today we have had many governments that have trampled [and] corrupted the South; but none . . . so systematically trampled our honor and dignity."[31]

Salvemini charged that Giolitti had taken the measure of the Reformists and had bought them off with essentially meaningless concessions.

> The great strength of Giolitti is the knowledge he has of the intimate character of the Italian democratic movement—and I mean by democratic all the factions of the *estrema.* . . . The Socialist Party is the least stupid of these parties, but it is always stupid enough to be good for nothing. Giolitti has understood . . . and has acted: he has let us cry, demonstrate, strike; meanwhile with laws on the municipalization of public services he impedes municipalization to the great joy of the shareholders of private organizations and he prepares to reestablish the *status quo* in the railroads while we have the freedom to hold mass meetings.[32]

The GPS had fallen into its difficulties supporting Giolitti. By seizing upon the issue of universal suffrage, the parliamentary group had the opportunity to revitalize itself and the PSI through a "serious, resolute, energetic opposition to the government and the parliamentary majority." If it failed to act, Giolitti would employ the suffrage reform issue for his own purposes.[33]

Salvemini's critique was powerful. He was correct in accusing the Reformists of ignoring the South and its problems, correct in his analysis of Giolitti's relationship to the PSI and GPS, and probably correct in his assessment of the effects of a campaign for universal suffrage conducted against Giolitti. He dealt with every major problem facing the PSI save one: modifying its organizational structure to exploit the power of the masses he wanted to bring into the Socialist party. Salvemini's paradoxical willingness to operate within the existing structure of the PSI doomed his effort to defeat.

Salvemini planned to capture control of the 1910 Party Congress, believing that if the Congress approved his program, the GPS would have to try to enact it. He ignored the previous decade's lessons, although he knew them by heart. Salvemini, like most Reformists, retained a great faith in the powers of moral suasion and believed that the deputies could be roused to shake off their ties to Giolitti and lead a crusade against the Piedmontese statesman. He badly underestimated the determination of Bissolati and his followers to support Giolitti, as well as the desire of the majority of Socialist deputies to partake in the division of favors which would mark another successful Giolitti ministry.[34]

While Bissolati and Bonomi were content to work slowly toward their goal, Salvemini believed that immediate action was needed to save the Party from its continued drift into impotence. For Salvemini, the first step in the resuscitation of the PSI was passage of a universal suffrage law. He expected a fierce struggle and planned a campaign of mass agitation to awaken the nation and its representatives to the need for this reform. The greatest danger he foresaw was a parliamentary compromise that would swell the voting rolls but still leave large segments of the masses disenfranchised. He personally envisioned a law that would enfranchise every male citizen able to read and write his own name, with provisions protecting voters from election fraud and intimidation. Salvemini planned to win the backing of the PSI at the 1910 Congress. With the Party mobilized behind universal suffrage, he foresaw a long period of agitation, climaxing in an obstructionist campaign within parliament.[35]

Salvemini's plans won little support within the PSI. Morgari, an ally, accurately estimated the mood of the GPS and the leadership: "I am sure that the Group will lack the energy necessary to bring to life a plan like yours. The Group is composed in a good part of Reformists by temperament. . . . Several . . . are only Socialists in name (for example, Bissolati). . . . Not to have Bissolati, that is *Avanti!*, is to be unable to carry out your campaign."[36]

Morgari was an excellent prophet. In the spring of 1910, a discouraged Salvemini wrote a friend that "men like Turati and Bissolati hate to hear about the Mezzogiorno. And, shamefully, they act in good faith." Turati accused Salvemini and Modigliani of embracing the discredited views of Arturo Labriola. Convinced that his old friends Turati and Bissolati had betrayed him, Salvemini sought the support of the Revolutionaries. They were equally unsympathetic, and Salvemini admitted, "Every day that passes, I feel [drawn] further away from the old parties."[37]

What began as a campaign to give new vigor and direction to Reformism ended as a violent personal clash. Kuliscioff, who supported Salvemini's objectives, if not his methods, tried to mediate between Turati and the young historian. Meanwhile, she continued to encourage his efforts to win the support of the Party Congress. In July 1910, Salvemini outlined the dissidents' plans:

> I am here at Milan to get in agreement with Kuliscioff, Schiavi, [and] Pagliari on the approach to be taken to the Congress. They are fully in agreement with me. The Socialist section of Milan will take a position in July, supporting . . . a series of resolutions in which it will back the positions of the "dissident Reformists." Then . . . several sections will support the Milan decisions and invite the Milan section to set up a propaganda and organization committee. We will propagandize and we will go to the congress as a group. At the congress, there will be a right: Bissolati, Bonomi, Cabrini, Podrecca, Chiesa, etc.; a Turati center right; a Morgari center left; a left (us); an extreme left, the Revolutionaries. . . . If the center supports us, we will have a majority, but we will not make any concessions on the ideological level . . . and in any case we will leave the governing of the Party to the center.[38]

The center-left coalition upon which Salvemini counted never coalesced. Turati had firm control of the majority. Six weeks before the Congress, Kuliscioff advised Salvemini that their chances of achieving a victory at the Milan Congress were virtually nonexistent. Salvemini agreed. "Dissident" left Reformism was stillborn.[39]

THE CONGRESS OF MILAN, 1910: STAGNATION ENSHRINED

The Congress of Milan was anticlimactic. In spite of all the ferment within the Reformist camp, Turati easily reaffirmed his leadership. The right Reformists chose not to act and the Salvemini-Modigliani left Reformists were impotent. The Revolutionaries had split. Turati gladly tolerated their presence within the PSI: they provided a weak alternative but had never posed a real threat to Reformist domination. Still, the Reformist *Direzione* was unwilling to permit the left an opportunity to bog down the Congress with their attacks. It modified the agenda so that discussion of the activities of the GPS, the *Direzione,* and *Avanti!* were placed near the end of the meeting.[40]

The Congress opened on October 21, 1910, at Milan's *Casa del Popolo.* The delegates elected a multiple presidency representing all the factions. The first day's meetings were taken up electing officers, hearing the left's protests over the agenda, and voting on a novel proposal that divided the Congress into five smaller discussion groups. These groups were to deal with one or more items on the agenda, adopt a resolution, and bring only unresolved questions back to a general meeting of the Congress. The motion was adopted over the objections of Lazzari.[41]

The next day Turati presented his views on political strategy. The Reformist leader presented himself as the chief of a broad centrist current whose objective was Party unity. He defended the activities of the GPS and the *Direzione.* Turati admitted that the Party faced serious trouble:

> It is very true that the Reformists, especially in the past two years, have not known how to obtain any great reforms, just as the Revolutionaries have not known how to make the smallest revolution: but this derives uniquely from the fact that the Party is exhausted, that the sections are dead organisms which galvanize themselves only during elections, without undertaking serious propaganda work, without attempting to infuse the working masses with the passion, sentiment, consciousness, [and] notion of politics.

Responsibility for the Party's failures lay with all of them. Turati rejected the idea that the Party's mission was over. It had just begun. Whatever was wrong with the PSI, responsibility lay with the individual members and not with the PSI's organization or its doctrine. To revive the Party, the rank and file would have to display a greater commitment to excellence and new leaders would have to emerge from the young.[42] This essentially empty analysis showed that Turati at that point was unwilling to promote serious internal change in the PSI.

Salvemini warned Turati that his Reformism had become nothing more than "state socialism" that sacrificed the needs of the masses to the requirements of the elite of Northern workers. He made an impassioned plea for opposition to Giolitti and support for universal suffrage.[43]

During the two days of debate on political strategy that followed, only one other delegate made a significant statement. Amid thunderous applause, Leonida Bissolati rose on the third day of the Congress to read the PSI its death warrant. The failings of the Party did not lie with the rank and file, nor was universal suffrage a cure for its ills. In fact, suffrage expansion would probably work against the PSI. What the Party needed, Bissolati told the Congress, was autonomy for the deputies in elections, a GPS freed from the control of the *Direzione*, and permission for the group to support a ministry. So long as the GPS could not give its full support to a ministry, it would remain impotent. The crisis of the PSI called for a new organization:

> We are constituted just as we were in 1895 at the Congress of Parma. Then we were being persecuted by Crispi who dissolved the leagues and even the mutual aid societies. In order to save the party we decided to reorganize it in a manner which would safeguard the economic organizations. We built it on the basis of individual membership, which was not without personal danger because we were engaged in a struggle in which we were candidates for jailing. . . . But when liberty was won, when, let me speak a great heresy, the Party had fulfilled its function, which was winning the right to participate in the nation's political life for the working class. From that moment, the Socialist Party as constituted, inevitably had the destiny of a dead branch.[44]

A labor party representing the real interests of the working classes would be able to meet the developing situation in Italy. The right Reformists were ready to move with the working class.

Three resolutions offered by Modigliani, Turati, and Lazzari were placed before the delegates at the end of the debate. Turati's won easily, gaining 13,006 votes to 4,547 for the Modigliani resolution and 5,928 for the Lazzari motion.

The voting totals indicated that Reformism's stronghold continued to be the small agrarian section of Emilia. Modigliani's resolution drew its support from essentially the same areas as Morgari's had in 1908 but had weaker backing among urban sections. The Revolutionaries continued to make inroads in Ravenna and Forli in the eastern part of the Romagna. The most significant addition to their strength came from Rome. The Rome Socialist Union, which had voted for Morgari's resolution in 1908, passed into the left's camp in 1910. The Reformists were generally stronger in north central Italy, the left in the southern half. The South almost ceased to participate in the Party. A number of provinces did not send any delegates. Naples and other sections that did had declined significantly in their membership. Between 1908 and 1910 the number of sections that represented Sicily and Sardinia dropped by half.[45]

Recognizing that the Congress's work was incomplete, delegates from all the factions were unanimous in recommending that a special congress meet in 1911 to continue the work of Party reform. Bissolati gracefully vacated his position, permitting Turati's dominant faction to install Treves as the new director of *Avanti!*.[46]

The Congress was a triumph for Turati but a hollow one. Tactically, he had a success. The Revolutionary faction remained small. The dissident Reformists were defeated and the right Reformists had surrendered the Party newspaper. On the other hand, Reformist-led sections included 6000 fewer Party members than in 1908. Moreover, Reformism was irrevocably split, and Turati was being abandoned by many of his oldest allies. The way lay open for the left to mount another challenge to Reformist control.

III

The
Revolutionary
Experiment

Revolutionaries

in the

Ascendant,

1911–1912

THE LEFT REORGANIZES

Following their defeat at the 1910 Congress of Milan, the Revolutionary Intransigent delegates met to decide upon a course of action. Benito Mussolini, a young demagogue from the Romagna, urged the delegates to withdraw from the Party and form their own organization. Lazzari, Angelica Balabanoff, Francesco Ciccotti, and G. M. Seratti, veteran leaders of the faction, supported continued participation within the Reformist-dominated PSI. The left decided to remain in the Party and adopted a resolution in which they disavowed the future action of the Reformist leadership. Next, the Revolutionary faction adopted a Mussolini proposal to establish a five-member central committee to coordinate their activities and agreed to publish their own national newspaper. The left established its headquarters at via Seminario 87, a few doors away from the office of the *Direzione*.[1]

The speedy creation of this central committee was the first step toward building a party within the Party. The Reformists chose both to tolerate and to ignore these developments. *Avanti!* carried little information on the activities of the left. Within six months the Revolutionary faction built a parallel organizational structure to the official Reformist-dominated one. On the local level, the left-wing members sought control of the sections. At the national level, the Revolutionary central committee established its own secretariat "to provide for the organization of the forces of the faction, [for] the distribution of propaganda in preparation for the national congress, and for the execution of the deliberations of the Central Committee." The new Revolutionary newspaper, *La Soffitta* ("the attic"), became one of the principal tools for coordinating the left's activities, a useful weapon for checking "deviation" by the Reformists, and a rival to *Avanti!*, which the Revolutionaries charged was simply the mouthpiece of the opposing faction of the PSI. The left even acquired its own parliamentary group when Agnini and Morgari resigned from the GPS, attacking its members for class collaboration.[2]

The Revolutionaries had two aims in establishing this structure: to capture control of the PSI at the next congress and to force Bissolati's right out of the Party. Even in defeat, the left was confident that events were already driving the PSI in their direction. Lerda told the delegates to the Milan Congress:

> The Revolutionary Intransigent force which numbered only 1000 at the Congress of Rome, today, after the ravages of four years of Reformism and *trasformismo* on the healthy body of Socialism will reach several thousand. This will be the true proof . . . that you have followed the wrong road. The proof that if you continue on this road . . . the Socialist Party will really become the dead branch about which friend Bissolati spoke.[3]

Statistical evidence to the contrary, the left felt that its progress, as measured by the growth of the faction, had been nothing less than spectacular. In August 1911, Giovanni Allevi, a Revolutionary spokesperson, commented that the left's vote at Milan had been "magnificent," adding wistfully, "If, at the last moment, the comrades of Ravenna had taken a more decisive attachment, the Party would have rediscovered itself."[4] Actually, the Revolutionary vote grew little at Milan, and even the defection of Ravenna's 1722 votes from the Reformist column would have left the Revolutionaries well short of a majority.

Nevertheless, establishing an organizational framework for a Revolutionary party within the PSI was the essential first step toward creating a left-wing majority. When the crisis of October 1911 shattered Reformist unity, the left was in position to build a new majority out of a disillusioned rank and file. Moreover, the left's decision to create a Revolutionary organization was consciously designed to encourage the right Reformists to act in a similar fashion, increasing the impetus for their break with the PSI.[5]

The leadership of this left-wing coalition was a mixed group. Lazzardi and Lerda, together with a number of other survivors of the Ferri and Syndicalist disasters, formed the inner core of leaders. Morgari and Agnini moved to the Revolutionary camp from Integralism. Support also came from a number of surviving Southern organizations. Two new elements, with fresh leaders, offered the promise of substantial assistance. One group was the Young Socialist Federation (FGS), led by Arturo Vella. The second group came from the Romagna, a traditional area of leftist extremism: the Socialist organizations of Forli province, under the command of the twenty-seven-year-old Benito Mussolini.

The Young Socialist movement had its roots in Tuscany, where its first provincial organization and newspaper came into being. The Young Socialists quickly aligned themselves with the Syndicalists in the internal Party battles of 1904–6. As a result, the Reformists, who were usually eager to promote decentralization, adamantly opposed granting autonomy to the Young Socialists. When the Syndicalists left the Party in 1907, most of the Young Socialists followed them out. At the 1907 national Congress of Young Socialist organizations, a Vella-led minority formed the "Young Socialist Federation adhering to the PSI." During the next five years Vella and his associates re-created a national organization and supported the struggle against Reformism.[6]

The new organization grew rapidly, but like the PSI, it was continuously troubled by serious financial problems. In 1910 FGS claimed to have 12,000 members but candidly admitted that "hardly one-third had yet paid" for the *tessera*. Like *Avanti!*, the Young Socialists' national weekly *La Avanguardia* existed on the financial borderline. The Young Socialists were incensed by the indifference of the Reformist-led Party to their problems.[7]

The FGS claimed three missions for itself: anticlerical and antimilitary propaganda, ousting the Reformists from Party leadership, and driving Masons out of the PSI. Their antimilitary propaganda was very tame and hardly distinguishable from that of the Reformists. Anticlericalism failed to fire much popular protest during the conciliatory era of Giovanni Giolitti. The FGS had somewhat more success with the other major targets of their hostility: the Reformists and those Socialists who belonged to the Masonic Order. The campaign against these two "evils" was conducted in close partnership with a variety of left-wing Socialists.[8]

The Revolutionary leadership paid a good deal of attention to the activities of FGS, regularly contributing to *La Avanguardia* and frequently speaking at Young Socialist political meetings. Vella emerged as one of the leaders of the Revolutionary faction, and his articles appeared regularly in *La Soffitta*. By 1912 he was secretary of the Rome Socialist Union. Subsequently, he became Lazzari's deputy in the Party secretariat. FGS directed many young workers into the Party's left wing and provided a cadre of young organizers to aid in the struggle against Reformism. Moreover, the FGS continued to grow while the Reformist-led Party was stagnating. By

1912 FGS had over 5600 members, equal to nearly one-sixth of the PSI's total enrollment. If sizeable numbers of Young Socialists joined the Party prior to its national Congress, they could powerfully reinforce the Revolutionary faction. Vella and the Revolutionaries' problem was retaining members allegiance to FGS. The Young Socialists were impatient with continuing Reformist domination of the PSI and attracted by the action-oriented anarchists and Syndicalists.[9]

The most influential of the younger Socialist leaders was a case in point. Mussolini and his Forli sections provided the leaders of the left with both great opportunities and great headaches. In 1910, after a decade of wandering about Italy, Switzerland, and the Austrian Empire, Mussolini accepted an invitation to return to his home province and set up a local newspaper. Utilizing this new paper, *La Lotta di Classe,* and his oratorical gifts, Mussolini built a party organization of about 2500. He had returned home at the right moment. Disaffection with Reformism was growing in the Romagna. At the 1908 Florence Congress, four sections of his home province, including Forli, voted for the left. In 1910 Mussolini made his first appearance on the national political stage, speaking to the Congress of Milan. Thirty-four Forli province sections supported the Revolutionary resolution.

An alliance with Mussolini presented some problems for orthodox Revolutionary socialists. He was more of an anarcho-Syndicalist than a Socialist, embracing many of the ideas that had provoked Lerda and Lazzari to break with the Syndicalists. Mussolini was also an outspoken champion of an elitist approach to politics. The Revolutionaries and Young Socialists were openly waging war against the elitism that both Reformism and the Masonic lodges represented. Mussolini, moreover, was hostile to all forms of parliamentary action, while almost all the other leaders of the left believed in the importance of Socialist participation in elections and in parliament. Finally, Mussolini's frequent calls for violence set him at odds with the rest of the left's leaders who were wary of provoking government repression of the Party and organized labor. Mussolini's views on violence aligned him with Sorel and the Syndicalists.[10]

Nevertheless, Mussolini was welcomed into the Revolutionary camp. Differences over ideological questions were commonplace in the PSI, and Mussolini took care to break publicly with both Sorel and his Italian disciples.[11] Moreover, Mussolini's views were not widely known outside his province. However, the old left's new ally initially failed to provide the support the Revolutionaries needed. When the Socialist party's 1911 Congress met, Mussolini was in prison, awaiting trial for leading violent protests against the Libyan war. The Forli Socialists failed to appear at the Congress.

The various factions which composed the Revolutionary coalition had little in common except their enemies: Reformism, class collaboration, Masonry, labor parties, and Socialist participation in a government. Past experience indicated that agreement on these points was unlikely to provide a formula for long-term unity. The positive side of the Revolutionary program was even more threadbare: intransigence and party discipline. Intransigence was the belief that the Socialist party could force concessions at a faster pace by means of confrontation with the bourgeois state than by the strategy of class cooperation recommended by the Reformists. The revolution was a long way off in the minds of these self-styled revolutionaries. The only other positive program around which the left was united was their demand that the PSI reorganize to restore discipline to the GPS and Party press. On this point Mussolini, Vella, Lerda, Lazzari, Morgari, and other leaders of the left were in complete agreement. Discipline "made the Party strong and feared in the past, and without it no organism can remain vital."[12]

As early as 1902 Lerda offered a plan for modification of the Reformist-designed structure of the PSI. He proposed to limit severely the wide powers of the sections, placing them in the hands of the provincial federations and the *Direzione.* Lerda wanted the give the *Direzione* control over the selection of provincial leaders and make these appointees salaried employees of the Party. While Lerda's proposal called for the continued participation of the director of *Avanti!* on the *Direzione,* it pointedly excluded any special representation for the GPS. Lerda wanted to place both the GPS and *Avanti!* under the direct control of the *Direzione.*[13] Ten years later, Lerda's ideas were a blueprint for the Revolutionaries, who took power with the twin objectives of internal centralization and of war against the bourgeois state.[14]

GIOLITTI'S FOURTH MINISTRY AND THE DISSOLUTION OF REFORMISM, MARCH–OCTOBER 1911

On March 18, 1911, Giolitti overthrew the ministry of his lieutenant, Luzzatti, by presenting a proposal for suffrage reform far more comprehensive than that offered by the government. Luzzatti handed in his resignation. King Victor Emmanuel III immediately began consultations for the formation of a new government. *Avanti!* observed that the only realistic options were either a second Luzzatti government or a new Giolitti ministry.[15] The consensus among the deputies favored Giolitti's return. The Piedmontese leader again asked the PSI for its support:

> I turned therefore to Leonida Bissolati, and had a long conversation with him. . . . Bissolati, speaking not only personally, but with the full approval of his colleagues, declared his full approval for my program; but he repeated what he had already told me several years before . . . that the Socialist party was not yet mature enough to participate in a government.
>
> Bissolati suggested that he could best aid the government in the achievement of its program by remaining outside it. . . . I then asked Bissolati if, when he was called by the sovereign to express his views on the political situation and on the government's program, he would accept the invitation. Bissolati responded affirmatively, and the next day was received in audience by the King.[16]

The Socialists divided along predictable lines in their response to this consultation between a Party leader and the monarch. No one doubted that Bissolati's meeting with the king at the Quirinale Palace was important. The Party officially disavowed Bissolati's action but hedged this by publicly defending the integrity of the Reformist leader.[17]

Turati was surprised by Bissolati's latest action. He had already talked Bissolati out of accepting Giolitti's offer of a cabinet position. Contrary to Turati's advice, however, Bissolati told the prime minister that the decision was based on personal factors rather than on obedience to Party policy. Turati was furious with Bissolati's latest deviation. He condemned the latest episode of Bissolati's revisionism, remarking: "Participation in power? If we could, perhaps; certainly, however, we can not. . . . The paths of Bissolati and of the workers are different, one to the Quirinale, the other to the Aventine."[18]

While Turati disapproved of Bissolati's actions, he remained committed to cooperation with a reform ministry. In June Giolitti presented his new program to the Chamber of Deputies. Its three main points were a state monopoly on life insurance, salaries for parliamentary deputies, and an expanded suffrage. The proposed suffrage law gave the vote to all literate males over the age of twenty-one, to all men who had served in the armed forces, literate or not, and to all males over thirty who failed to meet the literacy test.[19]

Bissolati's actions and Giolitti's reform package placed the Reformist leadership in a bind. Giolitti was offering major political reforms which were clearly in the interest of the PSI and the working classes it claimed to represent. Bissolati insisted that the Party follow the logic of its positions and back Giolitti. Since 1901 the Reformists had claimed that parliamentary action was transforming Italy into a state in which the working class could assume a governing role. Bissolati reiterated this position and attempted to lead the PSI into a greater role in the political process. Turati, however, commented that the new program "gives the impression of a very abundant meal offered at eight in the morning when the stomach isn't ready." He pulled back, fearful of an intra-Party schism and skeptical of Giolitti's motives.[20]

Bissolati's meeting with the king marked a second stage in the breakup of Italian Reformism. He went to the meeting with Victor Emmanuel fully cognizant of the impact this meeting would have. This and subsequent actions suggest that Bissolati sought a "positive polarization" on the model of the 1892 break with the anarchists that would separate the Reformist wheat from the Revolutionary chaff even at the price of a permanent division of the PSI. After telling the Milan Congress that the Party as constructed was no longer useful to the working class, Bissolati moved along the road he felt the working class must take: participation in power. The first step on this path was consultation with Italy's political leadership. These consultations illustrated the growing weight of the working classes while acquainting them with a new responsibility. The next steps were: a major suffrage reform, an election under expanded suffrage, and then participation in a coalition government. Bissolati realized that somewhere along this road the Party would split. He chose a gradual approach to delay this split while he sought to win over the majority of the rank and file. Foreseeing a fusion of the PSI and CGL, Bissolati made no effort to create new Party structures. Instead, he founded a newspaper to disseminate his views. Given sufficient time, Bissolati expected to carry most of the GPS and much of the Party into a new Italian labor party.[21]

LIBYA

Giolitti ended whatever chances Bissolati had to create a new political structure and destroyed Reformism's hold on the PSI when he abruptly led Italy into war with Turkey in order to seize a colonial empire in Libya.

Giolitti had bargained for the support of the left with a series of far-reaching domestic concessions. He also turned his attentions to the right side of the Italian political spectrum. New and disturbing forces were rising on the right, and Giolitti tried to neutralize them with the same strategy of concessions which had been so successful with the left.

The largest group on the right was the Catholic church. The Italian Church's political wing had emerged from a major internal struggle in which clerical-conservative elements had wrested control of the movement from the reform-oriented Christian Democratic forces. Giolitti recognized the growing force of the Church in Italy's politics and sought to bring the Vatican and the Italian Church into support of his regime. An expanded suffrage bill was part of Giolitti's effort to attract the support of Catholics. Passage of the bill would permit the Catholics to bring their weight more fully to bear in Italian politics. His governments had also favored the growing investments of the Banco di Roma in Libya. The bank's owners were closely associated with both the Italian Church leadership and with the Vatican. They employed its financial resources and links to build up support for an Italian occupation of Libya. Large segments of the popular Catholic press demanded intervention and exploitation of the reputed wealth of "the promised land."[22]

Italian Catholics were only one influential interest group favoring an interventionist foreign policy. Important segments of Italy's business community were already trading and investing heavily inside the Turkish Empire and in the newly independent Balkan states. Corporations and banks wanted to enjoy the greater security that an Italian political and military presence would bring and thus favored expansion into North Africa, the Middle East, and other areas of the tottering Turkish Empire. They provided financial support for the groups of intellectuals that lobbied for renewed colonial expansion.[23]

The Nationalists, a small, vocal, and influential minority of intellectuals, who possessed a considerable talent for propaganda, believed that expansion would revitalize Italy. The Nationalists were outspoken opponents of Giolitti, whose reform politics they blamed for a weakening of Italian national sentiment and for the encouragement of class divisions. While Giolitti could not win them over, he could blunt their attacks and steal much of their program with a successful colonial campaign.[24]

Giolitti stood at the center of a growing domestic polarization. The old formula of shifting a bit to the left or right to produce a malleable majority had become increasingly untenable as the Nationalists, Catholics, and new industrial right made inroads among the middle class. Giolitti bid for the support of the left and, to a more limited degree, the Catholics with domestic reforms. He reluctantly adopted an aggressive foreign policy to attract the support of the right. He led Italy into a war with Turkey and seized Libya in order to satisfy the demands of important elements of the middle classes for profits, national glory, and an outlet for emigration. By means of these concessions Giolitti sought to bring these elements back into his political coalition. Like many a politician before and since, Giolitti believed he could win a quick and easy military victory that would glue together his domestic support and then control the political and social forces wars unleash. He proved to be tragically wrong on both counts.

In his memoirs Giolitti claimed that he had been preoccupied with finding a favorable solution to the Libyan question for nearly a decade. The weight of available evidence suggests that he decided to act only after Libya became an unavoidable diplomatic and domestic issue. Giolitti had made a career as an anti-imperialist, arguing that liberalism must avoid colonial entanglements if it were to remain a viable political force.[25] On July 28, 1911, as the Second Moroccan crisis threatened to freeze Italy out of the scramble for North African colonies, the Marquis di San Giuliano, Italy's minister of foreign affairs, advised Giolitti that although it might still be possible to avoid a war, Italy must be prepared:

> From the complex of international affairs and the local situation in the Tripolitania, I am led to believe it probable that in a few months Italy will be forced to undertake a military expedition. . . . We should take this probability into account, even while attempting to avoid it . . . but . . . prepare our action to the twin ends of evading it, and of preparing its success, if, as appears always more probable, it becomes inevitable.[26]

San Giuliano's memorandum captured Giolitti's mood: the hesitant, fatal acceptance, combined with the opportunism that always characterized his politics. A few days after the war began, Giolitti took up these themes in one of his rare addresses outside parliament:

> Foreign policy cannot, like internal politics, depend entirely on the will of the government and of parliament, but by absolute necessity must take into account events and situations which are not in our power to modify nor even to accelerate or retard. There are events that impose themselves.[27]

Significantly, after dealing with the issue which preoccupied the Italian nation, Giolitti devoted most of this speech to issues of domestic reform. The war was a necessary but temporary interruption in the primary business of reform.[28]

Giolitti's decision to go to war was a tragic mistake. The Nationalists and the policies of military adventure which they advocated were reinforced by the success of the venture. Their opposition to Giolitti never softened. Moreover, the war further destabilized the international situation by encouraging Turkey's Balkan neighbors to carve up the remaining European portions of its empire. The final pacification of Libya's desert nomads took another generation with heavy losses of life on both sides and large investments of scarce Italian capital. Economically, the prize failed to merit the effort. Libya never supported large-scale colonialization or relieved Italy's overpopulation problems.[29]

The most immediate effect of Italy's march into Libya was to create a rupture within the Italian Socialist party and end the collaboration between the PSI and Giolitti. The war drove a permanent wedge between the workers' movement and the Liberal state.

Giolitti had seriously underestimated the devotion of the majority of the Reformist leadership to Marxism and to anti-imperialist politics. This misconception was undoubtedly fostered by his contacts with the pliable deputies of the GPS. Moreover, Giolitti misunderstood the effects which an invasion of Libya would have on the Party leadership. Knowing that several leading Socialists either favored the expedition or were at least neutral, he assumed that, as in the past, they could carry the Party along with them. Instead, the war widened the gap which separated Bissolati and his small group of supporters from the majority of Reformists. The failure of a Reformist-led general strike and the subsequent paralysis of the GPS destroyed Reformism's moral capital. The war left Italy more deeply polarized, and Giolitti became the principal target for both an aroused left and right.[30]

The Reformists' initial reaction to the possibility of a war was confusion. Most were surprised by Giolitti's actions. Foreign policy matters rarely entered into the political calculations of Socialist leaders. In general, they took traditional and rather idealistic positions on foreign policy issues. Reformists clung to pacifism and opposed both large standing armies and colonialism. Their pacifism was sincere but unlikely to win converts among the nationalist middle classes.

When they realized that war was imminent, the Reformist dominated council of the CGL met on September 20, 1911, to draw up plans designed to stop the war. The labor leaders agreed that a meeting with the *Direzione* and GPS was essential. They published a manifesto explaining the situation to the workers. Finally, they discussed using a general strike to halt the invasion and decided to issue a joint call for action following a meeting with the Party leadership.[31]

The PSI's Reformist leaders were equally shocked by Giolitti's moves.[32] They were in a very embarrassing position. For most of the decade, Reformists had placed their trust in Giolitti, the progressive middle-class leader who repeatedly implemented programs of reform favorable to working-class interests. Now Giolitti had taken the country into a war which the Socialists with good reason regarded as immoral and dangerous to Europe's peace. When their middle-class ally betrayed them, Reformism stood as politically bankrupt. The choice before Reformist leaders was either supporting Giolitti and abandoning the Party or abandoning Giolitti to embrace the Revolutionaries and the program of parliamentary intransigence. As usual, they equivocated.[33]

Reformist Party leaders and labor chiefs met in special session on September 25, 1911. Turati tried to get his reluctant colleagues to issue a statement condemning Giolitti for betraying the nation. They rejected this suggestion but agreed to call a twenty-four-hour general strike to force a halt to the war. This half measure was typical of the Reformist leadership. Turati, for example, disliked the concept of a general strike. When Giolitti's actions forced the Party to employ it, Turati sought to limit both its duration and impact. Shortly after the 1904 general strike, Turati outlined a set of rules for its future use. The strike had to be politically motivated; it must be a demonstration without insurrectionary objectives; it must not involve public services or the production of essentials such as food; and above all, it must remain firmly in the hands of its organizers. Turati deeply mistrusted any spontaneous action by the working class.[34]

The general strike of September 1911 conformed to all these norms. It was totally political in motivation, limited in its duration, and had severely restricted aims. In announcing the work stoppage on September 27, *Avanti!* assured its readers that the general strike was not aimed at toppling the government but only at forcing it to recall parliament. The government, its supporters, and large segments of the working class ignored the call for a strike. The ineffectiveness of the Italian protest created great disillusionment among the other European socialist parties. Pompeo Ciotti, the secretary of the *Direzione,* was hard pressed to defend the PSI's conduct before the International.[35]

After an initial period of confusion, lines hardened within the Reformist camp. The war began less than three weeks before the opening of the special Congress at Modena. The various Reformist factions speedily adopted positions. Bissolati believed that Giolitti had no alternative but to carry on a colonial policy that the public supported overwhelmingly. If Giolitti resisted, the government would fall and the nationalist right would take power. He suggested that by accepting the gains already made in the war, the PSI could convince the government to compromise with the Turks and bring the war to a speedy conclusion. In any case, Bissolati admonished, the Party could not allow the war to jeopardize the existence of the Giolitti government or the passage of its reform package: "The protest was made . . . the event is completed and a new order of things begins. Must we now immobilize ourselves to repeat the protest and . . . thus renounce . . . the attempt to influence later events?"[36]

Turati stood fast on the Party's traditional pacifism and anticolonialism. He denounced the war as a criminal folly. The Socialist party must oppose it in parliament as "a war against Italy" which contradicted all the nation's democratic traditions. Turati charged that Bissolati had become an accomplice in the war and deserted the PSI. On October 11, the Milan Socialist organization approved a Turati resolution demanding that the parliamentary group join the opposition.[37] Italian Reformism was disintegrating.

THE CONGRESS OF MODENA

The outbreak of the Libyan war was a godsend for the Revolutionary faction of the PSI. Coming after Bissolati's trip to the Quirinale, it was a crushing demonstration of the futility of cooperation with the bourgeois state. The close collaboration Bissolati envisioned was clearly the prelude to betrayal. The left called for a return to class struggle. Of even greater immediate value to the Revolutionaries than the proof of Giolitti's perfidy was the irremediable split in Reformist ranks. The left broke out of its geographic confinement and exploited the disunity and failure of the Reformists to capture a majority at the Congress. Up to 1911, Revolutionary strength was confined in relatively limited areas (Novara, Como, Mantua, Ravenna, Massa-Carrara, Florence, Rome, and Foggia provinces and the Umbria region). The collapse of the PSI in southern Italy made it difficult for the left to make inroads in an area which traditionally supported anti-Reformist politics. With the exception of their limited penetration in Milan, the Revolutionaries had been unable to build serious support in any of the major industrial cities. They had, however, made inroads in certain small industrial cities.[38]

The Revolutionary strategy was to attack the Reformists on three issues: mismanagement of *Avanti!*, the Libyan disaster, and the acquiescence of the *Direzione* and of *Avanti!*'s editorial board in the parliamentary group's co-operation with successive Italian governments.[39] In the weeks immediately preceding the Congress at Modena the left received two substantial boosts. First, the majority of the Reformists decided to support a policy of intransigence. Given the circumstances, the Reformist decision was both a courageous act and a confession of failure. Reformism had no alternative to offer. Its strategy of class cooperation had failed. Simultaneously, numerous sections instructed their delegates to support the left's proposed resolution on political strategy. While many rank-and-file Socialists were unsure what such a policy would entail, they were ready to embrace any option which would save the Party from continued domination by the right Reformists. The sections of Bergamo province, for example, voted for a resolution calling for intransigence but qualified it to permit the parliamentary group to decide when to return to the old policy of cooperation with the government. In view of the GPS's record, this was a vote to support the ministry.[40]

In contrast with the confusion among the sections and within the Reformist ranks, the Revolutionaries presented a solid front. In mid-July 1911 when the dates for the Modena Congress were formalized, *La Soffitta* urged its readers to pay for the *tessera* immediately in order to ensure that their sections would be represented. The Revolutionary Central Committee increased the frequency and impact of its propaganda campaign by distributing free copies of *La Soffitta* to every section and publishing the newspaper as a weekly. On October 1, the paper printed the text of a resolution which all Revolutionary-controlled sections were to adopt at pre-Congress caucuses and called a meeting of the left's delegates to coordinate strategy. The Revolutionary leadership appointed "fiduciaries" to represent those sections which could not send a delegate to the Congress. On October 8, the Central Committee instructed all Revolutionary delegates to meet in an October 14 evening caucus to work out the final details of strategy. The secretariat of the Revolutionary faction transferred its seat from Rome to Modena to oversee the action of its delegates and coordinate the left's effort.[41]

The Reformists were struggling to achieve a minimal unity. In 1911 and 1912 the Reformists paid heavily for their lack of organization and discipline but showed no inclination to copy the methods of the left. On October 13, *Avanti!* announced an emergency caucus of the "Reformists of the left."

The paper was not referring to the small coterie which followed Modigliani and Salvemini in 1910 but to Turati and all those who opposed Bissolati. The manifesto issued by this new "left" admitted that Reformism was in disarray. While the previously disorderly left moved through its deliberations at a brisk pace, the lawyers and professors who dominated the Reformist faction met in a tumultuous session and debated what to do if the Congress supported Bissolati.[42]

Gregorio Agnini, a Revolutionary leader, presided as the first session of the Modena Congress began at 10:15 A.M., October 15, 1911. During this brief opening meeting Ciotti presented a report on the state of the Party. In the afternoon, the Congress began debating the issues of participation in power and support for the government. Arnaldo Bussi, spokesman for the left Reformists, argued that the PSI should support the program of a future reform-oriented government but ruled out any participation in power for the present. He insisted that the Party firmly oppose the Giolitti ministry and its war.[43]

Lerda, who followed Bussi, accused the Reformists of so debasing the PSI that it had become indistinguishable from the parties of the middle class. He attacked *Avanti!* for its failure to represent the needs of the working classes and accused the Reformists of destroying the idealism which made Socialism attractive.[44] Finally, Lerda introduced a resolution calling for the PSI to return to a policy of strict and total intransigence.

Bonomi, the chief theoretician of the right, made his group's case the following morning. He warned the delegates that support for a government and participation in power were "two things as strictly connected as a tree and its branches." While opposition had been a useful policy once, its time was past. The Italian party system had broken down class lines and the only way the Socialists could achieve a partial fulfillment of their aims was participation in a governing coalition. Bonomi defended Giolitti's record of government as generally good and advised the Party to register its protest against the war and then cooperate with Giolitti to achieve domestic reform.[45]

The left Reformists caucused that afternoon. The Treves-Bussi resolution which they had presented to the Congress was modified to condemn the Giolitti government for all its previous activities as well as for the Libyan war. Ettore Reina, acting as the spokesmen for Bissolati's group, offered to support the left's resolution in return for certain modifications. Turati initially rejected the proposal, but following further discussion, the representatives of the two factions agreed upon a compromise. Modigliani and a group of followers walked out of the meeting.[46]

The compromise between the Turati and Bissolati factions broke down the next afternoon. Cabrini, a deputy and member of Bissolati's faction, urged the Congress to make a radical choice: either the Revolutionaries or the right Reformists. The session had to be suspended when he stated, "We too should be glad that victory smiles on our people's flag."[47]

Turati then addressed the meeting. Once again he tried to establish himself and orthodox Reformism as the unifying center of a Party threatened with schism. As he had at Milan, Turati laid the responsibility for the Party's troubles on the local bodies. He defended the accomplishments of Reformism while admitting they were not as great as he had hoped. Turati also justified the GPS's June 1911 decision to support the Giolitti ministry, citing the past record of accomplishments which flowed from cooperation with the Piedmontese leader.

> From 1901 to 1904, he was with us, he was sincerely and efficaciously democratic, and it would have been a crime to abandon him to the plots and furies of the reactionaries. In 1904, the general strike threw him into the arms of the conservatives; another man would probably have gone further than he did. If today he claims that the Tripoli expedition was undertaken with regret, if he invokes as his excuse "historic fatality" . . . I propose [that we] believe him sincere since Africa does not figure in his government's petit bourgeois geography.[48]

Bissolati defended his actions in an address the same evening. He reminded the delegates that he had been invited to the Quirinale by a monarch who felt it was important to know the views of the Socialist party. "I was invited. I did not go like a turncoat who leaves his ideals on the doorstep in order to ascend to power. I went as a man who carried . . . even there the total patrimony of his convictions." Bissolati recalled that he had refused Giolitti's offer of a ministry. As for the war, it was "an abstract question, a question of political philosophy." The real choice facing the PSI, Bissolati concluded, was whether it would continue to support a ministry which had the ability to enact needed reform.[49]

Five resolutions were offered on the issue of Socialist participation in power. The Basile resolution of the right Reformists instructed the GPS to continue to support the government and ensure the passage of a suffrage reform. Two left Reformist resolutions offered by Treves and Modigliani instructed the deputies to oppose the Giolitti ministry. Giuseppe Pescetti, a deputy from Florence, offered an "integralist" resolution calling for a policy of intransigence. The Revolutionaries introduced a motion condemning participation in power, reaffirming class struggle as Party doctrine, and demanding that the GPS act in a disciplined manner to carry out the will of the Party. The result of the vote on these resolutions was:

Basile	1,986
Treves	7,818
Modigliani	1,746
Pescetti	1,073
Lerda	8,594

After some hasty maneuvering behind the scenes, the Treves and Modigliani forces coalesced around the Treves resolution and staved off a Revolutionary victory.[50] Nevertheless, the forces of the left had scored a significant triumph.

In comparing the vote totals at Ancona with those of 1910, the decline of Reformism is obvious. In the North, the Reformists triumphed by a sizeable margin, but the combined vote total for all three Reformist resolutions of 1911 was less than that for the 1910 Turati resolution.[51] If the total vote for the Modigliani and Turati 1910 resolutions is added, the drop in Reformist support in less than one year was 30 percent. Revolutionary support rose by 25 percent over its 1910 totals.[52] The left showed a strong gain in urban areas of the Romagna. The Revolutionaries were still in the minority in urban-industrial areas in Piedmont and Lombardy. However, the support which these areas had given to the resolutions of Morgari (1908) and Modigliani (1910) indicated that they were not safe for Turati's Reformism. The decline in Reformist support in the Emilia was equally significant. Two hundred thirteen sections had supported the Turati and Modigliani resolutions in 1910. Only 137 sections supported three Reformist resolutions in 1911. Reformist-controlled large urban sections dropped from nine to seven, while Revolutionary strength grew from two to ten.

The left took control in central Italy. The sections of Tuscany had given an edge to Reformism in 1910. In 1911 they dramatically reversed their positions and voted overwhelmingly for the revolutionary resolution. Rome and Florence became the power bases of the Revolutionary camp. The Revolutionaries held their own in the Southern mainland, but Party organization continued to decline, as it did on the islands. In Sicily and Sardinia, Reformist support continued to dissolve slowly without any corresponding rise in Revolutionary strength. *Critica Sociale* admitted, "The rise of 2666

[Revolutionary] votes . . . is very significant . . . given the diminished number of delegates.[53]

Declining Party membership was of limited significance so long as the size of the Revolutionary faction remained stationary. It became extremely important with the Reformists split into three camps and the Revolutionary faction growing.[54] Of even greater significance, the Revolutionaries had an increasingly firm hold over the support of their sections. Between 1906 and 1911, the ability of the left to retain the support of sections rose independently of the faction's vote totals (see table 10). The Revolutionaries' growing ability to retain their support was a key factor in their eventual triumph.[55]

THE TRIUMPH OF THE LEFT, OCTOBER 1911–JULY 1912

The Congress of Modena was a frustrating experience for all the factions. The Revolutionaries had won a plurality but lacked a majority, enabling the Reformists to deny them victory with last-minute maneuvering. The Reformists were still numerically the largest group within the PSI but had lost their unity. All factions looked to the upcoming regular Party Congress in Reggio Emilia to break the deadlock.[56]

Anticipating that next test of strength, *Critica Sociale* analyzed the 1911 vote and concluded that the Reformists' situation was perilous:

These figures confirm our easy prediction of Revolutionary growth following the journeys of Bissolati to the Quirinale and Giolitti to Tripoli. . . . Certainly, the absent and non-voting—about 8000—were almost all Reformists. It is their custom! So, as things go, the total of anti-Revolutionary votes (12,632) overcame by 4029 the votes of the Revolutionaries (8594). And, if as honesty requires, we subtract the 1986 ministerialist [Bissolati] and the 1073 integralist . . . the advantage . . . is reduced to less than a thousand. A very unstable equilibrium.[57]

TABLE 10
Section Retention Rate

Year	No. Voting Revolutionary	Previously	%
1906	50	—	—
1908	178	10	5.6
1910	205	50	24.4
1911	235	106	45.1

SOURCE: PSI, *Resoconti dei VIII, IX, X, XI congressi.*

Turati had a strategy to deal with this threat: forming a coalition between the left Reformists and the more moderate elements in the Revolutionary camp led by Lerda. Negotiations between the factions broke down because Lerda insisted that Turati make a complete, public break with Bissolati. A second effort at reaching an accommodation with Lerda just prior to the Reggio Emilia Congress also failed. The left was able to patch over their differences. Realizing that the left coalition remained fragile, Turati hoped to undermine it by adopting their unifying principle: parliamentary opposition to the ministry. He also stressed a common commitment to antimilitarism, anticolonialism, and pacifism between the left Reformists and the moderate Revolutionaries. If Lerda agreed to an alliance, Turati planned to eliminate the two extreme factions (Bissolati and the far left) from the Party.[58]

Turati misjudged the opposition. A fundamental change in attitude was taking place within the PSI. In 1898–1900, the victory of the Reformists signaled the dominance of the middle-class specialist—the journalist and the deputy—within a cadre party. The views championed by Lazzari appeared out of date in part because Lazzari and the other chiefs of the operaist current were incapable of doing the specialized work demanded of leaders of a cadre party. The struggles which pitted the Reformists against Integralists and Syndicalists between 1900 and 1908 were battles for supremacy of a cadre party by rival factions of middle-class specialists. By 1911 the cadre party was slowly becoming obsolete. A growing element of the working class, through the CGL, had demonstrated that it was ready for a new style of political organization which would base itself on their growing numbers. Bissolati recognized this and tried to build a labor party. Some of the Revolutionaries, too, understood this development. While most of the older generation of the Revolutionary leadership were ex-artisans or members of the middle class, the younger leaders, many of whom came from working-class backgrounds, were more closely attuned to the proletariat's outlook and interests.[59] They opposed the concept of a highly disciplined movement to a party with multiple independent power centers built by the Reformists. The Young Socialist Federation became the training ground of a new generation of working-class editors, propagandists, intellectuals, and eventually deputies. This development diminished but did not immediately eliminate the Party's need for middle-class specialists. Nevertheless, the independence which their scarce talents afforded men like Turati and Bissolati was becoming a burden to a working class whose potential strength lay in disciplining its numbers. The clash of Reformist and Revolutionary over the strategies of class collaboration or intransigence, reflected a deeper struggle of value systems: of middle-class individualism against the discipline of the working classes. The struggle that climaxed between October 1911 and July 1912 was both the triumph of one ideological outlook over another and of an as-yet poorly articulated working-class political organization over the middle-class cadre party.[60]

The Revolutionaries firmly rejected Turati's approaches. They had no interest in a deal. Even before the Modena Congress, they had turned down the suggestion of an alliance with the left Reformists. In January 1912 as Turati and Treves pressed for an alliance, Lerda scornfully observed, "[Turati] has returned to us like a fatherless son . . . repenting the evil done. Quite ready to relieve himself of the baggage and the responsibility for the old doctrine and tactics."[61]

The left opted to battle all the Reformist factions. Meeting immediately after the Modena Congress, the Revolutionary delegates voted to continue publishing *La Soffitta;* to collect an even larger campaign chest; and to single out Bissolati, Bonomi, Cabrini and Podrecca, all deputies and right Reformists, as special targets. They acted speedily to ensure the continued existence of their paper. A lack of funds, the traditional nemesis of the socialist press, threatened to put *La Soffitta* out of business. A November 1911 meeting of the Central Committee imposed a special contribution on all members of the faction.[62]

Meanwhile, the Revolutionaries kept up a steady pressure on both the *Direzione* and the parliamentary group to prevent either from giving support to Giolitti. After initial success, the Italian army's drive inland from the cities of Tripoli had bogged down. With the Italian advances stymied, Giolitti's government decided to expand the war into the Aegean Sea to force European great-power intervention in favor of a quick settlement and build pressure on the militarily weak Turkish government to capitulate. Knowing that Bissolati favored a compromise peace based on the status quo, the Revolutionaries feared that he would talk the *Direzione* into a deal with Giolitti. The Socialist International also suspected that the *Direzione* was ready to compromise. The two groups applied various sorts of pressure to the *Direzione* and parliamentary group to check any defection from a policy of total opposition to the war. Revolutionary-dominated sections passed resolutions demanding a firm stand against the war. The Central Committee issued repeated warnings of the dire consequences of any deviation from the Party's stated policy of total opposition to the Libyan adventure. The left organized mass demonstrations against the war designed to put some backbone in the irresolute Reformists. The International demanded an accounting of the PSI's actions and repeatedly criticized the Party's inability to mount an effective opposition to the war. Prodded by the Revolutionaries and the International, the *Direzione* maintained its stand against the war. However, everyone was aware that the real crisis would come when the Socialist parliamentary delegation met to decide its course of action.[63]

Giolitti launched the war during a parliamentary recess and governed throughout the fall and early winter by means of royal decrees. He planned to achieve a quick victory and present parliament with a fait accompli. He apparently calculated that he could then pay off the left with promised reforms. Giolitti decided in early February to recall parliament to sanction his war and put added pressure on the Turks to capitulate. The first bill to be laid before the new session of the Chamber of Deputies was an act formally annexing Libya.

The GPS met in Bologna on February 8, 1912, to map its strategy for the new parliamentary session. The deputies agreed that the group's policy would be opposition but that each deputy was free to support Giolitti. *La Soffitta* reacted violently to this betrayal of Party unity and discipline, stating that a decision to give each deputy individual autonomy made the group's previous decision to oppose Giolitti meaningless.[64]

Parliament reconvened on February 22, 1912. At a preliminary caucus of the GPS, the deputies discussed their strategy for a response to the traditional speech from the throne outlining government policy and to the Libyan debate which would follow. Turati and Prampolini introduced a resolution calling for "clear and forceful intervention against the war" and for discipline within the group. Bissolati responded that he could not agree, and the GPS rejected the Turati-Prampolini motion in favor of a weaker one which expressed the Socialist party's opposition to the war.[65] In the parliamentary debate, Bissolati not only took a divergent line but associated part of the group with it:

> Voting against the decree, I and the colleagues whom I represent separate our responsibility from that of the government and the great majority of the Chamber. We do not intend to utilize our dissent as a means of liberating ourselves from the duties of national solidarity which the gravity of the moment imposes on us. (Approval) We must also recognize that the Libyan expedition, which we believe is an error that will cost Italy dearly, was the result of a movement which, except for that part of the working class belonging to the Socialist Party, swept up the entire nation in a single impulse. (Approval).[66]

The Bissolati statement virtually aligned his faction of the GPS with the majority supporting the war. On an initial voice vote over the government's war policy, a unified GPS voted with the opposition. On a later secret ballot, thirteen Socialist deputies voted for a decree of annexation. Turati admitted, "The Socialist Parliamentary group, which mirrors the Party, is irremediably split."[67] Then on March 14, 1912, Victor Emmanuel narrowly escaped an assassination attempt. Bissolati, Bonomi, and Cabrini hurried to the Quirinale to congratulate the king on his escape. Mussolini expressed widely felt sentiments:

> We know better than to be scandalized by the fact that the honorable Bissolati, Cabrini, and Bonomi, who by now comprise an indissoluble triad of future ministers and undersecretaries of state, have felt so overpowering a need to join the cortege of monarchist deputies who rushed to the Quirinale to congratulate Victor Emmanuel III for having escaped danger . . . Bisssolati and his friends once again proved that they have crossed the Rubicon.[68]

For the left, the actions of the deputies of the GPS were the last straw. One Revolutionary leader lamented:

> The crisis and convulsions that periodically occur in the Socialist Party are almost always the result of the actions of the parliamentary group. They represent the Party and are considered its highest political expression. Despite this, the Party has no legislative means to oppose the actions taken by the parliamentary group and must modestly limit itself to platonic votes of disapproval.[69]

The Revolutionaries condemned the group, making no distinctions between Turati's faction which resolutely opposed the war and Bissolati's collaborationists. In fact, the left accused Turati and his associates of maneuvering to save Bissolati and Bonomi from the just wrath of the Party. The left demanded a purge of the parliamentary group.[70]

By mid-1912, the Revolutionary campaign to gain power at the July Reggio Emilia Party Congress and purge the right was well underway. Throughout the winter and spring of 1911–12, the left dueled with the Reformists for control of two key Party organizations: Rome and Milan. The Revolutionaries won both battles, capturing the Rome Socialist Federation in April and the Milan section in June. Meanwhile, at its May 18 meeting, the Central Committee drafted a resolution calling for the "most absolute intransigence in principle and method" and for the revocation of the GPS's autonomy. It instructed all Revolutionary sections to adopt this resolution. The Central Committee also publicly demanded the elimination of "those elements which have given repeated proof that they are outside Socialist discipline."[71]

Leaders of the faction traveled throughout Italy to inform the rank and file of their plans and encourage local efforts against the Reformist enemy. *La Soffitta* publicized every new victory for the Revolutionary resolution, giving special attention to its success in large urban sections as part of an effort to build the image of an unstoppable grass roots revolt against Reformism. The Central Committee again instructed its supporters to pay their *tessera* fees immediately. Tasting victory, the Revolutionaries were sensitive to any attempt by the *Direzione* to modify the rules of procedure for the Congress. When the rules were published, the Revolutionaries heatedly protested against a procedure which permitted the election of representatives by secret ballot, fearing it would lessen their ability to apply pressure to voters in the sections. They suspected that the *Direzione*'s decision to raise the price of the *tessera* to five lire was a Reformist ploy to limit the number of Revolutionary-controlled sections participating in the Congress. No matter what the cost, the Central Committee instructed its members and sections, they must purchase the *tessera*.[72]

By June 15, 1912, three weeks before the Congress convened, the Revolutionary faction was confident that it held a majority. The capture of the Milan section was a harbinger of Revolutionary success. This triumph was followed by the creation of Revolutionary majorities in Turin, Rome, Venice, Modena, Forli, Carrara, Pisa, Livorno, and Bari. Provincial congresses in the Romagna, the Marche, Tuscany, Latium, and Umbria also adopted the Revolutionary resolution. The columns of *La Soffitta* were filled with discussions of the specific changes that a victorious left would implement once it had triumphed, particularly the reorganization of the *Direzione*. Vella admonished the paper's readers that they must be ready to accept the increased responsibility that accompanied leadership of the entire Party. They must also find a means to permit the defeated Reformists "to express [their] ideas in a dignified manner."[73]

While the Revolutionaries debated their post-Congress policy, the left Reformists were appraising the ruins of a policy. Turati reaffirmed his commitment to complete parliamentary intransigence. Treves urged the left Reformists to recognize that the split with Bissolati's faction was final. Giovanni Zibordi wrote a series of pieces in *Critica Sociale* attempting to exorcise Bissolati's demon and establish where the Reformists' erred. He concluded that neither the war nor Bissolati's trips to the Quirinale had caused the rupture in Reformism. They had been signposts along the path toward participation in government by the right. Faith in the possibility of cooperation with Giolitti and the middle classes had "deformed" Reformism.[74]

The left Reformists recognized that a policy of intransigence was "inevitable." A disillusioned Turati lamented that Reformism had been "too much a larva; a word; a method lacking tenacious and concrete application. Parliamentary action was almost always an illusion. Passing to intransigence is a symptom rather than a cure, but apparently must take place."[75] Prampolini sadly added that expelling the right from the PSI was inevitable.[76]

Having embraced intransigence but rebuffed in their efforts to coalesce with the more moderate Revolutionaries, the left Reformists were without a distinctive program, without workable options, without hope. They reminded the rank and file of the former failures of the left and plotted to retain control of *Avanti!*. On the eve of the Reggio Emilia meeting, Treves glumly noted that the Congress "has become something of a trial in which the Reformists are the accused and the Revolutionaries have the role of the public prosecutor." Echoing Turati, he insisted that "we must distinguish between the theory [of Reformism] and those who practice it. Reformism is the valid tactic of the Socialist Party."[77]

Reformism was politically bankrupt. The war fully uncovered its weaknesses. The Reformists' refusal to adapt their political strategy and mobilize the working classes left them without viable options when Giolitti attacked Libya. They declined to push a political general strike beyond symbolic protest. Dignified parliamentary criticism of the invasion was a sterile alternative because Giolitti had the votes to annex Libya and to pay for continued military operations. He confidently told King Victor Emmanuel that Socialist opposition to the war would be of "no importance."[78] Faced with the evidence of the impotence of Turati's strategy of parliamentary and class cooperation, Reformist support began to melt away within the PSI.

8

Consolidating

Power,

1912–1914

REGGIO EMILIA

Reggio Emilia had special meaning for Socialists of all factions. The Socialist party had taken form there twenty years previously. The local Party organization was a model of what agrarian socialism could accomplish. For the left, it was the city where in 1893 the Party voted for policies of intransigence and a disciplined GPS. For the Reformists, Reggio was the ultimate stronghold. In July 1912 Reggio was the city where the Reformist era came to its end.[1]

The atmosphere in which the Congress met was electric. For the right Reformists, the Congress meant the end of their participation in the PSI. The left Reformists, facing certain defeat, hoped to emerge with a few concessions, above all with continuing control of *Avanti!*. The left knew its hour had arrived and was determined to revenge itself and the Party on those who had betrayed the movement.

The right Reformists caucused on July 6, 1912, and decided to fight the expulsion effort. Since Bissolati's faction had already concluded that the Party was a dying organism whose continued existence only hampered the development of a truly representative labor party, why stay and fight? The Syndicalists had abandoned the Party when they recognized that it no longer served their needs. The right could not realistically expect to avoid expulsion since many of the left Reformists supported a purge. The decision to give battle was a last effort by the right to win a sizeable group of Reformists to their views. Their statements to the Congress were both defiant and dignified. They tried to win the delegates to the logic of their actions. To the last, Bissolati continued to evangelize the PSI.[2]

The Revolutionaries also caucused that evening. Vella reported a delegate count of 12,000 votes for the left. The Revolutionary delegates agreed that if victorious they would take control of *Avanti!*. Lazzari cautioned against being lured into an exhausting debate over election strategy. The left, he counseled, must concentrate its fire on the conduct of the men who had "betrayed the Party." The Revolutionaries voted to expel four: Bonomi, Bissolati, Cabrini, and Podrecca. They elected Agnini, Bacci, and Lazzari as their representatives in the Congress presidency.[3]

Lazzari presided at the initial session of the Congress on the morning of July 7, 1912. The Revolutionaries and left Reformists split the presiding officers almost evenly among themselves, freezing out the right. Rosetti and Ciotti read the reports of the *Direzione*. They informed the Congress that dues payments had dropped another 2000 in the previous two years. Vella attacked the performance of the *Direzione,* accusing it of weakness for its failure to respond adequately to the International's calls for effective action to halt the Libyan war. He lashed out at the GPS for its indiscipline.[4]

Following this session, the left Reformists caucused. Over 200 delegates attended, evidence that Reformism remained a powerful force. Confusion reigned in the ranks of the left Reformists. They were unable to decide how to respond to the Revolutionaries' demand for expulsion of the four deputies. After a prolonged debate, the delegates reaffirmed their support for policies of parliamentary intransigence and for a vigorous campaign against the government in upcoming national elections.[5]

The debate on the *Direzione*'s conduct during the Libyan crisis continued on July 8. Montemartini then read the report of the GPS. It was a confession of failure: admitting that the group had no cohesion, no means of imposing discipline, and no program. Montemartini disingenuously laid the blame for the indiscipline at the feet of the group's two Revolutionary members: Agnini and Morgari. He claimed that their decision to break with the GPS undermined its ability to discipline the rebellious right Reformists. Lazzari responded that indiscipline had been a characteristic of the GPS for twenty years.[6]

Agnini was the presiding officer when the Congress reconvened at 2:10 P.M. that afternoon. He recognized Mussolini and the trial of Reformism began. After condemning parliamentary democracy as useless, Mussolini presented a resolution condemning the group, revoking its autonomy, and expelling Bissolati, Bonomi and Cabrini. In a piece of effective stage management, a delegate then shouted out the name of Podrecca. Mussolini replied that he would gladly add him to the list. Podrecca protested furiously.

Mussolini replied that he had no personal animosity against any of the men targeted for expulsion:

> I accuse the Bissolati of 1912 with the words of the Bissolati of 1900 . . . "We must avoid the incoherence of the other political parties in Italy, we must be disciplined." . . . We are liberating you the accused to follow your own path. Bissolati, Bonomi, Cabrini and the others . . . can go to the Quirinale, even to the Vatican if they wish, but the Socialist party declares that it is not disposed to follow them, not today, not tomorrow, never. (Lively and prolonged applause).[7]

Cabrini was the first of the accused to face the hostile Congress. As he spoke many delegates derisively sang the royal anthem. Admitting he would not escape condemnation, Cabrini tried to "widen the discussion from our personal action to the question of the direction and goals" the Party should choose. He defended the parliamentary action of the right and urged the delegates to accept diversity within the PSI.[8]

Bonomi followed Cabrini to the docket. Ignoring the issue of his past actions, he concentrated on the larger question:

> The case you are asked to judge is not a question of the crisis of a few individual consciences, but rather the crisis of two conceptions: Revolutionary and Reformist. . . . Expulsion is not . . . a disciplinary action against a few dissidents, but . . . the separation of two methods, two conceptions, two modes of interpreting socialism. Thus, from this time on, there will no longer be one Italian Socialism but a Revolutionary Socialism and a Reformist Socialism. . . . While we Reformists of the right have an open view of society and of the Party, you men of the left are the champions of dogma, [acting] under the illusion that the expansion of the Party depends on the purity of dogma. . . . We believe that the rising force of the proletariat makes this the period to reform, you hold after Libya no reform is possible. In a few words, you restrict yourself to opposition, we enlarge ourselves in action.[9]

Bissolati spoke to the Congress the following morning. Once again, he stressed that the demand for expulsion was a clash of opposing conceptions of socialism. Socialism, he reminded his listeners, consisted "not only in its ends but in the means which produce change." As for Socialist participation in power, only a small distinction existed between the power the Party wielded in parliament and that of the executive. Turning to the war, he reminded the delegates that "I too opposed the decree of annexation." Interruptions broke out on the floor and Bissolati left the podium. Lazzari pleaded for order. Returning to the rostrum, Bissolati claimed that the right's contribution to the PSI had been introducing realism into its debates:

We can not abolish arms, but we can reduce them . . . We felt that leaving pa-
triotism in the hands of the Nationalists would seriously harm the liberalization
of the Italian state and the Party's work. This is what your intransigence in the
face of the war is accomplishing. . . . If I had been allowed to enter the ministry
it is possible that there would have been no Libya. I regret I did not join the
ministry.[10]

After hearing the statements of the right Reformists, the delegates debated their punishment. Turati, while condemning the acts of the right,
warned the Congress that it was "neither a church nor an ecumenical council." Both Turati and Riena, who followed him, urged the right to recant
and return to the fold. The Revolutionary spokesman, Francesco Ciccotti,
rejected a reconciliation. "Discipline must be maintained. We do not withdraw the Mussolini resolution." The possible expulsion of the four deputies
was put to a vote on the evening of July 10, 1912. Three resolutions were
tabled. The Mussolini resolution expelled the four, the Modigliani resolution stated that the right had placed themselves outside the Party through
their actions, and the Riena resolution simply deplored their acts. The right
rejected any censure and urged its supporters to abstain. The results of the
vote were:

Mussolini	12,556
Modigliani	3,250
Riena	5,633
Abstentions	2,027

Later that evening the four expelled members met with eight other deputies
and founded the Italian Socialist Reformist party (PSRI).[11]

The vote on expulsion produced the absolute majority which the Revolutionaries had sought since 1906. Eight months earlier they had won 37.5
percent of the vote at the Modena Congress. At Reggio Emilia they captured 53.5 percent of the vote and a bare but absolute majority (50.24 percent) of all the sections voting. In the North the Revolutionaries had the
support of the nation's two major industrial centers, Turin and Milan, and
doubled their vote in Lombardy and the Veneto. Their support in Piedmont
and the Emilia Romagna increased by 50 percent. Even the Reformist
stronghold of Emilia cracked slightly when four sections supported Mussolini's resolution. In central Italy, Revolutionary strength remained at the
high levels it achieved in 1911. The left Reformists picked up support in
Tuscany. In the mainland South, however, support for the Revolutionaries

almost doubled, while backing for the left Reformists was virtually nonexistent. The right Reformists won the support of seven sections in the South. Altogether, the Right managed to equal its total vote at the Modena Congress. Bissolati's efforts at persuasion had clearly failed to win a majority. So had Turati's attempt to form a new center. The two left Reformist resolutions presented at the Reggio Emilia Congress received a total of 36.8 percent of the vote, a drop of almost one-quarter from the support orthodox Reformism enjoyed at the Modena Congress. One hundred forty-seven sections that had not participated at the Modena Congress returned to vote at the Reggio Emilia meeting. They voted overwhelmingly for the Revolutionary resolution. Finally, the Revolutionaries' effort to turn out their vote paid off. Sixty percent of the sections which had voted for the Revolutionary resolution at Modena returned to support the left at Reggio Emilia. Reggio Emilia was the triumph of a disciplined party machine.[12]

The left consolidated its victory on the fourth day of the Congress. The new majority approved a resolution which praised Treves's work with *Avanti!* and instructed the new *Direzione* to take charge of the financial problems of the paper. The Congress then approved a Lerda resolution which forbade the GPS to support the program of any government and made opposition to the government a key element in the Party's platform for the upcoming general elections. The Reformists had put the question of the dissolution of the FGS on the pre-Congress agenda. Lazzari confirmed the Revolutionaries' support for the Young Socialists. The *Direzione* assumed direct supervision over FGS activities. Finally, the Congress elected an all-Revolutionary *Direzione* and appointed Giovanni Bacci to succeed Treves as director of *Avanti!*.[13]

In the wake of its success at Reggio Emilia, the left faced a great challenge: utilizing their triumph while maintaining their unity. The Reformists were surprisingly content with the results of the Congress. Turati commented, "The congress of Reggio Emilia represents an integral step . . . toward . . . socialist Reformism . . . a . . .concentration toward the right." He was unconcerned by the triumph of the left because "revolutionism has always been little more than a verbal montage." Turati made the obvious point that intransigence and revolution were not the same. Adopting intransigence as a parliamentary tactic did not imply accepting the rest of the left's program: "Revolution was the name; intransigence was the fact." Turati could live with intransigence for the time being. The new *Direzione,* however, had a much wider view of its mandate and was determined to force the Reformists to conform with its programs.[14]

DISCIPLINING THE PARTY

The Revolutionary coalition existed on the basis of a common agreement among its members that the Party must be firmly disciplined and maintain a net separation from the political parties of the middle class. The left Reformists had accepted the need for a policy of parliamentary intransigence prior to the Reggio Emilia Congress. When Bissolati and those favoring continuing collaboration with the middle classes were expelled, the left lost one of its unifying grievances. With all Socialists in accord on intransigence, the imposition of a firmer discipline had to be the policy that held together the unstable Revolutionary coalition. The left's long record of factional infighting indicated that the coalition would hold together only if it succeeded in its objective of disciplining all areas of the Party. The left Reformists were waiting for the latest left coalition to dissolve in order to create a new center bloc. Turati hoped to repeat the success of 1906–8 over Ferri and Integralism by reaching an accord with Lerda. By adopting intransigence he would be in a position to capture significant support from the left if the Revolutionary faction dissolved. To prevent another round of Turati's *trasformismo*, the leaders of the left acted quickly to remove all vestiges of Bissolati's influence and to subordinate all Reformist-controlled Party bodies to the orders of the *Direzione*. In the process, they laid the groundwork for a new type of political party: one based on mass recruitment, primarily from the working classes.

The *Direzione*'s first priority was to complete the purge of Bissolati's followers begun at Reggio Emilia. The *Direzione* instructed all sections with deputies who had joined Bissolati's party to expel them or face immediate excommunication and the creation of a new Socialist party section in their territory.[15]

By August 18, 1912, all but four sections agreed to comply with the orders of the *Direzione*. The *Direzione* expelled these four sections, Genoa, Borgo S. Donnino, San Giovanni, and Ostiglia, from the Party. It ordered local Socialists to form new sections. By August 22 Genoa had a new PSI section. Meanwhile, the *Direzione* forced a number of wavering deputies to make a decision. Graziadei, the theorist of Reformist syndicalism, had attended the meeting at which Bissolati and his allies created the PSRI. After weighing his options, Graziadei affirmed his allegiance to the PSI. Alfredo Bertesi, a deputy since 1895, went over to the PSRI. The sections in his electoral college split over whether to follow him. Bertesi established a section of the PSRI, but the PSI recaptured a majority of the rank-and-file Socialists and unseated Bertesi in the 1913 elections. On October 12, 1912, another veteran Socialist parliamentarian, Adolfo Zerboglio, quit the Party and simultaneously resigned his seat. In January 1913, the *Direzione* announced its intention to carry on a special campaign against the greatest apostate, Enrico Ferri, who had aligned himself with the PSRI. By the end of 1913 almost half of the deputies elected on the PSI list in 1909 had been driven out of the Party. Most refused to resign their parliamentary seats.[16]

The expulsion of Reformist sections continued spasmodically throughout 1912–14. In January 1914, the *Direzione* expelled the section of La Spezia for cooperating with middle-class parties during the 1913 election campaign. In May 1914 the Naples section, traditionally a strong supporter of the left, voted to oppose a decision taken at the Party national Congress. *Avanti!* responded that this action put it "and its deputies out of the Party." Other sections simply left the Party. The *Direzione* demanded declarations of acceptance from the sections which had voted against the Mussolini resolution at the Reggio Emilia Congress. On August 17, 1912, it ordered all sections to confirm their loyalty to the Party immediately. Simultaneously, a purge of individual Party members was underway. In the most extreme action, the section of Piombino expelled all Reformists. The *Direzione* made no effort to protect any left Reformists among them.[17]

Bonomi later claimed that the split within the Party paralyzed the entire working-class movement. While this is an exaggeration, a real preoccupation with the right's objectives gripped the Revolutionary leadership, and with the support of the left Reformists, they conducted a thorough purge of the PSI.[18]

While the purge was continuing, the *Direzione* was rebuilding the PSI's numerical base. On July 28, 1912, the *Direzione* announced that it would attempt to recruit the men who had left the PSI prior to the Reggio Emilia Congress. Historians have usually interpreted this effort at recruitment as an attempt to pack the Party with leftists and submerge the Reformist minority in a sea of Revolutionary militants. Other indications of the Revolutionaries' intention to pack the Party were the *Direzione*'s decision to readmit Arturo Labriola and to support the ex-Communard Amilcare Cipriani's bid for a parliamentary seat in a 1914 special election. Labriola had tried to destroy the PSI and had supported the Libyan war. Cipriani was closer to the anarchists than the Socialists. However, both men were militant anti-Reformists.[19]

The Revolutionaries had their greatest success in the area of recruitment. Between July 1912 and April 1914, Party membership rose by nearly 20,000 from 28,689 to 47,724.[20] Table 11 shows the progress of reorgani-

TABLE 11
Growth of the PSI, 1912–14 (by sections)

Region	1912	1914	% Increase or Decrease
North			
Piedmont	147	177	20.4
Lombardy	132	158	19.7
Veneto	76	65	−14.5
Emilia-Romagna	317	347	9.5
Liguria	29	40	37.9
Total for region	701	787	12.3
Central			
Tuscany	134	178	32.4
Marche	29	51	75.9
Umbria	18	21	16.7
Lazio	18	22	22.2
Abruzzi	13	16	23.1
Total for region	212	288	35.9
South			
Apulia	23	35	52.2
Campania	14	22	57.1
Basilicata	3	3	0
Calabria	0	8	100.0
Total for region	40	68	60.0
Islands			
Sicily	22	10	−54.5
Sardinia	2	10	400.0
Total for region	24	20	76.2
Total	977	1163	18.7

SOURCES: PSI, *Resoconti dei XIII e XIV congressi.*

zation among the sections during these two years. Significant gains occurred in all the regions of North Italy except the Veneto.[21] Recruitment lagged in Southern Italy and on the islands. In the mainland South, the Revolutionaries added an unimpressive total of twenty-eight new sections. Gains in Sardinia were more than counterbalanced by losses in Sicily. In addition, only ten of the seventy-six new sections the Revolutionaries established in Central Italy were in its three southern provinces.

The Revolutionaries soon came under fire for their neglect of the South.[22] In 1914 barely 1500 of the Party's 47,000 members came from the South. The same pattern of distribution of members and sections existed in 1914 as it had under Reformist leadership in 1910. (See table 12.)

TABLE 12
Distribution of Sections, 1910 and 1914

Area	1910 (%)	1914 (%)
North	68.5	67.7
Central	24.9	24.8
South	4.4	5.9
Islands	2.3	1.7

SOURCE: PSI, Resconti dei XI, XIV Congressi.

The area of the Party's greatest growth was Tuscany, where it added forty-four new sections (Cf. table 11). Overall, the Party grew most in the North and North Central areas where industrialization was underway. In addition to being an encouraging sign of the renewed health of the PSI, this growth indicated that the PSI was finding increasing support among the working classes. The Revolutionaries celebrated the creation of new sections and the reconstruction of old ones as proof that they were achieving their objectives. However, the disproportion between new organizations built in the North and South underlines the mixed success they achieved. The Revolutionary-led PSI was still a party with its base of support restricted primarily to the more developed areas of the North and the better-salaried portions of the working classes.[23]

In Sicily, a stronghold of Reformist sentiment, the Socialist organizations went over to the PSRI en masse immediately after the Reggio Emilia Congress. The Sicilian Socialists held a regional congress on July 19, 1912, and voted to support the right. Led by DeFelice Giuffrida, all the Sicilian deputies followed suit. The *Direzione* initially attempted to lure the Palermo province sections back to their old loyalty. Then it issued a proclamation to the workers of Sicily to reject their old leaders and form new sections. A new PSI section was set up in Palermo in August 1912. The PSI enlisted the aid of the veteran Sicilian organizer, Niccolo Barbato, in rebuilding its organizations on the island. Early in 1913, the *Direzione* dispatched Arturo Vella, Lazzari's deputy, to the island to review the organizational effort. During his five-day fact-finding mission, Vella created a commission to investigate the loyalty of applicants for admission and reiterated the *Direzione*'s instructions that the new sections avoid any type of cooperation with other parties. The Revolutionaries called a provincial organization congress for April 17, 1913. In their efforts to re-create a Sicilian provincial organization, the Revolutionary leadership pulled out all the stops. Both Lazzari and Filippo Turati became deeply involved.[24]

The PSI lost sixteen of the twenty-two sections on the island during 1912. It created four new sections. Membership in the Sicilian regional party stood at 381 in July 1912 and at 259 in 1914. The Revolutionaries' strenuous efforts to rebuild the Sicilian party resulted in a smaller but left-wing organizaton. The island's socialist voters, however, were solidly pro-PSRI and elected six right Reformist deputies in the 1913 parliamentary elections.[25]

In addition to its emphasis on rebuilding the local organization of the PSI, the *Direzione* attempted to strengthen the power of the Party's provincial bodies over the sections. Lazzari's secretariat began drafting a revised *statuto* for presentation to the 1914 Party Congress. Even without this new document, the *Direzione* continued to work for greater centralization. It exercised the powers of intervention that already existed in the Party constitution to purge the right and to create new sections, forcefully establishing its right to pass on the ideological orthodoxy of individuals and organizations. By forcing all sections to conform with its organizational and ideological views, the *Direzione* greatly reduced but did not totally eliminate their autonomy. A number of sections, including the Revolutionary-dominated ones, continued to oppose the drive for greater centralization.[26]

Party finances were another area in which the *Direzione* intervened effectively. On August 29, 1912, Adolfo Zerbini, the Party's administrative secretary, announced that all the sections had to pay for the *tessera* by October 31 or face expulsion. No data exist on the number of sections which defied this edict or on how many were actually expelled. However, evidence that the tough line produced results comes from the increasing number of sections which paid their dues promptly. Reformist pleas for support were replaced by blunt warnings from a Revolutionary *Direzione* that had proven its ability to enforce its will on the sections.[27]

Dues payments was not the only area in which the *Direzione* established Party finances on a better footing. It utilized a variety of strategies to expand its control over the sections' finances. In the spring of 1913 the *Direzione* investigated the finances of the Bari section and expelled one of its members for mismanagement of funds. In the winter of 1913–14, the *Direzione* bypassed provincial organizations to provide cash subsidies for sections. The Revolutionary leadership also imposed special contributions on members whenever it felt that the situation justified this action. In November 1913 the Party levied a special contribution to pay for the expenses of the parliamentary election campaign. The *Direzione* also pressured the sections to pay the full subscription price of 100 lire per year for *Avanti!* in an effort to overcome the paper's financial problems.[28]

As part of the process of centralization, the *Direzione* singled out the GPS for special attention. The Mussolini resolution placed the parliamentary group under the direct control of the *Direzione*. Lazzari assumed the role of watchdog over the GPS. The new leadership had given up on the existing group. Instead of attempting to reorganize it, the *Direzione* purged it. Once this process was completed and the reduced GPS had assumed a position of total intransigence, the *Direzione* turned to building an enlarged group in the 1913 elections.[29]

One of the delicious ironies of the left's insistence on opposing Giolitti was that the Revolutionaries expected to benefit from his suffrage law, electing a larger and more "revolutionary" GPS while demonstrating the popularity of the left's version of socialism. In the winter of 1912–13, the *Direzione* drew up a list of requirements for individuals who wished to become Socialist candidates. The *Direzione* asserted its right to pass on the "fitness of the Party's candidates," and annulled a number of the selections made by local Socialist organizations. Lazzari attempted to discourage the sections' long-established practice of nominating middle-class professionals as candidates. The PSI's gains in the October 1913 parliamentary elections were solid rather than spectacular, in great measure due to the defection of so many influential deputies to the PSRI. Once the election was over, the *Direzione*'s major concern was the ideological reliability and discipline of the GPS. It was determined to enforce conformity with its instructions. On November 26, 1913, Lazzari presided over a meeting of the new parliamentary group. He lectured the deputies on the policy they would follow and read a set of directives for their conduct. He stressed that the *Direzione*, acting through Lazzari, would be the group's direct superior. The GPS could select its own secretary, who would handle the distribution of the work load and report to the secretariat. The *Direzione* would set political guidelines for the group. Every deputy was required to give one-tenth of his new salary to the Party. Finally, Lazzari reaffirmed the Party's commitment to a policy of complete intransigence.[30]

On December 15, 1913, the group published a declaration of its parliamentary objectives for the upcoming session. The GPS pledged to bring "to light the violence and fraud perpetuated by the government in the last election," and "to establish firm financial control over the government forcing it to give a full account of the costs of the war in Libya." In his report to the Congress of Ancona (April 1914), Lazzari proudly stressed the "new discipline" imposed on the GPS. Examples of the *Direzione*'s growing power over the group's composition are plentiful. On January 7, 1914, the *Direzione* ordered the newly elected deputy from Oleggio, Aurelio Sarfatti, to resign his seat for making a "declaration contrary to Party policy." Sarfatti complied with the order. In the 1913 elections Treves won seats in both Milan and Bologna. The *Direzione* instructed Treves to take the Bologna seat and backed the candidacy of Amilcare Cipriani for Treves's former seat.[31] By enforcing its will on questions of the qualifications of candidates and their selection, the *Direzione* was taking the first step toward exercising full control over the GPS. Still at issue was the *Direzione*'s ability to enforce its will on the group during the parliamentary session.

The CGL was not ignored in the Revolutionary drive to consolidate its power and establish a coordinating role over the various elements of the workers' movement. The Confederation had followed an independent line in its relations with the PSI since its foundation. The Reformists generally accepted this separation of power in return for the CGL's backing in their battles with the Integralists and the Revolutionaries. Prior to the outbreak of the Libyan war, Rigola, the Confederation's secretary general, had continued to flirt with some of the ideas championed by Bissolati, notably the concept of a labor party. Forced to choose sides by the war, the CGL came down on the side of the left Reformists.[32] However, the lure of a labor party remained strong, and at its April 2–5, 1912, meeting the CGL leadership discussed "enlarging" the scope of their political action. Rigola continued to agree with Bissolati that vigorous protests against the war played into the hands of the Nationalists. The Confederation adopted a mild antiwar resolution.[33] The vote was another indication of the strength of right Reformist views within the CGL. After the Revolutionaries took control of the PSI and expelled the Bissolati faction, Rigola announced that the Confederation would "maintain the most absolute neutrality between the two wings of Socialism."[34] Two days later, the Directive Council of the CGL passed a resolution warning union members to avoid "permitting the crisis of the political party to have repercussions in the union movement."[35]

The *Direzione* refused to accept assertions of organized labor's independence. At its inaugural session (July 12, 1912), the Revolutionary *Direzione* demanded that the CGL accept class struggle as the formula for proletarian unity. The Italian historian G. A. Pepe notes: "This certainly was not a formality: faced with the Confederation's abandonment . . . the *Direzione* . . . clearly understood that it could not permit itself to be openly opposed and defeated at the beginning of its exercise of power by the largest organization of the Italian working class."[36]

The left Reformists, who badly needed the continued support of the CGL, pressed the union leadership to disavow publicly both Bissolati and the idea of a labor party. On November 12, 1912, the Confederation complied and issued the requested statement. For the first time it had publicly accepted a limitation on its freedom of operation, a serious setback for the union's leaders and a corresponding victory for the *Direzione*. For the *Direzione* this triumph represented only an initial step. The Revolutionaries were determined to force the CGL into a subordinate position. The leaders of the Confederation were equally determined to limit the left's penetration of their domain. Both sides looked for allies. The Confederation turned to the Socialist parliamentary group. The Revolutionaries unleashed Benito Mussolini and the FGS.[37]

Acting on its own, the Revolutionary *Direzione* piled up an impressive record of accomplishment: reducing the autonomy of the sections, GPS, and CGL; streamlining and centralizing lines of authority within the PSI; purging the Bissolati faction; and building a larger movement which was united around a tactical program of electoral and parliamentary intransigence. Centralization meant bureaucratization. Here, too, the Revolutionaries took the lead. They devoted great attention to the collection of minute statistical data, built a professional corps of salaried bureaucrats to administer the PSI, and instituted a welter of new forms and paperwork. The fascination and enthusiasm with which the Revolutionaries presented proof of their progress in building a Party bureaucracy might bring a sad smile to the face of a late-twentieth-century Italian. Nevertheless, the Revolutionaries' actions in this area enabled them to increase their direct control over the movement during the Giolittian era and paved the way for the creation of a mass party in the post-World War I years.[38] One task remained before the Party renewal could be completed: the subjection of the Reformists within the Party and within the CGL.

The objective of Lazzari and the older generation of Revolutionary leaders was to place the Reformists in a position of permanent subordination within the PSI. They wanted to avoid a split with Turati's faction because the loss of the Reformists would mean an approximately 40 percent loss in members. In addition, the left Reformists, once expelled, might ally with the Bissolati faction to form a formidable challenge to the PSI's claim to leadership of the workers' movement. The *Direzione*'s major weapon in its struggles with the Reformists and the CGL was *Avanti!*. The director of the paper, Bacci, although a proven soldier in the struggle against Reformism, was not the man to handle this task. His appointment as director had been a stopgap designed to ensure Revolutionary control of *Avanti!* during the critical period of transferring and consolidating power. Bacci took a conciliatory line with the Reformists and retained Treves to assist in the paper's management. Moreover, he was in poor health and recognized the need for quickly finding a successor. When one was found, he gracefully retired to the sinecure of president of the *Società Editrice Socialista*. In its search for a new director, the *Direzione* turned first to Gaetano Salvemini, whose reputation within the Party rested on his critique of Reformism and his calls for a war without quarter against Giolitti. As late as 1914, young militants such as Antonio Gramsci, Angelo Tasca, and Palmiro Togliatti urged Salvemini to become the parliamentary candidate of the Turin section. Salvemini had made favorable comments about the Revolutionary experiment. The historian declined, telling the Revolutionaries that as chief of *Avanti!* he would give the paper a more, rather than less, Reformist orientation.[39]

After a further search, the *Direzione* selected Benito Mussolini. This choice was primarily the work of Lazzari, who regarded the young Romagnol as a protégé. Mussolini's youth, his oratorical skills, and his semiproletarian extraction made him a symbol of a new leadership. Moreover, of all the militant young leaders of the Revolutionary faction, only Mussolini possessed the journalistic experience and temperamental qualities needed for the long struggle against Reformism in the Party and the CGL. The Revolutionaries lacked men capable of matching pens with Turati, Treves, or the leaders of the PSRI. Mussolini was the exception. Although not a match intellectually, Mussolini could more than hold his own in any kind of polemical contest. The obvious and serious danger in appointing Mussolini was that in his drive to take the leadership of the Party, he would stake out his own positions, independent of the Revolutionary leadership, creating a schism within the left coalition.[40]

Mussolini was admirably qualified to lead the left's battle against the Reformists and their value system. Parliament, he wrote, "is the force which is destroying democracy in Italy. Channeling the vital energies of the Socialist movement into parliament is destroying the vigor and revolutionary potential of the movement." Elections and universal suffrage were only two aspects of the great "fraud" which the bourgeoisie tried to inflict on the working class. The PSI should participate in parliament and in elections only with the objective of using these bourgeois institutions to radicalize the masses. Any concessions that the Party won in bourgeois politics were secondary to its continuing campaign to create a revolutionary consciousness among the working classes. As for the CGL, Mussolini stated that its business was to lead the fight for economic gains. Political matters were the preserve of the Party, and it would repulse any attempt by organized labor to cross into its territory.[41]

In his inaugural message to the readers of *Avanti!*, Mussolini stated that the paper would take a new approach to the Reformists. Bacci had promoted a measure of conciliation among the divided factions of the PSI. That period was over.[42]

Mussolini brought a new style of journalism to *Avanti!*. Its marks were: incendiary headlines and editorials, a free hand to the cartoonist Scalarini, a continuous attack on Reformism, and the increasing use of the shock value of photography. The intellectual level of the paper dropped from the years of Bissolati and Treves. Livelier, less inhibited, and often sensationalistic, *Avanti!*'s sales leaped. Along with the rising sales came a major improvement in the financial status of the paper. The average daily press run for Mussolini's *Avanti!* was 60,000 copies, and sales of 100,000 copies were not unknown.[43]

The *Direzione* gave Mussolini more generous support than any of *Avanti!*'s previous directors had enjoyed. In June 1913 it forced all the sections capable of paying to buy shares in the *Società Editrice Socialista*. Under Bacci's direction, the Society gradually reduced the paper's debts, although it abandoned plans to publish two regional editions of *Avanti!*.[44]

Mussolini put his personal stamp on the Party newspaper. His first objective was to end Reformist influence on the paper's staff. He dismissed Treves from the staff within days of his arrival in Milan and canceled the contracts of other Reformist journalists. Mussolini bluntly warned potential employees that they could not accept assignments from the bourgeois press. Utilizing his new position, Mussolini quickly built up an increasingly autonomous position within the Party. *Avanti!* became the mouthpiece of an individual director to a degree unseen since the Ferri era.[45]

Like Ferri, Mussolini soon began to explore the possibility of expanding the physical plant of his empire. On May 1, 1914, he announced that the paper needed new presses and proposed establishing a special fund to cover their purchases. World War I erupted before he could realize these ambitious plans.[46]

Mussolini also introduced a new group of collaborators, primarily from the non-Socialist left: Syndicalists like Leone, Labriola, and Panunzio.

Mussolini immediately demonstrated a tendency to overthrow the traditional bounds within which the PSI had demonstrated its inability for self-renewal. This explains the divergent backing which he attracted from those who for one reason or another were interested in breaking the Party's immobility: from the revolutionary Syndicalists to Salvemini . . . to the young of FGS . . . with the sympathy and initial protection of Lazzari.[47]

Mussolini recognized that the Party's factionalized left was incapable of defeating the Reformists and taking control of the CGL. He organized his own coalition of revolutionary forces; building alliances within and outside of the PSI with the individuals and groups that wanted to radicalize Italy's politics. When combined with the growing base of support that he was creating within the PSI, especially among younger Socialists, and his control of *Avanti!*, Mussolini had an independent power base from which he simultaneously waged war on the Reformists and sought to radicalize the Party and Italian politics.[48]

While acting as the left's watchdog over the GPS and CGL, Mussolini began a protracted polemical campaign against the left Reformists. He branded them a "Trojan Horse" inside the PSI and singled out Turati, Treves, and the Genovese journalist and deputy Giuseppe Canepa, as the chief culprits. Mussolini lambasted Turati's continuing opposition to the use of the general strike in the battle against the bourgeois state. He attacked Treves for refusing to accept the idea that an elite should organize the popular revolution. Mussolini demanded that the Party "cleanse" itself of deviationists like Turati and Treves. In November 1913, he launched an independent theoretical journal, *Utopia*. Mussolini's inaugural essay stressed the need to purge socialism of the distortions created by two decades of Reformist practice. He blamed the Fabian tactics of the Reformists and like-minded movements in Northern Europe for creating a climate of passivity among all European socialist parties. The battle between Mussolini and the Reformists continued until August 1914, with the tempo constantly escalating. The Reformists were never intimidated by Mussolini. They utilized the opportunity to defend themselves and to launch a counter-offensive against the Revolutionary faction. Nevertheless, Mussolini's attacks succeeded in impeding Turati's efforts to reach a compromise with Lerda and other moderates in the Revolutionary camp.[49]

The *Direzione* had chosen Mussolini as director of *Avanti!* to reinforce its effort to organize and discipline the working classes. In January 1913 the police killed a number of striking workers at Rocca Gorga. The *Direzione*, aided by Mussolini, utilized these tragedies to tighten its control over the

173

CGL and the Reformists. A meeting of the Confederation's Executive Committee passed a strongly worded resolution condemning the killings.[50] If Treves or another Reformist had been director of *Avanti!*, the paper would have added its protest and the issue would have receded, as occurred many times over the previous decade. Mussolini had other ideas. The January 7, 1913, edition of *Avanti!* described the police as "state assassins" and charged that the ruling classes were transferring their war from Libya to Italy. The following day, *Avanti!* published the CGL's declaration and a restrained *Direzione* statement condemning Giolitti and calling for a dignified mass protest, together with a Mussolini editorial insisting that violence was "a legitimate reaction to the killings."[51]

As Mussolini continued to incite violence in subsequent editions, the Reformists condemned both the director of *Avanti!* and the government. A February 1 article by Treves in *Critica Sociale* warned that the left's increasing militancy threatened to turn workers into cannon fodder. Mussolini countered with a full-scale attack on the leading Reformists.[52]

Recognizing that he had a popular issue, Mussolini continued to attack the Reformists. The *Direzione* sent a delegation to meet with the CGL's Directive Council. The Party spokesmen informed the labor leaders that the PSI would call a general strike if further killings occurred. Unable or unwilling to directly confront the PSI leadership on this issue, the Reformists of the CGL argued that the issue of using a general strike should be put to a national referendum. They made another important concession, edging further away from their previous declaration of neutrality between PSI and PSRI, and accepted resolutions that reaffirmed the mutual cooperation of PSI and CGL and the political leadership role of the Party.[53]

Following these successes, Mussolini let the Rocca Gorga killings slip off the front page. He continued his efforts to force the submission of the Reformists and CGL to the will of the *Direzione*. He encouraged the formation of a Syndicalist union to weaken the CGL and exploited strikes in Milan to undercut the rank and file's loyalty to the Confederation's leadership. In a May 1913 speech to the PSI's Milan section, Mussolini urged the public condemnation of the CGL's leaders for failing to support a metal workers strike. The following month Mussolini and the *Direzione* called a general strike to protest the arrest of Rigola. A badly embarrassed Rigola offered his resignation to the CGL's Executive Committee, which rejected it. Surveying the growing disarray of the CGL, the *Direzione* gave it a vote of confidence, coupled with the warning to the union leadership that to enjoy the PSI's continued support organized labor must accept the Party's leadership.[54]

The Young Socialists also played a role in the effort to firmly control the Reformists. The FGS wholeheartedly supported the effort to discipline the Reformists. During the election campaign of 1913 and later in the final assault on Masonic influence within the PSI, the FGS, the *Direzione*, and Mussolini's *Avanti!* achieved a high degree of coordination.[55]

The Young Socialists' decision to take a highly active role in the 1913 election campaign was a direct result of their campaign against Masonry within the PSI. The dispute over whether a Party member could also participate in the secret activities of the Masonic lodges had long troubled the PSI. The issue cut across factional lines. Giovanni Lerda, for example, was an avowed Mason and actively defended dual membership. The Reformist Giovanni Zibordi was a fierce critic of the lodges. In the decade prior to 1913, a series of referenda produced majorities opposed to Socialist membership in the Masonic movement.[56] The Masons remained within the PSI and successive *Direzione* preferred to leave a final decision on the matter to a national Congress. Meanwhile, argument raged over the nature of Masonry and the compatibility of joint membership in the lodges and the PSI.[57]

The views of the Young Socialists were set out in a 1910 pamphlet by Guido Feroci. He attacked the lodges for their secretiveness and warned that the Masons were plotting to take over the sections of PSI. Feroci also noted that the French Masons had opposed a general strike in 1907 and favored coalitions between socialists and middle-class parties in national elections.[58] An anonymous rejoinder by a "Socialist Mason" stressed the democratic tradition of the lodge and their nondogmatic views.[59]

FGS's campaign against Masonry was in high gear by 1910. A December 1910 declaration of the Young Socialists' central committee called on PSI members to unconditionally reject dual membership in an upcoming referendum.[60] The issue remained on the Party's back burner, however, until the Revolutionary victory at the 1912 Reggio Emilia Congress. On August 3, 1912, the *Direzione* authorized another referendum on the Masonic question. Socialists were polled on two propositions: whether membership in the PSI and the lodges was compatible and whether Masons should be expelled from the Party. Bacci had already begun a campaign against the Masons when Mussolini took over the directorship of *Avanti!*. As Italian Socialism's self-appointed chief prosecutor, he acted with his customary vigor. The *Direzione,* however, decided to put off the resolution of the issue until the 1914 national Congress. Moreover, in the summer of 1913, the attention of both Mussolini and the *Direzione* was increasingly riveted on the upcoming parliamentary elections. Mussolini admitted that the Revolutionaries wanted an impressive victory in 1913 and were willing to accept the Masonic ties of candidates who could win elections.[61]

No such considerations inhibited the Young Socialists, for whom ideological purity counted more than an enlarged parliamentary group. On June 29, 1913, the FGS central committee again demanded the expulsion of Masons and coupled this with a warning to Socialist candidates that the price of Young Socialist support was accepting the FGS's position on issues like Masonry.[62] Obviously the weight that individual candidates gave FGS varied. But, the Young Socialist Federation was increasing dramatically in size and could provide eager campaign workers. Moreover, the FGS was especially strong in the industrial areas where Socialist candidates had their best chances of election.[63]

The *Direzione* appreciated the FGS efforts to get out a large vote, one of its 1913 priorities. It was equally pleased with the outcome of the balloting. The decision to place the Masonic issue on the agenda for the Congress of Ancona and later maneuvers to make it the first order of business were part of the reward FGS received for its efforts.[64]

THE REVOLUTIONARY ACHIEVEMENT

As the Congress of Ancona approached, the dominant impression of the Socialist party, one carefully fostered by *Avanti!,* was that of a confident, unified, and disciplined organization, secure in its theory and methods, leading the Italian working class forward to the conquest of the bourgeois state. Salvemini, a knowledgeable observer, reflected this outlook: "The Libyan war, liquidating the Reformists . . . and restoring the Party to its natural function has created the conditions for the rebirth of Italian Socialism. And Benito Mussolini proved to be the essential man . . . expressing and representing . . . the need for a truly revolutionary movement in our nation."[65]

In fact, internal disputes had already damaged the fragile unity of the Revolutionary coalition. While these divisions did not appear to open the way for the Reformists to recapture the Party, they seriously limited the PSI's freedom of action, and during the two great crises of 1914 would reduce it to impotence.

The Italian historian Gaetano Arfe has noted, "On the political plane . . . the left soon demonstrated its immaturity. It lacked not only men with sufficient prestige and proper experience, but also a distinctive program or even a distinctive set of ideas."[66] *Avanti!* adopted the motto, "Socialism which does not die," claiming that the PSI had passed through its crisis and that "at Reggio Emilia we finished with equivocations." The *Direzione* consistently assured the faithful that its internal reform was a success and that the PSI was "in the field." The need to reassure both itself and the rank and file of the Party's vitality caused the *Direzione* to devote so much of its time to recruiting. Rising membership figures were the best assurances that the Italian Socialist party was still a viable political force. *Avanti!* played upon this theme, as did the orators at the 1914 national party Congress. Even the Reformists appear to have felt the need for this type of reassurance.[67]

Certainly the PSI found its numerical resurrection under the Revolutionaries. However, the left was unable to give the movement a real sense of direction. The Revolutionaries were keenly aware that they lacked a program. An August 1911 article in *La Soffitta* entitled "Our Reform Program" might have seemed familiar to many readers, since it was a restatement of the 1900 minimal program. The left, in effect, was saying that once in power, it would be more reformist than the Reformists while refraining from any deals with the middle class. Younger "orthodox" revolutionaries had little to offer in the way of a new program. In 1913, Giovanni Allevi, one of the younger Socialists, published his *Crisis of Socialism*. The book was intended as a refutation of Bonomi's *Vie Nuove* and contains a strong critique of Reformist practices. Allevi, however, never advanced beyond a critique of the right to establish a Revolutionary alternative. The overall impression created by Allevi's book was that although Reformism was an error, the left had no options to offer. Rather than a triumphant assertion of Revolutionary ideas, *The Crisis of Socialism* was a confession of sterility.[68]

The inability of the orthodox leadership of the left to provide a program for political action, to develop a Revolutionary alternative to Reformism, or even to advance beyond the goals of the minimal program opened the way to more radical leadership. The leading radical was *Avanti!*'s director, Benito Mussolini. An undoubted revolutionary, Mussolini was not an orthodox Marxist. He was strongly influenced by syndicalism. As late as 1909 Mussolini called himself a Syndicalist. He regarded syndicalism as an advance over socialism in its concepts of political organization, its stress on mobilizing mass participation, and its analysis of the role of elites in leading a revolution.[69]

Mussolini's personal experiences, particularly his success as the leader of the local socialist organizations of Forli and his rapid rise to national prominence, stimulated his ambition to seize the leadership of the Party. Aware that he possessed unusual talents as a journalist and orator, Mussolini was intent on crystallizing his support among both the masses and the Party's elite.[70]

Mussolini was convinced that an elite had to direct the masses toward a successful revolution. These beliefs made him a confirmed enemy of both Reformism and more moderate factions within the Revolutionary camp. While traditional Revolutionary leaders like Lerda and even Lazzari accepted a limited role for the Reformist minority in a disciplined PSI, Mussolini viewed Turati's faction as a roadblock to radicalization of the masses. His objective was to destroy Reformist influence with the masses and simultaneously drive them out of the PSI. Mussolini's determination to destroy alternative leadership elites extended to rival factions inside the Revolutionary coalition and to extra-Party bodies such as the Masons. Lerda was a major danger because of his association with the Masons and his tendency to seek an accommodation with the Reformists.[71]

In the campaign against the CGL, Mussolini exploited Syndicalist theories to challenge Reformist control of organized labor. In May 1913, Mussolini wrote a friend that he expected the bourgeoisie to react fiercely to political unrest, taking advantage of a weak and divided working class. He believed that the political strike could rally and unite the workers. In the late spring and summer of 1913, the workers of Milan went on strike with increasing frequency, encouraged by Mussolini. In May metal workers called a general strike in their sector of the city's economy. A June political strike enlisted the vast majority of the city's working class. A second city-wide general strike occurred in August.[72]

The Reformists strenuously opposed these strikes. Mussolini's role in them stirred up opposition in the *Direzione*. While the June 1913 strike initially enjoyed the *Direzione*'s support, Mussolini's actions went beyond the bounds of the permissible for many Revolutionary leaders. Compounding a growing dissatisfaction with Mussolini was his support for the Unione Sindacale Italiana (USI), a Syndicalist labor federation which contested the CGL's leadership of the working class. Even Lazzari objected. At the July 1913 meeting of the *Direzione*, Vella accused Mussolini of deviating from *Direzione* policy during the June strike and of creating confusion among

Milan's workers. Vella introduced a resolution censuring Mussolini's conduct as director of *Avanti!*. Agnini joined in the attack, accusing Mussolini of following an oscillating policy. Lazzari, however, continued to back the young director. Mussolini extracted a unanimous vote of confidence from the *Direzione* by offering his resignation. The left could ill afford to lose a journalist of Mussolini's talent. Moreover, *Avanti!*'s director enjoyed wide support within the PSI. A split within the Revolutionary coalition resulting from disciplining Mussolini would open the door for the return to power of the Reformists. The *Direzione* balanced off its retreat by adopting a resolution which reaffirmed its support for the CGL and instructed all PSI members to "retain their membership in the Confederation . . . the sole representative of the International Workers Association in Italy." The Revolutionary majority had rebuffed Mussolini and challenged his conduct.[73]

During the August 1913 strike, Mussolini initially was more circumspect. At first, he doubted the strike's utility. By August 9, however, his natural combativeness got the better of him, and he edged toward a call for a national general strike. Lazzari headed him off by releasing a declaration from the *Direzione* opposing any extension of the strike and instructing all PSI sections to refrain from joining it. On August 10, the Milanese workers approved a Syndicalist proposal for a national general strike. Mussolini commented that "no one has the right" to impede a solidarity strike. He also suggested that the strikers could move the Party to intervene in support by introducing political objectives into a strike which up to that point had solely economic motives. Recognizing that he had again overstepped the limits of Party discipline, Mussolini defended the CGL from Syndicalist attacks. Nevertheless, he continued to support the USI. Mussolini's support of the Syndicalist union created a serious division within the Revolutionary camp. Serrati, Vella, Lerda, Ratti, and eventually Balabanoff, Mussolini's deputy at *Avanti!*, became critics of his behavior.[74]

The *Direzione* faced opposition from other elements within the coalition. The powerful Rome Socialist Union criticized it for supporting the coalition government of Rome's republican mayor and Masonic leader, Ernesto Nathan. The Roman Socialists felt that the *Direzione* had reacted weakly to the killings at Rocca Gorga. The FGS, too, showed signs of unrest. Its leaders wanted speedy action to drive the Masons out of the PSI. Mussolini's influence over the Young Socialists was at its zenith. FGS leaders were embracing the Syndicalist views he promoted. The Young Socialists were equally receptive to Salvemini's impatient criticism of the PSI. Finally, the *Direzione*'s decision to welcome ex-Revolutionary Syndicalists such as Labriola back into the PSI created additional difficulties. The inclusion of these revisionists within the PSI augmented the mushrooming ideological confusion that had long plagued both the Party and the left.[75] By the summer of 1914, this confusion was so great that Mussolini was admonishing the strictly orthodox Lazzari:

> Permit me to manifest—if only confidentially—my total surprise at the proclamation of the candidacy of Avv. Marvasi in one of the districts of Rome. I do not have any animosity toward him, but I remind you that he has been one of the shameless proponents of the Tripoli expedition which he still defends, that he is a Syndicalist, and an opponent of parliamentary politics. I do not even know if and when he joined the Party. . . . Marvasi's candidacy is a more or less happy "contrivance" but still a contrivance. I ask you if politics in general, and Socialist politics in particular, ought to be based on contrivances. It seems this is the system from Rome south. However, the sincerity and coherence of the party go to the devil.[76]

The Revolutionary leadership continued to face serious problems from outside its ranks. The Reformists were a perpetual source of trouble from the left's perspective. In January 1913 Modigliani, who favored reducing the autonomy of the GPS, commented that while the group no longer led the Party it was still undisciplined. Less than two months later, the *Direzione* publicly appealed to the deputies for disciplined behavior. From the Revolutionary point of view, the elections created an improved group that included a higher percentage of working-class members and more leftist deputies. Even so, soon after the election, the *Direzione* was urging greater efforts in the struggle against Giolitti. In a June 1914 interview with the *Giornale d'Italia,* Mussolini admitted that the *Direzione* had to rely on the Reformist deputies because they continued to wield political clout within the Chamber. Despite the increase in Revolutionary representation, the Reformists dominated the GPS. Treves justly claimed that Cipriani's victory in Milan's sixth electoral college (district) was a result of the loyalty that he and Cabrini had created through nearly two decades of service to the section's rank and file.[77]

Treves also stressed the *Direzione*'s increasing tendency to deviate from its own rules of conduct. Cipriani's main political objective was to build a coalition between the parties of the *estrema* on one side and the anarchists and Syndicalists on the other. As a Reformist Treves was in the ironic and politically advantageous position of defending intransigence against the collaborationist tactics of Revolutionaries such as Cipriani and Mussolini.[78]

The splits within the Revolutionary camp and the embarrassing deviations by Revolutionary leaders boosted Reformist morale. As the Congress of Ancona approached, the Reformists hoped to exploit these divisions. Their main immediate objective was defensive: to prevent the left from raising intransigence from a tactical weapon to the status of Party dogma. The Reformists were also eager to capitalize on inconsistencies in the *Direzione*'s performance. Their main target was Mussolini, but the *Direzione*'s backing for candidates such as Labriola, Della Seta, and Cipriani provided inviting opportunities for telling Reformist criticism. By exposing the deviations of the left, the Reformists hoped to neutralize their past links to Bissolati—ties which still weighed heavily and negatively with the Party rank and file. Turati and Kuliscioff were revamping *Critica Sociale*. They hoped to rebuild their political base of support by recapturing the Milanese Socialist movement from Mussolini. With Milan in the Reformist camp, *Critica Sociale* reestablished as the PSI's leading ideological journal, and the Reformists' continuing to control the GPS, they would be able to reassert a leading role within the Party. Throughout North Italy, the Reformists were contesting Revolutionary control of the sections and regional organization. "Events had outrun the normal course of Italian politics," one Reformist commented, and a return to quieter conditions would permit his faction to reestablish their hegemony. Treves echoed this outlook. Peace in the Party was due to the "happy infelicity of the times." A truly reforming government, dedicated to arms reduction, would reopen the struggle for control between left and right within the PSI.[79] For now, however, the Reformists awaited the onslaught: "The disputes [at the Congress] will be between . . . those who propose to match the facts to the theory and those who propose to fit the theory to the facts.[80]

Revolutionary tactics were acceptable as long as a "reactionary" ministry held power. These conditions would not last forever. As for the growth of the Party since 1912, "We are somewhat cheered that enforced concord benefits the 'material' growth of the Party, although we are not disposed to give it an overriding value."[81]

One factor that may have encouraged Reformist optimism was the composition of the expanding PSI. Strong indications exist that the vaunted recruiting drive was producing results not totally in line with Revolutionary objectives. Historians have frequently interpreted the fleshing out of the Party after 1912 as "a throwing open of the gates of the Party to all malcontents," and the submerging of the Reformist "old guard."[82] However, an examination of three sample provinces reveals a different pattern. Two of the areas were traditional strongholds for the left, and the other, Milan, normally had a strong "revolutionary" presence. Table 13 examines the voting patterns of sections admitted after 1912 and of sections which were readmitted after the Revolutionary purge.

These figures suggest that recruitment was a goal in itself for the Revolutionaries, that they were not able to pack the PSI with "malcontents" who agreed with their views, and that the Reformists were in a position to recapture the Party if the political climate changed favorably.

There are other indications that the PSI's enlarged membership was not overwhelmingly leftist. All the sections of Teramo province (Sicily) broke with the PSI after Reggio Emilia. The Revolutionaries readmitted them on their promise to support an intransigent policy. At the Ancona Congress, these sections voted for a Reformist resolution on local elections.[83] Finally, the size of the PSI declined in the areas where the Revolutionaries were able to enforce an ideological hard line. In Sicily, the PSI lost 16 sections and about 130 members. In Parma, the Revolutionaries made a major effort to rebuild local organizations after the Reggio Emilia purge. They enjoyed limited success. (See table 14.) Revolutionary representatives built new sections quickly, but the provincial Party was smaller than in 1912.

The Parma PSI declined notably after the Syndicalist-led agrarian strikes of 1908 split the local labor movement. Within three years, however, the

TABLE 13
Voting Patterns in New and Readmitted Sections, 1914

Province	No. Sections	No. Sections Voting Revolutionary
New Sections		
Milan	8	2
Ravenna	10	7
Foggia	9	1
Total new sections	27	10
Readmitted Sections		
Milan	4	0
Ravenna	8	6
Foggia	2	0
Total readmitted sections	14	6
Combined Total	41	16

SOURCE: PSI, *Resoconto del XIV congresso.*

TABLE 14
Voting Pattern in the Parma Socialist party, 1908–14

Year	Sections	Members	Voting Revolutionary
1908	19	482	1
1910	9	213	0
1911	14	289	0
1912	15	312	0
1914	9	242	5

SOURCE: PSI, *Resoconto dei X, XI, XII, XIII, XIV congressi.*

Reformists had rebuilt the local organization. The Revolutionaries' purge undercut these efforts.

The success of the Revolutionaries' recruitment efforts revealed another critical weakness. Lazzari and his generation of Revolutionary leaders were unable to understand the political value of bringing the masses into the Party. In January 1914, Lazzari noted, "Those approximately one million electors distributed throughout every part of Italy, who have supported our program by voting for our Party's candidates in the recent elections, must be our greatest preoccupation in this new year. Certainly we cannot think of mobilizing all those one million electors in new sections of the Party. Only our comrades in Germany can."[84]

The older generation of Revolutionaries shared a common conceptual frame of reference with their Reformist opponents. Both factions looked for the distant triumph of socialism. They viewed the Party as a small body of activists whose job was to win concessions for the Italian masses who as yet were incapable of mature political action. They paid great attention to the activities of the GPS because they believed that parliament was the stage upon which the latest act in the struggle of working class and bourgeoisie was being played out. As a result, the older generation of Revolutionary leaders was eager to promote reform through parliamentary action. The triumph of the left altered the tactics employed by the Party in the Chamber of Deputies but not its concentration on parliament.[85]

The attitude of many of the younger Revolutionaries, best exemplified by their hero, Mussolini, was different. Commenting on the 1913 elections, the future leader of Italy's first successful mass movement, wrote:

Tomorrow, we have a single duty: . . . to attenuate in Socialist economic and political organization the too evident and strident disproportion between the effective contingents of the Party and the number of its votes.

It is not enough to collect votes in mass, it is necessary to collect new recruits for the party and for the organizations of [the working] class. A serious and large Party organization renders election contests less dependent on contingencies. The ideal is not the Socialist voter but the voting Socialist. As many Socialists as electors. This is perhaps an unreachable goal, but we must direct all our forces toward it.[86]

Mussolini recognized that the PSI could not bring all workers and peasants within its organizations. He believed that it could build a mass-based working-class organization incrementally. Noting the Party's 1909 vote, he commented that the PSI was capable of enrolling one of three Socialist voters to create an organization of 100,000. The next step was building an organization of about 1 million members, the size of the German Social Democrats (SPD). This size organization would be capable of rallying the support of the 20 million Italian workers and peasants. Replying to Reformist criticisms of Revolutionary emphasis on increasing the Party's membership, Mussolini stressed that rather than building a large number of sections with small membership, he wanted to create a party with a mass base in both the cities and the countryside.[87]

Mussolini believed that the key to mobilizing mass membership was creating political consciousness by identifying the Party with the interests of the masses. The bourgeois state used force to control the masses. The PSI must be willing and ready to meet state violence with force. By utilizing force, the Party could simultaneously win the loyalty of the masses, radicalize them, and turn them into a disciplined and powerful political force.[88]

Mussolini's call for different tactics and a new type of political organization struck a responsive chord because the Party's political base was undergoing important changes. In the wake of one and a half decades of accelerating industrial development, the working class component of the PSI was becoming more involved in Party affairs. The Reformists built their predominance on the agricultural workers of the Po Valley, the middle class, and the skilled workers of the small factories. From 1900 to 1912, the industrial proletariat in Turin, Genoa, and Milan swung between support for Reformism and the various left-wing currents. By 1912, newer, large-scale mechanical industries, such as automobiles, together with supporting industries such as rubber, petroleum, and steel, had developed in the North. Over 1 million Italians were employed in industry in Piedmont and Lombardy. Companies involved in textiles, chemicals, shipbuilding, construction, electricity, and transportation were also becoming large-scale employers. These new industries, employing large numbers of skilled and semi-skilled workers, broke the older type of relationship between employers and workers. Labor-management relations became more confrontational, and a true industrial proletariat emerged. The economic slowdown that began in 1908 hit the newer industries with special force. As these companies began to lose profitability, they cut the work force and attempted to roll back wages. Hardline corporate policies produced a wave of strikes that hit a peak in 1913 when 810 industrial strikes, involving 385,000 workers, took place.[89]

The emergence of an industrial proletariat as an important constituency within the PSI coincided with the industrial slowdown of 1907–13 and with the political and social polarizaton of Italy. The Libyan war accelerated this polarization. Spokesmen for the proletariat also emerged: young socialists such as Antonio Gramsci and Angelo Tasca in Turin, who sought to interpret the proletariat's demands to the Revolutionary leadership.[90]

Mussolini's vision of a new type of political movement had great appeal for these young socialists and to the radical groups led by Amadeo Bordiga in Naples and Nicola Bombacci in Rome.[91]

The young Revolutionaries for whom Mussolini was both prophet and spokesman and the older generation differed in their conception of the political party. Lazzari, Lerda, and their generation were attempting to create a sort of cadre party of the left, a small PSI, employing the tactics of intransigence to win concessions from parliament. The young Revolutionaries were anxious to build a mass party that could use its numbers in the streets and polling places to extract concessions from the middle classes while preparing itself for a revolutionary seizure of power.[92]

Mussolini, in particular, held fundamentally different views of political strategy and organization from those of the older Revolutionary leaders. He believed that revolution was the work of elites but also recognized that overthrowing the Italian state meant utilizing the numbers and discipline of the working classes. The elite would achieve a revolution by first building a disciplined mass movement. Once the masses had been thoroughly trained to follow orders, the political party could move from demanding concessions to seizing power. The Socialist party's initial objective had to be expanding its membership base in order to create the necessary identification between the elite that led it and the masses who would carry out the revolution.[93]

By insisting that a political movement had its own existence, independent from its leaders and that individuals and groups must accept subordination to the party, Mussolini challenged the views of both the older Revolutionary leadership and the Reformists. At the PSI's 1914 national Congress, Mussolini, in the process of staking out his leadership claims, pointedly warned both old leadership elites that their days were numbered: "Men are instruments of the Party and the Party must never be an instrument in the hands of men. The supreme act of intelligence is recognizing that each [of us] has his quarter hour, after which he must recognize that he cannot become a new barrier that has to be overcome, but instead must leave the way open to the new forces."[94] The fundamentally differing views of political strategy and party organization espoused by Mussolini and the young left-wing socialists created a widening gap between them and the Party's veteran leaders. When the older generation declined to either adopt new strategy and organizations or make way for new leaders, first Mussolini and then the younger leaders broke with the PSI to create new political movements.

The years 1911–14 were a watershed in the history of the Italian labor movement. The Libyan war revealed the bankruptcy of the Reformist-led cadre party. Internal Party reforms, a vastly expanded suffrage, the growth of the CGL, the emergence of a new generation of leaders, and the growing weight of the industrial proletariat brought to the fore the issues of new types of political organizations and strategy. Before exploring these alternatives, however, the Revolutionary leadership took the Party through a series of frustrating experiments with the lifeless strategy of intransigence and its cadre organization.

The Failure

of the

Revolutionary

Alternative,

1913–1914

THE REVOLUTIONARY PARTY

The changes in Party organization that the Revolutionaries introduced were grafted onto the PSI without major modifications in the structure inherited from the Reformists. The Revolutionary party remained a hybrid: a cadre party with certain of the features associated with mass-based political organizations like the SPD. The Revolutionaries introduced these features in order to discipline and control the Reformists rather than to build a new type of political party. In addition to their determination to control firmly the activities of the large Reformist minority, the Revolutionaries believed that a more disciplined party would make a strategy of intransigence workable: putting enough pressure on the bourgeois state to promote major reforms without involving the PSI in the sort of compromise that had undermined Reformism. The cadre party's demonstrated inability to achieve the left's objectives eventually led to changes in PSI organization. Younger leaders and the growing power of the industrial proletariat drove the old left to abandon its reliance on parliamentary politics and bring a large number of workers into the PSI.

The Revolutionary party of 1912–14 was a halfway house on the path to this mass organization. The basic elements of Reformist political organization remained: the national Congress, the *Direzione,* the GPS, *Avanti!,* and the sections. The Revolutionaries attempted to subordinate the sections, GPS, and *Avanti!* to the will of the majority as expressed at the national Congress by means of the actions of the *Direzione.* The Revolutionary *Direzione* did establish its control over the local organizations, over candidate selection for the GPS, and over the parliamentary group's political agenda. The left built a small permanent bureaucracy to facilitate the *Direzione*'s control over the sections and GPS. Through forced contributions and insistence on prompt, annual payment of the *tessera* fee the Revolutionaries put Party finances on a firmer footing. Building on the Reformists' efforts, they stabilized *Avanti!*'s finances and turned it into a mass circulation daily. Similarly, the Revolutionaries' never fully successful assertion of the Party's control over organized labor, undertaken to reduce Reformist power, was a significant step in the direction of harnessing the unions in a single broad-based political movement. However, in the crucial area of recruitment, the Revolutionaries betrayed their own mistrust of the masses. Like the Reformists, they concentrated on building a party of militants, leaving the organization of and ultimately control over the masses of workers and peasants to the CGL. The Revolutionary Party was more highly centralized but still lacked the degree of direct control over the masses that would permit the left to guide them toward achieving its political objectives.[1]

The Revolutionaries' factionalism severely limited the effectiveness of their policy of centralization. After wresting *Avanti!* from Reformist control, the Revolutionary leaders effectively surrendered control of the Party's national voice when they handed it over to the ambitious and talented Mussolini. The rising leader of a growing faction, Mussolini utilized *Avanti!* to indoctrinate Party members and the working classes with his particular vision of socialism. Mussolini's *Avanti!* was as independent of Party control as the journal had been under Bissolati or Ferri.[2]

Revolutionary factionalism also effectively limited the *Direzione*'s ability to impose control on any of the Party's diverse elements. Within the Revolutionary coalition, the "moderates" led by Lerda retained the tactical option of allying with the Reformist minority to build a new center majority, ending the left's experiment. As a result, the *Direzione* proceeded with caution in disciplining its own factions.[3]

The multiclass nature of both the Revolutionary faction and the PSI frustrated the left's efforts to achieve a coherent policy. Lower middle-class members played a disproportionate role in setting PSI policy. A highly radicalized coalition of government employees and artisans dominated the powerful Rome Socialist Union and consistently took hardline positions that brought it into frequent conflict with the *Direzione* over tactics. Meanwhile, the strongly left-wing Naples section, another longtime opponent of Reformist activities, insisted on autonomy in its local political operations. Eventually it broke with the PSI. The Reformists tried to widen these divisions in the Revolutionary ranks by championing local autonomy.[4]

Operating within a cadre party structure, the Revolutionaries made only limited progress toward their goals of controlling the Reformists and committing the Party to a permanent strategy of confrontation with the government. Their efforts to impose greater discipline on individual members, on the Party's constituent bodies, and on their opponents were partially undercut by the left's factionalism. Most critically, by continuing to regard political action as the preserve of a small body of Socialist militants while relying on the Party's peripheral organs and organized labor to mobilize the masses, the Revolutionary leadership put themselves and their policy in the hands of the Reformists and of Mussolini. At critical moments in 1913 and 1914, the Revolutionary leadership had to rely on the Reformist-dominated parliamentary group and labor organizations and on an increasingly independent Benito Mussolini to build support for its objectives. Both Mussolini and the Reformists had different goals. The Revolutionary leadership discovered that operating within a Reformist-built party structure limited its ability to mobilize the masses in support of its aims. Between October 1913 and September 1914, the cadre party structure severely limited Revolutionary options and ensured Reformist independence.

INTRANSIGENCE ON TRIAL

The period between the Congress of Reggio Emilia and the October 1913 national elections was marked by intense activity within the PSI. The Party's interventions in Italian politics were spasmodic, consisting primarily of Mussolini's repeated backing of strikes. The GPS, its numbers halved and without a program, was incapable of mounting a consistent opposition to the Giolitti ministry. In the year that followed the trauma of Reggio Emilia, Giolitti brought the Libyan war to a successful conclusion and guided his reform legislation through parliament. He then turned to the nation to renew his mandate to govern.

The electoral campaign of 1913 marked the reemergence of the PSI as a cohesive force. *Direzione*, FGS, *Avanti!*, Revolutionaries, and Reformists cooperated in the struggle against the man who had led Italy into Libya. The results of the election pleased all factions. The Revolutionaries saw the nearly 900,000 votes and fifty-two seats garnered by the PSI as a vindication of their leadership. The majority of the newly elected deputies were Reformists.[5]

The 1913 elections, the first under expanded suffrage, confirmed that the PSI was a northern movement with a growing working-class base. In 1913, the PSI presented 312 candidates in Italy's 508 electoral colleges. The vast majority of the candidates ran in the colleges of North and Central Italy. At the time of the elections, the PSI had only 78 sections south of Rome and approximately 1000 north of the capital. The Party collected its largest vote totals in strongly working-class districts.[6]

In the first round of voting, on October 26, 1913, the PSI elected thirty-six deputies and had thirty-four other candidates eligible for runoff elections the following week. Despite its concerns about the PSRI's ability to make inroads among its voters, the Party backed a small number of Socialist Reformists together with a few "independent" socialists against conservative candidates. The *Direzione* took this action over Mussolini's objections. Eleven of these Socialist-supported candidates won. Overall 20 PSRI deputies and 8 "independents" joined the 52 PSI deputies in the new Chamber of Deputies.[7]

In the wake of the elections, a revitalized parliamentary group went on the offensive. At the group's November 15, 1913, meeting Turati, Treves, Samoggia, and the Revolutionary deputies, Musatti and Morgari, worked out a common program of action: an assault on Giolitti's record, beginning with the demand for an investigation of electoral fraud in the South. Complimenting the group on its plans and energy, *Avanti!* joined in the attack.[8]

When the Chamber reconvened, the Socialist deputies turned the attack on Giolitti into a full-scale campaign of obstructionism. In a speech to the Party-supported Popular University of Milan, Treves explained that the struggle in Italy was between the PSI and the Nationalists, who now represented all sections of the bourgeoisie. With class differences exacerbated, the only strategy open to the PSI was to maintain its complete separation from the other parties.[9]

Treves's concentration on the Nationalist menace and lack of comment on Giolitti was extremely significant. In the conditions of political and social polarization which followed the attack on Libya, Giolitti represented the last barrier against the intensification of class warfare which both the Revolutionaries and Reformists desired, albeit for differing reasons. The era of class collaboration that began with the Zanardelli-Giolitti ministry was giving way to a decade of intense class struggle, of which the government of Antonio Salandra would be the harbinger.

In February 1914 the group intensified its efforts to topple Giolitti. On February 4, the GPS agreed to challenge additional appropriations for pacification operations in Libya. The *Direzione* lent its support by organizing nationwide demonstrations against both Giolitti and the continuing cost of colonial adventure. *Avanti!* unleashed a crescendo of articles and graphic photographic illustrations of the human and material cost of the Libyan war as part of a campaign of "War against the Kingdom of War." Giolitti rode out this onslaught. *Avanti!* called for renewed efforts to topple the government. The campaign received badly needed assistance from the Republicans and the Nationalists. They, too, were eager to put an end to the era of social tranquility that Giolitti symbolized.[10] Treves observed, "A great agony is commencing at Montecitorio; an agony comprised of many agonies; an agony which is not that of a ministry, but of an era, of a method, one could almost say of a civilization. *Giolittismo* is dying; victim of that which was its solemn double triumph: the Libyan war and universal suffrage."[11]

On March 7, 1914, the Radicals withdrew from the ministry, dealing it a death blow. For the first time since 1901, Giolitti had not resigned voluntarily. The king turned first to Sonnino and, after he declined, to Antonio Salandra to form a new ministry. The first Salandra ministry took office on March 20, 1914. The new government still had to depend on Giolitti's deputies to maintain its majority. Almost everyone expected the eventual return of Giolitti. Salandra, however, shrewdly exploited the growing polarization of the nation to preserve his tenuous position. He exploited a parliamentary system so thoroughly debilitated by Giolitti's *trasformismo* that "it could be maneuvered even against Giolitti. It proved possible to do this because the principal interest of most deputies of the majority was power."[12] Slightly more than a year later, Salandra led Italy into World War I over the opposition of Giolitti, the Socialists, and the weak-willed parliamentary majority. In the six months prior to the outbreak of war in Europe, Salandra gave the PSI what it wanted: clear-cut class warfare.[13]

During the political battles which followed the 1913 elections, the Reformist-dominated GPS took the leading role in carrying out a program favored by both currents of the Revolutionary-dominated Party. The PSI's reemergence as a significant factor in Italy's politics accompanied the reemergence of the Reformists as the Party's most influential spokesmen, underlining the serious weakness which beset the Revolutionaries. In the major political crises of 1914, the Revolutionary leadership consistently relied on the parliamentary group for the effective defense of working-class interests.[14]

The Revolutionaries' continuing strong hold on the loyalty of the Party's rank and file blocked a Reformist bid to reclaim Party leadership. The Congress of Ancona met in April 1914 and consecrated Revolutionary control of the Party machinery. The real drama at the meeting was the heated debate on the issue of Masonry that became a power struggle between two Revolutionary faction leaders: Mussolini and Lerda.

The themes of the Congress were growth, renewal, and harmony. The statistical proof was an increase of 20,459 members in less than two years. Lazzari underlined the firm discipline of the Party, citing the cases of the deputies of Turin and Oleggio, Treves and Sarfatti. Mussolini, greeted by prolonged applause, pointed to the wave of general strikes ("A record four in Milan alone") as proof of both the Party's vitality and the influence of *Avanti!*. Criticism of the *Direzione* and Mussolini was muted. Treves, in a statement strangely reminiscent of Giolitti's comments on the outbreak of the Libyan war, gave the *Direzione* grudging support. The Party's actions were the product of "historical necessity," he told the delegates.[15]

On the second day of the Congress Mussolini introduced a resolution ordering all sections to expel any members who were Masons. An angry Lerda replied by attacking Mussolini as an ideologue. Eventually, three resolutions on Masonry were tabled. The Poggi resolution stated there was no incompatibility between dual membership in the Party and the lodges. A Zibordi motion "invited" all socialist-Masons to leave the Masonic movement. Mussolini's called for a purge of the Masons.[16]

The Mussolini resolution won an overwhelming victory: 27,378 votes to 1819 for Poggi's. Lerda immediately resigned from the PSI. Mussolini had removed a powerful personal enemy and deprived the moderates within the Revolutionary coalition of one of their most effective leaders, employing an issue that cut across factional divisions and permitted Lerda's supporters to remain within the Revolutionary coalition. Angelo Ragghianti, *La Tribuna*'s specialist on the Socialist party, commented that Lerda's departure also constituted a victory for the Reformists over an old antagonist. In reality, the ouster of Lerda reduced Turati's already limited chances of creating a new center coalition to oppose Mussolini's growing dominance of the PSI.[17]

The Congress also addressed the issue of tactics for local elections. A Modigliani resolution proposed that intransigence remain the norm but that the Party grant limited flexibility to its local organizations to cooperate with the other parties of the *estrema* in specific instances. A Mazzoni resolution endorsed "flexibility" in tactics when the situation made cooperation a matter of the "general good" of the Party. A motion introduced by Ratti, reflecting the *Direzione*'s position, reaffirmed the policy of absolute intransigence in all circumstances. The result of the vote was:

Ratti	22,591
Modigliani	3,214
Mazzoni	8,584

The Reformists were anxious to avoid a test of strength on the local elections issue. Nevertheless, the victory of the Ratti resolution ended two decades of Socialist collaboration with the progressive middle class at the local level.

The left was pleased with the results of the Congress. The question of Masonry was finally settled; intransigence was reconfirmed as official Party strategy, and worker participation in Party activity had increased. Mussolini proclaimed that the factional struggle within the PSI had ended with the total defeat of the Reformists.[18]

The battle between Reformists and Revolutionaries simply took new directions. The left held the support of the majority of the rank and file and had power bases in the *Direzione* and *Avanti!*. For the moment, the Reformists accepted Revolutionary control of the Party. They retained two key power bases, the GPS and CGL, and were determined to resist further encroachments from the left.[19] The May 1914 congress of the CGL at Mantua enacted a resolution reaffirming that the "two movements [PSI and CGL] proceed on parallels in cordial and constant alliance while maintaining the reciprocal freedom of specific action."[20]

This standoff encouraged both factions to concentrate on building their power bases. By mid-1914 the chief preoccupation of the Revolutionaries was electioneering. Local elections took place in June 1914, and the Revolutionaries wanted a major success to bolster their control of the Party. The Reformists, of course, counted on a victory at the polls to solidify their position.[21]

In the midst of the campaign, an insurrection erupted in the Romagna and the violent clashes soon engulfed most of Italy. Red Week (June 7–14, 1914) surprised everyone: PSI, CGL, Mussolini, even the Ancona anarchists who helped to provoke it. Mussolini was the first to recover his poise. He claimed that the credit for the outbreak rested with the Revolutionary leadership and called for a national general strike.[22]

The reaction of the leaders of both the PSI and CGL contrasted markedly with Mussolini's opportunism. Arturo Vella, in Rome, appears to have been the first Revolutionary leader to receive reports of the outbreak at Ancona. At 10:15 P.M., June 7, 1914, he telephoned the editorial offices of *Avanti!* in Milan. The editors had no news from the Romagna. Vella declined to give them any instructions pending consideration of the situation by the *Direzione*. The next morning Vella, apparently after contacting the members of the *Direzione*, called CGL Secretary Rinaldo Rigola to coordinate the actions of the two movements. Vella asked, "What do we do?" "Strike," Rigola responded. He informed Vella that the CGL was calling a strike for the following day. Vella feared the PSI was in danger of losing its already limited control over events and had to take some dramatic act. He suggested a twenty-four-hour strike. Before taking any action, however, Vella wanted to consult with the leaders of the GPS. By the evening of June 8, the Party and Confederation had agreed on a joint declaration of a general strike. They made no decision on the duration of the strike. Vella informed Mussolini of the agreement and cautioned, "We are in accord on this point: you are not to speak of limits or no-limits to the strike."[23] *Avanti!* published the general strike declaration on June 9, 1914.

The strike had long since escaped anyone's control. By June 10, the strike was so complete that *Avanti!* was unable to publish and just barely managed to get out a June 11 edition.[24] The CGL leadership was highly upset by the uncontrolled nature of the strike and was anxious to end their active support for it. Early on the evening of June 9, Lodovico D'Aragona, Rigola's top deputy, called Lazzari:

D'ARAGONA: I would like to know if you have decided something about ending the strike.

LAZZARI: But we have hardly begun. . . .

D'ARAGONA: All right. But a number of Chambers of Labor want to know how long the strike will last.

LAZZARI: It must continue, become intense; we will see how they resolve the issue in parliament.

D'ARAGONA: All right. I want to know when you will meet and decide to stop [the strike].

LAZZARI: What stoppage! We have just begun. . . . We have to intensify it throughout Italy.

D'ARAGONA: Then I will call again tomorrow.[25]

In the early evening of June 10, the CGL issued its own call for an end to the strike. Lazzari called Rigola to request that the Confederation rescind this action. Rigola responded that many local labor organizations could no longer support the strike movement.

LAZZARI: I have sent you a telegram; can you suspend your order? . . . And you must respond that you are waiting the decision of the Party, from Rome!

RIGOLA: We must respond and say something. . . .

LAZZARI: Exactly. You must say that you are waiting. We are the ones with responsibility for this movement.

RIGOLA: But we have to think of our organizations and we have [already] sent the telegram. . . .

LAZZARI: But this telegram has put you in the government's hands. How can the deputies defend you today?

Lazzari continued to press for the reversal of the Confederation's action until an operator cut him off. He insisted that the strike had to continue because "today is a parliamentary session of extraordinary importance. . . . How can we sustain the struggle against the ministry which has been informed of your decision?"[26] In the midst of the most serious national crisis since the Libyan war, the Revolutionaries avoided provocative action, and turning to the GPS and organized labor for action, they effectively placed Party leadership in the hands of their Reformist opponents. Realizing that they lacked the ability to control the strike movement, the Revolutionaries relied on the CGL to capture control of the working classes. Meanwhile, the left relied on the Reformist-dominated GPS to exploit Red Week for the political advantage of the PSI.

For those who hoped that a new spirit and discipline existed in the GPS elected in 1913, Red Week proved disillusioning. The GPS's effort to topple Salandra failed. The group publicly blamed the failure of the general strike on the *Direzione,* charging that it had inadequately coordinated the working-class response to the events at Ancona.[27]

Mussolini, meanwhile, was again acting in an extremely independent manner. *Avanti!*'s editor was bent on pulling both the PSI and, through the Party, Italy into a social revolution. Red Week presented him with a unique opportunity to advance both the Party and Italian society toward that goal. On June 11 he ignored the *Direzione*'s call for a return to work and urged a mass meeting to continue the strike. The following day, as the strike slowly died out, Mussolini exulted, "Its intensity conferred a particular significance to the strike. It was an offensive not a defensive strike."[28]

The Reformists took a different line. Treves condemned the strike as a leaderless action that resulted in the needless deaths of workers. Even some of the Revolutionaries attacked the *Direzione* for supporting the strikes and violence of Red Week. At the June 16–17, 1914, meeting of the CGL's leadership, G. M. Serrati, an emerging force among the left's leaders, backed the Confederation's handling of the strike, claiming that the movement lacked a revolutionary character.[29]

Red Week revealed serious strains within the working-class movement. Fortunately for the Revolutionaries, the severity of these divisions was partially obscured from both the masses and the bourgeoisie. Moreover, elections under the expanded suffrage followed Red Week and the PSI did very well. At Milan, the center of the Party's effort, the PSI gained a near plurality of the vote and for the first time would nominate the city's new mayor. The choice of a Reformist, Emilio Caldera, graphically underlined the power of the minority and the left's continued reliance on the Reformists for electable candidates.[30]

Nevertheless, the election success raised the prestige of the Party leadership. The GPS resumed its parliamentary obstruction campaign in late June, providing a rallying point for all the PSI's factions. The group made a serious effort to defeat increased military expenses, an area where the Party's left and right were in substantial agreement. The *Direzione* energetically supported the deputies. By the end of June, the *Direzione* felt strong enough to mildly rebuke the CGL and sternly lecture the GPS for deviating from the Party's political line.[31]

The PSI was preoccupied with domestic political issues during the spring of 1914. The assassination of Archduke Franz Ferdinand of Austria on June 28, 1914, made little initial impression on Italian Socialists. Party press coverage of the assassination and its aftermath quickly receded. At the *Direzione*'s June 28 meeting the only foreign affairs issue discussed was a long-planned meeting with the chiefs of the Austrian Socialist party scheduled for August 22. During the first half of July, the Party's attention focused on yet another public exchange between Treves and Mussolini. The Salandra government's decision to occupy Albania should have awakened the PSI's leadership to the growing polarization of European politics. The Socialists, however, misread the import of the government's actions. The PSI was concerned that a coalition of France, Austria, and Russia was forming to impede further Italian colonial expansion. *Avanti!* expressed the hope that domestic pressure would convince Salandra to stay out of Albania.[32]

Mussolini was one of the first Socialists to correctly assess the gravity of the international situation. On July 26, 1914, *Avanti!* began to spread the alarm: war threatened in Europe.[33] The *Direzione* met the same day and issued a proclamation warning that "a new slaughter of the people is being prepared by bourgeois diplomacy." The Party's statement cautioned Salandra's government that secret pacts could not force the Italian working class to take up arms. The *Direzione* demanded that the Italian government openly state its objectives and call parliament back into session. Absolute neutrality became the rallying cry of the PSI. On July 27, the GPS met in Milan with the *Direzione*'s representatives, Ratti and Mussolini. Led by Turati, the deputies marched to the home of Giuseppe Marcora, the president of the Chamber, to present a petition demanding the immediate recall of parliament. The next day Balabanoff and Morgari left for Amsterdam, the seat of the International, to find out what action the other European socialist parties were taking to preserve the peace. On July 29, following Austria's declaration of war on Serbia, the Executive Committee of the CGL voted to follow the political lead of the *Direzione*. The Unione Sindacale Italiana and CGL issued strong statements condemning the war. In an effort to build up popular resistance to Italian involvement in the war, PSI leaders addressed antiwar rallies throughout the country. The Socialists achieved their most pressing objective when Italy formally declared its neutrality on August 3, 1914.[34]

Once the Salandra government had proclaimed Italy's neutrality, the PSI concentrated on preserving it. On August 3, the *Direzione* met, passed another resolution against the war and, noting the government's declaration of neutrality, urged the working classes to avoid any provocative action. The Revolutionary leadership recognized that Italy's neutrality was a very fragile plant. The Nationalists and other influential middle-class intellectuals were already demanding Italian entry in the conflict. The government's position remained ambiguous. The Socialists feared that any provocation by the working classes would aid the Nationalists' efforts to drive Italy into war. The *Direzione* threatened immediate action if the Salandra government violated Italy's neutrality. A policy of "neither sabotage nor support" was taking root. It would reduce the Party to impotence for the duration of the war.[35]

The war knit the entire working-class movement behind the Revolutionary leadership. On August 5, representatives of the CGL, USI, and Federterra, led by Rigola, placed their organizations under the command of the *Direzione*. The August 1 issue of *Critica Sociale* expressed Turati's full accord with the *Direzione*'s actions. The *Direzione*, however, lacked a coherent strategy for keeping Italy out of the war. Aside from continued neutrality, its only demand was to recall parliament.[36] Mussolini supported this demand, abandoning his initial hopes for a mass insurrection. He recognized that the PSI was in a corner, advising Lazzari: "Given this complex situation, I think that in case of mobilization or a declaration of war against Austria, the *Direzione* ought to establish its position by means of a manifesto to the nation while the Socialist deputies oppose military credits for the war. There is nothing else to do. We had decided on a revolutionary general strike for contingencies which by now no longer exist."[37]

The Party's impotence spurred Mussolini toward a break with the *Direzione*. Always an advocate of action, he manifested signs of interventionist leanings shortly after the outbreak of the war. After August 4, *Avanti!* took an increasingly marked anti-German tone. An August 13 editorial supported continuing Italian neutrality, pointing out that French troops on the quiet Italian border could be sent to face the German offensive. By late August, Mussolini concluded that Italy should enter the war as France's ally.[38]

Mussolini was not the only Socialist disoriented by the outbreak of the war. An August 9 article by Angelica Balabanoff stressed that the PSI was isolated from the other European socialist parties. The Second International was the first casualty of the war. Balabanoff assigned heavy responsibility for the war's outbreak on the German socialists' decision to vote for military credits. The failure of internationalism among the European socialists had set "brother against brother." Treves, in commenting on the collapse of the International, identified true Italian nationalism with the Socialist party's insistence upon continued neutrality.[39]

The events of August 1914 were the great test of the Revolutionary-led cadre Socialist party. Neither the strategy of intransigence nor the disciplined cadre organization proved capable of providing a more successful response to war than the Reformists had achieved in 1911 when Italy attacked Libya. In the battle against first Giolitti and then Salandra, during the Red Week crisis, and in August 1914, the Revolutionary *Direzione* relied on the Reformist-dominated GPS for effective action. Although they had introduced greater discipline within the Party, the left had failed conspicuously to develop a political strategy that improved on Reformism. The PSI approach to Italian politics in the wake of the 1913 election was a replay of its actions in 1900 and 1909. Once again, election gains appeared to open the way for the PSI to achieve its goals. Once again, the Party's structural limitations, especially its restricted popular base, hamstrung the achievement of its goals. The disciplined cadre party had been put to the test and repeatedly failed.

While Reformists like Treves and Revolutionaries like Balabanoff contemplated the paralyzed state of the Party, Mussolini took action. Among the Party's major leaders, he alone had an instinctive understanding of the dynamics of mass movements. Mussolini had observed the practical consequences of reliance on a cadre party. He had urged building a disciplined mass organization to capitalize on the expansion of suffrage and the 1913 election success. Mussolini believed that the wave of strikes that culminated in Red Week were significant steps in the creation of political consciousness among Italian workers. At the outbreak of the war, Mussolini stated that only a mass insurrection could stop the holocaust and ignite a revolution. By the fall of 1914, he became convinced that the PSI was incapable of leading such a mass movement and broke with it. One critical factor determining Mussolini's defection was his recognition that the continuation of the *Direzione*'s policy would result in subordinating the Revolutionary faction to the Reformist-dominated GPS. As early as July 28 Mussolini privately and bluntly warned Lazzari that if the *Direzione* was incapable of dynamic political action, it would lose its Party leadership to the GPS.[40]

The events which surrounded Mussolini's defection hardened the Revolutionary leadership in its position of inaction. Salandra's efforts to maneuver Italy into the war drove the *Direzione* into an even greater reliance on the GPS. By the spring of 1915, the Revolutionary faction had clearly demonstrated its inability to effectively lead the PSI. However, the war impeded a successful challenge for control by either the Reformists or by the increasingly discontented young socialists of the left.[41]

THE BALANCE OF AN ERA

A shared belief that the Giolittian era presented a remarkable opportunity for Italian socialism sparked the bitter factional infighting that plagued the PSI between 1900 and 1914. Following the defeat of the reactionary Pelloux government, Socialists expected major economic and political change. Reformism and its opponents altered Party leadership in a frustrating attempt to capitalize on the favorable conditions created by an expanding economy and increased political liberty. Both the Reformist strategy of class cooperation and the left's efforts to pressure the government into change failed in the face of Giolitti's intelligent exploitation of the governmental machinery. Reformism's strategy of cooperation with middle-class reformers produced significant social, economic, and political benefits but at the high cost of entwining the GPS in Giolitti's corrupting system of favors and bargains. The Reformists backed Giolitti because they believed that the Piedmontese leader was the main bulwark against the return to the politics of repression. Giolitti, in turn, kept Reformism afloat through most of the decade after 1901 with well-timed concessions and good administration. His policies reduced social tensions while Italy's expanding economy provided more goods for a slowly emerging industrial society.[42]

Prior to 1912 only one left-wing faction, the Syndicalists, actively challenged the political system within which the PSI operated. In general, the left, like the Reformists, attempted to operate within a system they condemned as reactionary. While refusing to cooperate with Giolitti or his methods, the Revolutionaries avoided violent challenges to the system's continued existence. Turati was contemptuous of these self-styled "revolutionaries." Their "revolutionary" program consisted of parliamentary intransigence and the impractical claim that the PSI could extract change by an ostentatious refusal to compromise with the parties of the middle class. Like the Reformists, the Revolutionaries flatly rejected Syndicalist plans to radicalize organized labor as the first step toward a revolution. Confident that "history" was on their side, the left preferred to conserve its organization, explore the possibility of exacting additional gains from the bourgeoisie, and wait on the working class to mount a revolution.

In agreeing to work within the existing political system, the PSI threw away one of its key advantages: numbers. It accepted all the restrictions that Italy's small ruling elite placed upon its opponents: a highly limited suffrage, single-district parliamentary elections, *trasformismo*, and government control of the South's deputies. During the Giolittian era a growing body of both workers and farm laborers developed a heightened degree of political consciousness and began to actively participate in trade unions and farm cooperative movements. Both PSI factions consistently underestimated the potential strength of this emerging political force. They continued to rely on an elite of highly motivated militants to win major concessions from Italy's rulers. When major concessions were not forthcoming, both focused their criticisms on the Party's lack of discipline. The Reformists insisted that greater cohesion within the GPS would lead to political success. The left countered that the whole Party needed discipline if the PSI was to overcome bourgeois resistance to political change.

A sense of missed opportunities inflamed interparty relations. The bitterness and exasperation that Turati expressed in his private correspondence with Kuliscioff were a product of his belief that the PSI's failures were the result of correctable human weakness: if the deputies attended to their parliamentary responsibilities, and individual Socialists actively participated in their sections, the Party could exploit the very real possibility of reform through cooperation with the progressive middle class.

The real story of Italian socialism during the Giolittian decade was not one of missed opportunities but of excessive expectations. Possessing a common set of principles and a more advanced political organization, the

PSI had the chance of obtaining a disproportionate influence but not necessarily a decisive one. A limited suffrage, the unicameral electoral system, and the corrupt electoral politics practiced in the South were major constraints on the PSI's influence in parliament. Giolitti further weakened Socialist influence by drawing individual deputies into his system of favors. In the last resolve, Socialist expectations were beyond the Party's reach because they lacked the type of organization that could translate their goals into reality and were unable to formulate a coherent political strategy that would enable the PSI to extract substantive concessions from the Italian state.

The spokesmen for an alternate approach to politics were Gaetano Salvemini and Benito Mussolini. Both created important followings among the young socialists. Both men based their strategy on bringing the masses into the PSI, utilizing their power to achieve Socialist political objectives. Salvemini insisted that the Party had to mobilize a mass base of support and impose its program of universal suffrage on Giolitti. He recognized that the GPS and the Party would only be able to break with the Giolittian system if overwhelming pressure developed from their political base of support. As long as the PSI simply represented the interests of a Northern aristocracy of labor, it would remain a captive of Giolitti's system of political management. Salvemini's solution was first to bring the masses, particularly the Southern peasantry, into the Party and then to change the restricted political system into a parliamentary democracy.

Benito Mussolini was the champion of a more radical vision: organizing the masses to make a revolution. Mussolini wanted to utilize election campaigns, universal suffrage, and the general strike to radicalize the union movement and build the political identification of the working classes with the PSI. A Mussolini-led revolutionary elite would develop the tactics and, utilizing its control over the unions, organize the masses to overthrow the state.

Reformist and Revolutionary leaders ignored the options offered by Mussolini and Salvemini. For the Reformists, the oversight was disastrous. Reformism postulated that the political education of the masses was the key to its program of social and political amelioration. By limiting contacts between the PSI and the working classes and leaving the task of political indoctrination primarily to the CGL, the Reformists lost their best chance to win the understanding and cement the support of the working classes for their strategy of gradual social change. Without this support, Reformism was incapable of staying its course. During the crisis of 1911, large elements of the rank and file deserted the Reformists for good.

The Revolutionaries discovered that a disciplined cadre party was no substitute for mass participation in 1914. The Party postured its way through the major crises of June and August 1914 because it was unable to either control or direct the working classes. These crises demonstrated that the Party could not remain within the ideological and organizational halfway house of Revolutionary intransigence. As Mussolini had foreseen, a policy of avoiding a direct confrontation with the government in the piazza surrendered the Party's trump card: mobilization of the strong antiwar sentiment that existed throughout the working classes and, indeed, Italian society in general. The *Direzione*'s decision to avoid provoking the government with mass protests left the Revolutionary leadership without any alternative to reliance on the GPS to express the Party's opposition to Italian participation in the war. The group, however, was an isolated minority in the Chamber of Deputies. During the next nine months, the GPS and Party were incapable of braking the Salandra government's steady movement toward participation in the war.

Epilogue:
Toward
Mass Politics,
1915–1922

The war accelerated the twin processes of Italian industrialization and the radicalization of the industrial working class. It undercut the legitimacy of parliamentary institutions while creating a deep social chasm between the industrial workers who enjoyed deferment from military service and the primarily peasant army that endured the privations, misery, and dangers of three and a half years of trench and mountain warfare.

Italy's entry into the war dramatically demonstrated the ability of a political elite to force its will upon the nation by the utilization of mass political pressure. In May 1915, the proponents of military intervention poured into the piazzas to demand Italy join the war. The carefully organized demonstrations of "Radiant May" intimidated the pro-neutrality majority in parliament and overrode the objections of a predominantly neutralist nation. Mussolini, who played an important role in organizing the demonstrations for war, saw his theories of mass political organization and mobilization by a radical elite triumphantly vindicated.

The Italian Socialist party was a major loser in the battle over intervention. The Revolutionary leadership of the PSI avoided a direct clash with the inflamed forces of nationalism by surrendering the streets to its opponents and relying on parliament and, ironically, Giovanni Giolitti, to save Italy from war. When Giolitti and his deputies capitulated to the Interventionists, the PSI, as in 1911, became a helpless parliamentary minority opposing the apparent national will.

Throughout the war, the PSI was isolated and ineffective. Thousands of its members were called into military service. The Italian government, fearful of subversion, arrested Socialist leaders, repressed organized labor, and severely restricted the Party's ability to recruit. The government's actions were probably unnecessary. The PSI remained divided internally. The battle of Reformist and Revolutionary continued within the truncated PSI. The Reformists held on to control of the GPS, the unions, and municipal administrations. While urging a quick, compromise peace, they cautiously supported "patriotic" cooperation with national defense, particularly after Italy's stunning defeat at Caporetto in 1917.

The Revolutionaries continued to control *Avanti!* and the *Direzione*. They emphasized noncooperation with the Italian war machine but balanced this by insisting that the Party and working class avoid provocative actions. In practice, the Revolutionaries policy of neither supporting nor sabotaging the war condemned the PSI to political inaction.

In spite of its ineffectiveness, the PSI not only survived the war but gained potential adherents. The rapid, victorious conflict that the interventionists imagined would follow an Italian declaration of war turned into a series of futile mountain assaults and bloody Austrian counteroffensives. War weariness grew in both the army and the civilian population as months and years passed without victory. The PSI's steadfast call for an immediate peace settlement solidified working-class loyalty. Simultaneously it aroused the enduring hatred of the largely peasant army and their middle-class officers.

As soon as the war was over, government repression lapsed. The PSI mushroomed. Between 1918 and 1920, Party membership rose from approximately 22,000 to more than 200,000. The radicalized working classes poured into both the PSI and CGL, which grew to 2 million members.

The PSI had become a mass party almost against the will of its traditional leadership elites. Neither the Party's left nor right knew what to do with a potentially revolutionary mass party dominated by the industrial proletariat. The success of the Bolshevik revolution in Russia inflamed their expectation of emulating the success of Russian workers. For the first two postwar years, the PSI followed the lead of its radicalized mass base. The industrial proletariat engaged in a dramatic confrontation with both factory owners and government that climaxed in the occupation of factories in Turin in September 1920.

The Reformists and their traditional constituencies were submerged in the radicalized PSI. The passage of an expanded suffrage act and proportional representation law in 1919 broke their control over the GPS. By January 1921, the Reformists were a small, isolated, and increasingly powerless minority of approximately 15,000 within a Party of 200,000.

The old Revolutionary leadership, now rechristened Maximalists, fared little better. Party leaders, especially Seratti, resisted pressure both within the PSI and from Moscow to emulate the Russian model and to join the Third International. The old left was still incapable of providing a coherent alternative to the vision of democratic socialism that Turati championed. Faced with a potentially revolutionary situation in 1919–20, they lacked the stomach for a violent confrontation with the Italian state.

The old leaders' failure to act and the example of the triumphant Russian revolution fractured the PSI. The younger generation of Socialist leaders— Gramsci, Togliatti, Terracini, and Tasca in Turin; Bordiga in Naples; and Bombacci in Rome—recognized that the Maximalist-led Party was incapable of carrying out a coherent revolutionary strategy.

Probably no Italian Marxist had meditated more deeply on the problems of the organization of a socialist party than Gramsci. His conception of the political party evolved rapidly in the postwar years. Gramsci tried to marry the lessons of Bolshevik Russia with the Italian national experience to produce a socialist revolution. By 1920 he concluded that, in Italy, only a mass party could successfully fulfill the role of the vanguard of a victorious proletarian revolution.

Gramsci recognized that the PSI's existing organization was totally unsuited for leading a working-class movement:

> The Socialist Party with its web of sections . . . with its provincial federations . . . with its annual congresses . . . with its *Direzione* . . . constitutes a machine of proletarian democracy that, in political fantasy, could easily be seen as exemplary. . . . The Socialist is a model of "libertarian" society, voluntarily disciplined through an explicit act of conscience.[1]

Unfortunately, the Party was incapable of revolutionary action:

> The Socialist party remains . . . a mere parliamentary party that stands immobilized within the narrow limits of bourgeois democracy . . . neither the *[D]irezione* of the Party nor *Avanti!* oppose a truly revolutionary conception to the incessant propaganda that the [R]eformists . . . are continually making in parliament and in the unions. The central organs of the Party do nothing to provide the masses with a communist political education.[2]

Gramsci insisted on the urgent need for immediate renovation of the Party because, "the present phase of the class struggle in Italy precedes either the revolutionary proletariats' conquest of power . . . or a tremendous reaction by the propertied classes and governing cast."³ In order to seize the leadership of a radicalized proletariat and direct it toward a successful revolution, the Party first had to carry out a purge of its leaders, centralize its control over the sections, and win the understanding and support of the working class for its objectives.⁴

By the early months of 1920, Gramsci was convinced that the PSI as constituted was incapable of such self-reform. Initially, he thought that the "factory councils" of Turin modeled on the Soviets of Petrograd could serve as the revolutionary vanguard in place of the PSI. However, he soon realized that only a political party could provide the leadership required for a revolution. In April 1920 Gramsci wrote, "The existence of a cohesive Communist Party . . . is the fundamental and indispensable condition for attempting any Soviet experiment."⁵

Gramsci envisioned a mass party drawing its power from the proletariat and performing three essential functions: providing political education, creating a consensus within the working class, and leading the revolution. Unlike the PSI's Marxists, Gramsci stressed that the party, operating within strict time limits, had to build a consensus for the revolutionary insurrection and then initiate action. If the party waited until a revolutionary insurrection was already underway and then attempted to intervene, it would possess little credibility or support and would be incapable of assuming its natural and correct role of guide for the proletariat.⁶

Gramsci insisted that only a mass party could successfully carry out these three functions. In debate with Amadeo Bordiga, another rising socialist leader, Gramsci argued that creating an elite of revolutionaries, an Italian Bolshevik party, would produce problems similar to those existing within the PSI. This revolutionary vanguard would lose contact with the proletariat and would be incapable of creating the conditions for revolution. A mass party, Gramsci stressed, would enable the communists to guide the revolution in the manner of the Russian Bolsheviks.⁷

While they disagreed on issues of party organization and strategy, the young socialists united around the demand that the Socialist party accept the ideological leadership of the newly created Third (Communist) International. Encouraged by the Bolsheviks, they demanded a purge of the Reformists as the essential first step in the creation of a disciplined mass organization capable of carrying out a socialist revolution. When the January 1921 Congress of Livorno rejected this demand, the radicals led nearly 50,000 members out of the PSI and formed the Communist party of Italy (PCdI). Continuing Socialist infighting culminated in the expulsion of the

Reformists and the defection of a faction under Serrati. These losses, combined with the earlier defection of the Communists, severely limited the Party's ability to cope with the emergence of a multiclass Catholic mass party and a rapidly developing right-wing totalitarian movement.

The Catholics, too, had discovered the advantages of a mass political organization. The Italian Popular party (PPI), founded in 1919, had 3137 branches and 251,740 members by April 1920. In addition, the PPI boasted eighty-two daily and weekly newspapers and a growing trade union movement. In spite of major internal factionalism and continuing problems with a conservative Catholic church hierarchy, the multiclass Catholic party adopted a political platform that included woman's suffrage, together with educational, agrarian, and fiscal reforms that would favor the interests of the Italian working class and peasantry.[8]

Between 1919 and 1922, rival Catholic and Socialist parties with their allied unions and cultural and educational associations brought Italy's masses into active political participation. Their mutual mistrust paralyzed parliament and opened the way for an extremist mass movement to seize power. Benito Mussolini developed and refined his theories of political organization and tactics within the prewar PSI. In the postwar era, he blended together elements of his socialist-syndicalist theories with the nationalism and imperialism of the right to create a contradictory but highly attractive ideology. He exploited the middle class's fear of the left and its aroused nationalism to build an alliance with Italy's traditional ruling elites.

Mussolini organized his new political movement on the model of the PSI: individual dues-paying members, party sections (*fasci*), regional organizations, congresses, and a national executive. By December 1921, Mussolini led a movement with 834 sections and a membership of approximately 250,000 that was developing peripheral supporting bodies such as a party press and trade unions. Fascism drew its support from all classes but was primarily a middle-class movement, plagued with the classic problem of indiscipline. Mussolini had a particularly difficult time controlling the local chieftains (*ras*) in North and Central Italy.

The glue that held fascism together was hatred, particularly hatred of the Socialists. Antisocialist feeling ran highest among the *ras* and their squads of toughs. Mussolini's march on Rome began as an assault on the organizations of the PSI and CGL. Lacking agreement on a program of action, the PSI fell victim to further internal schism and to Fascist violence. Mass politics triumphed in Italy but in the guise of right-wing authoritarianism. After debilitating his potentially most formidable rival with the use of violence, the *Duce* of Italian fascism challenged the continuing rule of the elite that had governed Italy since unification.

In 1922, the ruling elites surrendered political power to Mussolini and his Fascists as part of a complex social compromise that left their economic and social predominance relatively intact. Repressing the Catholic, Socialist, and Communist parties while conciliating the crown, army, Church, and business, fascism preserved the essential privileges of Italy's ruling elites for a further twenty years. When he completed the political consolidation of a dictatorship in 1926, Mussolini turned to the effort to organize mass consensus among both the middle and working classes. Fascist labor unions, recreational clubs, media, schools, and popular-culture organizations attempted to create a bond of loyalty and obedience between the individual and the state. Combining these organizations with coercion and appeals to nationalism, fascism created a broad but paper-thin consensus while preserving the economic and social privileges of the traditional elites.

The consensus collapsed when Mussolini allied Italy with Nazi Germany and led the nation into a series of wars in search of an expanded empire and control of the Mediterranean. By 1940, even before military defeats revealed the military impotence of fascism, Mussolini had lost the support of his most important backers.

When fascism collapsed under the weight of its military defeats, the three pre-Fascist mass parties, Communist, Socialist, and Christian Democratic, reemerged from years of exile and underground activity. In spite of continuing differences, they temporarily buried their hostilities to cooperate in an armed resistance against fascism and in the building of a democratic state.

The truce fell apart in 1947–48, but forty years of democratic politics have gradually attenuated their mutual mistrust and created a new set of political rules of conduct. Postwar Italy's economic prosperity and wide political freedoms, as well as many of the democratic state's less attractive features, are the product of the competition, cooperation, and talent for self-perpetuating compromise of these mass parties. The political system, in turn, is the culmination of developments that began during the industrialization of Liberal Italy when Italian Socialists embarked on the tortuous process that brought the working masses into active participation in politics through the creation of a new type of party.

Abbreviations Used in Notes

AC/S	Archivio Centrale dello Stato, Rome
AP	Atti Parlamentari
b	busta
CC	Ganci, *Democrazia e Socialismo in Italia*
CM	Carte Morgari
CR	Carte Rigola
CS	*Critica Sociale*
DS	*Divenire Sociale*
f	fascicolo
GC	Carocci, et al., *Quarant'Anni*
IF	Istituto Giangiacomo Feltrinelli (archives)
LL	Zanardo, "Lettere di Antonio Labriola"
LLB	Procacci, *Antonio Labriola e la rivisione*
LLE	Labriola, *Lettere a Engels*
s	sottofascicolo
SC	Salvemini, *Carteggio*
TA	Schiavi, *Filippo Turati attraverso*
TKC	*Turati-Kuliscioff Carteggio*

Notes

Preface and Acknowledgments

1. *Political Parties; Storia critica del movimento socialista italiano;* and *Proletariato e borghesia.* Also, *L'imperialismo italiano.* Other interesting contemporary comments include Allevi, *Crisi del socialismo;* Bonomi, *Vie nuove;* and Ragghianti, *Uomini rossi.*

2. Candeloro, *Movimento sindacale;* Bassi "Rinaldo Rigola"; Preti, "Giolitti e le leghi"; Rigola, *Storia;* Arfe, *Storia;* Basso, *Salvemini;* Colapietra, *Bissolati;* Colombi, *Pagine;* Mondolfo, Nenni, and Gonzales, *Turati;* Romita, *Origini;* Schiavi, *Pionieri* and *Omaggio.* During the 1950s and 1960s *Critica Sociale* published a number of interesting occasional pieces on the early Socialist party.

3. "Discorso su Giolitti," (1950) reprinted in Togliatti, *Momenti,* pp. 79–116. Two interesting analyses of the historiographical debate from the Marxist perspective are Detti, "Anna Kuliscioff," and Manacorda, "Formazione."

4. Ganci, *Democrazia e socialismo;* Salvemini, *Opere;* Zanghieri, *Lotte agrarie;* and in the *Annali Istituto Feltrinelli* series, Cortesi, "Corrispondenza Engels-Turati"; Masini, "Lettere di Salvemini"; Procacci, "Antonio Labriola"; Zanardo, "Lettere di Antonio Labriola." In addition, Feltrinelli published Carocci, *Quarant'anni,* and has issued facsimile copies of a number of early radical newspapers including *Lotta di Classe.*

5. In addition to the Turati-Kuliscioff correspondence, Giolitti, *Discorsi extraparlamentari.*

6. Ragionieri, *Sesto Fiorentino,* was a pioneering work which served as a model for many Communist and non-Communist scholars. Among the useful recent studies of local and regional Socialist party activity are Badaloni and Bartolotti, *Movimento operaio;* Casella, *Democrazia, socialismo;* Diomide, *Associazione operaie;* Manconi, Melis, and Misu, *Storia dei partiti popolari;* Mazzoni, "Molinella e Giuseppe Massarenti"; Marianelli, "Movimento operaio a Pisa"; Onofri, *Grande guerra;* Riosa, *Socialismo riformista a Milano;* and the multivolume *Storia del movimento operaio in Piemonte.*

7. *Storia della cooperazione; Libia;* Degl'Innocenti also prepared the second volume of Sabatucci, ed., *Storia del socialismo,* covering the Giolitti era.

8. *Giolitti e Turati; Il PSI;* "Italian Socialism and the First World War"; and "Il suffragio universale."

9. *Dilemmas.* Also "Filippo Turati e la scissione"; "Filippo Turati, the Milanese Schism"; and "Parliamentary Socialists."

Introduction

1. On the role of elites in Italy's Risorgimento and post-Risorgimento politics, see Lovett, *Democratic Movement;* Grew, *Sterner Plan;* Mack Smith, *Cavour and Garibaldi* and *Cavour.*

2. On Italy's efforts to conduct a great power foreign policy on its limited resources base, cf. Chabod, *Storia,* and Bosworth, *Italy.*

3. On Italy's industrial development, see Clough, *Economic History;* Carracciolo, *Formazione;* Romeo, *Risorgimento e capitalismo* and *Breve storia;* Fossati, *Lavoro e produzione;* Cohen, "Financing" and "Economic Growth"; Castronovo, *Economia e societa,* "Italian Take-Off," and "La storia economica"; Romano, *Le classi sociale;* Sereni, *Capitalismo.*

4. Gerschenkron, "Notes"; Coppa, *Planning,* pp. 16–35, 39, 50–64; Neufield, *Italy,* pp. 292–94; Clough and Levi, "Economic Growth"; Castronovo, "Italian Take-Off."

5. Schacter, *Italian South,* pp. 5–11, 31; Banfield, *Moral Basis;* Cornelisen, *Torregreca;* Villari, *Il Sud;* Clough and Levi, "Economic Growth"; Coppa, *Planning,* pp. 16–45.

6. Hobsbawm, *Primitive Rebels,* pp. 20–24, 105, and Romano, *Fasci siciliani.*

7. Hobsbawm, *Primitive Rebels,* pp. 40–44.

8. Ibid, p. 31; Gramsci, "The Southern Question," in *Modern Prince,* pp. 42, 46–47; and Coppa, "Italian Tariff."

9. Seton-Watson, *Italy,* p. 247.

10. Ibid. Cf. comments of D. Brogan in his introduction to Duverger, *Political Parties,* p. vii.

11. Salomone, *Giolittian Era,* pp. 13–19; Candeloro, *Storia dell'Italia,* 6:343–44; and Salvemini, *Opere,* 4, pt. 1: 544.

12. Jemolo, *Chiesa,* pp. 27–33; Halperin, *Italy and the Vatican,* pp. 18–19; and von Aretin, *Papacy,* pp. 87–92, 118–20, 130.

13. Halperin, *Italy and the Vatican,* p. 24, and Jemolo, *Chiesa,* pp. 71–72.

14. Halperin, *Italy and the Vatican,* pp. 27–28, 105–66, and von Aretin, *Papacy,* p. 129.

15. Jemolo, *Chiesa,* pp. 106–9, and Candeloro, *Movimento cattolico,* pp. 244–304.

16. *LL,* p. 460, and von Aretin, *Papacy,* p. 122.

17. "Relazione politica della direzione," *Avanti!,* 22 April 1914, and Rigola, *Storia,* p. 396.

18. Michels, *Proletariato,* p. 162.

Chapter 1

1. Lazzari, "Memorie," pp. 613ff. On the origins of the Italian workers movement, Manacorda, *Movimento operaio;* Romano, *Storia;* Hostetter, *Italian Socialist;* Rosselli, *Mazzini e Bakunin;* and Gonzales, *Andrea Costa;* Manacorda, "Formazione."

2. Lazzari, "Memorie," p. 619; *CC,* p. 226; *TA,* p. 89; and *LLE,* pp. 29–35. Hembree, "Costantino Lazzari," pp. 1–71, is a useful introduction to operaism.

3. Lazzari, "Memorie," p. 789; Cortesi, *Costituzione,* p. 522; and *TA,* p. 78.

4. Cortesi, *Costituzione,* pp. 9–12; DiScala, *Dilemmas,* p. 15; *LLE,* p. 12; Briguglio, *Congressi socialisti,* p. 7; *TA,* p. 65; and Cortesi, *Turati giovane,* p. 417. An account of the congress is in Spinella, *Critica Sociale,* pp. 17–25.

5. Cortesi, *Turati giovane,* pp. 421–26. Data on the contributors to *Critica Sociale* were assembled from *I 508 Deputati;* Cerchiari, *L'opera;* Ghisalberti, ed., *Dizionario biografico;* and *Enciclopedia biografica.* Cf. Zacan, *Stampa periodica,* p. 18; Schiavi, *Pioneri;* Manzotti, "Giovanezza di Bissolati"; Ganci, "Formazione positivistica"; and DiScala, *Dilemmas,* pp. 2–10, 16–19.

6. PLI, *Rendiconto del I congresso* in Cortesi, *Socialismo,* pp. 10–17, 20–21, and DiScala, *Dilemmas,* pp. 19–22.

7. *Programma e Statuto* of the PLI in Cortesi, *Socialismo,* pp. 20–21.

8. DiScala, *Dilemmas,* pp. 20–21; Arfe, *Storia,* pp. 9–21; Cortesi, *Costituzione,* pp. 9–12, 48–54; *SC* 1:197–98; and *LL,* p. 319.

9. Valiani, *Historiographie,* pp. 115–16; Schiavi, "La giovanezza," pp. 353–55; and Miller, "Italian Socialist Party," pp. 81–87.

10. *Rendiconto del I congresso nazionale* in Cortesi, *Socialismo,* pp. 18–19; and Pedone, *Partito socialista attraverso,* 1:20–23. On the foundation of *Lotta di Classe,* see Cortesi, *Costituzione,* pp. 48–54, and Zacan, *Stampa periodica,* pp. 24–27.

11. DiScala, *Dilemmas,* pp. 20–21.

12. Pedone, *Partito socialista attraverso,* pp. 20–23.

13. *Rendiconto del I congresso* in Cortesi, p. 19. See also the observations of Warner Sombart, "Der gegenwartige Stand des italienischen Arbeiterbewegung," *Sozialpolitisches Centralblatt* 1(1892): 479–83.

14. E. Ciccotti, "L'organizzazione socialista in Italia," *CS,* 1 May 1893, pp. 132–34; DiScala, *Dilemmas,* p. 22; and Ragioneri, *Giudicata,* pp. 230–31.

15. PSI, *Da Parma a Firenze,* p. 4.

16. *LLE,* pp. 79–81, 116–18; Lazzari, "Memorie," pp. 806–7; Cortesi, *Costituzione,* p. 54; Casella, *Democrazia,* pp. 35–39, 170–75; and Ciuffoletti, "La fondazione del partito socialista italiano e l'opera di Filippo Turati," in Arfe, et al., *Storia,* pp. 1–60. Hembree ("Costantino Lazzari," pp. 124–25) notes that Lazzari became administrator of *Lotta di Classe* in 1893 and attempted with some success to color the paper's reporting. However, effective editorial direction remained with the Reformists.

17. Lazzari, "Memorie," p. 802; PSLI, *Rendiconto del II congresso,* in Cortesi, *Socialismo,* pp. 34–37; *LLE,* pp. 62–63, 86–87; and Spinella, *Critica Sociale,* pp. 28–34. The five "socialist" deputies were Prampolini, Agnini, Maffei, Costa, and Colajanni. Cf. DiScala, *Dilemmas,* pp. 22–24.

18. *Rendiconto del II congresso,* in Cortesi, *Socialismo,* pp. 40–41.

19. *Lotta di Classe,* 16–17 Sept. 1893.

20. Hughes, *Fall and Rise,* p. 17, and Romano, *Fasci siciliani,* pp. 295ff.

21. Lazzari, "Memorie," p. 804; *Lotta di Classe,* 19–20 Jan. 1895; and DiScala, *Dilemmas,* pp. 20–31.

22. Engels, "La futura rivoluzione italiana e il Partito socialista," *CS,* 16 Feb. 1895, pp. 35–37. On the editing of the letter, see Cortesi, "F. Engels–F. Turati, Corrispondenza, 1891–1895," pp. 253ff.

23. Spinella, *Critica Sociale,* pp. 28–34; Cortesi, *Turati giovane,* p. 295; *TA,* p. 79; and DiScala, *Dilemmas,* pp. 28–29.

24. "Tattica elettorale," *CS*, 15 Jan. 1895, pp. 20–22; "Fierezza allegra," *CS*, 1 Nov. 1894, pp. 337–39; and Lazzari, "Memorie," pp. 806–7.

25. PSI, *Rendiconto del IV congresso*, in Cortesi, *Socialismo*, pp. 60–61, 67–69.

26. Ibid., p. 62.

27. Arfe, *Storia del Avanti!*, p. 13.

28. No proceedings of the congress were published. For information see *Lotta di Classe*, 25–26 Sept. 1897, and *Avanti!*, 19, 20, 21 Sept. 1897. Briguglio, *Congressi socialisti*, pp. 24–27, 155. The scandals in the Central Committee were outlined in a letter from Antonio Labriola to Engels, 22 August 1893, in Labriola, *Lettere*, pp. 116–18. On the professionalization of the Party, see Michels, *Political Parties*, p. 80.

29. Bonomi, "Riccordi d'un redattore dell'Avanti!" in Negro and Lazzarini, *Uomini e giornale*, pp. 32–36, *TKC*, 1:484–85.

30. *TKC*, 1:166; *GC*, 1:343; and *AP* Camera, 20th Legislature, pp. 4329–33, 4334–43.

31. Treves, "Giolitti," *CS*, 11–12 June 1899, pp. 182–84.

32. "Dichiarazioni necessarie," *CS*, 1 Jan. 1900, pp. 1–2.

33. PSI, *Rendiconto del VI congresso*, pp. 66–67.

34. Ibid., pp. 71–84.

35. Ibid., pp. 92–93, 112–14.

36. Mammarella, *Riformisti*, pp. 73–74. Cf. the comments of DiScala, *Dilemmas*, p. 53.

37. "Per la riforma del programma minimo," *CS*, 16 June 1900, pp. 228–34. Only later when they came under intensified pressure from the Party's left did the Reformists fall into the habit of justifying their actions as fulfilling the minimal program. The minimal program, however, did not give its blessing to any specific tactical political approach. It said nothing at all about tactics. Historians have tended to take the Reformists at their word, reading into the minimal program a significance which it did not possess. The actions of the Party's left support this view. Throughout the Giolittian era, the left directed its fire at Turati's tactics, not at the minimal program. In power, the left made no attempt to repeal or modify the minimal program. What Socialist was likely to oppose universal suffrage, a reduction of military spending, or abolition of the appointed Senate?

38. "La sentenza del congresso di Roma," *CS*, 16 Sept. 1900, pp. 273–75, and PSI, *Rendiconto del VI congresso*, pp. 92–94.

39. DiScala (*Dilemmas*, p. 53) takes the opposite view, arguing that the "streamlining" of the *Direzione* introduced by the Ferri resolution actually reinforced the powers of that body. However, the effect of packing the *Direzione* with deputies was to undercut any tendency toward the control of the parliamentary group of the PSI at the moment when the political issues critical to the Party were being settled within parliament.

40. Vigezzi, *Il PSI*, p. 27.

41. For details and a defense of Giolitti's involvement, see Thayer, *Italy and the Great War*, pp. 54–77. *GC*, 1:418–19; Giolitti, *Memorie*, pp. 123–24; [Salvemini], "Il ministero delle tendenze," *CS*, 16 April 1901, pp. 111–14; and *GC*, 2:405.

42. On the historical debate, Salomone, *Giolittian Era*, intro., pp. 117–69, and *Risorgimento to Fascism*, pp. 3–34, 303–74. Coppa, *Planning*, pp. 1–15, 41–49, 241–42; Marianni, *Storia*, p. 231; Giolitti, *Memorie*, pp. 111–17, and *Discorsi extraparlamentari*, pp. 105–6, 122–23, 181–86.

43. Giolitti, *Discorsi extraparlamentari*, pp. 116, 186–88, 237–46; and Perticone, *Italia*

contemporanea, pp. 487, 510. On Giolitti's conservatism, see Giolitti, *Memorie*, p. 125; and Coppa, *Planning*, p. 107. Bosworth, *Italy and the Approach*, pp. 71–76, 140.

44. Salvemini, *Opere*, 4, pt. 1: 136–38, 554, and "Il diversivo anticlericale," *L'Unità*, 28 Nov. 1913.

45. Giolitti, *Discorsi extraparlamentari*, pp. 96, 133–34, 181, 220, and Coppa, "Economic Liberalism." For a conservative critique of Giolitti's politics, see Albertini, *Vent'anni*, p. 147.

46. Salvemini, "Il ministero delle tendenze," *CS*, 16 April 1901, pp. 114–19.

47. *Avanti!*, 27 May 1900; "La lezione delle cose," *Rivista popolare di politica*, 30 Jan. 1900, pp. 21–23; and Salomone, *Giolittian Era*, p. 58.

48. *TKC*, 2:52–53, and DiScala, "Parliamentary Socialists."

49. Angiolo Cabrini, "La legislazione sociale e il GPS," *Avanti!*, 26 Feb. 1901.

50. Mammarella, *Riformisti*, p. 95. Bonomi commented that this policy paid extra dividends by allowing the Socialists to assume "an attitude of virtual indifference in regards to the institutional [monarchy] problem" (Bonomi, *La politica italiana*, p. 215).

51. *GC*, 2:18–19, 23–24, 26, 28–30.

52. *GC*, 2:24.

53. Ibid., pp. 38–39. See also the texts of telegrams from Giolitti to various prefects quoted in Natale, *Giolitti e gli italiani*, pp. 441–44.

54. Natale, *Giolitti e gli italini*, pp. 430–31, 436, 438–39; *GC*, 2:30, 40, 53; and Coppa, *Planning*, pp. 111–12.

55. Salomone, *Giolittian Era*, p. 58.

56. *GC*, 2:55, 217–19, 284–85, 294. For details, see DiScala, *Filippo Turati*.

57. Enrico Ferri, "Una replica al caso di Milano," *Avanti!*, 21 Aug. 1901, and "Il ministero e noi," *Avanti!*, 5 Dec. 1901. Coppa, *Planning*, pp. 244–45, passim. I disagree strongly with Coppa's analysis of the relationship of Giolitti with the PSI. While the PSI and its parliamentary group were frequently in a formal position of "opposition" to the Giolitti governments, the prime minister was always able to cut deals with individual deputies, that is, to carry them into the majority on particular issues and thus to negate the formal opposition of the Party.

Chapter 2

1. *LLB*, p. 333, and Michels, *Political Parties*, p. 197.

2. Kolakowski, *Main Currents*, 2:1–2.

3. Braunthal, *History*, pp. 195–96; McInnes, *Western Marxists*, pp. 12–71; and Kolakowski, *Main Currents*, 2:7–8.

4. Lichtheim, *Marxism*, pp. 235, 250–52.

5. Ibid., pp. 236–37.

6. Ibid., p. 237.

7. Braunthal, *History*, pp. 208–9, Lindemann, *History*, pp. 164–65; and Joll, *Second International*, pp. 7, 12–14, 47.

8. DuVeger, *Political Parties*, p. 64.

9. Ibid., p. xxxiv.

10. Ibid., p. 63.

11. Ibid., p. 63.

12. Steensen, *Not One*, pp. 26, 32–33, and *Kautsky*, p. 84; and Joll, *Second International*, pp. 89–90.

13. Lindemann, *History*, p. 150, and Gay, *Dilemma*, pp. 239–40.

14. Kolakowski, *Main Currents*, pp. 99, 114, and Morgan, "The Father of Revisionism."

15. Joll, *Second International*, pp. 95–96.

16. Santarelli, *Revisionismo*, p. 62; Gay, *Dilemma*, p. 143; and "Riformismo e socialismo," *CS* 13 (16 March 1903): 83–87.

17. "Il partito socialista e l'attuale momento politico," *CS* 11 (16 July 1901):209–15. Cf. also Turati, "La conquista di Libia," *CS* 22 (1 March 1912):67–73, for later reflections on this theme. Braunthal, *History*, p. 237.

18. N. Colajanni, "La crisi del socialismo," *Rivista popolare di politica*, 30 July 1901, pp. 268–71; and Arfe, *Storia*, p. 32.

19. Kolakowski, *Main Currents*, p. 17; Croce, *Storia d'Italia*, pp. 121–37; and Mammarella, *Riformisti*, pp. 14, 87, Cf. comments on the SPD in Shorske, *German Social Democracy*, p. 20, and Gay, *Dilemma*, p. 235.

20. Michels, *Storia critica*, pp. 240–41. Cf. Michels, *Political Parties*, pp. 212, 372–73.

21. Cortesi, ed., *Socialismo*, pp. 341–42; Labriola, *Storia*, pp. 285–86; and Arfe, *Storia*, p. 163.

22. Picone, *Italian Marxism*, pp. 67–73, 80, 101–2.

23. In 1908, Michels estimated that 256,874 workers were eligible to vote under Italy's restricted suffrage laws in the election of 1904. The Socialist vote in that election was 326,016. Michels, *Proletariato*, p. 206. Cf. the comments of Degl'Innocenti in Sabatucci, *Storia del socialismo* 2:231–41.

24. *Avanti!*, 22 April 1914; Schiavi, *Come hanno votato*, p. 86; and PSI, *Resoconto del XIV congresso*, pp. 25–26. As noted in chap. 1, in the aftermath of the 1900 election, PSI membership rose from 19,194 to 47,098 in 1901.

25. Duverger, *Political Parties*, pp. 63–71; Ragionieri, *Socialdemocrazia tedesca;* and Degl'Innocenti, *Storia della cooperazione*, pp. 121–23, 257. On Turati's relations and problems with extraparliamentary organizations, see *TKC*, 2:775. Sabatucci, *Storia del Socialismo*, 2:49–50, 190–204; Riosa, et al., *Socialismo riformista*, pp. 388–91; Schorske, *German Social Democracy*, chaps. 4 and 5; Treves, *"Debbono le camere del lavoro diventare socialiste?" CS*, 1 Dec. 1901, pp. 353–55; Zibordi, "L'opera dei giovani socialisti," *CS*, 1 and 16 March 1909, pp. 70–73; statements of Rigola, Dugoni, and Graziadei to 1908 Congress in PSI, *Resoconto del X congresso*, p. 202–20, 283–88, 295–96; *LLE*, p. 184; and Michels, *Borghesia*, p. 98.

26. Michels, *Storia critica*, p. 286; Salvemini, *Opere* 4, pt. 2: 287; and Spinella, *Critica Sociale* 2:20, 29–38.

27. Mariani, *Storia*, pp. 235–36, and Santarelli, *Revisione*, p. 65.

28. Marazio, *Partito*, p. 5. Cf. Shorske, *German Social Democracy*, p. 5.

29. See the comments of Prampolini in *CC*, pp. 301–2. Michels, *Political Parties*, p. 150.

30. Michels, *Political Parties*, pp. 152–53, and Pischel, *Antologia*, pp. 279–82.

31. "La lotta di classe in parlamento," *CS* 23 (Nov. 16–Dec. 16): 338–41.

32. Neufield, *Italy*, p. 318; Davidson, *Theory*, p. 30; Michels, *Political Parties*, p. 51; and Bertelli, "Socialismo."

33. See the caustic comments of Antonio Labriola to Turati in *TA*, p. 79. Bissolati, *L'Azione*, pp. 13–15.

34. Satta, "I Socialisti."
35. "I socialisti e la monarchia," *CS* 12 (1 Oct. 1902): 291–92; *SC*, 1:70–71; and Mammarella, *Riformisti*, p. 98.
36. PSI, *Rendiconto del VIII congresso*, p. 115.
37. Sabatini, *Storia* 2:215–27.
38. *TKC*, 2:52–53, 105, 281–83, 358, 419, 434–39. Cf. Colajanni, "La crisi del socialismo," *Rivista popolare di politica*, 30 July 1901, pp. 268–71; *SC*, 1:197–98; and Valiani *L'Historiographie*, pp. 115–16. Turati never underestimated Giolitti's political skill or overestimated his commitment to the objectives of the PSI. Giolitti, he wrote Kuliscioff, was "a very cool headed man . . . and more clever than the devil." The issue, he felt, was one of opportunities. A parliamentary party had to deal with the government, Turati told Kuliscioff, "because single-minded opposition to the ministry gained nothing" (*TKC*, 2:47, 3:261–63). Turati, *Discorsi*, 1:181.
39. PSI, *Statuto*, arts. 1, 3, 5; PSI, *Rendiconto del VIII congresso*, pp. 175, 181; and *Avanguardia Socialista*, 10 Sept. 1904.
40. PSI, *Statuto*, art. 2.
41. Marazio, *Partito*, pp. 39–42; *Statuto* of the section of Nasiano, arts. 2–4, in Cerrito, "Il circolo di lavoratori"; *Statuto* of the section of Naples, art. 2, in Arfe, "Per la storia"; PSI, Sezione di Torino, *Statuto*, art. 2; PSI, *Statuto*, arts. 1, 3, 4, 7; and *Avanti!*, 8 Sept. and 24 Nov. 1900, 4 Aug. 1902, 22 Jan. and 11 Feb. 1903, 21 Oct. 1903, 27 April 1905, 17 Dec. 1909, 5 June 1910. See also the comments of Ciotti in PSI, *Resoconto del XIII congresso*, pp. 16–17.
42. PSI, *Statuto*, art. 4, and PSI, *Rendiconto del VI congresso*, pp. 21–25. The appeals process is outlined in articles 11, 14, and 17 of the *Statuto*. Nonpayment of the *tessera* was supposed to carry with it automatic suspension from membership.
43. In 1912, Michels observed that the story of the PSI in the period 1900–1912 was one of oscillations by the proletariat between two groups of intellectuals. The figures cited in the text tend to give substance to this observation and also to clarify why the shifts were so sudden. Michels, *Storia critica*, p. 243.
44. On daily life in a socialist section, see Arfe, "Per la storia," and Cerrito "Il circolo di lavoratori." Information on the Rome section of the Party is plentiful for most of the Giolittian era because *Avanti!* was published in that city until 1911. For Milan, see *Il Tempo*, 1902–10; *Avanguardia Socialista*, 1902–6; and *Avanti!*, 1911–14. *Avanti!* published capsule reports of the activity of other sections on a daily basis. *Statuto* of Naples section, arts. 3–5, 8, 13–17, 25–26; *Statuto* of Naso section, arts. 11–14; and *Statuto* of Turin section, arts. 10–17.
45. On the duties of the secretary, see "Prima del Congresso," *Avanti!*, 7 Sept. 1900. A. Novelli, *La missione dei nostri circoli*.
46. PSI, *Statuto*, art. 9; E. Ferri, "La lotta nel mantovese," *Nuova Antologia* (1901): 668–75; I. Bonomi and C. Vezzani, "Il movimento proletariato nel mantovano," *CS* 11 (16 March–1 June 1901): 83–85, 99–102, 119–122, 130–33, 151–53, 166–70; and PSI, *Rendiconto del VIII congresso*, pp. 175, 187.
47. PSI, *Statuto*, arts. 10, 11.
48. *Avanti!*, 17 and 18 Feb. 1904.
49. PSI, *Statuto*, arts. 12, 14. On the PSI's generally unsatisfactory relationship with the Socialist International, see Franco Andreucci, "Il Partito Socialista Italiano e la seconda internazionale," in Riosa, et al., *Anna Kuliscioff*, pp. 33–58. The Ciccotti resolution on the organization of the *Direzione* is in PSI, *Rendiconto del VI congresso*, pp. 88–92.

50. Rigola, *Rinaldo Rigola*, p. 184; PSI, *Rendiconto del VIII congresso*, pp. 164–65; PSI, *Resoconto del IX congresso*, p. 296; and PSI, *Statuto*, art. 15.

51. Zibordi, *Organizzazione del Partito*, p. 7. On the functions of the secretaries, see also Costa and Verazzini, *Relazione*, esp. pp. 9–10.

52. PSI, *Statuto*, arts. 6, 17, 20.

53. PSI, *Statuto*, arts. 20, 22, and PSI, *Rendiconto del VIII congresso*, pp. 155–56. At every Congress the representatives of these three sections controlled between 3000 and 3500 votes.

54. For an example of this pattern, see PSI, *Rendiconto del VIII congresso*, p. 187. See also the comments of Paolini in PSI, *Resoconto del XIII congresso*, p. 119.

55. PSI, *Statuto*, arts. 18, 26. For efforts by the left to amend an agenda, see PSI, *Resoconto del XI congresso*, pp. 17, 25.

56. Michels, *Proletariato*, p. 100, and Procacci, *Lotta di classe*, pp. 238–39, 254.

57. Information on the census is in Michels, *Storia critica*, p. 286. On the class makeup of the delegates in 1904, see PSI, *Rendiconto del VIII congresso*, pp. 172–89. Lawyers, doctors, professors, school teachers, accountants, and engineers were considered middle-class professionals. The totals for 85 *relatori* (1906–14) were: middle class backgrounds, 53; workers, 8; background unknown, 23. Besides the occupations listed above, state employees, shopkeepers, Party functionaries, journalists, contractors, senior railroad employees, and landowners were considered as members of the middle classes.

58. See "Il congresso d'Imola," *Nuova Antologia* (1902), p. 379. For an example of a speaker being laughed down, see PSI, *Resoconto del X congresso*, p. 353. See also *Avanti!*, 11 April 1904, for an example of problems keeping order. On the seating arrangements at a PSI Congress, see the ironic comments of *La Nazione*, 8–9 April 1904. For the seizure of the podium, see PSI, *Resoconto del XI congresso*, pp. 320–32. On delegate absenteeism, ibid., p. 287. On the uncoordinated nature of the Congresses, see E. Leone, "Aspettando il congresso," *Avanti!*, 11 August 1902. *La Tribuna*, 23 Oct. 1910, on late arrivals. The issue of autonomy in elections and inside parliament occupied the Congresses of 1900, 1912, and 1914. The meetings of 1902, 1904, and 1906 debated the "general line of the Party" (Reformism). The 1908 Congress discussed the emergency financial situation of *Avanti!* and the relationship of the PSI with organized labor. In 1911, the Party dealt with the impact of the Libyan war. Only the 1910 Congress tried a novel committee procedure to deal with a variety of issues, but it too quickly bogged down on tactical issues.

59. C. Lazzari, "La nostra conquista," *Avanti!*, 20 Oct. 1913, and Degl'Innocenti, "Il socialismo italiano nell'età giolittiana: l'egemonia riformista," in Arfe, et al., *Storia*, pp. 73–143, esp. p. 85.

60. The "safe" seats included those of Turati (Milan V), Cabrini (Milan VI), Morgari (Turin II), Ferri (Gonzaga), Costa (Imola), Sichel (Guastella), Agnini (Mirandola), Prampolini (Reggio Emilia), Gatti (Ostiglia), Badaloni (Badia), Berenini (Borgo S. Donnino), Bertesi (Carpi). Some of the seats were safe because of the composition of the voters in a district ensured a Socialist victory. Others, however, were safe because of the influence which a given deputy enjoyed in his district. In 1912, the PSI discovered that in expelling certain Reformist deputies, it was also forfeiting secure seats.

61. Cortesi, *Origini del PCI*, pp. 138–41, 192–93, 196–200, and Arfe, *Storia*, p. 270.

62. Marazio, *Partito socialista*, pp. 42–43; Galli and Prandi, *Patterns*, pp. 90–100; and Duverger, *Political Parties*, pp. 40–51.

63. Mocchi statement in PSI, *Rendiconto del VIII congresso*, pp. 71–80.

64. Lazzari is perhaps the best example of this. The left-wing chief ran in every election from 1885 onward, usually in Milan. He was finally elected in 1919 after the passage of a universal suffrage act and under proportional representation. Mussolini, who was one of the most popular leaders of the late Giolittian era, was unable to win election in 1913, despite the wide expansion of suffrage approved in 1912. Lazzari, *Necessità*, and "La nostra conquista," *Avanti!*, 20 Oct. 1913. Statements by Lazzari and Lerda in PSI, *Resoconto del XI congresso,* pp. 81–100, 212–20. Cf. the article "Ufficio di soccorso o *Direzione* del Partito," *Avanti!*, 6 July 1901. On the impact of proportional representation, see DiScala, "Parliamentary Socialists."

65. "Ufficio del soccorso o *Direzione* del Partito," *Avanti!*, 6 July 1901.

66. "La sintesi del Congresso di Roma," *CS*, 16 Sept. and 1 Oct 1900, pp. 273–75, 289–91.

67. G. Cassola, "La *Direzione* del Partito," *CS*, 1 Oct. 1901, pp. 289–91.

68. See "La sintesi del Congresso di Roma," *CS*, 16 Sept. and Oct 1, 1900, pp. 273–75, 289–91, and "La vittoria delle cose," *CS*, 1 Oct. 1908, pp. 289–90.

69. *Avanti!* gave almost weekly coverage to Ferri's activities as a propagandist, the basis of his personal standing in the PSI. The importance of the role of the propagandist for both the individual deputy and for the Party is discussed in chapter 5.

Chapter 3

1 Lazzari, "Memorie," pp. 806–13, 816–17, and Briguglio, *Congressi socialisti*, p. 7. On Lazzari, see Hembree, "Politics of Instransigence." In the brief memoir he wrote after World War I, Lazzari often reduced the events which culminated in the triumph of Reformism into terms of a personal struggle between Turati and himself.

2. *CC*, p. 226; Briguglio, *Congressi socialisti*, pp. 108–13; *SC*, 1:197; Lazzari, "Memorie," pp. 613–19; Procacci, *Lotta di classe*, p. 236; and DiScala, "Filippo Turati, the Milanese Schism."

3. Cortesi, *Bonomi*, pp. 7–8, and Bonomi, *Bissolati*, pp. 91–92.

4. Hughes, *Consciousness and Society*, pp. 19, 35–36. In 1906 Croce wrote the preface to the first Italian edition of *Reflections on Violence*. Selections of their correspondence were printed by Croce in *La Critica*, 1927–28.

5. de Clementi, *Politica e società*, pp. 73–74.

6. DiScala, *Dilemmas*, pp. 74–77, and Roberts, *Syndicalist Tradition*, pp. 53–57, 64.

7. de Clementi, *Politica e società*, p. 75.

8. See the comments of Arturo Labriola in Schiavi, *Omaggio*, pp. 42–43. Labriola, *Spiegazione*, pp. 84–89. There was no family relation between Arturo and Antonio Labriola. Sorel to Croce, 30 Nov. 1897, reprinted in *La Critica* 25:49–50; Meisel, *Genesis*, pp. 30–31; and Labriola, *Spiegazione*, p. 89.

9. Santarelli, *Lettere*, pp. 569–70.

10. Statement of Leone in PSI, *Resoconto del IX congresso*, pp. 228–29; Labriola, *Spiegazione*, pp. 111–13, 116–17. Labriola's stress on republicanism has led Procacci and others to judge him more a middle-class radical than a socialist (*Lotta di classe*, p. 223). On this issue, however, Labriola was on solid ground as a Marxist. In 1894 Engels wrote Turati,

"Marx and I have repeated for forty years . . . that for us the democratic republic is the only form in which the struggle between the working classes and the capitalist classes . . . can arrive at its end" (*CS*, 16 Feb. 1894. pp. 35–37). Moreover, in May 1898, Turati wrote to Salvemini, "This will be the hour of the republicans. . . . The monarchy in Italy is strong . . . from the weakness . . . of the nation. A united Italy would be the end of the monarchy" (*SC*, 1:70–71). Speech of Mocchi in PSI, *Rendiconto del VIII congresso*, pp. 71–80, and the statement of Labriola in ibid., p. 135; Mocchi, "Per farci intendere una buona volta," *Avanguardia Socialista*, 10 Sept. 1904; Labriola speech in PSI, *Resoconto del IX congresso*, pp. 106–8; and Labriola, *Ministro e socialismo*, pp. 9, 22, 31. On problems with the bureaucracy, see Labriola, "Questioni di libertà," *Avanti!*, 11 March 1901.

11. Procacci, *Lotta di classe*, p. 222.

12. Bonomi, "Ricordi," pp. 31–32, and Ferri speech in PSI, *Rendiconto del VI congresso*, pp. 73–77, 92. For an evaluation of his character, see Balabanoff, *Life*, p. 30

13. *LLF*, p. 334, and Schiavi, "La giovanezza," p. 356.

14. *CC*, p. 416.

15. "I give my work above all for the ultimate end. . . . It is necessary to keep the Italian people focused on the ultimate end" (Ferri, "Il metodo rivoluzionario," *Il Socialismo*, 25 May 1902, pp. 97–106).

16. Ferri statement in PSI, *Resoconto del IX congresso*, pp. 39–42, 184, 186–88. On Ferri's appeal to the rank and file, see Marconi, *Storia dei partiti popolari*, pp. 56–57. On the growing disillusion with Ferri, evident by 1908, see PSI, *Resoconto del X congresso*, p. 139.

17. Ferri, "Il metodo rivoluzionario," *Il Socialismo*, 25 May 1902, pp. 97–106.

18. Ferri, "Dopo il congresso di Amsterdam," *Il Socialismo*, 10 Sept. 1904, pp. 209–11. "Dopo la Battaglia," *Il Socialismo*, 10 Nov. 1904, pp. 273–75.

19. For details and an analysis of the failures of the Reformists, see Procacci, *Lotta di classe*, pp. 184–223. Riosa, *Socialismo riformista a Milano*, pp. 403, 416, on *Tempo; GC*, 2:217–18; and *TKC*, 2:52–53, 64–65, 74–75. On *Il Socialismo*, cf. comments of Bissolati to Turati, *TA*, pp. 161–63. For Turati's stress on the importance of Socialist cooperation with Giolitti during this period, cf. DiScala, *Dilemmas*, pp. 70–73.

20. PSI, *Rendiconto del VII congresso*, pp. 12–18.

21. Ibid., pp. 18–19, 55–68.

22. Ibid., pp. 77–84.

23. Bonomi, "Al congresso finito," *Avanti!*, 16–18 Sept. 1902, and Ferri, "Il congresso unitario," *Il Socialismo*, 15 Sept. 1902, pp. 209–10.

24. Labriola, "Il fabianismo italiano," *Il Socialismo*, 10 June 1902, pp. 113–16, and Santarelli, *Lettere*, p. 571. For details of the takeover, see *Avanti!*, 25 Feb., 10 March, 1 April 1903. Procacci, *Lotta di classe*, pp. 260–75. Kuliscioff's evaluation of the importance of the loss of *Avanti!* is in *TKC*, 2:102–4.

25. Ferri, *L'Avanti!: Resoconto morale del giornale*, p. 9. Ferri's efforts to explain away his deficit makes amusing reading. The report is one of the first attempts at a statistical analysis of the newspaper's condition. *Il Socialismo*, Dec. 25, 1902. On the "*succhioni*" campaign, see Coppa, *Planning*, pp. 97–103.

26. DiScala, *Dilemmas*, pp. 72–74; *TKC*, 2:105–8, 125–27, 145; and Giolitti, *Memorie*, p. 134.

27. *GC*, 2:324–25, and Giolitti, *Memorie*, p. 135.

28. Labriola, *Ministero e Socialismo*, and *TKC*, 2:102–5, 145.

29. F. Ciccotti, "Dopo il Congresso di Brescia," *Avanti!*, 27 Feb. 1904, and A. Bertini, "Dopo il Congresso di Brescia," *Il Tempo*, 18 Feb. 1904. On the Ferri coalition's increasing power, see Badaloni and Bartollotti, *Movimento Operaio*, pp. 28–20. *TKC*, 2:159.

30. Duverger, *Political Parties*, p. 143. Cf. Turati's 1906 comments in *TKC*, 2:364–65.

31. Evans, *Coexistence*, pp. 3–16.

32. PSI, *Rendiconto del VIII congresso*, pp. 7–9, 13–16.

33. Ibid., pp. 21–22, 55–63.

34. Ibid., pp. 130–35, 160–61.

35. The minutes of the first Congress of Federterra are in Zanghieri, *Lotte agrarie*, pp. 8–131. A. Schiavi, "L'organisation des paysans en Italie," *Mouvement Socialiste*, 1901, pp. 716–24.

36. On the Imola section, see Salvemini, *Opere* 4, pt. 2: 26–43.

37. *Avanti!*, 13 April 1904. PSI, *Rendiconto del VIII congresso*, pp. 181, 189.

38. Ferri, "Il compito pratico del Congresso di Bologna," *Il Socialismo*, 10 April 1904, pp. 49–50, and PSI, *Rendiconto del VIII congresso*, pp. 162–69. Cf. the analysis of the Congress in DiScala, *Dilemmas*, pp. 78–82.

39. Mocchi's statement is in PSI, *Rendiconto del VIII congresso*, pp. 71–73.

40. *Avanti!*, 13 April 1904; *TKC*, 2:205; and PSI, *Rendiconto del VIII congresso*, pp. 71–72. In 1906 Ferri succeeded in leading the GPS into support of an anti-Giolitti government of Sidney Sonnino, reversing five years of Reformist practice. See Ferri's statement to the 1906 Congress in PSI, *Resoconto del IX Congresso*, pp. 184, 187–88, 194, also *TKC*, 2:125.

41. *Avanti!*, 9 April 1904.

42. PSI, *Rendiconto del VIII congresso*, p. 105.

43. Ibid., pp. 106–7. Writing before the Congress of Bologna, Leone remarked that the Reformists' ability to obscure the differences between the two Party factions had been central to their success. "Imola a Bologna." *Il Socialismo*, 10 March 1904, pp. 17–20. On Turati's strategy for the congress, see *TKC*, 2:205, 209–11, 263, 279.

44. Catalano in the introduction to Marchetti, *Confederazione*, p. viii.

45. Gualtieri, *Labor Movement*, pp. 167–69; Neufield, *Italy*, 320–22; Rigola, *Storia*, pp. 224–25; Procacci, *Lotta di classe*, pp. 61, 163; and Rigola, *La CGL nel triennio 1908–1911*, p. 15.

46. Catalano's introduction to Marchetti, *Confederazione*, p. viii, and Corbino, *Annali*, 5:453–54.

47. For details of the general strike of 1904, see Procacci, *Lotta di classe*, pp. 272–74. The term *general strike* had two meanings for the Syndicalists: either a complete work stoppage by all categories of workers or the complete stoppage of labor in one area. The 1903 Rome, *general strike* fitted into the second category. The 1902 railway workers strike was a national strike but not a general strike since only one economic sector was involved. By 1912 the term *general strike* had been so watered down that it also meant a work stoppage by all the workers in one industry. Leone, "A congresso finito," *Avanti!*, 15 April 1904; Labriola, "Che fare?" *Avanti!*, 23 April 1904; Arfe, *Movimento giovanile*, p. 9; *Avanti!*, 15 Sept. 1904; Spadolini, "1904: Primo sciopero generale"; Procacci, "Lo sciopero"; and Giolitti, *Memorie*, p. 146.

48. Leone, "Dopo lo sciopero," *Avanti!*, 20 Sept. 1904; Leone, "Lo sciopero generale e la politica proletariato," *Il Socialismo*, 10 Oct. 1904, pp. 241–43; Chiesa and Muraldi, *Il Partito Socialista e l'organizazzione economica*, pp. 17, 49; Procacci, "Lo sciopero"; Ferri, "Lo

sciopero generale e l'estrema sinistra," *Avanti!*, 25 Sept. 1904; and Mammarella, *Riformisti*, pp. 167–68.

49. Giolitti, *Memorie*, 146.

50. Albertini, *Vent'anni*, 1:143.

51. Tommaso Tittoni, "Ricordi personali di politica interna," *Nuova Antologia* 342:304–27, 441–67.

52. "Camera Nuova e politica vecchia," *CS*, 1 Nov. 1904, pp. 321–22; *Avanti!*, 15 Nov. 1904; and *SC*, 1:265–67. Cf. table 1. Oddly, the maneuvers to which Giolitti restored to rig the 1904 elections against the PSI may have saved the Reformists from a serious setback in their interparty battles. The doubling of the total Socialist vote was offset by the reduction in the size of the parliamentary group. If Giolitti had allowed the elections to proceed unimpeded, the PSI would probably have won nearly as many seats as it did in 1909 with a similar number of votes. The left would have had proof of its success by electing more deputies than the Reformists. The Italian electoral system and its workings as they affected the PSI are analyzed in DiScala, "Parliamentary Socialists."

53. Santarelli, *Lettere*, pp. 576–77.

54. Ibid., pp. 573–74; Ferri, "Dieci anni o dieci secoli," *Avanti!*, 2 Oct. 1904; and *Avanguardia Socialista*, 15 Dec. 1904.

55. See Santarelli, *Lettere*, pp. 580–81, for the Syndicalist view of the crisis of *Avanti!*.

56. *Avanti!*, 8 March and 12 May 1906; Leone, "Reazione intelligente e riformismo evanescente," *DS*, Mar. 16, 1906, pp. 81–84; Bonomi, "Situazione nuova," *CS*, 16 Feb. 1906, pp. 51–53; "Coll'armi ai piedi," *CS*, 16 Feb. 1906, pp. 149–51; and Ferri, "Le dimissione del Gruppo parlamentare socialista," *Avanti!*, 14 May 1906. The reaction of the Syndicalists to the Sonnino adventure was spelled out in "Dopo l'ultimo sciopero generale," *DS*, 16 May 1906, pp. 145–47. Sabatucci, *Storia del Socialismo*, 2:163. The growing weakness of his position within the PSI induced Ferri to seek closer ties with the Socialist International. Ferri to the Bureau of the International, 6 Feb. 1905, "Ferri," Huysmans Papers, IF. Cf. *TKC*, 2:364–65.

57. *TKC*, 2:364–69, 372–73.

58. PSI, *Resoconto del IX congresso*, pp. 185, 187–188, 194; Sabatucci, *Storia del Socialismo*, 2:245; and *TKC*, 2:125.

59. PSI, *Resoconto del IX congresso*, pp. 196–223, and *TKC*, 2:369.

60. On Lerda, see Finale, "Gli anni genovese di Giovanni Lerda," and Perrilo, "Socialismo e classe operaio." Mammarella, *Reformisti*, pp. 205–6.

61. PSI, *Resoconto del IX congresso*, pp. 273–81.

62. Perrilo, "Socialismo e classe operaio." Thirteen sections in this province voted for the left, while fifteen voted the Integralist motion.

63. Balestrazzi, "Lo sciopero parmense."

64. PSI, *Resoconto del IX congresso*, pp. 286–96. In fact, Ferri included at least six well-known Reformists on the enlarged *Direzione*. The central directive committee, however, was solidly Integralist.

65. *Avanti!*, 12 Oct. 1906. "Per prepararci il congresso," *CS*, 1 July 1906, pp. 196–98.

66. "Previsione ottimistiche," *CS*, 1 Sept 1906, pp. 257–59; *TKC*, 2:424, 494; Labriola, "Sindicalista e il partito socialista, *DS*, 16 June 1906, pp. 181–82; and Mantica, "L'organizzazione del partito," *DS*, July 16, 1906, pp. 209–10. On Turati's successful drive to oust the Syndicalists, see Cortesi, *Socialismo*, p. 294.

67. Rubbiano, *Pensiero politico,* pp. 72–73; *TKC,* 2:364–65, 424; Cortesi, *Storia,* pp. 229–30; and Pepe, "La costituzione."

68. Rigola, *Storia,* pp. 228–30, 245, and Pepe, "La costituzione."

69. Rigola, *Storia,* pp. 306–8, and Cartiglia, *Rigola,* p. 52. The text of the minutes of this Congress is in Marchetti, *Confederazione,* pp. 3–16. The results of the vote are included. Degl'Innocenti, *Storia della cooperazione,* pp. 62–63, 72.

70. Pepe, "La costituzione"; Rigola, *Storia,* p. 288; and D'Aragona to Rigola, 24 Dec. 1908, "D'Aragona," Rigola Papers, IF. Rigola's speech is in PSI, *Resoconto del X congresso,* pp. 202–220.

71. The text of the minutes of the meeting of the CGL's directive council is in Marchetti, *Confederazione,* p. 47.

72. Marchetti, *Confederazione,* pp. 23–24. *TKC,* 2:815–16. Speaking to the 1908 Party Congress, Cabrini commented: "We were, up to the formation of the Confederation of Labor, a bit the shepherds of the spirit of socialist educational [propaganda] and a little bit the technicians of proletarian organization. [Then] came the Confederation, with its ample and complete political program. . . . [A] great part of the policy which before was under the control of the Socialist Party, today is the field of action of organized labor" (PSI, *Resoconto del X congresso nazionale,* pp. 158–59).

73. Labriola, "Che fare?" *Avanti!,* 23 April 1904, and *Il Socialismo,* 25 Feb. 1903, 10 Feb. 1905. On Ferri's abandonment of the PSI, see *Avanti!,* 4 and 5 Jan. 1910.

74. *TKC,* 2:64–65, 205, 236, 434–39, 489; Santarelli, *Lettere,* pp. 573–75; *SC* 1:464; and Balabanoff, *My Life,* p. 30.

Chapter 4

1. PLI, *Rendiconto del I congresso,* in Cortesi, *PSI Attraverso,* p. 19. In a generally unfavorable report to Engels on the outcome of the Congress, Antonio Labriola added, "[There] remains one plausible result of the Congress, the newspaper. It is enough that it exists and I will do whatever I can to aid it" (*LLE,* p. 73). The best study of the paper is Arfe, *Storia del Avanti!.*

2. See the analysis of the paper's prospects by Salvemini, "Per il giornale quotidiano," *Opere* 4, pt. 2: 3.

3. *Lotta di Classe,* 14–15 Aug., 12–13 Sept., and 24–25 Oct. 1896. Two previous attempts to found a daily had failed. Schiavi, "Enquête."

4. *Lotta di Classe,* 21–22 Nov. 1896, and Salvemini, "Per il giornale." A major factor in the decision to publish in Rome was the desire of the Party leadership to avoid the appearance that the PSI was simply another Lombard party on the model of the POI. *Avanti!,* 25 Dec. 1896, and Schiavi, "Enquête." Cf. Sabatucci, *Storia del Socialismo,* 2:186. The copy of *Avanti!* which I used at Rome's Istituto Gramsci was mailed to Turin, and the postmarks indicated that it arrived one to two days late.

5. *Lotta di Classe,* 6–7 Aug. 1892. In order to get a special edition of *Avanti!* on the newsstands at a low price, the paper's administration sent it free to the distributors. Distributors then charged one centesimo to the newsstand dealers, who passed this cost on to public.

Avanti!, 29 Dec. 1902. Normally, the cost to vendors was 3 lire per 100, with the right to a further 10 percent markup. Schiavi, "Enquête."

6. In its first four and a half years of existence, *Avanti!* was confiscated about 150 times by government censors and had to pay 20 to 30,000 lire in fines and court costs. On the tactics of sequestration, see *Avanti!*, 20 Aug. 1898, 21 June 1901, 12 July, 7 Dec. 1904, 22 April 1905, 18 Sept. 1910. For examples of subscription drives, see *Avanti!*, 9 March 1899, 22 May, 18 Nov. 1900, 2 May 1905, 28 Aug. 1908, 13 Feb. 1909. In 1900 Schiavi commented that as a matter of policy "the paper has never given and does not give prizes." On 7 Dec. 1902, *Avanti!* introduced a cash raffle. This practice increased under subsequent directors. Schiavi, "Enquête."

7. Schiavi, "Enquête"; Ferri to Morgari, 14 June 1904, s 1, f 5, b 3, CM, AC/S; and Pontermoli to Morgari, 14 May 1902, s 2, f 5, b 3, CM, AC/S.

8. Mussolini, *Opere*, 5:356, and *Avanti!*, 6, 12 Aug. 1905. The paper utilized telephonic reports for its coverage of the Party Congresses. The Italian state press agency, Stefani, was the source for most domestic and foreign news that appeared in *Avanti!*. The paper's foreign correspondents usually covered news from other Socialist parties. E. Bottazzi, "Leonida Bissolati in via Seminario," in Negro and Lazzarini, *Uomini e giornale*, p. 40, and Balabanoff, *Life*, p. 100.

9. On the sequestration of *Avanti!*, see *Avanti!*, 15 May 1898, 7 Dec. 1904, 22 April 1905. For an example of sequestration motivated by an offending word, see, *Avanti!*, 7 June 1898. Mussolini, *Opere*, 5:356.

10. *Avanti!*'s preference in literature ran strongly toward the social novel. Dickens was approved, presumably for his sympathy with the downtrodden lower classes. Italian and foreign socialists who tried their hands at writing were also published. Russian novelists were esteemed above all others. Between 1897 and 1907, eleven of thirty-four serialized novels were by Russians. On Rigola's role, see Cartiglia, *Rinaldo Rigola*, p. 55. Ferri to Rigola, 19 Feb. 1906, "Ferri," CR, IF.

11. The type of advertising which appeared in *Avanti!* did not differ greatly from that which appeared in other newspapers. Still, for a paper with the self-proclaimed mission of educating the working classes, *Avanti!* might have exercised a bit more prudence and probably would have if its financial condition permitted. Examples of advertising include a full-page ad for a fortune teller (31 Dec. 1901), hair-growing tonics (almost daily), antisyphilis medicine (16 Sept. 1902), cures for impotence (4 Aug. 1903), cure-all "Pilloles Pink" (9 June 1907), brass knuckles (11 Aug. 1908), as well as virility restoratives (11 Aug. 1908).

12. *Avanti!*, 3, 4, 9, 11 Jan. 1897, 14 Feb., 17 April 1898. Schiavi, "Enquête." Morgari to the Administrative Council of *Avanti!*, 22 Jan. 1898, s 1, f 5, b 3, CM, AC/S. On Galantra, see Santarelli, *L'Asino*, and Neri, *Galantra*.

13. *Avanti!*, 9 May 1898, and Bonomi, "Ricordi."

14. *Avanti!*, 10, 14, 15, 17, 20 May, 11 June, 17 July, 6, 8 Sept., 22–25, 29, 30 Oct., 1, 7 Nov. 1898; Bonomi, "Ricordi"; and Schiavi, "Enquête."

15. *Avanti!*, 19 May, 28 June, 22–23 Sept., 17, 25 Dec. 1898.

16. Ibid., 3–5, 7, 16–17 Feb., 7, 15 March, 1 April 1899.

17. *LL*, p. 319.

18. PSI, *Rendiconto del VI congresso*, pp. 27–29, 32–39, and *Rendiconto del VII congresso*, pp. 87–90. See also the supplement to *Lotta di Classe*, 10 Sept. 1902.

19. *LLB*, p. 326.

20. Ibid., p. 327. On the various factions attempting to revise Marxism in Italy, see Santarelli, *Revisione.*

21. *Avanti!*, 25 April, 3, 9, 21 May, 4 June 1900, 20 June 1901.

22. Ibid., 18 Nov., 25, 30 Dec. 1900.

23. Ibid., 9 March, 20 Dec. 1899, 27 Dec. 1900, 30 Dec. 1901.

24. PSI, *Rendiconto del VII congresso*, pp. 88–89, and *Avanti!*, 24 Feb. 1903.

25. *Avanti!*, 24 Feb., 19 March, 1, 3–4 April 1903. Cf. "Abdicazione," *CS*, 16 May, 1 June 1903, pp. 149–51. TKC, 2:102–4.

26. *Avanti!*, 12, 24 May 1903.

27. On anticlericalism in Ferri's *Avanti!*, see the coverage of the last illness of Leo XIII and subsequent election of Pius X in *Avanti!*, 9–14, 17–19, 22–31 July, 1–5 Aug. 1903. Examples of Ferri's self-promotion proliferate. See, for example, the coverage of the slander trial against *Avanti!* in the period Nov. 1903–Jan. 1904; the coverage of Ferri's visit to Paris, *Avanti!*, 22–26 Feb. 1904; and his participation at the 1904 Congress of the Socialist International, *Avanti!*, 17–23 Aug. 1904. For the return of sequestration, see *Avanti!*, 18 Sept., 14 Oct. 1903.

28. *Avanti!*, 4 April, 11, 22 May, 2 June 1903; PSI, *Rendiconto del VIII congresso*, pp. 10–11, 169; and Ferri, *L'Avanti!: Resoconto morale del giornale*, p. 9. Ferri was particularly anxious to create the impression that he had restored the paper to good financial health. When the Turin daily, *La Stampa*, reported the paper's financial situation was shaky, *Avanti!* heatedly denied the story. Ferri's 1904 claims of a restored financial balance were based on projections of expenses which his own plans upset.

29. *Avanti!*, 31 Aug., 14 Oct. 1904.

30. Ibid., 8, 18 April, 26 July 1906.

31. Ibid., 26 Aug. 1906. The expenses of the newspaper showed a gradual but continuous rise under Ferri. Arfe, *Storia*, pp. 65, 69.

32. Aside from the cost of new machines, the move to new offices were expensive, costing 4000 lire. Signs of the worsening condition of *Avanti!* included the decision to threaten all non-paid-up vendors with court action and their suspension, the decision to impose a forced loan from all Party leaders, and revelations during the investigation of reputed Syndicalist misappropriation of funds in the *Avanti!-Azione* case that Ferri had taken out a personal loan to help the paper in addition to the disclosure that the Syndicalists were tapping the paper's funds. *Avanti!*, 26–27 Aug. 1906, and Ferri circular letter, June 1907, "Ferri," CR, IF.

33. *Avanti!*, 10 March 1906.

34. On the return of the Reformists, see *Avanti!*, 24 Sept. 1907. On the *Azione* inquiry, see *Avanti!*, 30–31 March, 1, 18–21 April 1907. The results of the *Direzione*'s inquiry were published in the edition of 21 April.

35. *Avanti!*, 21 April, 1, 5 May, 2, 4 Aug., 1 Oct., 30 Nov. 1907. Included among the prizes were books by the right-wing Reformist Guido Podrecca and Syndicalist leader Arturo Labriola.

36. *Avanti!*, 6 Feb., 27 June, 18 Aug. 1908.

37. PSI, *Resoconto del X congresso*, pp. 109–73.

38. Ibid., pp. 181–98, 363–64.

39. *Avanti!*, 1 Oct. 1908.

40. For the guidelines, see *Avanti!*, 18 Oct. 1908, and also 17 Dec. 1908, 22 April, 28 Aug. 1909. In 1909 the paper lost 46,224.30 lire. PSI, *Relazione sull' Avanti!*, 1910, p. 8. Also see *Avanti!*, 20 Sept. 1909.

41. *Avanti!*, 28 Dec. 1909, 13, 21 Feb., 2, 3 March, 10 June, 20, 24 July, 12 Sept. 1910. PSI, *Relazione sull' Avanti!*, 1910, p. 6–8, and Cortesi, *Socialismo*, p. 406. Cf. the comments of Bergamasco, Lazzari, and Turati in PSI, *Resoconto del XI congresso*, pp. 312–31. *TKC*, 2:1154, 1159–60, and 3:21–22.

42. *TKC*, 2:303, 1128–29, 1159–60, 3:21–22, 70.

43. *TKC*, 3:350–51, 357–60, 362, 431, 440, 456–59, 572. Cf. Turati to Morgari, 13 March 1911, s 1, f 16, b 10, CM, AC/S, and Treves to Rigola, 12 Jan. 1911, "Treves," CR, IF.

44. *Avanti!*, 5 Dec. 1910, 27 May, 5, 14 June 1911. On Scalarini, see *Avanti!*, 14 Dec. 1913. Prior to his retirement, Bissolati came under harsh criticism for his lack of enthusiasm for universal suffrage; see *Avanti!*, 8 June 1910, 23 March, 1 May 1911.

45. Ibid., 24, 28 July 1911.

46. Ibid., 7, 17 Sept. 1911. Balabanoff indicates that the decision to leave a Roman staff may have been influenced by the low incomes of several of the editors. *Life*, p. 98.

47. *La Soffitta*, 1 July 1911; PSI, *Resoconto del XII congresso*, pp. 259–93; and *TKC*, 3:21–22.

48. *Avanti!*, 10 Feb. 1912; "Relazione della Società editrice socialista," *Avanti!*, 20 April 1914; and Arfe, *Storia*, pp. 101–2.

49. See the letter of Treves in *Avanti!*, 23 July 1912, and the judgment of Arfe, *Storia*, pp. 101–2.

50. *TKC*, 2:1128–29, 3:231, 572, 726.

Chapter 5

1. Information on the secretariat is derived from Costa, *Il Gruppo parlamentare;* Montemartini, *Il Gruppo parlamentare;* PSI, *Relazione del gruppo;* Morgari, "Relazione del GPS," *Avanti!*, 1 Dec. 1904, 21, 24, 25 April 1914; and *I 508*.

2. On non-PSI members in the GPS, *La Nazione*, 17–18 Feb., 18–19 Nov. 1909. PSI members who remained outside the GPS included E. Ferri (1909–11), Morgari and Mussatti (1912), and even Turati (1904). See *Avanti!*, 23 March 1902, for the nomination of an orator, *Avanti!*, 13 March 1902, on the use of the unit rule, and *Avanti!*, 14 March 1902 on the division of the work load.

3. Sources used in preparing this group biography include those listed in n. 5, chapter 1, together with the obituaries of deputies which ran in *Avanti!* and the series "I 508 moribundi" which ran in the paper beginning on 7 August 1904. The other Socialist deputies greeted the maiden parliamentary speech of one of the working class deputies with cries of "Silence, labor speaks!" *Avanti!*, 7 Feb. 1901.

4. Galli and Prandi, *Patterns*, p. 43. The PSI won its first seat in Rome in the 1909 elections and took a second seat in a special election in 1910. In 1912, a Socialist orator noted that 900 PSI sections existed in the 308 parliament seats north of Rome. South of Rome there were 201 electoral colleges but only 78 Socialist sections. PSI *Resoconto del XIII congresso*, p. 262.

5. For example, in 1900 Turati was editor of *Critica Sociale*, president of the Milan Socialist party, a member of the *Direzione*, president of the mailmen's union, a practicing attorney,

and a deputy. Ferri and Ciccotti were university professors, chiefs of their local Party organizations, and of course, deputies. Letter from the Turin Chamber of Labor to Morgari, 15 July 1906, insert 1, s 6, f 8, b 5, CM, AC/S; Ciotti to Morgari, 14 Aug. 1909, and Ciotti to all GPS deputies, 11 July 1909, s 1, f 16, b 10, CM, AC/S; and *TKC*, 2:39, 312. Cf. the correspondence in b 7, f 12, CM, AC/S. "Previsione," *Lotta di Classe*, 22–23 Oct. 1894; *Avanti!*, 16 April 1900, 25 May, 29 June 1902, 6 May 1904, 21 Feb. 1905; and Turati, "Agli amici," *CS*, 16 Feb. 1909, p. 49. Todescini was elected to a seat from Gonzaga.

6. *Avanti!*, 14 and 24 Oct. 1900, 23 Nov. 1901; *La Nazione*, 20–21 Jan 1908; and "La Propaganda socialista nel VI collegio," *Avanti!*, 1 Jan. 1901.

7. Ciccotti, "L'opere dei deputati socialisti," *Avanti!*, 17 July 1901. Cf. the letters to Morgari in s 1, b 4, f 6, CM, AC/S.

8. For an example of the nomination procedure, see *Avanti!*, 25 May 1900. Morgari to the "comrades" of Turin, n.d., s 2, b 4, f 5, CM, AC/S. Zerboglio to Morgari, 13 March 1910, s 1, b 6, f 12, CM, AC/S.

9. In 1902, for example, Costa arranged for reduced railway fares for delegates to the PSI Congress. *Avanti!*, 23 August 1902. On the initial reaction of Socialists to the Ferri interview, *Avanti!*, 15 Nov. 1909. *Avanti!*, 13, 22 Dec. 1909; *La Nazione*, 27–28 Dec. 1909; and *TKC*, 3:211. On Ferri's 1912 activities, Viani, "L'azione politica di I. Bonomi," and Manzotti, *Il Socialismo riformista*, pp. 183–86.

10. *Statistica della elezione (1904)*, p. 87. *Avanti!*, 15 Dec. 1901, 20 March 1902, 4 Jan. 1903, 5 April 1904.

11. Leone and Mantica to Morgari, 24 June 1906, s 2, b 3, f 5, CM, AC/S. A good example of how the combination of proportional representation and the selection of organizational candidates from the central organs can discipline a party was provided by the Italian Communist party in the 1972 parliamentary elections. In selecting its candidates, the PCI dropped one-third of its sitting senators and deputies in good part to create the image of a more youthful party.

12. *Avanti!*, 13 March 1897.

13. "I deputati socialisti. Ciò che fanno e ciò che possono fare," *Lotta di Classe*, 26–27 May 1894.

14. "Il Gruppo socialista parlamentare," *Lotta di Classe*, 8–9 June 1895.

15. PSI, *Rendiconto del VI congresso*, pp. 71, 77–78, 82–84; E. Ferri, "Prima del congresso," *Avanti!*, 12, 13 Aug. 1900; and *Avanti!*, 6 Feb., 6 April, 17, 27 May 1900. Even the fairly radical Socialist proposal for a constituent assembly was couched in terms of constitutional rather than social reform; *Avanti!*, 27 March 1900.

16. "La Vittoria," *CS*, 1 July 1900, pp. 193–94. "The Zanardelli government, as Ferri clearly noted in his March address to the Chamber, is the principal if not the exclusive fruit of two years of work by the *estrema*." Turati, "Ministerialismo," *Avanti!*, 16 April 1901. Even the usually negative Antonio Labriola felt the GPS was following the proper course by cooperating with the progressive forces of the bourgeoisie. See his comments, *Avanti!*, 28 Aug., 12 Sept. 1901.

17. *Avanti!*, 29 May 1901, and "La politica nostra," *CS*, 1 June 1901, pp. 161–63.

18. *TKC*, 2:911–13, 3:929.

19. *AP*, Camera, 21st Legislature, 1st session, 2622–25, 6017–18, 6128–29, 6475–79.

20. *Avanti!*, 11, 21 Dec. 1901; *AP*, Camera, 21st Legislature, 2d session, pp. 5685–87; and DiScala, "Parliamentary Socialists."

21. Labriola, *Ministero e socialismo,* pp. 9, 22, 31; *Avanti!,* 22 Feb. 1902; Ferri, "Il coraggio della libertà," *Socialismo,* 10 March 1902, pp. 17–18; and Labriola, "Il Fabianismo italiano," *Socialismo,* 10, 25 June, 10 July 1902, pp. 113–16, 129–31, 145–47.

22. "Sciopero parlamentare," *CS,* 16 May 1902, pp. 145–46, and *TKC,* 2:11, 52–53, 74–75, 94, 102–5, 281–83. In 1904 Kuliscioff proposed a congress of Reformists to create a program of action for a parliamentary group, TKC, 2:178. Vigezzi, *Il PSI,* pp. 27–28.

23. "Sciopero parlamentare," *CS,* 16 May 1902, pp. 145–46. See *TKC,* 2:105, 145, 283, 358, 776, for the views of Turati and Kuliscioff. Bertesi, Turati, and others to Morgari, 17 Sept. 1904, s 4, f 6, b 5, CM, AC/S.

24. *TKC,* 2:74–75, 102–4, 281–83.

25. Ferri, "La Bancarotta del popolarismo," *Socialismo,* 10 Aug. 1902, pp. 177–80; "Il Partito socialista e Italia meridionale," *Socialismo,* 10 Oct. 1902; and *Avanti!,* 5 Feb., 24 June 1903. On the Ferri-Turati duel, see Mammarella, *Riformisti,* p. 151.

26. *Avanti!,* 7 Oct. 1904, and *TKC,* 2:80, 115–16, 205, 209–11, 358, 361–62, 434–39. Cf. D. Sachi to Morgari, 15 March 1906, s 4, f 6, b 4, CM, AC/S. Morgari to the Turin section, 16 March 1905, s 4, f 6, b 4, CM, AC/S.

27. *Avanti!,* 1 Dec. 1904, and *TKC,* 2:207–11.

28. E. Ferri, "Duplice crisi," *Avanti!,* 8, 23 March 1905, and *TKC,* 2:419, 434–39. See DiScala, *Dilemmas,* pp. 107–12, on the debacle of the first Sonnino ministry.

29. Zerboglio, "La funzione e l'opera del Gruppo parlamentare socialista," *CS,* 16 July 1906, pp. 209–10.

30. "La nostra azione parlamentare," *CS,* 1 Jan. 1907, pp. 2–3.

31. "L'inazione parlamentare socialista," *CS,* 16 Jan. 1907, pp. 17–20.

32. "Spettri e realtà," *CS,* 1 March 1907, pp. 67–71. Cf. Kuliscioff's comments in *TKC,* 2:963.

33. Marchetti, *Confederazione,* pp. 36–37; *Avanti!,* 29 March 1907; "Bisogna decidersi," *CS,* 1 April 1907, pp. 97–98; and "La riapertura," *CS,* 1 Dec. 1907, pp. 353–54. For Integralist comments on the GPS's problems, see *Avanti!,* 27 April 1907.

34. *TKC,* 2:776–78.

35. *TKC,* 2:257, 762, 776–79, 870, 911–13.

36. *Avanti!,* 9 June 1908, and *La Nazione,* 9–10, 11–12 June 1908. Cf. *TKC,* 2:698–99, 776–78.

37. On the transformation of DeFelice, see Renda, "Giuseppe DeFelice-Giuffrida." *TKC,* 2:721–22.

38. Mussolini, *Opere,* 4:18.

39. Cf. comments of *La Nazione,* 20–21 Nov. 1909. On growing problem of absenteeism, see *Avanti!,* 22 May 1899, 4 Dec. 1902, 21 Nov. 1903, 25 May 1904.

40. *TKC,* 2:587. Cf. "Ripresa d'armi," *CS,* 16 Aug. 1905, pp. 241–42.

41. *TKC,* 2:308, 1118; *Avanti!,* 18 April 1907; and Spinella, *Critica Sociale,* pp. 272–78.

42. *TKC,* 2:728–29, 781, 884–85, 1047.

43. PSI, *Resoconto del X congresso,* pp. 305–8, and *TKC,* 2:1096–97, 3:152–53.

44. *TKC,* 2:886.

45. *TKC,* 2:912.

46. *TKC,* 2:929, 935; "Blocco e non più blocco," *CS,* 1 Sept. 1908, pp. 237–39; and *Avanti!,* 14 Feb., 27 March 1909.

47. *TKC,* 2:1080, 1090–91; and *Avanti!,* 8 July 1909. Cf. Cortesi, *Storia,* pp. 294–95.

48. *La Nazione*, 30–31 Aug. 1909, and *Avanti!*, 10 Sept. 1909.

49. *TKC*, 3:9–10, 13, 31, 73–74, 106. *SC*, 1:427–28. *Avanti!*, 22 Feb. 1910.

50. *TKC*, 3:102–3.

51. *TKC*, 3:122, 152–53, and *CS*, 1 May 1910, p. 129, and 16 May 1910, pp. 145–49.

52. Vigezzi, *Giolitti e Turati*, pp. 3–8, passim, and *TKC*, 3:505–21.

53. DiScala, "Parliamentary Socialists"; *TKC*, 3:444; and Giolitti, *Memorie*, p. 211.

Chapter 6

1. Marchetti, *Confederazione*, pp. 39–40, 51–62, 68, 125.

2. Ibid., pp. xvi, 42, 63–64, 77–80; Rigola, *La CGdL, 1908–1911*, p. 5; Rigola, *Storia*, pp. 343–44, 396–97; and Cortesi, *Socialismo*, p. 294.

3. Turati, "La leva elettorale," *CS*, 1 May 1908, pp. 129–32; *Avanti!*, 9 Feb., 4 Sept. 1909; Perlstein, "Le Congrès socialiste," *La Tribuna*, 27 Oct. 1910; Bello, *L'Azione*, pp. 75–76; and *TKC*, 2:968.

4. *Avanti!*, 21 Sept. 1908, and PSI, *Resoconto del X congresso*, pp. 202–20, 222–39.

5. PSI, *Resoconto del X congresso*, pp. 250–65.

6. *Avanti!*, 23 Sept. 1908, and PSI, *Resoconto del X congresso*, pp. 279–309.

7. Cf. Miller, "Italian Socialist Party," pp. 201–2.

8. PSI, *Resoconto del X congresso*, pp. 348–51, 354–60; *Avanti!*, 24 Sept. 1908; and Vigezzi, *Il PSI*, p. 33.

9. *Avanti!*, 8 March 1909, and Cortesi, *Socialismo*, pp. 294–95.

10. "Spettri e realtà," *CS*, 1 March 1907, pp. 67–71.

11. "Rinnovazione," *CS*, 16 Dec. 1906, pp. 369–72.

12. *SC*, 1:439; PSI, *Vigilia del congresso*, p. 16; and *TKC*, 2:1033.

13. *SC*, 1:449, and *TKC*, 3:9–10.

14. "E il partito?" *CS*, 16 July 1911, pp. 209–10. For a different view, see Mammarella, *Riformisti*, p. 204. See also the comments of Vigezzi, *Giolitti e Turati*, pp. 294ff.

15. "Sindacalismo, riformismo e rivoluzionarismo," *CS*, 1 August 1905, pp. 195–97. See DiScala, *Dilemmas*, pp. 103–4, for Turati's analysis.

16. Bonomi, *Vie nuove*, pp. 7, 9–10, 13, 15–16, 21, 27, 34–36, 38, 41, 44, 47.

17. Ibid., pp. 54–55, 65, 75.

18. Ibid., pp. 109, 116, 120–21, 123–24.

19. Ibid., pp. 196–97.

20. Bonomi, "Il partito socialista," *Il Viandante*, 17 Oct. 1909, pp. 153–54.

21. *Avanti!*, 4 June 1910, and Bonomi, "Il partito socialista." On Turati's reaction, as well as an analysis of his role in the development of "Reformism of the right," cf. DiScala, *Dilemmas*, pp. 106–7.

22. Balabanoff, *Life*, p. 30.

23. DiScala, *Dilemmas*, pp. 126–29; *Avanti!*, 7, 11 April, 6 May 1909; *La Nazione*, 30 June–1 July 1909; and Valiani, "Problema."

24. *Avanti!*, 6 May 1909, 4 June 1910; Cartiglia, *Rinaldo Rigola*, pp. 64, 73, and "La CGdL e il progetto"; Bissolati, "Socialismo e governi," *CS*, 1 March 1904, pp. 68–70; and Bonomi, "Incubazione" *CS*, 1 Feb. 1904, pp. 33–35. Rigola's statement is in *Il Viandante*, 5

Dec. 1909, pp. 213–14. Cf. Cartiglia, "La CGdL e il progetto," and *Rinaldo Rigola*, p. 74.

25. Schiavi, "Lettere Bonomi," pp. 118–20. See also Kuliscioff, "Verso nuovi lidi," *CS*, 1 Jan. 1908, p. 2. *TKC*, 2:963. On Modigliani and Salvemini, see Arena, "Formazione ideale"; Badaloni and Bartolotti, *Movimento operaio;* Basso, *Salvemini;* and Colapietra, "Il maestro."

26. Salvemini, "Nord e sud nel partito socialista," *CS*, 16 Dec. 1902, pp. 373–74.

27. Salvemini, "I socialisti meridionali," in *Opere*, 4, pt. 2: 314–16, and "Nord e sud." Cf. Kuliscioff's comments in *TKC*, 2:1096–97.

28. Salvemini, "I socialisti meridionali."

29. PSI, *Resoconto del X congresso*, p. 258.

30. Salvemini, *Opere*, 4; pt. 2: 301–2; "Il suffragio universale e le riforme," in Salvemini, *Opere*, 4, pt. 1: 65–72; PSI, *Resoconto del X congresso*, pp. 250–66. For Turati's view of Salvemini, see DiScala, *Dilemmas*, pp. 113–14.

31. PSI, *Resoconto del X congresso*, p. 225.

32. *SC*, 1:265–67, and Salvemini "Il pericolo," *Avanti!*, 21 May 1899.

33. *CS*, 16 Jan. 1907, pp. 67–71; Salvemini and Turati, "Che fare," *CS*, 1 Jan. 1911, pp. 1–5; and PSI, *Resoconto del XI congresso*, p. 66.

34. *SC*, 1:433–36; Salvemini, *Opere*, 4; pt. 2: 355–56; and *TKC*, 3:11–12.

35. *SC*, 1:419–22, 432–33, and *TKC*, 3:21–22.

36. *SC*, 1:426–27.

37. *SC*, 1:423, 437–38, 454, and Turati, "In vista del congresso," *CS*, 1 June 1910, pp. 161–64. Cf. *TKC*, 3:63, 92–93.

38. *SC*, 1:455–58. On Kuliscioff's mediation, see *TKC*, 3:284, 286, and DiScala, *Dilemmas*, p. 117.

39. *SC*, 1:465–67. Cf. DiScala, *Dilemmas*, pp. 118–19.

40. *Avanti!*, 11, 16 Sept. 1910; Turati, "La vittoria delle cose," *CS*, 1 Oct. 1908, pp. 289–90; and PSI, *Resoconto del XI congresso*, pp. 29–34.

41. PSI, *Resoconto del XI congresso*, pp. 14, 23–27.

42. Ibid., pp. 43–56. Cf. *TKC*, 3:152–53, 372.

43. PSI, *Resoconto del XI congresso*, 59–70, and *TKC*, 3:160–61, 168, 261.

44. PSI, *Resoconto del XI congresso*, pp. 174–89.

45. Cf. Miller, "Italian Socialist party," pp. 225–26.

46. PSI, *Resoconto del XI congresso*, pp. 287–91, 330–32, and *TKC*, 3:92–93.

Chapter 7

1. *Avanti!*, 26 Oct. 1910, and *La Soffitta*, 15 June 1911.

2. *La Soffitta*, 15 June, 15 July 1911. For information on how this conquest was carried out, see Guerrini, *Movimento operaio empolese*, and Ragionieri, *Comune socialista*. On the newspaper, see *La Soffitta*, 1 May, 15 Aug. 1911. *Avanti!*, 7 April 1911.

3. PSI, *Resoconto del XI Congresso*, p. 219.

4. *La Soffitta*, 15 Aug. 1911.

5. F. Ciccotti, "Il Partito socialista si dissolve?" *Rivista d'Italia*, Sept. 1911, pp. 411–22. *Avanti!*, 29 Oct. 1910.

6. See note 5. On the Young Socialists, see Arfe, *Movimento giovanile*, pp. 6, 38–52, 78.

Mammarella, *Riformisti,* pp. 280–95, and Martinelli, "I giovanni." The 1904 Reformist resolution on the Young Socialists read in part "The congress recognizes that the so-called young
peoples circles lately flourishing in Italy are either a useless duplication of the socialist circles
or create a pernicious dualism. . . . [They are] a most dangerous form of puerile ambition and
of deplorable stagnation" (Zibordi, *Relation,* p. 8).

7. On membership, see *La Avanguardia,* 28 August 1910. Three weeks later, at the FGS
national congress, these claims were scaled down to a membership of 4330. FGS, *Resoconto
del III congresso,* p. 33. This represented a threefold growth in FGS since 1907. On the press,
see *Avanti!,* 31 Aug. 1908, and *La Avanguardia,* 31 Dec. 1910. *La Avanguardia* aimed at 2000
subscriptions and a newsstand run of 10,000 copies per issue. On the Young Socialists views,
cf. FGS, *Resoconto del III congresso,* pp. 20, 38. *La Avanguardia,* 14 Aug. 1910.

8. Mammarella, *Riformisti,* p. 290. Typical antimilitarist outbursts are found in FGS, *Resoconto del III congresso,* p. 52, and PSI, *Resoconto del IX congresso,* pp. 366–69. When the
conscription of a new "class" was announced the following year, the FGS, in a published
statement, denounced conscription and militarism but advised draftees to serve and try to
undermine the system. It also urged Socialist draftees not to flee Italy. *La Avanguardia,* 16
Oct. 1910. On the Reformists and the Masons, see *La Avanguardia,* 14 Aug. 1910, and *TKC,*
3:180.

9. Among the most frequent contributors to *La Avanguardia* were "Sylva Vivani" (Giovanni Martinelli), the Party specialist on military affairs, and Angelica Balabanoff. On FGS
membership, see *La Avanguardia,* 14 Aug. 1911, and *Avanti!,* 31 Aug. 1908. Among the future
leaders of the working-class movement passing through FGS in these years were Gramsci,
Tasca, Togliatti, Bordiga, and Bombacci, the future founders of the Italian Communist party.
Arfe, *Movimento giovanile,* p. 108, and Mammarella, *Riformisti,* p. 289. Arfe has pointed out
that FGS became a party in itself for the young, who tended to remain inside it for as long as
possible, showing great reluctance to join the parent PSI. FGS probably failed to provide all
the support the Revolutionaries desired. There are no figures for the passage of members from
the FGS to the PSI, but in December 1911, the Party had 30,220 members, and in July 1912,
it had a membership of 30,233. This suggests little movement. Degl'Innocenti, *Libia,* pp.
247–48, and Hembree, "Lazzari," p. 272.

10. *La Soffitta,* 15 June 1911, gave figures for the Forli sections as 2100 Socialists and 360
FGS members. On elitism, Mussolini, *Opere,* 1:128. *La Avanguardia Socialista,* 3 Sept. 1904;
F. Ciccotti, "Il Partito socialista si dissolve?" *Rivista d'Italia,* Sept. 1911, pp. 411–22; and
Feroci, *Socialismo e massoneria.* On parliament, Mussolini, *Opere,* 3:43–44. On violence,
Avanguardia Socialista, 10 Dec. 1904. Mussolini, *Opere* 1:147–49, 174–84.

11. Mussolini, *Opere,* 2:163–68.

12. Lazzari, *Principi e metodi;* Detti, "Serrati, il partito"; Mussolini, *Opere,* 2:115; Lerda,
Sull'organizzazione, pp. 8–14; *La Soffitta,* 15 Oct. 1911; and Degl'Innocenti, *Libia,* p. 244.
The quote is from a resolution of the Rome Socialist Union in *La Soffitta,* 12 Nov. 1911.

13. The proposed constitution is an appendix to Lerda, *Sull'organizzazione.* Cf. Lerda proposed constitution arts. 6, 8, 9, 10, 11, 14 with PSI, *Statuto,* arts. 6, 11, 14.

14. The resolution is reprinted in *La Soffitta,* 1 Sept. 1911.

15. *Avanti!,* 20 March 1911.

16. Giolitti, *Memorie,* pp. 192–93. Cf. *TKC,* 3:516–21.

17. *Avanti!,* 24 March 1911. Judging from the reaction of the local Socialist press that
Avanti! published, a sizeable minority of sections supported Bissolati's action.

18. Turati, "Dura salita," *CS*, 1 April 1911, pp. 97–99, and DiScala, *Dilemmas*, pp. 122–23.

19. Giolitti, *Memorie*, p. 206 for details.

20. "Impreparazione," *CS*, 16 June–1 July 1911, p. 177, and *TKC*, 3:509, 516–21. Giolitti did not agree with Turati and Bissolati on the political "immaturity" of the Italian working class. He cuttingly noted, "It seemed that the Socialists could mature individuals for government and its responsibilities but not the Party itself" (*Memorie*, pp. 135, 192). Valiani, "Problema," and Vigezzi, *Giolitti e Turati*, pp. 3–8.

21. See Rigola's statement in *Il Viandante*, 5 Dec. 1909, pp. 213–14, and the comments of Bissolati and Lerda in PSI, *Resoconto del XI congresso*, pp. 174–89, 212–20. Mussolini understood Bissolati's plans very well, cf. *Opere*, 3:366–42.

22. On the Catholics, Santarelli, *Revisione*, p. 133. Palazzi, "Opinione." Cf. the bibliographical information in Degl'Innocenti, *Libya*, p. 21. Coppa, *Planning*, pp. 116–22; Candeloro, *Movimento*, pp. 341–52; Candeloro, *Storia*, 7:315, 318–20; and Bosworth, *Italy*, p. 119.

23. Webster, *Industrial Imperialism*, pp. 191–246; Bosworth, *Italy*, pp. 126, 144–46; Vigezzi, "Imperialismo"; and Sori, "Penetrazione."

24. On the Nationalists, see Salomone, *Giolittian Era*, pp. 86–101. Thayer, *Italy and the Great War*, pp. 192–232, and De Grand, *Italian Nationalist Association*, pp. 132–35, 141–45, 150–52.

25. Salomone, *Giolittian Era*, p. 87; Bosworth, *Italy*, pp. 133, 142; Giolitti, *Memorie*, pp. 213–16; Askew, *Europe and Italy*, p. 41; Seton-Watson, *Italy*, p. 367; and Angiolini, *Socialismo*, pp. 585–86.

26. *GC*, 3:52–56.

27. Giolitti, *Discorsi Extraparlamentari*, p. 261. Cf. Bosworth, *Italy*, p. 163.

28. A number of Italian historians have suggested that Giolitti was seeking consciously to utilize the Libyan war as the final act in the transformation of the PSI, securing a renunciation of its ideology and entry into the Giolitti government. Pepe, *Storia*, pp. 6–7, takes this line. However, in view of Giolitti's own correspondence, his lifelong adversion to colonial adventures, his later opposition to Italy's entry into World War I, and the statements cited in the text, this is a difficult position to hold. Cf. Bosworth, *Italy*, pp. 127–60.

29. Cunsolo, "Libya"; Giolitti, *Memorie*, p. 295; and Askew, *Europe and Italy*, p. 249.

30. The most famous example of Giolitti's mistaken evaluation was his 8 April 1911 statement to the Chamber that "Marx has been sent to the attic" by the Socialists. *GC*, 3:40, 61. See the comments of Bissolati, *Politica estera*, pp. 229–30. Degl'Innocenti, *Libia*, pp. 33, 36, 41, 46–48, and Vigezzi, *Giolitti e Turati*, pp. 352–53.

31. Marchetti, *Confederazione*, pp. 146–47, and DeCleva, "Anna Kuliscioff."

32. Degl'Innocenti, *Libia*, p. 155. Margherita Sarfatti, a member of Turati's circle then and later Mussolini's mistress and official biographer, provides an unlikely but entertaining version of the initial reaction of Turati and his closest associates to the threat of war. Sarfatti claimed that both Treves and Turati were initially inclined to support the war, but Kuliscioff convinced them that the PSI must oppose it. *Life*, p. 171.

33. "Soli!" *CS*, 1 Oct. 1911, p. 289, and Vigezzi, *Giolitti e Turati*, pp. 334–40, 352–53, 382.

34. Turati, "L'ora della responsibilità," *CS*, 16 Sept.–1 Oct. 1904, pp. 237–77. The Directive Council of the CGL adopted a position analogous to that of Turati in February 1910. Marchetti, *Confederazione*, p. 109, and DiScala, *Dilemmas*, p. 129.

35. *Avanti!*, 27 Sept 1911. *La Tribuna*, 27 Sept. 1911. On 28 October *La Tribuna* crowed, "The miserable strike against the nation has miserably failed." Pepe, *Storia del CGL*, pp. 18–19. Mussolini's critique of the strike is in *Opere*, 4:61–73. Ciotti to Huysmans, Milan, 22 Oct. 1911, in Haupt, "L'internazionale socialista," and Degl'Innocenti, *Libia*, pp. 151–56.

36. Bissolati, *Politica estera*, pp. 229–30, 232–34.

37. Turati, "La guerra contra l'Italia," *CS*, 16 Nov. 1911, pp. 337–39; *La Tribuna*, 12 Oct. 1911; *TKC*, 3:648–50.

38. *Avanti!*, 25 Sept., 14 Oct. 1911. An example of the problems which the PSI faced in the South was that of the largest section in the region, Naples, which dissolved twice between 1908 and 1910. Each time that the organization was rebuilt it had fewer members.

39. Ciccotti, "Il partito socialista si dissolve?" *Rivista d'Italia*, Sept. 1911, pp. 411–22. *La Soffitta*, 15 June, 15 Oct. 1911.

40. *Avanti!*, 2, 3, 13 Oct. 1911; *La Soffitta*, 15 Sept., 1, 8, 15 Oct. 1911; and Degl'Innocenti, *Libia*, p. 159.

41. *La Soffitta*, 15, 31 July, 1, 8, 15 Oct. 1911.

42. *Avanti!*, 13, 15 Oct. 1911, and *TKC*, 3:648–50.

43. PSI, *Resoconto del XII congresso*, pp. 9–13, 19–26.

44. Ibid., pp. 26–36.

45. Ibid., pp. 62–74.

46. *Avanti!*, 17 Oct. 1911.

47. PSI, *Resoconto del XII congresso*, pp. 156–70.

48. Ibid, pp. 183–211.

49. Ibid., pp. 235–42.

50. Ibid., pp. 246–50, 256. Even if the Revolutionaries had maintained the majority for their resolution, the left would have been unable to achieve a total victory. The 1911 Congress was a special meeting, and the already existing *Direzione* would continue to sit. Both at the Congress and later the *Direzione* underlined its determination to follow a Reformist course. *La Soffitta*, 3 Dec. 1911. PSI, *Resoconto del XII congresso*, p. 256.

51. In 1910 Turati's resolution had the support of 307 sections and 13,006 votes. In 1911 the three Reformist resolutions were supported by 277 sections and 10,637 votes.

52. The actual figures were Reformists, -29.87 percent; Revolutionary, $+24.82$ percent.

53. "La statistica del congresso," *CS*, 1 Nov. 1911, p. 328.

54. Both factions claimed with some justification that the losses in membership came from their followers. The losses came in areas where both sides had shown support in the past, so that it is likely that they both lost backing as a result of the declining strength of the PSI.

55. For the importance of retention, see *La Soffitta*, 2 June 1912.

56. PSI, *Resoconto del XII congresso*, p. 256.

57. "La statistica del congresso," *CS*, 1 Nov. 1911, pp. 327–30.

58. "Quel ha detto il congresso," *CS*, 1 Nov. 1911, pp. 323–25, and "La accordo dei contrari," *CS*, 16 Nov. 1911, pp. 340–41.

59. The FGS was especially proud of losing its middle-class composition. Most middle-class students followed the Syndicalists out of the PSI in 1907. *La Avanguardia*, 14 Aug. 1910; Santarelli, "Socialismo rivoluzionario"; and Spriano, *Socialismo e classe operaio*, and "La terza generazione."

60. Cf. the comments of Degl'Innocenti, *Libia*, 247–48, 255–56, 320–22, with those of Vigezzi, *Giolitti e Turati*, p. 425 n. 41.

61. *La Soffitta*, 1 Oct 1911, 15 Jan. 1912.
62. *La Soffitta*, 29 Oct., 9, 17 Nov., 3 Dec. 1911, and Degl'Innocenti, *Libia*, pp. 242–43.
63. *La Soffitta*, 12, 17 Nov., 11 Dec. 1911; PSI, *Contro la guerra;* and Degl'Innocenti, *Libia*, p. 178. A majority of the deputies opposed the decision for a general strike taken by the Party and CGL on 25 Sept. 1911. The pressures which the International laid on the *Direzione* appear in the correspondence exchanged by Huysmans and Ciotti between October and December 1911 in f "Ciotti a BSI" and "BSI a Ciotti," Fondo Huysmans, IF.
64. *Avanti!*, 9 Feb. 1912, and *La Soffitta*, 15 Feb. 1912.
65. *Avanti!*, 23 Feb. 1912, and Degl'Innocenti, *Libia*, pp. 175–77.
66. Bissolati, *Politica estera*, p. 254.
67. *Avanti!*, 24 March 1912; *La Soffitta*, 4 March 1912; "La scissione del gruppo social-ista," *CS*, 1 March 1912, pp. 65–67; Degl'Innocenti, *Libia*, pp. 175–77; and *TKC*, 3:664, 667, 682–83, 699–704.
68. Mussolini, *Opere*, 4:113.
69. *La Soffitta*, 15 March 1912.
70. Ibid., 16 April, 1 May 1912. Mussolini, *Opere*, 4:125–28.
71. *La Soffitta*, 19 May 1912; Prefect of Ancona to the minister of the interior, 18 June 1912, f K5-Ancona, b 50, Interior Ministry Files, AC/S; prefect of Milan to the minister of the interior, 6 June 1912, f K5-Milano, b 50, Interior Ministry files, AC/S; and Hembree, "Laz-zari," pp. 271, 273.
72. *La Soffitta*, 2, 15 June, 6 July 1912. On the Revolutionary takeover in Sardinia, see Mancini, Melis, and Misu, *Storia dei partiti popolari*, pp. 122ff. Prefect of Florence to the minister of the interior, 3 June 1912, f K5, b 51, Interior Ministry files, AC/S, and prefect of Milan to minister of the interior, 26 Feb. and 2 July 1912, f K5, b 51, Interior Ministry files, AC/S.
73. *La Soffitta*, 15, 22, 29 June, 6 July 1912; *Avanti!*, 2 July 1912; and Prefect of Turin to the minister of the interior, 26 Feb. and 2 July 1912, f K5 Torino, b 51, Interior Ministry files, AC/S.
74. "All'Opposizione," *CS*, 16 March 1912, pp. 81–82; *Avanti!*, 24 March, 22 June 1912; "La crisi del riformismo italiano," *CS*, 16 May, 1, 16 June, 1 July 1912, pp. 146–47, 183–84, 197–98; and Degli'Innocenti, *Libia*, pp. 188, 190, 192, 221–26.
75. "A Reggio Emilia," *CS*, 1 July 1912, pp. 193–94, and *TKC*, 3:712–13, 741.
76. *Avanti!*, 3 July 1912.
77. *Avanti!*, 4, 6 July 1912; *TKC*, 3:712–13, 726; and Degl'Innocenti, *Libia*, p. 186.
78. *GC*, 3:61.

Chapter 8

1. See, for example, Malagodi, "Il socialismo nell'Emilia," in Spinella, *Critica Sociale*, 2:20. *Avanti!*, 7 Dec. 1907, and Turati, "A Reggio Emilia," *CS*, 1 July 1912, pp. 193–94.
2. *TKC*, 3:726, and *Avanti!*, 7 July 1912.
3. *Avanti!*, 7 July 1912; *TKC*, 3:741; and Prefect of Ancona to the minister of the interior, July 18, 1912, f "K–5 Ancona," b 50, Interior Ministry files, AC/S.
4. PSI, *Resoconto del XIII congresso*, pp. 10–11, 13–16, 18–21.

5. *Avanti!*, 8 July 1912.

6. The test of the report is in *Avanti!*, 7 July 1912. PSI, *Resoconto del XIII congresso*, pp. 59–66. Turati referred to the report as an "alibi" (*TKC*, 3:747).

7. PSI, *Resoconto del XIII congresso*, pp. 69–73. Podrecca had been listed on the Revolutionary resolution as one of those to be expelled. However, since he had not gone to the Quirinale with the other three, the Left probably felt it useful to refresh the minds of the delegates about the nature of his crimes. The Bissolati statement quoted by Mussolini was made during the 1900 Party Congress in defending the expulsion of DeMarinis from the PSI.

8. PSI, *Resoconto del XIII congresso*, pp. 75–89, and *Avanti!*, 9 July 1912.

9. PSI, *Resoconto del XIII congresso*, pp. 96, 101, 104–6.

10. Ibid., pp. 151–65.

11. PSI, *Resoconto del XIII congresso*, pp. 23–24, 187–216, and *Avanti!*, 11 July 1912. The first Congress of the new Party took place the following December. For the history of the right Socialists, see Manzotti, *Socialismo riformista*. The studies by Bonomi cited in the bibliography also provide some information on the activities of the new Party.

12. Degl'Innocenti, *Libia*, pp. 256–57, 282.

13. PSI, *Resoconto del XIII congresso*, pp. 238–49, 266–68, 273–86, 289–91. Modigliani, acting as spokesman for the left Reformists, declined the offer of two seats on the *Direzione*. The Reformists preferred "to leave the experiment in your hands."

14. "I risultati del congresso," *CS*, 16 July 1912, pp. 209–14, and "Dopo la vittoria," *La Soffitta*, 20 July 1912. The text of the new *Direzione*'s manifesto is also in *Avanti!*, 13 July 1912. *La Soffitta* ceased publication with its 20 July issue.

15. *Avanti!*, 24 July 1912.

16. *Avanti!*, 5, 18, 22, 29 Aug., 12, 15 Oct. 1912, 2, 11, 25 Jan. 1913, and prefect of Pisa to the minister of the interior, 11 Sept. 1912, f "K–5 Pisa," b 51, Interior Ministry files, AC/S. The deputies involved were Canepa, Berenini, Bonomi, and G. Ferri. All had participated in the foundation of the PSRI. On the struggle between PSI and PSRI in the Mantua area, see Viani, "L'azione politica." *TKC*, 3:825.

17. *Avanti!*, 16 Jan., 9 May 1914. For background on the problems of the Naples section, see *Avanti!*, 7 March 1913, and Fatica, "Movimento socialista napolitano." Prefect of Naples to the minister of the interior, 30 Nov. 1913, f "K–5 Naples," b 48, Interior Ministry files, AC/S. *Avanti!*, 18, 23, 25, 28 July, 2, 6, 14, 17 Aug. 1912. Reporting to the *Direzione* on 5 January 1914, Lazzari stated that 137 sections had left the Party since the Reggio Emilia Congress. Prefect of Genoa to the ministry of the interior, 30 Aug. 1912, f "K–5 Genova," b 50, Interior Ministry files, AC/S; prefect of Bologna to the minister of the interior, 5 Nov. 1912, f "K–5 Bologna," b 50, Interior Ministry files, AC/S; and prefect of Agrigento to the minister of the interior, 13 Sept. 1912, f "K–5 Agrigento," b 50, Interior Ministry files, AC/S.

18. Bonomi, *From Socialism to Fascism*, pp. 10–12. PSI fears about the objectives of the PSRI were well founded. At its initial meeting the leaders of the Socialist Reformists had decided to contest the Socialist party's control of certain sections. *La Tribuna*, 11, 12 July 1912. Vegezzi, *Giolitti e Turati*, p. 402.

19. *Avanti!*, 28 July, 14 Dec. 1912, 20 Jan., 23 March 1914; Arfe, *Storia*, p. 157; and prefect of Milan to the minister of the interior, 19 July 1912, f "K–5 Milano," b 51, Interior Ministry files, AC/S. Mussolini, defending the choice of Cipriani, told the members of the

Milan section that whatever his flaws, the old revolutionary was the *Direzione*'s choice (*Avanti!*, 2 Dec. 1913).

20. Zerbini, *Relazione*, p. 3.

21. Sabatucci, ed., *Storia del socialismo*, 2:425–26. The Veneto, an area of traditional Catholic loyalties, was the scene of a clash of Catholic and Socialist recruitment efforts.

22. PSI, *Resoconto del XIII congresso*, pp. 25–26, 73–85.

23. *Avanti!*, 3 Nov., 14 Dec. 1912, 3 March, 27 April, 3 June, 14 July 1913, 6 Jan., 23 March 1914, and Zerbini, *Relazione*, pp. 3–4. Cf. the observations of Degl'Innocenti, *Libia*, pp. 255–56, 320–22.

24. For the causes of the split in Sicily and the subsequent activities of the right, see Micciche, "Suffraggio universale." *Avanti!*, 20 July, 6, 22 Aug., 30 Sept. 1912, 5, 15 Jan. 1913. On the Vella mission and the maneuvers to retain the Palermo sections within the PSI, see the reports of the prefect of Palermo to the minister of the interior, 11, 17 Aug., 15 Oct. 1912, 13 Jan. 1913, f "K–5 Palermo," b 48, Interior Ministry files, AC/S.

25. Figures are from PSI, *Resconto del XIII congresso*, pp. 303–18, and *Resoconto del XIV congresso*, pp. 305–19.

26. *Avanti!*, 9 Aug. 1912, 7 March 1913. The revised *Statuto* was not presented in 1914. On resistance, see Hembree, "Lazzari," pp. 289–90.

27. *Avanti!*, 29 Aug. 1912, 3 March, 2 April, 20 Nov. 1913, 23 March 1914. At the 13 July 1913 meeting of the *Direzione*, Lazzari reported that 34,000 *tessere* had already been purchased. The previous high for the same period was 22,000. *Avanti!*, 13 July 1913.

28. *Avanti!*, 7 March, 20 Nov. 1913, 6 Jan., 27 April 1914. The Revolutionary *Direzione* did nothing to erase the Party's long-standing debt to the Socialist International. In September 1912, the International dunned Lazzari for back dues owed since 1907. This debt continued to mount, and Lazzari ignored later demands for repayment. Cf. the correspondence in f "a Lazzari," and "Lazzari a BSI," Huysmans Papers, IF.

29. See Morgari's report on the GPS and PSI in PSI, *Resoconto del XIV congresso*, pp. 76–80. *TKC*, 3:804, 851, 919, 989, 993, and Vella to Morgari, 19 June 1913, S 1, f 6, b 10, CM, AC/S.

30. *Avanti!*, 25 Feb., 7 July, 27 Oct., 3, 12, 20, 27 Nov., 1913.

31. Lazzari to Morgari, 12 Jan. 1914, s 1, f 16, b 10, CM, AC/S; *TKC*, 3:1100–1101, 1108, 1117, 1120; *Avanti!*, 15 Dec. 1913, 15, 20 Jan. 1914; Vigezzi, *Giolitti e Turati*, pp. 489–90; PSI, *Resoconto del XIV congresso*, pp. 19–24; and Hembree, "Lazzari," pp. 291–92.

32. Pepe, *Storia del CGL*, pp. 9–11; Castiglia, "La CGdL"; and Castiglia, *Rigola*, pp. 76–77, 82–83, 86–87.

33. Marchetti, *Confederazione*, pp. 154–55.

34. *Avanti!*, 20 July 1912, and Castiglia, "Partito del Lavoro."

35. Marchetti, *Confederazione*, p. 161.

36. *Avanti!*, 13 July 1912, and Pepe, *Storia del CGL*, p. 43.

37. Schiavi, "Il partito del lavoro in Francia e in Italia," *CS*, 1 Aug. 1912, pp. 225–26; Pepe, *Storia del CGL*, pp. 48, 175, 199; and *Avanti!*, 20 Dec. 1912, 15 Feb. 1913.

38. See Lazzari's report to the 1914 Congress, reprinted in *Avanti!*, 22 April 1914. PSI, *Relazione amministrativa*, pp. 4–9, 90–91. Examples of this zeal for bureaucratization include the data provided on the numbers of messages sent, minute lists of the expenses of the *Direzione*, and statistics on Party growth. Cf. Lazzari, *La necessità*, pp. 43–44.

39. Arfe, *Storia del Avanti!*, pp. 102–3, and *L'Unità*, 1 May 1914.

40. De Felice, *Mussolini*, pp. 133–39, and Riboldi, *Vicende Socialiste*, p. 32. Balabanoff tried to minimize the role she and other revolutionary leaders had in the selection of Mussolini, claiming these decisions were made on the spur of the moment. She seems to have been particularly anxious to protect Lazzari's reputation. Balabanoff, *Life*, pp. 96, 98, and Arfe, *Storia del Socialismo*, p. 165. Cf. Hembree, "Lazzari," p. 285.

41. *Avanguardia Socialista*, 2 July 1904. Mussolini, *Opere*, 1:69–72, 4:121–24; 5:8–9.

42. *Avanti!*, 1 Dec. 1912.

43. *Avanti!*, 3 Jan. 1914; Mussolini, *Opere*, 5:356; and DeFelice, *Mussolini*, p. 188.

44. *Avanti!*, 3 June 1913, 20 April 1914.

45. Mussolini, *Opere*, 3:187–91, 5:356; Balabanoff, *Life*, pp. 99–100; and Dorso, *Mussolini*, p. 72. During the course of his directorship, Mussolini also fired a number of Revolutionary collaborators, including Balabanoff. By 1914 only one staff member, F. Ciccotti, carried any weight within the Party high command.

46. *Avanti!*, 21 Jan. 1913 (Modigliani comments), 1 May, 14 Aug. 1914.

47. Cortesi, *Socialismo*, p. 551.

48. De Felice, *Mussolini*, pp. 83–86, 137, 163–64; Festa, "Socialismo."

49. Mussolini, *Opere*, 5:87–91, 6:5–8; 16–18; *Avanti!*, 9 March 1913; and *TKC*, 3:845, 890–91, 902–5.

50. Marchetti, *Confederazione*, pp. 165–66, and *Avanti!* 8 Jan. 1913.

51. *Avanti!*, 7, 8, 10, 11, 12, 13 Jan., 10 Feb. 1913.

52. *Avanti!*, 16, 18 Jan. 1913, and Treves, "La politica della protesta," *CS*, 16 Jan., 1 Feb. 1913, pp. 18–20.

53. *Avanti!*, 4 March 1913, and Marchetti, *Confederazione*, p. 169.

54. When the USI exhausted its usefulness, Mussolini quickly dropped it. Pepe, *Storia del CGL*, pp. 182–92, and *Avanti!*, 24 May, 16, 17 June, 1, 17 July 1913.

55. Report on the FGS congress, 11 Sept. 1912, f "K–5 Alessandria," b 50, Interior Ministry files, AC/S.

56. Licata, *Notabili*, pp. 17–33; Lerda statement in PSI, *Resoconto del XIV congresso*, p. 109; and *Avanti!*, 7 April 1914 for the text of Zibordi's report on Masonry. See also "Un congresso di transizione," *CS*, 16 May 1914, pp. 147–49. *Avanti!*, 9 June 1905, 22 Jan. 1911, 14 Aug. 1912; Mola, *Storia della massoneria*, pp. 292–93, 313, 331; and Martinelli, "I giovanni."

57. Labriola, *Storia di dieci anni*, p. 125.

58. Feroci, *Socialismo e massoneria*, pp. 3–10.

59. *Partito socialista*, pp. 3–10. Mongini, the semiofficial press of the PSI, published both Feroci's work and the rejoinder, another indication of the divergent views existing within the Party.

60. *L'Avanguardia*, 25 Dec. 1910, and PSI, *Resoconto del XI congresso*, pp. 10–11.

61. *Avanti!*, 4, 26 Aug. 1912, 25 Feb., 16 July 1913, and Mussolini, *Opere*, 6:230.

62. *Avanguardia*, 21 Aug. 1910; *Avanti!*, 30 June 1913; and Arfe, *Movimento giovanile*, p. 145.

63. Information on the growth of FGS is in the interview with Lido Ciani, *Avanti!*, 22 Dec. 1913. For FGS development in Lombardy, see *Avanti!*, 30 March 1914.

64. *Avanti!*, 16 July, 27 Oct. 1913; Mussolini, *Opere*, 5:360; and PSI, *Resoconto del XIV congresso*, pp. 104–7.

65. *L'Unità*, 1 May 1914.

66. Arfe, *Storia*, p. 164.

67. Santarelli, *Revisione*, p. 147; *Avanti!*, 10 Sept., 15 Nov. 1912, 19 Jan. 1913, 24 April 1914; and CS, 16 May 1914, pp. 145–46.

68. *La Soffitta*, 15 Aug. 1911, and Allevi, *Crisi*, pp. 28–29, 58–59, 71.

69. Mussolini, *Opere*, 2:124–28.

70. De Felice, *Mussolini*, pp. 23–31.

71. Ibid., pp. 90–91, 126.

72. Mussolini, *Opere*, 5:358; *Avanti!*, 14 June, 11, 13 Aug. 1913, 12, 14 June 1914; and PSI, *Resoconto del XIV congresso*, pp. 26–30.

73. *Avanti!*, 23 Nov. 1912, 15 Feb., 14, 15, 17 July 1913; Arfe, *Storia dell'Avanti!* p. 114; and Sabatucci, *Storia del Socialismo*, pp. 395–415.

74. *Avanti!*, 4, 9, 11, 13 Aug., 7, 8 Dec. 1913. On Serrati's views, see Detti, "Serrati." Santarelli, *Rivisione*, pp. 152–54; Cortesi, *Socialismo*, pp. 550–51; and PSI, *Resoconto del XIV congresso*, pp. 137–42.

75. Bartelli, "Socialismo e movimento operaio"; Arfe, *Movimento giovanile*, p. 114; Spriano, "La terza generazione"; and *Avanti!*, 17 July 1913.

76. Mussolini, *Opere*, 6:437.

77. *Avanti!*, 21 Jan., 13 March 1913, 6 Jan. 1914; Mussolini, *Opere*, 6:230–33; and "L'elezione di Ciprinai," CS, 1 Feb. 1914, pp. 33–35.

78. Ibid.

79. CS, 1 April 1914, pp. 99–110, April 16, 1914, pp. 113–18; TKC, 3:1114, 1147, 1152; Vigezzi, *Giolitti e Turati*, pp. 420, 436, 474, 484; Mancini, Melis, and Misu, *Storia dei partiti*, pp. 132–40, 144.

80. CS, 16 April 1914, pp. 113–15.

81. Ibid.

82. Arfe, *Storia*, p. 156.

83. *Avanti!*, 14 April 1914, and PSI, *Resoconto del XIV congresso*, p. 320.

84. *Avanti!*, 5 Jan. 1914.

85. Lazzari, *Principi e metodi*. Statements of Dugoni in PSI, *Resoconto del X congresso*, pp. 282–89, of Lazzari in PSI, *Resoconto del XI congresso*, pp. 80–101, and of Savelli on pp. 56–59.

86. *Avanti!*, 29 Oct. 1913.

87. *Avanti!*, 27 Jan. 1913, and Mussolini, *Opere*, 5:87–91.

88. See note 87; Mussolini, *Opere*, 6:276–80; and Festa, "Socialismo."

89. Degl'Innocenti, *Libia*, pp. 255–57, 282, and *Avanti!*, 6 Nov. 1913.

90. Degl'Innocenti, *Libia*, pp. 320–22.

91. Lotti, *Settimana*, pp. 40–41, and Spriano, "Terza."

92. Prefect of Ancona to the minister of interior, 20 May 1912, f "K–5 Ancona," b 50, Interior Ministry files, AC/S. Cammett, *Gramsci*, pp. 192–200.

93. De Felice, *Mussolini*, pp. 41–42, 88–89, 122, 137.

94. PSI, *Resoconto del XIV congresso*, pp. 134–35.

Chapter 9

1 Vigezzi, *Giolitti e Turati*, p. 484; Degl'Innocenti, *Libia*, p. 186; and Mancini, Melis, and Misu, *Storia*, pp. 122, 126, 132–40.

2. De Felice, *Mussolini*, pp. 143–44, 188.

3. Ibid., pp. 116–17, 177.

4. Bertelli, "Socialismo"; Fatica, "Movimento"; and Mancini, Melis, and Misu, *Storia*, p. 102.

5. *Avanti!*, 20 Oct. 1913, and Mancini, Melis, and Misu, *Storia*, pp. 133–40.

6. *Avanti!*, 12 Oct. 1913, and Schiavi, *Come*, p. 87.

7. *Avanti!*, 30 Oct. 1913, 24–25 April 1914, and Degl'Innocenti, *Libia*, pp. 423–24.

8. *Avanti!*, 16 Nov. 1913.

9. *TKC*, 3:1152, 1159, 1171, and *Avanti!*, 3, 4, 15 Dec. 1913, 20 Jan. 1914.

10. *Avanti!*, 4, 5, 9, 16, Feb. 1914; Lotti, *Settimana rossa*, pp. 48, 52; and De Grand, *Italian Nationalist*. Ironically, the slogan that Mussolini adopted came from the words Turati wrote for the Party's anthem, the "Inno dei lavoratori."

11. "Aspettando un annunzio mortuario," *CS*, 16 Feb. 1914, pp. 49–50.

12. DiScala, "Parliamentary Socialists."

13. *Avanti!*, 8, 18 March, 7 April 1914; *TKC*, 3:1171, 1173; *CS*, 1 April 1914, pp. 97–99; and Vigezzi, "Suffraggio universale."

14. Cf. Arfe, *Storia*, p. 161, and concluding comments in Mammarella, *Riformisti*. Cortesi, *Origini del PCI*, pp. 54–55, 60–70, 102ff notes the reemergence of the GPS in a leadership role during World War I. Cf. the comments of Degl'Innocenti, *Libia*, p. 323.

15. *Avanti!*, 25 April 1914; Mussolini, *Opere*, 4:151–55; and PSI, *Resoconto del XIV congresso*, pp. 18–30, 60–62.

16. PSI, *Resoconto del XIV congresso*, pp. 107–57.

17. *La Tribuna*, 26 April 1914.

18. *Avanti!*, 1 May 1914.

19. *CS*, 16 May 1914, pp. 145–47. The decision to adopt a policy of absolute intransigence caused unrest in a number of sections. See Onofri, *La Grande guerra*, pp. 31–33, 71ff.

20. Marchetti, *Confederazione*, p. 189.

21. The electoral manifesto of the *Direzione* is in *Avanti!*, 7 June 1914.

22. *Avanti!*, 8, 9 June 1914.

23. The intercepted conversations are reprinted in Lotti, *Settimana rossa*, pp. 265–66, 270–71.

24. *Avanti!*, 11 June 1914.

25. Lotti, *Settimana rossa*, p. 271.

26. Ibid., pp. 274–76; telegrams from Baldini to Morgari, 13 and 22 June 1914, and telegram from FGS to Morgari, 8 June 1914, s 1, f 18, b 10, CM, AC/S.

27. The motion of censure, proposed by Turati, was adopted with only two dissenting votes. *Avanti!*, 21 June 1914.

28. *Avanti!*, 12 June 1914. On Red Week and Mussolini's determination to exploit its revolutionary potential, see Spencer DiScala, " 'Red Week' 1914: Prelude to War and Revolution," in Coppa, *Studies*, pp. 123–33.

29. *CS*, 16 June 1914, pp. 177–79; Marchetti, *Confederazione*, p. 195; and telephone conversation between Vella (Rome) and Marabini (Bologna), 26 June 1914, f A–14, b 13, Direzione Generale della Pubblica Sicurezza, Ministry of the Interior files, AC/S.

30. In the Milan elections, the Socialists won 33,430 votes to 28,810 for the clerical and moderate parties and 8240 for the middle-class democrats. The victory was a major success for both Mussolini and the Reformists. Onofri, *Grande guerra*, pp. 71, 82–84.

31. *CS*, 16 June 1914, pp. 177–79. *Avanti!*, 18, 26, 29 June, 1 July 1914.

32. *Avanti!*, 29 June, 13, 16 July 1914, and *CS*, 1, 15 July 1914, pp. 193–95.

33. *Avanti!*, 26 July 1914. Giolitti, too, was surprised by the war's outbreak, *Discorsi extraparlamentari*, pp. 277–78.

34. *Avanti!*, 27–31 July 1914; Valiani, "Italian-Austro-Hungarian Negotiations"; and Bosworth, *Italy*, pp. 377–417.

35. *Avanti!*, 4, 15 Aug. 1914. Lazzari coined the phrase. Vigezzi, "Italian Socialism," and De Grand, *Italian Nationalist*, pp. 57–71. On the PSI's wartime immobility and its effects, see Valiani, *Partito socialista*, and Cortesi, *Origini del PCI*. Onofri, *Grande guerra*, p. 125.

36. *Avanti!*, 5, 6 Aug. 1914, and *CS*, 1 Aug. 1914, pp. 225–26. At the 6 August meeting of the *Direzione*, Socialist mayors were urged to conduct referenda among their city councils on the war question in order to reinforce antiwar sentiments in Italy. Cf. Onofri, *Grande guerra*, p. 125. Even the usually dynamic FGS was infected by the immobilism. Prefect of Bologna to the minister of the interior, 26 October 1914, f K–5 "Bologna," b 48, Interior Ministry files, AC/S.

37. Mussolini, *Opere*, 6:440. On his idea of an insurrection, see 6:438.

38. *Avanti!*, 4, 6, 13 Aug. 1914, and Vigezzi, *Giolitti e Turati*, pp. 523, 563.

39. *Avanti!*, 9 Aug. 1914, and *CS*, 16 Aug. 1914, pp. 242–44.

40. DeFelice, *Mussolini*, pp. 224–33, 257–87, for a discussion on the causes and effects of Mussolini's defection.

41. Cortesi, *Origini del PCI*, pp. 102–4, and Vigezzi, *Giolitti e Turati*, p. 612.

42. I am in substantial agreement with the views of Coppa, *Planning*, pp. 89–122, on Giolitti and his achievements. Coppa makes some particularly acute observations on the relation of mass parties to the eventual postwar collapse of the Giolittian system on pp. 250, 252–53.

Epilogue

1. Gramsci, *Ordine Nuovo*, p. 67.

2. Ibid., pp. 118–19.

3. Ibid., p. 117.

4. Ibid., pp. 121–22.

5. Gramsci quoted in Femia, *Gramsci's Thought*, p. 146.

6. Sassoon, *Gramsci's Politics*, pp. 68–72.

7. Ibid., pp. 96–97. De Grand, *Stalin's Shadow*, p. 23.

8. Molony, *Emergence*, pp. 56, 78–79, 85–89.

Bibliography

I. Primary Sources: Archives

Archivio Centrale dello Stato, Rome
  Carte Oddino Morgari
  Ministero del Interno, Direzione Generale della Sicurezza Pubblica
Istituto Giangiacomo Feltrinelli
  Fondo Camille Huysmans, Sezione Italia
  Carte Rinaldo Rigola

II. Published Documents

A. Italian Government

Atti parlamentari: Discussioni della Camera dei deputati, 1898–1914.
Direzione generale della statistica. *Statistica delle elezioni generali politiche.* Rome, 1900, 1904, 1909, 1914.
Manuale ad uso dei deputati al parlamento nazionale. XXI Legislatura. Rome, 1904.
——— . *XXII Legislatura.* Rome, 1909.
Pagliano, Emilio, ed. *La Libia negli atti del parlamento e nei provvedimenti del governo.* 3 vols. Milan: Pirola, 1912.

B. Italian Socialist Party

Bacci, G. *Socialismo e antimilitarismo.* Rome: Tipografia Popolare, 1908.
Bacci, G., and B. Mussolini. *L'Avanti!: Relazione morale.* Rome: Direzione del Partito Socialista Italiano, 1914.

Bibliography

Bonomi, Ivanoe. *Azione dei socialisti nei comuni*. Rome: Tipografia Popolare, 1908.

————. *L'azione politica del Partito Socialista e i suoi rapporti con l'azione parlamentare*. Imola: Cooperativa Tipografia, 1902.

Cabrini, Angiolo. *Il Partito Socialista Italiano e la politica dell'emigrazione*. Rome: Tipografia Operaia, 1908.

Cerchiari, G. Luigi. *L'opera dei deputati socialisti durante l'ultima legislatura*. Rome: Mongini, 1904.

Cheisa, Pietro, and Gino Muraldi. *Il Partito Socialista e l'organizzazione economica del proletariato industriale*. Imola: Cooperativa Tipografia, 1902.

Costa, Andrea. *Il gruppo parlamentare socialista*. Imola: Gruppo, 1902.

————. *Relazione del gruppo parlamentare socialista*. 2 parts. Imola: Cooperativa Tipografia, 1902.

Costa, Andrea, and Savino Verazzani. *Relazione sulla direzione del partito*. Imola: Cooperativa Tipografia, 1902.

Direzione del PSI. *Contro la guerra*. Milan: Socialista, 1911.

————. *Programma e statuto del Partito Socialista Italiano*. Rome: Direzione del Partito Socialista Italiano, 1919.

Federazione Italiana di Giovani Socialisti. *Resoconto del III congresso nazionale*. Rome: Tipografia Popolare, 1911.

Ferri, Enrico. *L'Avanti!: Resoconto della direzione del giornale*. Rome: Romana, 1904.

Labriola, Antonio. *Le convenzioni ferroviarie e il Partito Socialista*. Imola: Cooperativa Tipografia, 1902.

Lazzari, Costantino. *Rapporti fra gruppo parlamentare e partito*. Rome: Avanti!, 1910.

————. *Relazione sulla tattica e programma per le prossime elezioni politiche e consequente azione parlamentare*. Rome: Operaio, 1908.

Lerda, Giovanni. *Sull'organizzazione politica del Partito Socialista Italiano*. Imola: Cooperativa Tipografia, 1902.

Longobardi, E. *Direttiva del partito in rapporto al movimento operaio*. Rome: Operaio, 1908.

Modigliani, G. E. *Per le prossime elezione generale politiche*. Rome: Tipografia Popolare, 1908.

Mongini, Luigi. *Relazione del segretario amministrativo*. Rome: Tipografia Popolare, 1908.

Montemartini, Luigi. *Il gruppo parlamentare socialista*. Rome: Tipografia Popolare, 1908.

Partito Socialista Italiano. *Da Parma a Firenze: Relazione morale e statistica*. Milan: Operaio, 1896.

————. *Dopo il congresso di Imola*. Genoa: Operaio, 1902.

————. *L'Avanti!: Resoconto della direzione del giornale*. Imola: Cooperativa Tipografia, 1902.

241

Bibliography

——— . *L'Avanti!*. Rome: Romana, 1904.

——— . *L'Avanti!: Rendiconto del consiglio d'amministrazione*. Rome, *Avanti!*, 1908.

——— . *L'Avanti!: Relazione del consiglio amministrativo al XI congresso*. Rome: *Avanti!*, 1910.

——— . *Rapport du Parti Socialiste Italien sur son activité depuis 1907 jusqu'au mois de juin 1910*. Rome: *Avanti!*, 1910.

——— . *Relazione amministrativa, 1914–1917*. Rome: Direzione del Partito, 1917.

——— . *Relazione del gruppo parlamentare e relazione politica e amministrativa della direzione del partito*. Reggio Emilia: Lavoranti, 1912.

——— . *Rendiconto del VI congresso nazionale*. Rome: Libreria socialista italiano, 1901.

——— . *Rendiconto del VII congresso nazionale*. Rome: Libreria socialista italiano, 1903.

——— . *Rendiconto del VIII congresso nazionale*. Rome: Mongini, 1905.

——— . *Resoconto stenografico del IX congresso nazionale*. Rome: Mongini, 1907.

——— . *Resoconto stenografico del X congresso nazionale*. Rome: Mongini, 1908.

——— . *Resoconto stenografico del XI congresso nazionale del Partito Socialista Italiano*. Rome: Officina poligrafica italiano, 1911.

——— . *Resoconto stenografico del XII congresso nazionale del Partito Socialista Italiano*. Milan, *Avanti!*, 1912.

——— . *Resoconto stenografico del XIII congresso nazionale del Partito Socialista Italiano*. Città di Castello, Unione arti grafiche, 1913.

——— . *Resoconto stenografico del XIV congresso nazionale del Partito Socialista Italiano*. Rome: Partito Socialista Italiano, 1914.

——— . *Statuto*. Rome: Mongini, 1905.

——— . *Statuto del PSI*. Milan: Officio Esecutive del Partito, 1896.

——— . *Statuto—modello di regolamento per le sezioni*. Rome: Direzione del Partito, 1909.

——— . *Statuto. Programma massimo e minimo del PSI*. Florence: n.p., 1900.

——— . Sezione di Milano. *I socialisti al comune*. Milan: Operai, 1910.

——— . Sezione di Torino. *Programma elezione amministrativa, 28 gennaio 1906*. Turin: Cooperativo, 1906.

——— . *Vigilia del congresso*. Biella: Tipografia Rigola, 1910.

Soldi, Romeo. *L'azione politica del proletariato e suoi rapporti coll'azione parlamentare*. Imola: Cooperativa Tipografia, 1902.

Treves, Claudio. *Relazione morale sul Avanti!*. Milan: *Avanti!*, 1912.

Turati, Filippo. *L'azione politica del partito socialista, criterie generali*. Milan: Critica Sociale, 1910.

Zerbini, Adolfo. *Relazione amministrativa della direzione, 1912–1914*. Rome: Direzione del Partito, 1914.

Zibordi, G. *Organizzazione del partito e azione relativa*. Rome: Galiati, 1904.

C. General Confederation of Labor

La confederazione del lavoro nel sessennio 1914–1920. Milan: La Tipografia, 1921.
Rigola, Rinaldo. *Il Partito Socialista e il movimento operaio.* Rome: Tipografia Popolare, 1908.
——— . *La CGL nel triennio 1908–1911.* Turin: Cooperativo, 1911.
——— . *La CGL nel triennio 1911–1913.* Milan: Operaio, 1914.

III. Published Documentary Collections

Albertini, Luigi. *Epistolario.* Edited by O. Barié. Vol. 1. Milan: Mondadori, 1968.
Andreucci, Franco, ed. *Programmi e statuti socialisti (1890–1903).* Florence: La Nuova Italia, 1974.
Arfe, Gaetano, ed. "Per la storia del socialismo napolitano: Atti della sezione del PSI di Napoli dal 1908 al 1911." *Movimento Operaio* 5 (March 1953): 201–93.
Basso, Lelio, and Luigi Anderlini, eds. *Le riviste di Piero Gobetti.* Milan: Feltrinelli, 1961.
Battaglia, Roberto, ed. *Un popolo in lotta.* Florence: La Nuova Italia, 1961.
Bella, Carlo, ed. *L'Azione, 1905–1922.* Rome: Cinque Lune, 1967.
Bissolati, Leonida. *La politica estera dell'Italia dal 1897 al 1920.* Milan: Treves, 1923.
Brown, Benjamin, ed. *Opera omnia di Sidney Sonnino.* 8 vols. Bari: Laterza, 1972–75.
Carocci, G., P. d'Angiolini and C. Pavoni, eds. *Quarant'anni di politica italiana: Dalle carte di Giovanni Giolitti.* 3 vols. Milan: Feltrinelli, 1962.
Cerrito, Gino, ed. "Il circolo dei lavoratori e la sezione socialista di Naso, 1889–1913." *Movimento Operaio* 6 (January 1954): 50–108.
Cortesi, Luigi, ed. "Correspondenza F. Engels–F. Turati, 1891–1895." *Annali del Istituto Feltrinelli* 1 (1958): 220–82.
——— . *Il socialismo italiano tra riforme e rivoluzione, 1892–1921.* Bari: Laterza, 1969.
Della Peruta, Franco, ed. "Lettere di Filippo Turati a Felice Cavalotti." *Movimento Operaio* 6 (January 1954): 109–15.
Ganci, S., ed. *Democrazia e socialismo in Italia: Carteggi di Napoleone Colajanni.* Milan: Feltrinelli, 1959.
Giolitti, Giovanni. *Discorsi extraparlamentari.* Turin: Einaudi, 1952.
Gnocchi-Viani, Osvaldo. "Lettere ad Andrea Costa." *Movimento Operaio e Socialista* 1 (November 1949): 41–46.
Gramsci, Antonio. *L'ordine nuovo, 1919–1920.* Turin: Einaudi, 1954.
——— : *Scritti politici.* Edited by P. Spriano. Rome: Riuniti, 1967.
Kuliscioff, Anna. *Lettere d'amore a Andrea Costa, 1880–1909.* Edited by P. Albonetti. Milan: Feltrinelli, 1976.

Bibliography

Labriola, Antonio. *Lettere a Engels*. Rome: Rinascita, 1949.

———. *Scritti politici*. Edited by V. Gerratana. Bari: Laterza, 1970.

Marchetti, Luciana, ed. *La Confederazione generale del lavoro negli atti, nei documenti, nei congressi, 1906–1926*. Milan: *Avanti!*, 1962.

Masini, Pier Carlo, ed. "Lettere di Gaetano Salvemini a Archangelo Ghisleri (1898–1900)." *Annali del Istituto Feltrinelli* 3 (1960): 342–87.

Mussolini, Benito. *Opera Omnia*. Edited by E. and D. Susmel. 35 vols. Florence: La Fenice, 1951.

Nogare, Lileana Dalle, ed. "Il carteggio F. Turati–A. Ghisleri." *Movimento Operaio* 8 (January 1956): 201–311.

Pareto, Vilfredo. *Lettere a Maffeo Pantaleoni*. 3 vols. Rome: Banca Nazionale del Lavoro, 1960.

Passerin d'Entreves, Ettore, ed. *Dal nazionalismo al primo fascismo*. Turin: Giappichelli, 1967.

Pedone, Franco, ed. *Il Partito Socialista Italiano nei suoi congressi*. 2 vols. Milan: *Avanti!*, 1959.

Perticone, G., ed. *L'Italia in Africa*. Rome: Instituto Poligrafico dello stato, 1965.

Pischel, Guiliano, ed. *Antologia della Critica Sociale (1891–1926)*. Milan: Gentile, 1945.

Procacci, Guiliano, ed. "Antonio Labriola e la revisione del marxismo attraverso l'epistolario con Bernstein e con Kautsky." *Annali del Istituto Feltrinelli* 3 (1960): 264–341.

Ragionieri, Ernesto. "La formazione del programma amministrativo socialista in Italia." *Movimento Operaio* 5 (September 1953): 685–749.

———, ed. *Italia giudicata, 1861–1945*. Bari: Laterza, 1969.

Rubbiani, Ferruccio, ed. *Il pensiero politico di Leonida Bissolati*. Florence: Battistelli, 1922.

Salvatorelli, Luigi, ed. *Giolitti*. Milan: Risorgimento, 1920.

Salvemini, Gaetano. *Carteggio, 1895–1911*. Edited by E. Gencarelli. Milan: Feltrinelli, 1968.

———. *Carteggio, 1912–1914*. Edited by E. Tagliacozzo. Bari: Laterza, 1984.

Santarelli, Enzo, ed. "Lettere di Arturo Labriola a E. C. Longobardi." *Revista Storica del Socialismo* 5 (September 1962): 563–84.

Schiavi, Alessandro, ed. "Anna Kuliscioff e Andrea Costa, lettere inedite, 1872–1909." *Nuova Antologia* 441 (October 1947): 109–28.

———. *F. Turati attraverso le lettere di correspondenti, 1881–1925*. Bari: Laterza, 1947.

———. *Uomini della politica e della cultura*. Bari: Laterza, 1949.

Spinella, M., et al., eds. *Critica Sociale*. 3 vols. Milan, 1959.

Spriano, Paolo, ed. *Opere complete di Piero Gobetti*. 3 vols. Turin: Einaudi, 1960.

Treves, Claudio. *Polemica socialista*. Bologna: Zanichelli, 1921.

Turati, Filippo. *Discorsi parlamentare*. 3 vols. Rome: Tipografia della Camera, 1950.

————. *Le vie maestre del socialismo*. Edited by R. Mondolfo. Bologna: Capelli, 1921.

————. *L'organizzazione socialista*. Edited by A. Schiavi. Rome: Opere Nuove, 1951.

————. *Socialismo e riformismo nella storia d'Italia*. Edited by F. Livorsi. Milan: Feltrinelli, 1979.

————. *Trent'anni di Critica Sociale*. Bologna: Zanichelli, 1921.

————. *Turati giovane*. Edited by A. Schiavi. Milan: *Avanti!*, 1962.

Turati, Filippo, and Anna Kuliscioff. *Carteggio*. 6 vols. Turin: Einaudi, 1949–77.

Tych, F., A. Kochanski, and G. Haupt, eds. "Corrispondenza B. A. Jedzedjowski– A. Labriola (1895–1897)." *Annali del Istituto Feltrinelli* 3 (1960): 226–63.

Valiani, Leo, ed. "Lettere di Antonio Labriola ai socialisti tedeschi e francesi." *Critica Sociale* 47 (October 20–November 20, 1955): 300–303, 316–19, 332–35.

Zandardo, Aldo, ed. "Lettere di Antonio Labriola a L. Mariano e J. Guesde, a V. Adler e W. Ellenbogen, a G. V. Plechanov, 1892–1900." *Annali del Istituto Feltrinelli* 5 (162): 422–85.

Zangheri, R., ed. *Lotte agrarie in Italia: La federazione nazionale dei lavoratori della terra, 1901–1926*. Milan: Feltrinelli, 1960.

IV. Memoirs

Albertini, Luigi. *Vent'anni di vita politica, 1898–1914*. 5 vols. Bologna: Zanichelli, 1950–52.

Balabanoff, Angelica. *My Life as a Rebel*. New York: Harper, 1938.

Balestrazzi, Umberto. "Lo sciopero parmese del 1908 nel ricordo e nelle considerazione di un vecchio sindacalista." *Movimento Operaio e Socialista* 11 (January 1965): 129–44.

Costa, Andrea. "Annotazione autobiografiche per servire alla memorie della mia vita." *Movimento Operaio* 4 (March 1952): 314–56.

Gentile, Panfilo. *Cinquant'anni di socialismo in Italia*. Milan: Loganesi, 1948.

Giolitti, Giovanni. *Memorie della mia vita*. Milan: Garzanti, 1967.

Graziadei, Antonio. *Memorie di trent'anni*. Rome: Rinascita, 1950.

Lazzari, Costantino. "Memorie." Edited by A. Schiavi. *Movimento Operaio* 4 (July 1952): 598–633; and 5 (September 1952): 789–837.

Mussolini, Benito. *My Autobiography*. New York: Scribners, 1928.

Negro, Silvio, and Andrea Lazzarini, eds. *Uomini e giornale*. Florence: Salani, 1947.

Riboldi, E. *Vicende socialista*. Milan: Azione Comune, 1964.

Rigola, Rinaldo. *Rinaldo Rigola e il movimento operaio nel Biellese*. Bari: Laterza, 1930.

Tittoni, Tommaso. "Ricordi personali di politica interna." *Nuova Antologia* 342: 304–27, 441–67.

V. Secondary Sources: Books, Pamphlets, and Articles

A. General

Abrate, Mario. *La lotta sindacale nella industrializzazione in Italia*. Milan: Angeli, 1967.

Albrecht-Carrie, Rene. *Italy from Napoleon to Mussolini*. New York: Columbia University Press, 1950.

Allevi, Giovanni. *La crisi del socialismo*. Bari: Humanitas, 1913.

Ansaldo, Giovanni. *Il ministro della buonavita*. Milan: Longanesi, 1950.

Are, Giuseppe. *Alle origini dell'Italia industriale*. Naples: Guida, 1974.

——— . "Economic Liberalism in Italy: 1845 to 1915." *Journal of Italian History* 1 (Winter 1978): 409–31.

Aron, Raymond. "Social Structure and the Ruling Class." *British Journal of Sociology* 1 (March, June 1950): 1–16, 126–43.

Askew, William. *Europe and Italy's Acquisition of Libya*. Durham, N.C.: Duke University Press, 1942.

Baglioni, Guido. *L'ideologia della borghesia industriale nell'Italia liberale*. Turin: Einaudi, 1974.

Bairati, Piero. *Valletta*. Turin: Utet, 1983.

Barberis, Corrado. *Da Giolitti a DeGasperi*. Rocca S. Casciano: Cappelli, 1953.

Barclay, Glen St. John. *The Rise and Fall of the New Roman Empire*. London: Sidgwick and Jackson, 1973.

Barié, Ottavio. "Luigi Albertini, il *Corriere della Sera* e l'opposizione al Giolitti." *Clio* 3 (January and October 1967): 66–112, 508–53; and 4 (January 1968): 40–76.

Barnes, Samuel. *Party Democracy*. New Haven, Conn.: Yale University Press, 1967.

Bassi, Enrico. "Argentina Altobelli e la Federazione dei lavoratori della terra." *Critica Sociale* 59 (March–May 1967): 176–77, 236–37, 297–99.

——— . "Rinaldo Rigola e la Confederazione Generale del Lavoro." *Critica Sociale* 45 (June 5, 1953): 154–57.

Blalock, Hubert. *Theory Construction*. Englewood Cliffs, N.J.: Prentice Hall, 1967.

Bobbio, Aurelia A. *Le riviste fiorentine del principio del secolo, 1903–1916*. Florence: Sansoni, 1936.

Bibliography

Bonelli, Franco. *Lo sviluppo di una grande impresa in Italia: La Terni dal 1884 al 1962.* Turin: Einaudi, 1975.

Bonomi, Ivanoe. *From Socialism to Fascism.* London: Hopkinson, 1924.

────── . *La politica italiana da Porta Pia a Vittorio Veneto.* Turin, Einaudi, 1946.

────── . *Le vie nuove del socialismo.* Rome: Sessante, 1944.

Bosworth, Richard. "The English, the Historians and the *Età Giolittiana.*" *Historical Journal* 12 (June 1967): 353–67.

────── . *Italy: The Least of the Great Powers.* Cambridge: Cambridge University Press, 1979.

────── . *Italy and the Approach of the First World War.* London: Macmillan, 1983.

Braunthal, Julius. *A History of the International.* Vol. 1. New York: Praeger, 1967.

Bulferetti, Luigi. *Introduzione alla storiografia socialista in Italia.* Florence: Le Monnier, 1949.

Cabrini, Angiolo. *La legislazione sociale (1859–1913).* Rome: Bontempelli, 1914.

Caizzi, Bruno. "Nord et Sud en Italie depuis un siècle." *Cahiers d'Histoire Mondiale* 3 (1956): 142–69.

Cameli, Illemo. *Dal socialismo al sacerdozio.* Cremona: Unione, 1911.

Candeloro, Giorgio. *Il movimento sindacale in Italia.* Rome: Cultura Sociale, 1950.

────── . *Storia dell'Italia moderna.* Vols. 1–8. Milan: Feltrinelli, 1956–79.

Cantono, Alessandro. *La crisi del marxismo.* Rome: Cooperativa, 1901.

Caracciolo, A., ed. *La formazione dell'Italia industriale.* Bari: Laterza, 1963.

Carista, Carmelo. *L'ultima crisi del socialismo.* Rome: Unione, 1913.

Carocci, Giampiero. *Giolitti e l'età giolittiana.* Turin: Einaudi, 1961.

Cartiglia, Carlo. "La CGdL e il progetto del 'Partito del Lavoro,' 1907–1910." *Movimento Operaio e Socialista* 20 (January 1974): 17–48.

────── . *Rinaldo Rigola e il sindacalismo riformista in Italia.* Milan: Feltrinelli, 1976.

Castronovo, Valerio. *Economia e società in Piemonte dall'unità al 1914.* Milan: Banca Commerciale Italiana, 1969.

────── . *Giovanni Agnelli.* Turin: Einaudi, 1977.

────── . "The Italian Takeoff: A Critical Reexamination of the Problem." *The Journal of Italian History* 1 (Winter 1978): 492–510.

────── . *La stampa italiana dall'unità al fascismo.* Bari: Laterza, 1970.

Cataluccio, Francesco. *Antonio di San Giuliano.* Florence: Le Monnier, 1935.

Chabod, Federico. *De Machiavel à Benedetto Croce.* Geneva: Droz, 1970.

Chiapetti, Francesco. *Gli scioperi.* Rome: Pistolesi, 1904.

Ciacchi, Eugenio. *Il congresso socialista.* Milan: La Grande Attualità, 1910.

Ciccotti, Francesco. *Il congresso socialista di Milano.* Rome: Operaia, 1910.

────── . *Dopo il congresso nazionale socialista di Firenze.* Rome: Operaia, 1908.

────── . *Il partito socialista si dissolve?* Rome: Unione, 1911.

Cilibrizzi, S. *Storia parlamentare, politica e diplomatica d'Italia.* Vols. 3 and 4. Rome: Tosi, 1939–52.

Bibliography

Clough, Shepard. *Economic History of Modern Italy.* New York: Columbia University Press, 1964.

Clough, Shepard, and Carlo Levi. "Economic Growth in Italy: An Analysis of the Uneven Development of North and South." *Journal of Economic History* 16 (September 1956): 334–49.

Clough, Shepard, and Salvatore Saladino. *A History of Modern Italy.* New York: Columbia University Press, 1968.

Cohen, Jon. "Financing Industrialization in Italy, 1894–1914: The Partial Transformation of a Late Comer." *Journal of Economic History* 27 (December 1967): 363–82.

Colajanni, Napoleone. *I partiti politici in Italia.* Rome, Libreria politica moderna, 1912.

Colapietra, Raffaele. *Il Novantotto.* Milan: *Avanti!,* 1959.

Coppa, Frank J. "Economic and Ethical Liberalism in Conflict: The Extraordinary Liberalism of Giovanni Giolitti." *Journal of Modern History* 42 (June 1970): 191–215.

——— . "The Italian Tariff and the Conflict between Agriculture and Industry: The Commercial Policy of Liberal Italy, 1860–1922." *Journal of Economic History* 30 (December 1970): 742–69.

——— . *Planning, Protectionism and Politics in Liberal Italy.* Washington, D.C.: Catholic University of America Press, 1971.

——— , ed. *Studies in Modern Italian History.* New York: P. Lang, 1986.

Corbino, Epicarmo. *Annali dell'economia italiana.* 5 vols. Città di Castello: da Vinci, 1938.

——— . *L'economia italiana dal 1860 al 1960.* Bologna: Zanichelli, 1962.

Cortesi, Luigi. *Le origini del PCI.* Bari: Laterza, 1972.

Costa, Andrea. *Il socialismo.* Florence: Nerbini, 1901.

Croce, Benedetto. *Storia d'Italia, 1871–1915.* Bari: Laterza, 1927.

Crotty, W. J. *Approaches to the Study of Party Organization.* Boston: Allyn and Bacon, 1967.

D'Angiolini, Piero. "La svolta industriale italiana negli anni del secolo e le reazioni dei contemporanei." *Nuova Rivista Storica* 56 (January 1972): 53–121.

Davidson, Alastair. *The Theory and Practice of Italian Communism.* London: Merlin, 1982.

de Donno, Alfredo. *L'Italia dal 1870 al 1944.* Rome: Moderna, 1946.

De Grand, Alexander. *Italian Fascism.* Lincoln, Neb.: University of Nebraska Press, 1982.

——— . *The Italian Nationalist Association and the Rise of Fascism in Italy.* Lincoln, Neb.: University of Nebraska Press, 1978.

Destree, I. *Figures italiennes d'aujourd'hui.* Brussels: n.p., 1918.

Drake, Richard. *Byzantium for Rome.* Chapel Hill, N.C.: University of North Carolina Press, 1980.

Bibliography

DuVerger, Maurice. *Political Parties.* New York: Wiley, 1963.

Edinger, Lewis, and Donald Searing. "The Social Background in Elite Analysis." *American Political Science Review* 61 (June 1967): 428–45.

Einaudi, Luigi. *Le lotte del lavoro.* Turin: n.p., 1924.

Federzoni, Luigi. *Italia di ieri.* Milan: Mondadori, 1967.

Feiling, K. *Italian Policy since 1870.* London: Oxford University Press, 1914.

Feroci, Guido. *Socialismo e massoneria.* Rome: Mongini, 1910.

Fonzi, Fausto. *Storia e storiografia dei movimenti cattolici in Italia.* Rome: Elia, 1976.

Fossati, Antonio. *Lavoro e produzione in Italia della metà del secolo XVIII alla seconda guerra mondiale.* Turin: Giapichelli, 1951.

Frassati, A. *Giolitti.* Florence: Parenti, 1959.

Galizzi, Vincenzo. *Giolitti e Salandra.* Bari: Laterza, 1949.

Ganci, S. M. *L'Italia antimoderata.* Parma: Guanda, 1968.

Garlanda, Frederigo. *The New Italy.* New York: Putman, 1911.

Garrone, Alessandro Galante. *I radicali in Italia, 1849–1925.* Milan: Garzanti, 1973.

Gay, Peter. *The Dilemma of Democratic Socialism.* New York: Columbia University Press, 1952.

Gerschenkron, Alexander. "Notes on the Rate of Industrial Growth in Italy, 1881–1913." *Journal of Economic History* 15 (December 1955): 360–75.

Gerschenkron, Alexander, and Rosario Romeo. "Lo sviluppo industriale italiano." *Nord e Sud* 8 (November 1961): 30–56.

Ghisalberti, A., ed. *Dizionario biografico degl'italiani.* Rome: Trecanni, 1960.

Goodstein, Phil. *The Theory of the General Strike from the French Revolution to Poland.* Golden, Colo.: East European Monographs, 1984.

Granone, Liboro. *La crisi socialista.* Catania: "Il Domani," 1914.

Grifone, Pietro. *Il capitale finanziario in Italia.* Turin: Einaudi, 1945.

Gualtieri, Umberto. *The Labor Movement in Italy.* New York: Vanni, 1946.

Gustapone, Enrico. "Giolitti Giovanni Federico: dottore in legge." *Storia Contemporanea* 12 (February 1981): 137–73.

Halperin, S. W., *Italy and the Vatican at War.* New York: Greenwood Press, 1968.

——— . *Separation of Church and State in Italian Thought.* Chicago: University of Chicago Press, 1937.

Hentze, Margaret. *Pre-Fascist Italy.* London: Allen and Unwin, 1939.

Hughes, H. Stuart. "The Aftermath of the Risorgimento in Four Successive Interpretations." *American Historical Review* 61 (March 1956): 70–76.

——— . *Consciousness and Society.* New York: Vintage, 1958.

Hughes, Serge. *The Fall and Rise of Modern Italy.* New York: Macmillan, 1967.

I 508 deputati al parlamento per la XXIV Legislatura. Milan: Treves, 1914.

Il nazionalismo giudicato. Genoa: Moderna, 1913.

"Il socialista massone." *Il partito socialista e la massoneria.* Rome, 1910.

Bibliography

Jemolo, Arturo Carlo. *Chiesa e stato in Italia.* Turin: Einaudi, 1965.

Joll, James. *The Second International.* New York: Harper, 1955.

King, Bolton, and T. Okey. *Italy Today.* London: Nesbit, 1904.

Kolakowski, Leszek. *Main Currents of Marxism: The Golden Age.* Oxford: Oxford University Press, 1978.

Labriola, Arturo. *Ministero e socialismo.* Florence: Nerbini, 1901.

——— . *Storia di dieci anni.* Milan: Il Viandante, 1910.

Lazzari, Costantino. *I principii e i metodi del Partito Socialista Italiano.* Milan: Presso C. Lazzari, 1911.

——— . *Le necessità della politica socialista in Italia.* Milan: Milanese, 1911.

Lemonon, Ernest. *L'Italie Economique et Sociale, 1861–1912.* Paris: Felix Alcan, 1913.

Levra, Umberto. *Il colpo di stato della borghesia.* Milan: Feltrinelli, 1975.

Licata, Glauco. *Notabili della terza Italia.* Rome: Cinque Lune, 1968.

Lichtheim, George. *Marxism.* New York: Praeger, 1965.

Lindemann, Albert S. *A History of European Socialism.* New Haven, Conn.: Yale University Press, 1983.

Lotti, Luigi. *La settimana rossa.* Florence: Le Monnier, 1965.

Lovett, Clara M. *The Democratic Movement in Italy, 1830–1876.* Cambridge, Mass.: Harvard University Press, 1982.

Ludwig, Emil. *Talks with Mussolini.* Boston: Little Brown, 1933.

McClellan, G. *Modern Italy.* Princeton: Princeton University Press, 1933.

McInnes, Neil. *The Western Marxists.* London: Alcove Press, 1972.

Mack Smith, Denis. *Cavour.* New York: Knopf, 1985.

——— . *Cavour and Garibaldi, 1860.* Cambridge: Cambridge University Press, 1954.

——— . *Da Cavour a Mussolini.* Catania: Bonano, 1968.

MacRae, Duncan. "A Method for Identifying Issues and Factions from Legislative Votes." *American Political Science Review* 59 (December 1965): 909–26.

Malatesta, Alberto. *Ministeri, deputati, senatori del 1848–1922.* Rome: EBBI, 1941.

Maltese, Paolo. *La terra promessa.* Milan: Sugar, 1968.

Mandurino, Silvia. "Questioni del Mezzogiorno e problema della scuola nel pensiero di Gaetano Salvemini." *Studi Salentini* 33 (March 1969): 24–29.

Maranini, Giuseppe. *Storia del potere in Italia.* Florence: Vallecchi, 1967.

Marazio, Annibale. *Il Partito Socialista Italiano e il governo.* Turin: Unione, 1906.

Melograni, Piero. *Storia politica della grande guerra.* Bari: Laterza, 1972.

Michels, Robert. *L'imperialismo italiano.* Milan: Libreria, 1914.

——— . *Political Parties.* New York: Dover, 1959.

——— . *Proletariato e borghesia nel movimento socialista italiano.* Turin: Bocca, 1908.

——— . *Storia critica del movimento socialista italiano.* Florence: La Voce, 1922.

Bibliography

Mola, Aldo. *Storia della massoneria italiana dall'unità alla repubblica.* Milan: Bompiani, 1976.

Molony, John N., *The Emergence of Political Catholicism in Italy.* London: Croom Helm, 1977.

Morgan, David. "The Father of Revisionism Revisited: Eduard Bernstein." *Journal of Modern History* 51 (September 1979): 525–32.

Mori, Giorgio. *Il capitalismo industriale in Italia.* Rome: Riuniti, 1977.

Natale, Gaetano. *Giolitti e gl'italiani.* Milan: Garzanti, 1949.

Neufield, Maurice. *Italy.* Ithaca, N.Y.: Cornell University Press, 1961.

Nicolai, Renato. *Emilia riformista e Italia giolittiana.* Milan: Mazzotta, 1977.

Novelli, A. *La missione dei nostri circoli.* Florence: Nerbini, 1901.

Novelli, Renzo. *Albo biografico dei deputati e senatori comunisti e socialisti.* Rome: EMEA, 1948.

Omodeo, Adolfo. *L'età del Risorgimento italiano.* Naples: Scientifiche, 1960.

Palazzi, Maura. "L'opinione pubblica cattolica e il colonialismo: *L'Avvenire d'Italia*, 1896–1914." *Storia Contemporanea* 10 (February 1979): 43–87.

Paoloni, Francesco. *Salviamo il partito!* Rome: Mongini, 1906.

Pareto, Vilfredo. *The Ruling Class in Italy before 1900.* New York: Vanni, 1950.

Pepe, Adolfo. "La costituzione della Confederazione Generale del Lavoro, 1906–1908." *Storia Contemporanea* 1 (December 1970): 691–824.

———. *Storia del CGdL, 1905–1911.* Bari: Laterza, 1972.

———. *Storia del CGdL, 1911–1915.* Bari: Laterza, 1971.

Perticone, G. *Gruppi e partiti politici nella vita pubblica italiana.* Modena: Guanda, 1946.

———. *La formazione della classe politica nell'Italia contemporanea.* Florence: Leonardo, 1954.

———. *L'Italia contemporanea dal 1871 al 1948.* Milan: Mondadori, 1962.

———. *Scritti di storia del post-Risorgimento.* Milan: Guiffre, 1969.

Pompei, C., and I. G. Paparazzo. *I 508 della XXV legislatura.* Rome: Ausonia, 1920.

Preti, Luigi. "Giolitti e le leghi contadini." *Critica Sociale* 44 (May 1, 1952): 493–94.

Rabuazzo, Antonio. *Dalla sinistra storica all'avvento della Repubblica italiana.* Bologna: Minerva, 1968.

Reale Accademia Nazionale dei Lincei. *Cinquanta anni di storia italiana.* Milan: Hoepeli, 1911.

Rigola, Rinaldo. *Cento anni di movimento operaio.* Milan: Problemi del Lavoro, 1935.

———. *Storia del movimento operaio italiano.* Milan: Domus, 1947.

Roberts, David. *The Syndicalist Tradition and Italian Fascism.* Chapel Hill, N.C.: University of North Carolina Press, 1979.

Romano, Salvatore. *Le classi sociale in Italia.* Turin: Einaudi, 1965.

Bibliography

Romeo, Rosario. *Breve storia della grande industria in Italia*. Bologna: Cappelli, 1961.

——— . "La storiografia italiana sul Risorgimento e l'Italia unitaria nel secondo dopoguerra." *Clio* 1 (July 1965): 407–33.

——— . *Risorgimento e capitalismo*. Bari: Laterza, 1959.

Ronchi, Mario. "Le origini del movimento contadino cattolico nel Soresinese, 1901–1913." *Movimento Operaio* 7 (May 1955): 423–39.

Sacco, Mario. *Storia del sindacalismo*. Milan: ISPI, 1942.

Saladino, Salvatore. *Italy from the Unification to 1919*. New York: Crowell, 1970.

Salomone, A. William. *Italy from the Risorgimento to Fascism*. New York: Doubleday, 1970.

——— . *Italy in the Giolittian Era*. Philadelphia: University of Pennsylvania Press, 1960.

Salucci, Arturo. *Il crepuscolo del socialismo*. Genoa: Chiesa, 1910.

Schachter, Gustav. *The Italian South*. New York: Random House, 1965.

Schiavi, Alessandro. *Come hanno votato gli elettori italiani*. Milan: *Avanti!*, 1914.

Schmidt, Carl T. *The Plough and the Sword*. New York: Columbia University Press, 1938.

Schorske, Carl. *German Social Democracy, 1905–1917*. New York: John Wiley, 1955.

Serini, Emilio. *Il capitalismo nelle campagne*. Turin: Einaudi, 1947.

Seton-Watson, Christopher. *Italy from Liberalism to Fascism*. London: Methuen, 1967.

Sforza, Carlo. *Contemporary Italy*. New York: Dutton, 1944.

Sori, Ercole. "La penetrazione economic italiana nei territori dei Slavi del Sud." *Storia Contemporanea* 12 (April 1981): 217–69.

Spadolini, Giovanni. *Giolitti e i cattolici*. Florence: Mondadori, 1971.

——— . *Il mondo di Giolitti*. Florence: Le Monnier, 1969.

Sprigge, Cecil. *The Development of Modern Italy*. New Haven: Yale University Press, 1944.

Steensen, Gary P. *Karl Kautsky*. Pittsburgh: University of Pittsburgh Press, 1978.

——— . *Not One Man! Not One Penny! German Social Democracy, 1863–1914*. Pittsburgh: University of Pittsburgh Press, 1981.

Tagliacozzo, Enzo. *Risorgimento e postrisorgimento*. Caglieri: Fossarto, 1969.

Tannenbaum, Edward, and Emiliana Noether. *Modern Italy*. New York: New York University Press, 1974.

Tasca, Angelo. *The Rise of Italian Fascism*. New York: Howard Fertig, 1966.

Thayer, John. *Italy and the Great War*. Madison, Wisc.: University of Wisconsin Press, 1964.

Tittoni, Tommaso. *Modern Italy*. New York: Macmillan, 1922.

Togliatti, Palmiro. *Momenti della storia d'Italia*. Rome: Riuniti, 1963.

Tommasini, Francesco. *L'Italia alla vigilia della guerra*. 3 vols. Bologna: Zanich- elli, 1937.

Toscano, Mario. *Pagine di storia diplomatica contemporanea*. 2 vols. Milan: Guif- fre, 1963.

Underwood, F. M. *United Italy*. London: Methuen, 1912.

Uva, B. "Per una storia del periodo giolittiano." *Clio* 5 (January 1969): 66–99.

Valeri, Nino. *Lezioni di storia moderna*. Milan: La Goliardica, 1951.

Valiani, Leo. *L'Historiographie de L'Italie contemporaine*. Geneva: Droz, 1968.

Vigezzi, Brunello. *Da Giolitti a Salandra*. Florence: Vallecchi, 1969.

Villari, Rosario. *Conservatori e democratici nell'Italia liberale*. Bari: Laterza, 1964.

Volpe, G. *Italia moderna, 1815–1915*. 3 vols. Florence: Sansoni, 1943–1952.

————. *L'Italia in cammino*. Milan: Treves, 1927.

von Aretin, K. O. *The Papacy and the Modern World*. New York: McGraw Hill, 1970.

Webster, Richard. *The Cross and the Fasces*. Stanford, Calif.: Stanford University Press, 1960.

————. *Industrial Imperialism in Italy, 1908–1915*. Berkeley: University of Cali- fornia Press, 1975.

Whittam, John. *Politics of the Italian Army, 1861–1918*. London: Croom Helm, 1977.

B. Italian Socialist Party

Angiolini, Alfredo, and Eugenio Ciacchi. *Socialismo e socialisti in Italia*. Florence: Narbini, 1920.

Anzi, Felice. "C. Lazzari." *Nord e Sud* 2 (June 30, 1946): 29–30.

Arfe, Gaetano. *Il movimento giovanile socialista*. Milan: Gallo, 1966.

————. *Storia dell'Avanti!* Milan: *Avanti!*, 1956.

————. *Storia del socialismo, 1892–1926*. Turin: Einaudi, 1965.

Arfe, Gaetano, et al. *Storia del Partito Socialista Italiano, 1892–1976*. Florence: Cooperativa editrice universitaria, 1977.

Badaloni, Nicola, and Franca Pieroni Bartolotti. *Movimento operaio e lotta politica a Livorno, 1900–1926*. Rome: Riuniti, 1977.

Basso, Lelio. *G. Salvemini socialista e meridionalista*. Lacaiata: Monduria, 1959.

————. "Turati, il riformismo e la via democratica." *Problemi del Socialismo* 1 (February 1958): 87–103.

Benini, Aroldo. "Come nacque *Critica Sociale*." *Il Risorgimento* 8 (October 1956): 175–77.

Berlin, Isaiah. "Georges Sorel." *Times Literary Supplement* (London), December 31, 1971.

Bibliography

Bonomi, Ivanoe. *Leonida Bissolati e il movimento socialista in Italia.* Rome: Sessanti, 1945.

Borghi, Armando. *Mussolini in camicia.* Naples: Scientifiche, 1961.

Briguglio, Letterio. *Congressi socialisti e tradizione operaista, 1892–1904.* Padua: Tipografia Antoniana, 1972.

Bulferetti, Luigi. *Introduzione alla storiografia socialista in Italia.* Florence: Olschki, 1949.

————. *Le ideologie socialistiche in Italia.* Florence: Le Monnier, 1951.

Carli-Ballola, Renato. *Avanti!* Milan: *Avanti!,* 1946.

Cartiglia, Carlo, ed. *Il Partito socialista italiano, 1892–1962.* Turin: Loescher, 1978.

Casella, Mario. *Democrazia, socialismo, movimento operaio a Roma, 1892–1894.* Rome: Elia, 1979.

CIVIS. "Antonio Graziadei." *Critica Sociale* 45 (February 20, 1953): 62–63.

————. "Giorgio Sorel." *Critica Sociale* 47 (April 5, 1955): 109–10.

Clark, Martin. *Antonio Gramsci and the Revolution That Failed.* New Haven: Yale University Press, 1977.

Colapietra, Raffaele. "Bilancio di Turati." *Belfagor* 12 (September 30, 1957): 567–78.

————. "Il maestro della buona vita (Gaetano Salvemini)." *Belfagor* 13 (September 1958): 535–54.

————. *Leonida Bissolati.* Milan: Feltrinelli, 1958.

Colombi, Arturo. *Pagine di storia del movimento operaio.* Rome: Cultura Sociale, 1951.

Coppari, Paolo. "Il movimento socialista nel maceratese dalle origine al 1913." *Storia Contemporanea* 10 (February 1979): 109–44.

Cortesi, Luigi. *Ivanoe Bonomi.* Salerno: Internazionale, 1971.

————. *La costituzione del Partito socialista italiano.* Milan: *Avanti!,* 1961.

Cunsolo, Ronald. "Libya, Italian Nationalism and the Revolt against Giolitti." *Journal of Modern History* 37 (June 1965): 186–207.

deBegnac, Ivon. *Vita di Mussolini.* 3 vols. Milan: Mondadori, 1937.

de Clementi, Andreina. *Politica e società nel sindacalismo rivoluzionario, 1900–1915.* Rome: Bulzoni, 1983.

Decleva, Enrico. "Anticlericalismo e lotta politica nell'Italia giolittiana." *Nuova Rivista Storica* 52 (May 1968): 291–354.

DeFelice, Renzo. *Mussolini il rivoluzionario.* Turin: Einaudi, 1965.

Degl'Innocenti, Maurizio. *Il socialismo italiano e la guerra di Libia.* Rome: Riuniti, 1976.

————. *Storia della cooperazione in Italia.* Rome: Riuniti, 1977.

De Grand, Alexander. *In Stalin's Shadow.* DeKalb, Ill.: Northern Illinois University Press, 1986.

Detti, Tommaso. "Anna Kuliscioff, Filippo Turati e la tradizione socialista." *Studi Storici* 18 (January 1977): 171–87.

Bibliography

————. "Serrati, il partito e la lotta di classe in Italia." *Movimento Operaio e Socialista* 18 (October 1972): 5–36.

DiScala, Spencer. *Dilemmas of Italian Socialism*. Boston: University of Massachusetts Press, 1980.

————. "Filippo Turati, the Milanese Schism and the Reconquest of the Italian Socialist party, 1901–1909." *Il Politico* 44 (1979): 153–62.

————. "Filippo Turati e la scissione del Partito Socialista Milanese del 1901." *Rassegna di Politica e di Storia* 16 (January 1970): 1–6.

————. "Italia 1905, echi della rivoluzione russa." *Critica Sociale* 70 (July 25, 1978): 53–58.

————. "Parliamentary Socialists, the *Statuto* and the Giolittian System." *Australian Journal of Politics and History* 25 (August 1979): 155–68.

————. *Renewing Italian Socialism*. New York: Oxford University Press, 1988.

Dorso, Guido. *Benito Mussolini alla conquista del potere*. Turin: Einaudi, 1949.

Ente per la storia del socialismo e del movimento operaio italiano. *Bibliografia del socialismo e del movimento operaio italiano*. 5 vols. Rome: ESSMOI, 1956.

Faggi, John A. "The Beginnings of the Italian Socialist Party." Ph.D. diss., Columbia University, 1954.

Femia, Joseph. *Gramsci's Political Thought*. Oxford: Oxford University Press, 1981.

Ferretti, Aldo. *Messenzatico nella Reggia rossa, 1885–1925*. Reggio Emilia: Rinascita, 1973.

Festa, Elio. "Il socialismo di Benito Mussolini e la Settimana Rossa." *Nuova Rivista Storica* 46 (May 1962): 312–36.

Finer, Herbert. *Mussolini's Italy*. New York: Grossett, 1965.

Foa, Vittorio. *Italian Social Democracy*. Reading: Reading University Press, 1968.

Galli, Giorgio, "La strategia gradualista." *Critica Sociale* 59 (June 20, 1967): 351–52.

Gonzales, Manuel. *Andrea Costa and the Rise of Socialism in the Romagna*. Washngton, D.C.: University Press of America, 1980.

Gozzini, Giovanni. "La Federazione giovanile socialista tra Bordiga e Mussolini, 1912–1914." *Storia Contemporanea* 11 (February 1980): 103–25.

Gregor, A. James. *Young Mussolini and the Intellectual Origins of Fascism*. Berkeley: University of California Press, 1979.

Guerrini, Libertario. *Il movimento operaio empolese*. Florence: Rinascita Toscana, 1954.

Hembree, Michael. "The Politics of Intransigence: Costantino Lazzari and the Italian Socialist Left, 1882–1919." Ph.D. diss., Florida State University, 1981.

Hilton-Young, W. *The Italian Left*. London: Longman's, 1949.

Hobsbawm, E. J. *Social Bandits and Primitive Rebels*. Glencoe, Ill.: Free Press, 1959.

Horowitz, Irving. *Radicalism and the Revolt against Reason*. Carbondale, Ill.: Southern Illinois University Press, 1968.

Bibliography

Hostetter, Richard. *The Italian Socialist Movement*. Princeton: Princeton University Press, 1958.

"Il riformismo socialista di Modigliani." *Critica Sociale* 59 (October 20, 1967), pp. 547–49.

Ivone, Diomede. *Associazione operaie, clero e borghesia nel mezzogiorno tra ottocento e novecento*. Milan: Giuffre, 1979.

Jacini, Stefano. *La riforma dello stato e il problema regionale*. Bresica: Morcelliana, 1968.

Kirkpatrick, Ivon. *Mussolini*. New York: Avon, 1968.

Labriola, Antonio. *Essays on the Materialistic Concept of History*. Chicago: Kerr, 1908.

Labriola, Arturo. *Il socialismo contemporaneo*. Naples: Morano, 1922.

Labriola, Lucio. *Storia e leggenda di Arturo Labriola*. Rome: Europa, 1967.

Lenin, V. I. *Sul movimento operaio italiano*. Rome: Rinascita, 1947.

Lovecchio, Antonio. *Il marxismo in Italia*. Milan: Bocca, 1952.

Mack Smith, Denis. *Mussolini*. New York: Knopf, 1982.

Mammarella, Giuseppe. *Riformisti e rivoluzionari nel Partito Socialista Italiano, 1900–1912*. Padua: Marsilio, 1968.

Manacorda, Gastone, ed. "Formazione e primo sviluppo del Partito Socialista in Italia." *Studi Storici* 4 (January 1964), pp. 23–50.

——— . *Il socialismo nella storia d'Italia*. Bari: Laterza, 1966.

——— . *Storiografia e socialismo*. Padua: Liviana, 1967.

Mancini, Pietro. *Il Partito Socialista Italiano nella provincia di Cosenza, 1904–1924*. Cosenza: Pelligrini, 1974.

Manconi, Francesco, Guido Melis, and Giampaolo Misu. *Storia dei partiti popolari in Sardegna, 1890–1926*. Rome: Riuniti, 1977.

Mandurino, Silvia. "Questioni del mezzogiorno e problema della scuola nel pensiero di Gaetano Salvemini." *Studi Salentini* 33 (March 1969): 14–121.

Marianelli, Allessandro. "Il movimento operaio a Pisa sul fine dell'eta giolittana." *Movimento Operaio e Socialista* 24 (July 1978): 209–46.

Mariotti, Giovanni. *Filippo Turati*. Florence: La Voce, 1946.

Marmiroli, Renato. *Storia amara del socialismo italiano*. Parma: La Nazionale, 1964.

Martinelli, Renzo. "I giovani nel movimento operaio italiano dalla FGS alla FGC." *Movimento Operaio e Socialista* 22 (July 1976): 247–84.

Mazotti, Fernando. *Il socialismo riformista in Italia*. Florence: Le Monnier, 1965.

——— . "La giovinezza di Leonida Bissolati ricostruita su documenti inediti." *Nuova Rivista Storica* 41 (January 1957): 107–29.

——— . "Turati e Bissolati." *Critica Sociale* 59 (July 20, 1967): 412–13.

Mazzoni, Gianna. "Molinella e Giuseppe Massarenti nell'età giolittiana." *Movimento Operaio e Socialista* 20 (October 1974): 317–54.

Meda, Filippo. *Il Partito socialista italiano*. Milan: Vita e pensiero, 1921.

Bibliography

Megaro, Gaudens. *Mussolini in the Making*. London: Allen, 1938.

Meisel, James. *The Genesis of Georges Sorel*. Ann Arbor, Mich.: University of Michigan Press, 1951.

Mondolfo, Ugo, Pietro Nenni, and E. Gonzales. *Filippo Turati*. Milan: Rizzoli, 1947.

Monteleone, Renato. *Turati*. Turin: UTET, 1987.

Natale, Gaetano. "Ivanoe Bonomi, uomo di stato e cospiratore." *Nuova Antologia* 58 (May 1951): 16–21.

Neri, Guido. *Gabriele Galantra*. Milan: Feltrinelli, 1965.

Onofri, Nazario. *La grande guerra nella città rossa: Socialismo e reazione a Bologna dal 1914 al 1918*. Milan: del Gallo, 1966.

Partito Socialista Italiano, Sezione di Milano. *Sessant'anni di socialismo a Milano*. Milan: *Avanti!*, 1952.

Partito Socialista Italiano, Sezione di Prato. *Sessant'anni di lotta socialista in Prato*. Prato: n.p., 1951.

Peccerini, Renzo. "L'opera di G. Sorel." *Nuova Rivista Storica* 24 (January, May, July, November 1940): 25–45, 200–15, 352–77, 473–94, and 25 (January 1941): 50–74.

Perticone, Giacomo. *Storia del socialismo*. Rome: Leonardo, 1945.

———— . "Sulle 'tendenze' nei congressi del partito socialista italiano." *Socialismo* 2 (April 1946): 93–96.

Picone, Paul. *Italian Marxism*. Berkeley: University of California Press, 1983.

Pinzani, Carlo. "I socialisti italiani e francesi nel periodo della neutralità italiana." *Studi storici* 15 (April 1974): 364–99.

Procacci, Giuliano. *La lotta di classe in Italia agli inizi del secolo XX*. Rome: Riuniti, 1970.

Ragghianti, Angelo. *Gli uomini rossi all'arrembaggio dello stato*. Bologna: Zanichelli, 1914.

Ragionieri, Ernesto. *Social democrazia tedesca e socialisti italiani, 1875–1895*. Milan: Feltrinelli, 1961.

———— . *Un comune socialista: Sesto Fiorentino*. Rome: Rinascita, 1953.

Renda, Francesco. "Giuseppe De Felice Giuffrida capo del movimento popolare catanese," *Movimento Operaio* 5 (November 1954): 893–950.

———— . *I fasci siciliani*. Turin: Einaudi, 1977.

———— . *Socialisti e Cattolici in Sicilia*. Caltanissetta: Sciascia, 1972.

Riccio, Peter. *On the Threshold of Fascism*. New York: Columbia University Press, 1929.

Riosa, Alceo. *I leaders del PSI*. Bergamo: Minerva italica, 1980.

———— . *Il Partito socialista italiano, 1892 al 1918*. Rocca San Casciano: Cappelli, 1969.

———— . *Il sindacalismo rivoluzionario in Italia*. Bari: De Donato, 1976.

———— . "Il sindacalismo rivoluzionario in Italia dal 1907 alla 'settimana rossa.' " *Movimento Operaio e socialista* 2 (1979): 51–87.

————. *Il socialismo riformista a Milano agli inizi del secolo*. Milan: Angeli, 1981.

Riosa, Alceo, et al. *Anna Kuliscioff e l'età del riformisimo*. Rome: Mondo Operaio: *Avanti!*, 1978.

Romano, Aldo. *Storia del movimento socialista in Italia*. Bari: Laterza, 1969.

Romano, Salvatori. *Antonio Gramsci*. Turin: UTET, 1965.

Romita, Giuseppe. *Origini, crisi e sviluppo del socialismo italiano*. Rome: Opere Nuove, 1952.

Rosetti, Amerigo. "Leonida Bissolati, un cavalier dell'idea." *Nuova Antologia* 86 (June 1951): 118–33.

Rosselli, Carlo. *Filippo Turati*. Cairo: Giustizia e Libertà, 1945.

————. *Filippo Turati e il movimento socialista italiano*. Bari: Istituto Socialista di Cultura, 1945.

Rossi, Cesare. "Ricordando Bonomi." *Idea* 7 (June 1951): 362–63.

Roth, J. J. "The Roots of Italian Fascism: Sorel and Sorelism." *Journal of Modern History* 39 (March 1967): 30–45.

Ruffolo, Ugo. "Scioperi, servizi pubblici e riforma dello stato." *Critica Sociale* 59 (September 20, 1967): 506–8.

Sabbatucci, Giovanni, ed. *Storia del socialismo italiano*. Vols. 1 and 2. Rome: Il Poligono, 1980.

Sacerdote, Gustavo. *Breve storia dell'Avanti!*. Rome: *Avanti!*, 1945.

Sadun, Carlo. *Il socialismo in Italia*. Florence: Facoltà di scienze sociali e politiche—Cesare Alfieri, 1954.

Salvadore, Rinaldo, et al. *I socialisti e il movimento operaio*. Mantua: n.p., n.d.

Salvadori, Massimo L. *Gaetano Salvemini*. Turin: Einaudi, 1963.

Salvemini, Gaetano. *Opere*. Part 3, *Scritti di politica estera*. Vol. 3, *La politica estera italiana dal 1871 al 1914*. Edited by A. Torre. Part 4, *Il Mezzogiorno e la democrazia italiana*. Vol. 1, *Il ministero della malavita e altri scritti sull'Italia giolittiana*. Edited by E. Apih. Vol. 2, *Movimento socialista e questione meridionale*. Edited by G. Arfe. Milan: Feltrinelli, 1962–63.

Santarelli, Enzo. *La revisione del marxismo in Italia*. Milan: Feltrinelli, 1964.

Sarfatti, Margherita. *The Life of Mussolini*. London: Butterworth, 1925.

Sassoon, Anne Showstack. *Gramsci's Politics*. New York: St. Martin's Press, 1980.

Satta, Vladimiro. "I socialisti e i problemi dello sviluppo economico italiano." *Clio* 22 (April 1986): 247–73.

Schiavi, Alessandro. "Giovanezza litteraria e polemica di Filippo Turati." *Nuova Antologia* 85 (August 1951): 342–58.

————. *I pioneri del socialismo in Italia*. 4 vols. Rome: Opere Nuove, 1955.

————. *Omaggio a Turati*. Rome: Opere Nuove, 1957.

————. "Sessant'anni di socialismo." *Critica Sociale,* November 16, 1952, pp. 666–68.

Schiavi, Alessandro, et al. *Figure del primo socialismo italiano*. Turin: ERI, 1951.

Bibliography

Sighele, Scipio. *Ultime pagine nazionaliste.* Milan: Treves, 1912.

Solari, Francesco S. "Lotte agrarie a Molinella, 1905–1915." *Storia Contemporanea* 9 (December 1978): 843–75.

Spadolini, Giovanni. "1904: Primo sciopero generale." *Il Mondo* 1 (December 10, 1949): 11–12.

Spini, Giorgio, et al. *Trent'anni di politica socialista.* Rome: Mondo Operaio: *Avanti!*, 1977.

Spriano, Paolo. "La terza generazione del socialismo italiano," *Rivista Storica del Socialismo* 2 (April 1959): 217–42.

——— . *The Occupation of the Factories.* London: Pluto Press, 1975.

——— . *Socialismo e classe operaio a Tornino dal 1892 al 1913.* Turin: Einaudi, 1958.

Tagliacozzo, Enzo. "Gaetano Salvemini nei primi anni del secolo, 1901–1908." *Nuova Rivista Storica* 34 (May 1950): 265–86.

Toscani, Italo. *Costantino Lazzari.* Rome: n.p., 1921.

Treves, Claudio. *Un socialista, F. Turati.* Milan: n.p., 1946.

Valeri, Nino. *Turati e la Kuliscioff.* Florence: Le Monnier, 1974.

Valiani, Leo. "Gli sviluppi ideologici del socialismo democratico in Italia." *Critica Sociale* 4 (February 16 and March 1, 1952): 411–14, 429–32.

——— . "Il partito socialista italiano dal 1900 al 1918." *Rivista Storica Italiana* 75 (June 1963): 269–326.

——— . *Il partito socialista italiano nel periodo della neutralità, 1914–1915.* Milan: Feltrinelli, 1977.

——— . "L'azione di Leonida Bissolati e il revisionismo." *Rivista Storica Italiana* 71 (May 1959): 653–64.

——— . *Questioni di storia del socialismo.* Turin: Einaudi, 1958.

——— . *Storia del socialismo nel secolo XX.* Rome: Edizione "U", 1945.

Vigezzi, Brunello. *Giolitti e Turati: Un incontro mancato.* 2 vols. Milan: Ricciardi, 1976.

——— . *Il PSI, le riforme e la rivoluzione, 1898–1915.* Florence: Sansoni, 1981.

——— . "Il suffragio universale e la 'crisi' del liberalismo in Italia." *Nuova Rivista Storica* 48 (September 1964): 529–78.

——— . "Italian Socialism and the First World War: Mussolini, Lazzari and Turati." *Journal of Italian History* 2 (Autumn 1979): 232–57.

Villari, Pasquale. *Scritti vari sulla questione sociale in Italia.* Florence: Sansoni, 1902.

Woolf, Stuart. "Mussolini as revolutionary." In *Left-Wing Intellectuals Between the Wars, 1919–1939,* edited by W. Laqueur and G. Mosse. New York: Harper, 1966.

Zacan, Marina. *Stampa periodica e formazione del Partito Socialista, 1890–1892.* Padua: Tipografia antoniana, 1973.

VI. Periodicals and Newspapers

A. Periodicals

Divenire Sociale
Il Socialismo
Il Viandante
La Civiltà Cattolica
La Critica
La Critica Sociale
L'Unità
Mouvement Socialiste
Nuova Antologia
Rivista Popolare

B. Newspapers

Avanti!
Il Tempo
L'Avanguardia
L'Avanguardia Socialista
La Lotta di Classe
La Nazione
La Soffitta
La Tribuna

Index

Index

Index

Index

Sozialdemokratische Partei Deutschland (SPD): vii, viii, 32, 33, 36, 64, 114; model for PSI, 37, 38, 184, 187

Stampa, La, 82

Syndicalists: critique of Reformism, 56–57; theory discussed, 55–56

Tasca, Angelo, 171, 185, 205

Tempo, Il, 60, 61, 95

Terracini, Umberto, 205

Tittoni, Tommaso, 69

Todescini, Mario, 102

Togliatti, Palmiro, x, 171, 205

Trasformismo: discussed, 4–6

Treves, Claudio: 16, 22, 52, 149, 150, 153, 157, 162, 169, 171, 172, 173, 190, 191, 192, 196, 198; director of *Avanti!,* 85, 95–97, 132; on state of party, 181

Triple Alliance, 106

Turati, Filippo: ix, x, xi, 38, 40, 52, 57, 59, 62, 63, 101, 122, 148, 161, 166, 173, 190, 197; analyzes Giolitti's actions, 149; attitude toward opposition, 54, 76; clashes with Bissolati, 125, 131–32; conflicts with Lazzari, 18, 54, 76; efforts to reform GPS, 106, 108–16, 130–32; emerges as leader of party, 15–25; ideology of Reformism, 34–35; laments state of PSI, 157; opposes Libyan war, 145–46, 154; Reformist convictions, 18, 22–24; role in move of

Avanti!, 95–96; role in organization of PSI, 11–15; seeks coalition on left, 152–53, 163; strategy for defeating left, 67, 71, 73; views on party organization, 52, 61

Umberto I, 21, 23

Unione Sindicale Italiana (USI), 178, 197

Unione Socialista Milanese, 54

Utopia, 173

Varazzani, Savino, 107

Vella, Arturo, 137, 139, 156, 159, 166, 178–79, 193–94

Victor Emmanuel II, 5

Victor Emmanuel III, 23, 25, 139–41, 155

Young Socialist Federation (FGS): 170; campaign against masonry, 175–76; origins and objectives, 137; reinforces left, 137, 152; support for Mussolini, 179

Zanardelli, Giuseppi, viii, 22, 25, 27, 28, 29, 53, 62, 63, 107–9

Zerbini, Adolfo, 167

Zerboglio, Adolfo, 111, 164

Zibordi, Giovanni, 156, 175, 192